ダスティーディ　りえごです。

こんにちわおげんきですか!

Paragraphs and Beyond

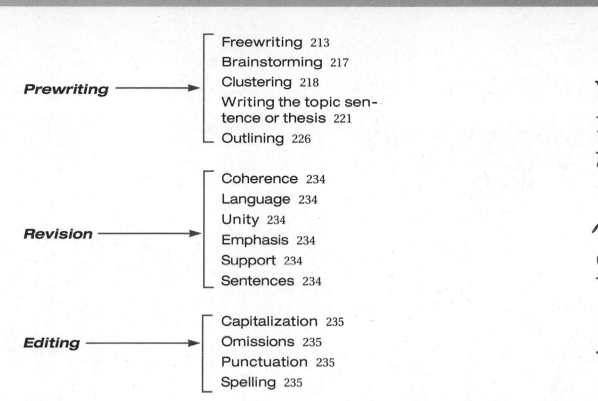

Prewriting

Revision

Editing

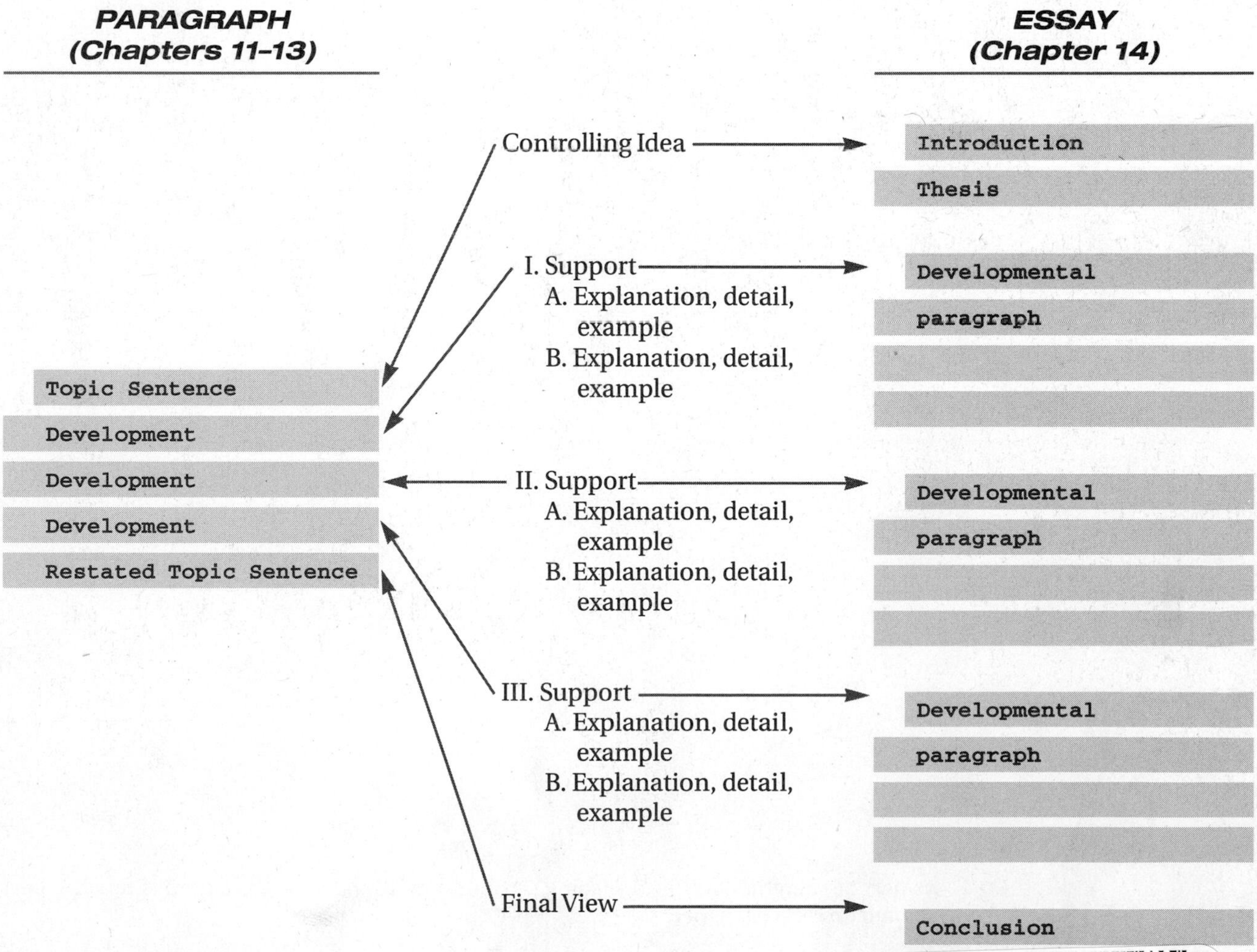

As part of Houghton Mifflin's ongoing commitment to the environment, this text has been printed on recycled paper.

Sentences, Paragraphs, and Beyond

With Culturally Diverse Readings

Dustin Day

Second Edition

Lee Brandon
Mt. San Antonio College

Kelly Brandon
Rancho Santiago College

Houghton Mifflin Company Boston New York

To Shane, Lauren, and Jarrett

Senior Sponsoring Editor: Paul A. Smith
Sponsoring Editor: Renée Deljon
Senior Associate Editors: Linda Bieze, Ellen Darion
Project Editor: Elizabeth Gale Napolitano
Production/Design Coordinator: Jennifer Waddell
Manufacturing Manager: Michael O'Dea
Senior Designer: Henry Rachlin

Cover Design: Henry Rachlin
Cover Image: © Tony Stone Images / Joe Cornish

Text Credits:
From *I Know Why the Caged Bird Sings* by Maya Angelou. Copyright © 1969 by Maya Angelou. Reprinted by permission of Random House, Inc.
"La Vida Loca: Crazy Life, Crazy Death," by Carlos Chavez and Antonio Rodriguez, from the *Los Angeles Times,* August 17, 1995. Reprinted by permission of the authors.
(Text Credits continue in the endmatter on page TC-1.)

Printed in the U.S.A.

Library of Congress Catalog Number: 96-76871

Student Text ISBN: 0-669-41597-9

Instructor's Edition ISBN: 0-669-41598-7

3456789-CS-00-99-98-97

Contents

Part Two Writing Paragraphs and Beyond

Section 3

1) Difference between Act, Rule, and Preference

Act Utilitarianism- holds that the principle should be applied to particular acts in particular circumstances.

Rule Utilitarianism- maintains that the principle should be used to test rules that in turn can be used to decide the rightness of particular acts.

Preferences- has the advantage of suggesting more explicit methods of analysis and rules for decision making than the classical formulation. Preferences and decision

Nancy Versteegt

Nursing: 455

Preface

Working on another edition of this textbook has given us the opportunity to improve our material through the evaluations of those who use it, as well as through observing what works in our own classes. We believe that a good textbook should cover the field broadly but with direction, serve instructors with differing pedagogies and personalities, present instruction pertinent to the needs of society, and energize students to learn with enthusiasm. Such a vision must address a two-part audience of instructors and students, and we believe that *Sentences, Paragraphs, and Beyond,* Second Edition, will serve this audience well. We have worked to produce a book that is comprehensive, adaptable, relevant, and stimulating.

Principal Features

Comprehensiveness

The text's three sections and the appendixes cover the full array of topics needed at this level:

Part One: Writing Sentences covers parts of speech, parts of sentence structure, phrases and clauses, sentence problems, sentence combining, parallel structure, pronoun usage, modifiers, punctuation.

Part Two: Writing Paragraphs and Beyond covers freewriting, listing, clustering, topic sentence writing, outlining, revision, editing.

Part Three: The Reading Connection provides suggestions for critical reading, summary writing, reaction writing (simple, critical evaluation, parallel experience), forms of discourse dually grouped with thematic arrangements of paragraphs and essays by students, and essays by professional writers.

Appendixes cover spelling, vocabulary building (word analysis, contextual clues), critical thinking (fact and opinion, fallacies of logic), taking tests, job applications, writing the resume, and the DCODE process (with a brief guide and a blank worksheet for the writing process).

Adaptability

The first two parts, "Writing Sentences" and "Writing Paragraphs and Beyond," move from short to long units of discourse. The third and final part, "The Reading Connection," adds reading selections and suggestions for written responses. The instructor can move easily within and between the parts according to his or her pedagogy and students' needs.

Relevance and Stimulation

Each requires the other. Relevance without stimulation equals boredom. Stimulation without relevance equals emptiness. Presented at the developmental level without condescension, the text has been successfully class-tested with college students. The examples and reading passages reflect a wide range of current and enduring concerns, as these chapter titles show: "Growing Pains and Pleasures," "Prized and Despised Possessions," "Heroes: Who Are They?," "The Joy and Grief of Work," "Girls and Guys in Gangs," "Cross-Cultural Encounters," and "Walking in Different Shoes."

Changes in the Second Edition

New Title

The change from *Sentences and Paragraphs* to *Sentences, Paragraphs, and Beyond: With Culturally Diverse Readings* highlights the unit on transition from the paragraph to the essay (though the book continues to feature the sentence and the paragraph). The new subtitle indicates the rich cultural diversity of ethnic, gender, and class sources for the reading selections.

Improved Organization

- Simpler organizational plan

  The book is now divided into three major sections:

  1. Writing Sentences
  2. Writing Paragraphs and Moving to the Essay
  3. Writing about Readings

- Table of Contents with page numbers at the beginning of each chapter
- Checklist Summary with Review Exercises at the end of each chapter

Emphasis on Writing Sentences, Paragraphs, and the Short Essay

- More sentence-writing exercises dealing with fundamentals
- Extended chapters on writing the paragraph
- A strong chapter on writing the essay

  Because many students in developmental English programs are either taking college transfer classes or will soon be taking them, we introduce the students to the essay. We present the essay in a separate chapter, explaining that a well-developed paragraph is often an essay in miniature. The essays used here for instruction, examples, and assignments are brief and they are within the ability of students in developmental programs. Both instructors who prefer to concentrate on the paragraph and those who feature the short essay will feel at ease with the instruction in this book.

- Strengthened verb section with time lines
- New Guide for ESL Students

Enhancement of The Reading Connection

- More activities related to writing responses to readings

  We have included a separate chapter (with discussion, examples, and exercises) on types of writing responses: summary, simple reaction, critical writing, and spin-off (parallel experiences).

- Anthology materials grouped according to topic and form of discourse
- Student work prominently featured
- Greater variety of subject material in exercises

Support Material for Instructors

- Annotated Instructor's Edition

  This annotated edition provides immediate answers or possible answers to exercises and activities, along with some instructional suggestions.

- Test Book

  A separate test book is also available to instructors. It includes two comprehensive tests for fundamentals, two quizzes for each unit of Part 1, and quizzes on the seventeen reading selections by professional authors.

- Instructor's Guide

- Heath Developmental Writing Software and Heath Grammar Review Software

Acknowledgments

We are grateful to the following instructors who have reviewed this textbook: Marilyn Black, Middlesex Community College; Kathryn Beckwith, Arizona State University; John Bell, New York City Technical College; Christena T. Biggs, DePauw University; Wendy Bishop, Florida State University; Betty Bluman, Community College of Allegheny; Marlene Bosanko, Tocoma Community College; Elizabeth Breen, Pierce College; Deborah Burson-Smith, Southern University—A&M; Nicole Greene, University of Southwestern Louisiana; Roslyn J. Harper, Trident Technical College; Carolyn G. Hartnett, College of the Mainland; Bradley S. Hayden, Western Michigan University; Grady Hinton, Jr., St. Louis Community College at Forest Park; Wayne P. Hubert, Chaffey Community College; Anna Jo Johnson, Community College of Western Kentucky University; James C. McDonald, University of Southwestern Louisiana; James Rice, Quinsigamond Community College; Susan Schiller, University of California—Davis; Ann Shackleford, Bacone College; and David White, Walters State Community College. Thanks also for the faculty members at Mt. San Antonio College (with special appreciation to the Basic Courses Review Committee) and Rancho Santiago College for their suggestions.

We also thank Paul A. Smith, Linda M. Bieze, Ellen Darion, Margaret Roll, Craig Mertens, Elizabeth Napolitano, Renée Deljon, and Henry Rachlin. We are grateful to our families for their affection and their enduring, cheerful support, especially Sharon, Jeanne, Erin, and Michael.

Lee Brandon
Kelly Brandon

Sentences, Paragraphs, and Beyond

PART One

Writing Sentences

An Overview for Student Writers

Writing effectively is not as difficult as you think. You can learn to be a good writer if you practice effective techniques. The operative words are the last three: "practice effective techniques." A good piece of written material includes clear organization, solid content, and good use of language skills. In other words, you should have something to say, present it in appropriate order, and write correctly. All of those points will be covered in the three main parts of this book: **Writing Sentences, Writing Paragraphs and Beyond,** and **The Reading Connection.**

Part One: Writing Sentences

The first section, **Writing Sentences,** concentrates on effectiveness. Beginning with the simplest aspects of sentences such as parts of speech and subjects and verbs, the text moves to the larger word units of clauses and sentences, with their numerous patterns. It shows you the difference between complete sentences and incomplete sentences, between sound and unsound arrangements of words, and between correct and incorrect punctuation. While giving you the opportunity to experiment and develop your own style, it leads you through the problem areas of verbs, pronouns, and modifiers. If you are not sure when to use *lie* and when to use *lay,* when to use *who* and when to use *whom,* or when to use *good* and when to use *well,* this book can help you. If you're not sure whether the standard expression is *between you and I* or *between you and me,* or if you're not sure about the difference between a colon and a semicolon, you will find the answers here. That line of *if* statements could be applied to almost every page in this book. Perhaps you are not sure of the correct answer to most of these questions. But the good news is that by the end of the course, you will be sure—and if your "sure" is still a bit shaky, then you will know where to find the rules, examples, and discussion in this book.

The text in **Part One: Writing Sentences** follows a pattern: rules, examples, exercises, writing activity. Again, you learn by practicing sound principles. As you complete assignments, you can check your answers to selected exercises in the Answer Key in the back so that you can monitor your understanding.

Part Two: Writing Paragraphs and Beyond

The second part, **Writing Paragraphs and Beyond,** presents writing as a process, not as something that is supposed to emerge complete on demand. Instead, writing begins with a topic, either generated or provided, and moves through stages of exploration, development, revision, and editing. If you have suffered, at least at times, from writer's block, this book is for you. If you have sometimes produced material that was organized poorly so that you did not receive full credit for what you knew, then this book is for you. If you have sometimes had ideas, but you did not fully develop them, so that your work was judged as "sketchy" or "lacking in content," then this book is for you.

Part Three: The Reading Connection

The third part, **The Reading Connection,** gives you models of good writing and lively ideas for discussion and writing. The selections are presented with observations and exercises to help you develop effective reading techniques. In working with these assignments, you may discover that you can learn a great deal from other writers—if you can read perceptively, understanding both what the writers say and how they say it.

Some reading selections are paragraphs and others are essays. They are rich in invention, style, and cultural perspective. Several are written by celebrated writers such as Maya Angelou, Gary Soto, and John Lame Deer. Some are written by students, individuals like you who entered college, worked on language skills, and learned. Well-written and fresh in thought, these models are especially useful because they were done as college English assignments. Each of the students whose writing is included in this book learned writing skills in a developmental program before taking freshman composition. Several of them also studied in English as a Second Language programs.

The selections are grouped in two ways: according to theme and according to form of writing. For example, the writings in "Prized and Despised Possessions" are all descriptions. Of course, no one selection is entirely in a single form, though one may predominate. Many forms are presented—narration, description, exemplification, functional analysis, process analysis, cause and effect analysis, comparison and contrast, and persuasion—because you will need to use many of these forms in your college work. Topics such as "Write an essay on causes of *(a war, depression, a disease)*" and "In a short essay, compare and contrast *(two theories, two leaders, two programs)*" abound across the curriculum. Studying the principles for these forms and reading good examples of pieces that demonstrate the effective use of these forms will help you get full credit for what you know in your college classes and elsewhere.

Appendix

This book also has an **Appendix,** a collection of support materials that were too valuable to be omitted from a college book on writing: spelling, vocabulary building, test-taking, writing a letter of job application and a résumé, guide for ESL students, the DCODE writing process, and a self-evaluation chart.

Strategies for Self-Improvement

Naturally, this textbook is only one component of several in the course you are taking. Two more important ones are your instructor and you. Take advantage of your instructor's classroom expertise by being an active class member—one who takes notes, asks questions, and contributes to class discussion. If you are to function well in the English classroom and in other departments, you should be systematic in addressing your needs. Here are two specific things you can do.

1. Write Frequently

How you will do this depends on you and your situation. Regular class assignments may meet your need for practice. One good activity is journal writing. These are some ideas for daily or almost daily writing:

1. Summarize, evaluate, or react to what you have learned in other classes. The results will be two-fold. You will master subject material while gaining writing experience.
2. Summarize, evaluate, or react to reading assignments in this class.
3. Summarize, evaluate, or react to what you see on television, in movies, in newspapers or magazines.
4. Use Reading-Related Writing suggestions for paragraphs and essays following reading selections in Part 3.
5. Describe, narrate, and analyze what you encounter in your daily life.

Get in the habit of writing frequently in a journal whether you are required to or not. Your instructor may ask you to write on specific subjects for your journal. Although he or she may be reading your journal, you will be writing in it especially for yourself, developing confidence and ease in writing, so that it comfortably becomes a part of your everyday activities.

These journal entries may read much like an intellectual diary, recording what you are thinking about at certain times. They will help you understand reading material, develop your writing skills, and think more clearly. Because these entries are more spontaneous than structured writing assignments, organization and editing will be of less concern to you. But do not discount the usefulness of your journal entries; they will help you develop skills, and they may provide you with subject material for longer, more carefully written pieces.

The important step now is to get into the habit of writing something each day. If you have writer's block or you need some techniques for generating ideas, read the chapters in Part 2.

2. Evaluate Yourself

Use the chart that follows this overview to perform a self-evaluation. Incorporating instructor comments, make notes about what you need to concentrate on, such as organization, development, spelling, vocabulary, grammar, or punctuation. Use this chart for review and for a checklist during revising and editing. As you master the problems, you can erase or cross out entries. An additional blank form is included in the Appendix.

Organization/Development/Content: These aspects include the techniques of prewriting such as freewriting, brainstorming, and clustering; the phrasing of a good topic sentence or thesis; and the design, growth, and refinement of your ideas.

Spelling: List common spelling words marked as incorrect on college assignments. Here, *common* means words that you would ordinarily use with some frequency. If you are misspelling these words now, you have probably been doing so for ten years or so. Look at your list. Is there a pattern to your misspelling? Consult the Spelling section in the Appendix for rules that may be useful. Whatever it takes, master the words on your list. Continue to add words as you accumulate assignments.

Grammar: List recurring problems in your writing assignments. Use the correction symbols and page number references listed just inside the back cover or obtain the same information from the book index. Then consult the relevant pages and work on the problem. Finally, use these symbols as reminders of what to look for in revising and editing.

Punctuation: Treat this in the same way as problems with grammar. Note that the punctuation chapter lists all rules with numbers; therefore, you can give very detailed locations of the remedies for your problems.

3. Be Positive

All of these elements are covered in detail in *Sentences, Paragraphs, and Beyond.* The table of contents, the index, and the correction guide inside the back cover will direct you to instruction that has been used successfully in developmental English classes.

While improving your English skills, write with freedom and revise and edit with rigor. Work with your instructor to set reasonable goals, and proceed at a reasonable pace. Your Self-Evaluation Chart will give you direction and purpose. Seeing what you have marked off your list as a result of mastery will give you a sense of accomplishment.

But don't expect near-perfection immediately, and don't try to work on all areas covered in this book at once. Instead, list and rank your needs, and concentrate on a few areas at a time. And don't compare yourself with others. Compare yourself with yourself. As you move through your developmental English course, notice how you are getting better at working with content, organization, and correctness as you read, think, and write.

However, you should understand that writing is more than content, organization, and correctness in relation to reading and thinking; it is also a matter of attitude. In this course, using this book, you will do a lot of writing, learn what works in writing, and become rather good at writing. Of course, it naturally follows that you will soon, if not already, look forward to writing with an attitude of enthusiastic anticipation.

Let the pleasing and satisfying experience begin as you move on to write *Sentences, Paragraphs, and Beyond!*

Self-Evaluation Chart

(examples)

Organization/ Development/ Content	Spelling	Grammar/ Sentence Structure	Punctuation
needs more specific information such as examples	receive, p. A-6	difference between who and whom, p. 145	difference between semicolons and commas, p. 189
	Your, you've, p. A-10	fragments, p. 47	commas after long modifiers, p. 183
	its, it's, p. A-9	subject-verb agreement, p. 126	

Basic Problems I Need to Work on in My Writing

(examples)

Spelling	Grammar	Punctuation
receive, p. A-6	difference between who and whom, p. 145	difference between semicolons and commas, p. 189
your, you're, p. A-10	fragments, p. 47	comma after a long modifier, p. 183
its, it's, p. A-9	subject-verb agreement, p. 126	

1

Parts of Speech

You already know a great deal about parts of speech. In fact, you started learning about parts of speech when you were little more than a year old. If English is not your first language, you learned parts of speech in your native language at the same time and basically in the same way the English-speaking child did—through imitation.

If you ask a four-year-old child to finish the sentence "I would like to eat a ___________," the child will use a noun. If you ask that child to complete the sentence "They might ___________ me," the child will use a verb. The child knows which part of speech to use. After all, parts of speech pertain to grammar, and grammar is concerned with how we—all users of the language, not just teachers, textbook authors, and students who have taken the course in which you are now enrolled—put words together.

Your concern here should be with learning terms, patterns, and principles so that you can examine and adjust your language for even more effective expression.

Words are classified as **parts of speech** according to their use and form.

Nouns

Nouns are naming words. Nouns may name persons, animals, plants, places, things, substances, qualities, or ideas—for example, *Bart, armadillo, Mayberry, tree, rock, cloud, love, ghost, music, virtue.*

Nouns can have a plural form. The most common plurals are formed by adding *-s* or *-es.* Some examples are *trees, rocks, clouds, ghosts.* But some nouns change to plural in other ways: *mouse–mice, ox–oxen.* Only a few, such as *deer–deer,* have the same form for both singular and plural.

Nouns are often pointed out by noun indicators:

the slime	*a* werewolf	*an* aardvark
the green slime	*a* hungry werewolf	*an* angry aardvark

These noun indicators—*the, a, an*—signal that a noun is up ahead, though there may be words between the indicator and the noun itself.

EXERCISE 1

In the blanks indicate whether each italicized word is a noun (n) or not (x). (See Answer Key for answers.)

______ ______ 1. The *buzzard* is one of the largest *birds* in North America.

______ ______ 2. It has brown and *black* feathers and a red, unfeathered *head*.

______ ______ 3. Instead of singing, it makes a low *hiss* or *moan*.

Fill in each blank with an appropriate noun.

4. The buzzard performs a useful ____________ by eating the ____________ of dead animals.
5. It often competes with ____________ for ____________.
6. Though beautiful in flight, their ____________ can be tolerated only by other ____________ .

Pronouns

A pronoun is used in place of a noun. Some pronouns may **represent persons:**

I	*him*	*himself*
me	*her*	*herself*
we	*they*	*itself*
us	*them*	*ourselves*
you	*who*	*themselves*
she	*whom*	*yourselves*
he	*myself*	*that*
it	*yourself*	

Some pronouns **refer to nouns** (persons, places, things) in a general way: *each, everyone, nobody, somebody.*

Other pronouns **point out** particular things:

Singular:	*this, that*	**Plural:**	*these, those*
	This is my treasure.		*These* are my children.
	That is your junk.		*Those* are your brats.

Note that if words like *this* and *these* modify nouns rather than replace them, as in the above example, they become adjectives:

This treasure delights me. *These* children are adorable.

That junk disgusts me. *Those* brats are obnoxious.

Still other pronouns **introduce questions:**

Which CD player is the best?

What are the main ingredients of a Twinkie?

EXERCISE 2

In the blanks indicate whether each italicized word is a pronoun (pro) or not (x). (See Answer Key for answers.)

______ ______ 1. *He* was big and strong, but he was far from *home.*

______ ______ 2. *People* gave *him* the name King Kong.

______ ______ 3. *Those* same people had taken *him* captive.

In each blank, fill in an appropriate pronoun.

4. The people ____________ treated ____________ that way would soon be sorry.

5. He attacked ____________ after he broke out of his cage and left ____________ in shambles.

6. At one point ____________ captured a maiden and held ____________ in the palm of his hand.

Verbs

Verbs are words with certain forms that show action or express being. They occur in set positions in sentences. The **action** should make them easy for you to identify.

The aardvark *ate* the crisp, tasty ants. (action verb)

The aardvark *washed* them down with a snoutful of water. (action verb)

The **being** verbs are few in number and are also easy to identify. The most common being verbs are *is, was, were, are,* and *am.* These words are always verbs.

Gilligan *is* on an island in the South Pacific. (being verb)

I *am* his enthusiastic fan. (being verb)

The form of a verb refers to its tense, meaning the time of the action or being. The time may be in the present or past.

Roseanne *sings* "The Star-Spangled Banner." (present)

Roseanne *sang* "The Star-Spangled Banner." (past)

A **helping** verb or verbs may be used with the main verb to show other tenses.

She *had sung* the song many times in the shower. (helping verb and main verb to show a certain time in the past)

She *will be singing* the song no more in San Diego. (helping verbs and main verb to show a certain time in the future)

Some helping verbs can be used alone as main verbs: *has, have, had, is, was, were, are, am.* Certain other helping verbs function only as helpers: *will, shall, should, could.*

The most common **position** for the verb is directly after the subject or after the subject and its modifiers.

At high noon only two men (subject) *were* on Main Street.

The man with the faster draw (subject and modifiers) *walked* away alone.

EXERCISE 3

In the blanks indicate whether each italicized word is a verb (v) or not (x). (See Answer Key for answers.)

_____ _____ 1. Elvis *was born* in Tupelo, Mississippi, and later *moved* to Memphis, Tennessee.

_____ _____ 2. As a child he *learned* gospel music on his mother's *knee.*

_____ _____ 3. He *liked* to play his guitar and tap his little foot *merrily.*

Fill in each blank with an appropriate verb.

4. Later Elvis became famous for the way he __________ his hips and __________ songs.

5. He __________ a flashy Cadillac and __________ his show on the road.

6. He __________ in many movies and __________ much money.

EXERCISE 4

Identify the part of speech of each italicized word or group of words by writing the appropriate abbreviations in the blanks: n (noun), pro (pronoun), v (verb), x (other). (See Answer Key for answers.)

_____ _____ 1. Edgar Allan Poe's *parents were* unsuccessful actors.

_____ _____ 2. Edgar's father died when Edgar was one year old, and *his* mother died when *he* was two.

_____ _____ 3. He *was taken* into the *home* of John Allan, a wealthy merchant.

_____ _____ 4. Edgar went with the *Allan* family to England, where he *was educated.*

_______ _______ 5. Edgar and *his* foster *father* did not get along.

_______ _______ 6. Following a *quarrel*, Edgar *tried* unsuccessfully to be a gambler.

_______ _______ 7. After dropping out of college, *he enlisted* in the army under an assumed name.

_______ _______ 8. Later Edgar's foster father *helped* him obtain an *appointment* to West Point.

_______ _______ 9. Soon after he *was admitted* to West Point, *he* was dismissed for bad behavior.

_______ _______ 10. On one occasion, he appeared *naked* in a *military* formation.

_______ _______ 11. After leaving West Point, Poe *devoted himself* to his writing.

_______ _______ 12. He *lost* one important job because of his *drinking* problem.

_______ _______ 13. In 1835 he *married* his *cousin* Virginia, who was thirteen.

_______ _______ 14. During the next *several* years, he *wrote* numerous short stories and poems.

_______ _______ 15. *His* most famous poem is *entitled* "The Raven."

_______ _______ 16. His best short *stories include* "The Pit and the Pendulum" and "The Tell-Tale Heart."

_______ _______ 17. To Poe, the most *dramatic* situation *was* a beautiful woman dying.

_______ _______ 18. His own *wife* Virginia *died* of tuberculosis.

_______ _______ 19. He is best known for his *tales* of *horror.*

_______ _______ 20. Edgar Allan Poe *died* under *mysterious* circumstances when he was only forty years old.

EXERCISE 5

Identify the part of speech of each italicized word or group of words by writing the appropriate abbreviations in the blanks: n (noun), pro (pronoun), v (verb), x (other).

_______ _______ 1. In "The Tell-Tale Heart" by Poe, the narrator (the teller of the story) *has* an unbalanced *mind.*

_______ _______ 2. Yet *he* insists that he is *sane.*

_______ _______ 3. He *tells* the *reader* what he did, how he did it, and how he was arrested.

_______ _______ 4. He had lived with an old man *who* had a *cataract* on one eye.

______ ______ 5. The narrator *came* to see the eye as *evil.*

______ ______ 6. He *called* the eye a "*vulture* eye."

______ ______ 7. Using a *lantern,* the narrator *spied* on the old man at night.

______ ______ 8. For several nights, *he watched* the old man, waiting for him to open that eye.

______ ______ 9. At last on the eighth *night,* the old man *opened* his eye.

______ ______ 10. He *believed* that he heard the beating of the old man's *heart.*

______ ______ 11. The narrator *pounced* on the man and *suffocated* him.

______ ______ 12. Then the narrator cut up the body and *buried it* under the floor of the house.

______ ______ 13. Soon the *police arrived* to investigate.

______ ______ 14. The *narrator set* out to prove that he was not insane.

______ ______ 15. *He* invited the police to come in and search the *house.*

______ ______ 16. After *they found* nothing, he invited them to sit.

______ ______ 17. He placed his own *chair* over the *dismembered* body.

______ ______ 18. He *tried* to remain calm, but he heard the *sound* of a beating heart.

______ ______ 19. A reader may think the narrator only *imagined* that he heard the sound, actually heard the sound of *his* own heart, or perhaps heard the sound of a watch left on the body of the old man.

______ ______ 20. The narrator *screamed* out in a *frenzy* and was arrested.

Adjectives

Adjectives modify nouns and pronouns. An adjective usually answers one of the questions What kind? Which one? or How many?

Adjectives answering the **What kind?** question are descriptive. They tell the quality, kind, or condition of the nouns or pronouns they modify.

red convertible *noisy* muffler *dirty* fork *wild* roses

Adjectives answering the **Which one?** question narrow or restrict the meaning of the modifier. Some of these are pronouns used as adjectives.

my money *our* ideas *their* house *this* reason *these* apples

Adjectives answering the **How many?** question are, of course, numbering words.

some people *each* pet *few* goals *three* dollars *one* glove

The words *a, an,* and *the* are **article adjectives.** They point out persons, places, and things.

EXERCISE 6

In the blanks indicate whether each italicized word is an adjective (adj) or not (x). (See Answer Key for answers.)

______ ______ 1. The *whoopie* cushion was invented in the *seventeenth* century in France.

______ ______ 2. It was made of *pig* bladders and sold to the *aristocrats.*

______ ______ 3. Even the *French* kings played tricks on *their* guests.

Fill in each blank with an appropriate adjective.

4. Whoopie cushions are now made of ____________ plastic and can be purchased at ____________ stores everywhere.

5. ____________ people believe that a person's sense of humor can be judged by his or her reaction to a ____________ prank.

6. The world would be a ____________ place if this ____________ item had not been invented.

Adverbs

Adverbs modify verbs, adjectives, and other adverbs.

Modifying verbs: They did (v) their work quickly (adv).

He replied (v) angrily (adv).

Modifying adjectives: They were somewhat (adv) happy (adj).

The jewelry was quite (adv) dazzling (adj).

Modifying other adverbs: He was almost (adv) always (adv) sleepy.

He ran very (adv) swiftly (adv).

An adverb answers one of the questions How? Where? When? Why? or How much? Adverbs that answer the **How?** question are concerned with manner or way.

She ate the snails *hungrily.* He snored *noisily.*

Adverbs that answer the **Where?** question show location.

They drove *downtown.* She climbed *upstairs.* He stayed *behind.*

Those that answer the **When?** question indicate time.

The ship sailed *yesterday.* I expect an answer *soon.*

Those that answer the **How much?** question express degree.

She is *entirely* correct. He was *somewhat* happy.

Most words ending in -*ly* are adverbs.

He completed the task skillfully.
adv

She answered him courteously.
adv

However, there are a few exceptions.

The house provided a lovely view of the valley.
adj

Your goblin mask is ugly.
adj

EXERCISE 7

In the blanks indicate whether each italicized word is an adverb (adv) or not (x). (See Answer Key for answers.)

______ ______ 1. Jim Bob *proudly* owned a *friendly* skunk with a big furry tail.

______ ______ 2. The skunk *followed* Jim Bob *closely* wherever he went.

______ ______ 3. *Soon* the skunk was Jim Bob's only friend, and Jim Bob grieved *deeply* about his loneliness.

Fill in each blank with an appropriate adverb.

4. ____________, he consulted a ____________ trained psychiatrist.

5. The psychiatrist said, "Get off my couch ____________ with your ____________-smelling companion."

6. Jim Bob could ____________ believe the rudeness of the remark and said ____________ that he would not pay for the appointment.

EXERCISE 8

Identify the part of speech of each italicized word or group of words by placing the appropriate abbreviations in the blanks: adj (adjective), adv (adverb), x (other). (See Answer Key for answers.)

______ ______ 1. In the *original* classic horror thriller *Frankenstein,* Victor Frankenstein was a *gifted* student who went to the university to study science.

______ ______ 2. While studying science, he *somewhat mysteriously* came upon the secret of how to create life.

______ ______ 3. Being more interested in *practical* matters than in theory, he set out to construct a *living* creature.

______ ______ 4. He *first* needed to gather up the materials *necessary* for his experiment.

______ ______ 5. He went all around town picking up *spare parts* wherever he could.

______ ______ 6. The dissecting room at a local hospital provided him with the *most basic* parts.

______ ______ 7. Local *butcher* shops had plenty of items, perhaps including some *spare* ribs.

______ ______ 8. *Finally* he was *ready* to begin construction of a human-like creature.

______ ______ 9. He made a creature that was eight feet tall and *very strong.*

______ ______ 10. The face of the creature, which could *only* be described as *hideous,* was not easy to look upon.

______ ______ 11. One night while Victor was sleeping *lightly,* the monster came to *his* bedroom.

______ ______ 12. Victor screamed *loudly,* and the monster ran *away* in disappointment.

______ ______ 13. Victor developed *brain* fever as a *result* of the encounter.

______ ______ 14. When Victor *recovered* from his illness, he discovered that one of his brothers had been murdered by an *unknown* person.

______ ______ 15. In despair Victor went away to a *remote* wilderness to sort *out* his problems.

______ ______ 16. There he saw a *strange creature* running into the mountains.

______ ______ 17. Victor chased after the creature, but he was *unable* to *catch* it.

______ ______ 18. *Soon* after he had sat *down* to rest, the creature appeared before him.

______ ______ 19. It was *Victor Frankenstein's* monster who had come to talk to *him.*

______ ______ 20. The monster was *very sad* because people were unkind to him.

EXERCISE 9

Identify the part of speech of each italicized word or group of words by placing the appropriate abbreviations in the blanks: adj (adjective), adv (adverb), x (other).

_____ _____ 1. Frankenstein's monster told a *sad story* of loneliness.

_____ _____ 2. After leaving *Victor Frankenstein's* house, he had *gone* to live in the country.

_____ _____ 3. He had tried *diligently* to help the *simple* people by bringing them firewood.

_____ _____ 4. They took the firewood, but they were at first frightened and *then angry.*

_____ _____ 5. The monster had become *very upset* and had gone back to the city.

_____ _____ 6. There he killed Victor's brother and *cleverly* tried to place the *blame* on someone else.

_____ _____ 7. The *full* realization of what he had done came *swiftly* to Victor.

_____ _____ 8. The monster started making *strong* demands that he would force Victor to carry *out.*

_____ _____ 9. He said that if Victor did not make a *female* companion for him, he would begin killing human beings at *random.*

_____ _____ 10. Victor went *away,* gathered up some *more* parts, and started building a bride for the monster.

_____ _____ 11. The monster waited in *eager* anticipation, but he was to be *sorely* disappointed.

_____ _____ 12. Victor became disgusted with *his* project and destroyed all the tissue *just* before it came to life.

_____ _____ 13. Needless to say, the monster was *deeply* disappointed with *this* development.

_____ _____ 14. Before the monster ran away, he swore to get *revenge* on Victor's *wedding* night.

_____ _____ 15. When Victor got married, he armed himself *fully,* expecting a visit from the *vengeful* monster.

_____ _____ 16. That very night, the monster slipped into the *bridal* chambers and strangled the *unlucky* bride.

_____ _____ 17. Victor himself *vowed* to revenge the murder by killing the monster, but the monster was *not* to be found.

_____ _____ 18. Victor *finally* died in a cabin in the *frozen* lands of the North, where his body was found by a friend.

______ ______ 19. The monster dropped by for one *last* visit, so that he could complain about the sadness of *his* life.

______ ______ 20. He said that Victor had created a man without a friend, love, or even a soul, and, therefore, Victor was *more wicked* than anyone.

Prepositions

A preposition functions as a connective. The preposition connects its **object(s)** to some other word(s) in the sentence. A preposition and its object(s)—usually a noun or pronoun—with modifiers make up a **prepositional phrase.**

Bart worked against great odds and completed the fourth grade.
(against = prep; odds = object; against great odds = prepositional phrase)

Everyone in his household cheered his effort.
(in = prep; household = object; in his household = prepositional phrase)

Some of the most common prepositions are the following:

about	above	across	after	against
among	around	before	behind	below
beneath	beside	between	beyond	but
by	despite	down	for	from
in	into	like	near	of
off	on	over	past	to
toward	under	until	upon	with

Some prepositions are composed of more than one word and are made up from other parts of speech:

according to	ahead of	along with	as far as
as well as	aside from	back of	because of
in spite of	instead of	in front of	together with

Caution: Do not confuse adverbs with prepositions.

I went *across* slowly. (without an object—adverb)

I went *across* the field. (with an object—preposition)

We walked *behind* silently. (without an object—adverb)

We walked *behind* the mall. (with an object—preposition)

EXERCISE 10

In the blanks indicate whether each italicized word is a preposition (prep) or not (x). (See Answer Key for answers.)

______ ______ 1. *Of* all cacti, the saguaro is the oldest and the largest *in* North America.

______ ______ 2. It can live *for* three hundred years *and* can grow to a height of fifty feet.

______ ______ 3. It has provided the Indians *of* the Southwest *with* food from its fruit.

Fill in each blank with an appropriate preposition.

4. ____________ the main trunk run ribs ____________ tough fibers that expand when the cactus absorbs water.

5. These ribs have been used ____________ settlers and Indians ____________ building shelters.

6. Woodpeckers chisel out holes ____________ the trunks ____________ the saguaros and build their nests there.

Conjunctions

A conjunction connects and shows a relationship between words, phrases, or clauses. A phrase is two or more words acting as a part of speech; we have discussed verb phrases and prepositional phrases. A clause is a group of words with a subject and a verb. One kind is **independent** and can stand by itself: *She plays bass guitar.* The other kind is **dependent** and cannot stand by itself: *When she plays bass guitar.*

There are two kinds of conjunctions: the coordinating and the subordinating.

Coordinating conjunctions connect words, phrases, and clauses of equal rank: noun with noun, adjective with adjective, verb with verb, phrase with phrase, main clause with main clause, and subordinate clause with subordinate clause. The seven common coordinating conjunctions are *for, and, nor, but, or, yet,* and *so.* One simple way to remember them is to think of the acronym FANBOYS; each letter in that word is the first letter of one of the common coordinating conjunctions. The coordinating conjunctions will take on special significance in our discussion of compound and compound/complex sentences in Chapter 4.

Two nouns: Bring a pencil (noun) and (conj) some paper (noun).

Two phrases: Did she go to the store (phrase) or (conj) to the game (phrase)?

Paired conjunctions such as *either/or, neither/nor,* and *both/and* are usually classed as coordinating conjunctions.

Neither the coach nor the manager was at fault.
conj conj

Subordinating conjunctions connect dependent clauses with main clauses. These conjunctions will be important in our discussion of complex and compound/complex sentences in Chapter 4. The following are among the most common subordinating conjunctions:

after	although	as	as if
as long as	as soon as	because	before
besides	but that	if	in order that
notwithstanding	provided	since	so that
till	until	when	whenever
where	whereas	wherever	

Sometimes the dependent clause comes *before* the main clause and is set off by a comma.

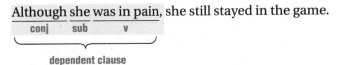

Although she was in pain, she still stayed in the game.
conj sub v
dependent clause

Sometimes the dependent clause comes *after* the main clause and is *not* set off by a comma.

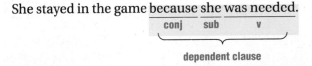

She stayed in the game because she was needed.
conj sub v
dependent clause

Caution: Certain words can function as either conjunctions or prepositions. It is necessary to look ahead to see if the word introduces a clause with a subject and verb—conjunction function—or takes an object—preposition function. Some of the words with two functions are these: *after, for, since, till, until.*

After the concert was over, we went home. (clause follows—conjunction)

After the concert, we went home. (object follows—preposition)

EXERCISE 11

In the blanks indicate whether each italicized word is a conjunction (conj) or not (x). (See Answer Key for answers.)

______ ______ 1. *Although* they are different varieties of butterflies, the Monarch *and* the Viceroy have some common characteristics.

______ ______ 2. They are similar *in* color, shape, *and* size.

______ ______ 3. *Because* the Monarch caterpillar feeds *on* the milkweed plant, it is bitter to the taste of birds.

Fill in each blank with an appropriate conjunction.

4. ____________ the Viceroy does not have a bitter taste, it is safe ____________ it looks like the Monarch.

5. This technique is a form of mimicry, ____________ it is widely used by insects ____________ reptiles.

6. Thus certain animals survive ____________ prosper ____________ they assume the bad reputation of other creatures.

EXERCISE 12

Identify the part of speech of each italicized word or group of words by placing the appropriate abbreviations in the blanks: conj (conjunction), prep (preposition), x (other). (See Answer Key for answers.)

_____ _____ 1. *Before* meteorology was well developed, people *in* the country did their own forecasting of weather.

_____ _____ 2. Their main method was to look around *at* their surroundings *for* signs.

_____ _____ 3. Animals provided them *with* many indications of whether winter would be bad *or* good.

_____ _____ 4. For example, thick fur or hair *on* horses, dogs, squirrels, *and* cattle was regarded as a sign of a cold winter.

_____ _____ 5. When squirrels had especially bushy tails *and* rabbits grew thick fur on the bottom of their feet, people prepared *for* deep snows.

_____ _____ 6. *If* the owls *in* the mountains hooted more often than usual, a bad winter was coming.

_____ _____ 7. There was *even* a saying, "*When* the owl hoots and hoots, put on your coat and boots."

_____ _____ 8. *When* worms crawled into houses, people expected sleet *and* snow.

_____ _____ 9. *If* the miller moths frequently bumped *against* the screen as if trying to enter the house, winter would be bad.

_____ _____ 10. Many people believed that the woolly worm provided many signs *of* both good *and* bad weather.

_____ _____ 11. If many of them were crawling about in the early fall *and if* they had heavy coats, the people forecasted a brutally cold season.

_____ _____ 12. *But* if the woolly worm was still crawling around just before the first frost, *then* the people expected that the winter would be mild.

_____ _____ 13. Plants were watched carefully *during* the summer *for* tell-tale signs.

_____ _____ 14. Moss growing heavily on trees *and* leaves growing in great numbers were interpreted *as* signs of nature getting ready for the cold.

_____ _____ 15. *When* the bark of trees grew thick or the bark grew thicker *on* the north side of the trees, some country people prepared for the worst.

_____ _____ 16. These people looked well beyond their immediate environment *with* its plants *and* animals for signs.

_____ _____ 17. Some maintained that the twelve days after Christmas were good predictors *of* weather *for* the following twelve months.

_____ _____ 18. Even weather was taken *as* a good indicator *of* weather.

_____ _____ 19. A long, hot summer was regarded *as* the sign *of* a long, cold winter.

_____ _____ 20. *By* counting the rings around a moon, a farmer could calculate how many days *before* a rain would come.

EXERCISE 13

Identify the part of speech of each italicized word or group of words by placing the appropriate abbreviations in the blanks: conj (conjunction), prep (preposition), x (other).

_____ _____ 1. Horse trading is a *declining* art *in* American society.

_____ _____ 2. Once many thousands *of* people made their living *by* trading horses.

_____ _____ 3. These traders traveled from farm *to* farm, riding one horse *and* leading several others.

_____ _____ 4. They traded *for* other horses, but they also traded for poultry, cattle, land, *and* personal items.

_____ _____ 5. Some horse traders were honest *and* some were *not.*

_____ _____ 6. A farmer buying a horse *from* a trader had to be careful *or* he could purchase a bad horse.

_____ _____ 7. *Because* a horse's teeth grow longer *with* age, some traders filed the teeth to shorten them.

_____ _____ 8. *When* a horse is in poor condition, it often develops a depression *over* each eye.

______ ______ 9. Dishonest traders used needles *for* pumping these depressions full *of* air.

______ ______ 10. *As* horses grow older, the hair *on* their face begins to turn gray.

______ ______ 11. Some traders dyed the gray hair, *often with* shoe polish.

______ ______ 12. Traders often gave pain killers *to* lame horses *and* sold them.

______ ______ 13. Many *of* the farmers were shrewd in selecting horses, *but* some were gullible.

______ ______ 14. The farmers were looking mainly *for* workhorses to pull a plow *and* other farm equipment.

______ ______ 15. They wanted horses *with* large feet that would not easily sink *into* the soil.

______ ______ 16. They also wanted horses *with* broad chests *and* strong hindquarters for pulling.

______ ______ 17. Some were looking *for* a handsome matching pair *of* horses to pull their wagons and buggies into town.

______ ______ 18. Horse trading was a big business *because* the farmers' livelihood depended *on* their having good work animals.

______ ______ 19. *Now,* most people who own horses use them only *for* recreational riding.

______ ______ 20. *Whereas in* past times the horses worked to support people, now people work to support horses.

Interjections

An interjection is one or more words used to convey strong emotions or surprise. When an interjection is used alone, it is usually punctuated with an exclamation mark: Wow! Curses! Cowabunga! Yabba dabba doo! When it is used as part of a sentence, an interjection is usually followed by a comma: Oh, I did not consider that problem. The interjection presents no significant structural problem and is seldom used in college writing.

Chapter Checklist

Consider word order (*the round book*), word composition (*rounded, see, saw, boys*), and word meaning (What does *round* mean?) when determining **parts of speech.**

1. **Nouns** name persons, animals, plants, places, things, substances, qualities, and ideas; they can take a plural form (girl, girls), and are often pointed out by noun indicators like *a, an, the.*

    a book, *an* elephant, *the* girls

______ ______ You went (5) ______________ and spent my hard-earned (6) ______________.

______ ______ Then you (7) ______________ a dozen bouncing (8) ______________.

______ ______ And then (9) ______________ had to go and hurt my (10) ______________

______ when you ran (11) ______________ with my best friend named Tex.

Chorus:

______ ______ You (12) ______________ my feelings, and I'm feeling (13) ______________.

______ ______ You hurt my (14) ______________ (15) ______________ I'm feeling sad.

You hurt my feelings, ran away with my friend.

______ ______ (16) ______________ hurt my feelings, and (17) ______________ is the end.

______ You went out drinking on my (18) ______________.

______ ______ Then you (19) ______________ my mother is a (20) ______________.

______ You made (21) ______________ of my special mustache.

______ You (22) ______________ it gives you a funny itch.

______ You broke all my Dolly Parton (23) ______________.

______ Then you went (24) ______________ dancing with your ex.

______ And then you had to go and (25) ______________ my feelings

______ when you ran away with my best (26) ______________ named Tex.

Chorus:

You hurt my feelings, and I'm feeling sad.

______ ______ You hurt my (27) ______________, and I'm feeling (28) ______________.

______ You (29) ______________ my feelings, and I'm feeling sad

______ because Tex was the best (30) ______________ I ever had.

Scale for correctly labeled parts of speech (have your instructor check your answers):

0–10 = need help with grammar

11–20 = starting to catch on to parts of speech

21–25 = becoming highly capable with parts of speech

26–30 = excellent knowledge of parts of speech

Scale for correct answers (exact matches with the Answer Key or close enough, as determined by your instructor) of word selections:

0–10 = need help with basic song writing

11–20 = ready for simple ditties

21–25 = becoming highly capable in dealing with sentimentality

26–30 = ready for advanced country song writing

REVIEW 5

Write ten sentences of ten words or more on the subject television, *and label the nouns (n), verbs (v), and pronouns (pro).*

1.

2.

3.

4.

5.

6.

7.

8.

9.

10.

REVIEW 6

Write five sentences of ten words or more on the subject of family, *and label each word as a part of speech.*

1.

2.

3.

4.

5.

2

Verbs and Subjects

The two most important parts of any sentence are its subject and verb. **The subject is what the sentence is about, and the verb indicates what the subject is doing or is being.** Sentence structure requires both, though occasionally the subject will be understood rather than stated. Many times the subject and verb taken together will carry the basic meaning of a sentence. Consider this example: *The woman left for work.* The subject *woman* and the verb *left* carry the basic meaning. Naturally, putting the right words into these key positions makes writing more effective. Identifying and creating subjects and verbs are prime concerns of this chapter.

Topics covered in this chapter:

Verbs

We begin with the verb because verbs are usually more easily recognized than subjects. The verb (sometimes called a simple predicate) as a part of sentence structure is also a verb part of speech. Therefore, the verb is easy to identify because it shows different time periods (for example, *see, saw, seen* or *am, was, been*). But it must also be related to the subject. When you find the verb and ask the question Who? or What? you will find the subject. Hence, **verbs show action or express being in relation to the subject of the sentence.**

Types of Verbs

Action verbs suggest movement or accomplishment in idea or deed. We can "consider the statement" or "hit the ball." Here are other examples:

She *left* the arena.

He *bought* the book.

They *adopted* the child.

He *understood* her main theories.

Being verbs indicate existence. Few in number, they include *is, was, were, am,* and *are.*

The movie *is* sad.

The book *was* comprehensive.

They *were* responsible.

I *am* concerned.

We *are* organized.

Verb Phrases

Verbs may occur as single words or as phrases. A **verb phrase** is made up of a main verb and one or more helping verbs such as the following:

be	*was*	*can*	*have*
is	*were*	*could*	*had*
are	*will*	*would*	*has*
am			

Here are some sentences that contain verb phrases:

The judge *has presided* over many capital cases.

His reputation for order in the courtroom *is known* to all.

His rulings *are* seldom *overturned* on appeal.

Compound Verbs

Verbs that are joined by a coordinating conjunction such as *and* or *or* are called **compound verbs.**

As a district attorney, she *had presented* and *won* famous cases.

She *prepared* carefully and *presented* her ideas with clarity.

Verbals

Do not confuse verbs with **verbals.** Verbals are verb-like words in certain respects, but they function as other parts of speech. There are three kinds:

The *infinitive* is made up of the word *to* (sometimes omitted) and a verb. It provides information, but unlike the true verb it is not tied to the subject of the sentence. Usually the infinitive acts as a noun.

He wanted *to go* to work.

To go to work has her main objective.

(In the first example, the word *wanted* is the verb for the subject *He.* The word *go* follows *to,* and *to go* is an infinitive.)

The *gerund* is a verb-like word ending in *-ing* that acts as a noun.

Going to work was her main objective.

He thought about *going* to work.

Going in each sentence acts as a noun.

The *participle* is a verb-like word that has an *-ing* or a past-tense verb ending (usually *-ed*). It acts as an adjective or adverb.

Walking to town in the dark, he lost his way.

Wanted by the FBI, she was on the run.

In the first example, the word *walking* acts as an adverb, answering the question *when.* In the second, the word *wanted* is an adjective, answering the question *which one* and modifying *she.*

Main points: Verbals are not connected to subjects, but verbs are. Verbals act as nouns, adjectives, or adverbs. A verb linked to the word *to* is no longer a verb, and a word that ends in *-ing* and does not have a helping verb cannot be a verb.

Trouble Spots

Do not confuse **adverbs** such as *never, not,* and *hardly* with verbs. They only modify verbs.

The attorney could *not* win the case without key witnesses. (*Not* is an adverb. You can't "not" something, but you "could win." The verb phrase is *could win.*)

The jury could *hardly* hear the witness. (*Hardly* is an adverb, and *could hear* is the verb phrase.)

Do not overlook a part of the verb that is separated from another in a question such as "Where had the defendant gone on that fateful night?" If you have trouble finding the verb phrase, recast the question, making it into a statement form: "The defendant *had gone* where on that fateful night." The result will not necessarily be a smooth or complete statement, but you will be able to see the basic elements more easily.

Can the defense lawyer *control* the direction of the trial?

Change the question to a statement to find the verb phrase:

The defense lawyer *can control* the direction of the trial.

EXERCISE 1

Underline the verb(s) in each sentence. (See Answer Key for answers.)

1. Chimpanzees live and travel in social groups.
2. The composition of these groups varies in age and gender.
3. The habitat of the chimpanzees is mainly forests.
4. They spend more time in the trees than on the ground.
5. Each night they make a nest of branches and leaves in trees.
6. Sometimes a proud male will beat on his chest.
7. Chimpanzees are violent at times, but usually they live peacefully.
8. When a chimp finds food, he or she hoots and shakes branches.
9. Other chimps hear the commotion and go to the food source.

10. Can chimps use sophisticated tools?

11. Chimp tools, such as leaf sponges for collecting water and sticks for digging out termites, are primitive.

EXERCISE 2

Underline the verb(s) in each sentence.

1. Do chimpanzees share many features with human beings?
2. More than ninety percent of basic genetic make-up is shared.
3. Both human beings and chimps can use reason.
4. Some scientists maintain that chimps have a remarkable talent for communication.
5. Chimps do not have the capacity for human speech.
6. However, there is evidence that chimps can use other symbols.
7. In one experiment, chimps learned American Sign Language.
8. Are chimps able to learn a complex system of language?
9. Chimp scholar Washoe has learned more than 160 signs and can ask questions.
10. Another chimp, Lana, can carry on conversation with human beings by using a computer.

Subjects

The **simple subject** is what the sentence is about. You can recognize the simple subject by asking **Who?** or **What?** causes the action or expresses the state of being found in the verb. It is usually the main noun or pronoun occurring before the verb.

The court selected the jury members. Who "selected"? The "court" (subject).
action verb

The judge was happy. Who "was"? The "judge" (subject).
being verb

Types of Subjects

The simple subject may also be compound:

The *prosecutor* and the *attorney* for the defense made opening statements.

The *judge* and *jury* listened carefully.

Location

Although the subject usually occurs before the verb, it may follow the verb:

Into the court stumbled the *defendant* in chains.

There was little *support* for him in the audience. (*There* is an adverb and can never be a subject.)

The command, or **imperative**, sentence has "you" as the implied subject and no stated subject:

(You) Now take the oath.

(You) Sit in that chair.

(You) Read the notes.

Trouble Spot

Be careful not to confuse subjects with objects of prepositions. The prepositional phrase is made up of a preposition (words such as *of, in, to, at, with*) and one or more nouns or pronouns with their modifiers (*of the problem, in the courtroom, in the jury, to the judge and media, at the wrong time, with anger*). The object of a preposition cannot be a subject or any other main part of sentence structure.

The foreman (subject) of the jury (obj. of prep.) directs deliberation.

The bailiff (subject) of the court (obj. of prep.) is directed by the judge.

The smallest room (subject) in the building (obj. of prep.) is used for deliberation.

EXERCISE 3

Underline the subjects in the following sentences. (See Answer Key for answers.)

1. Mahatma Gandhi gave his life for India and for peace.
2. Through a practice of nonviolent resistance, he led his people to freedom from the British.
3. (You) Ponder his preference for behavior rather than accomplishment.
4. There was only good in his behavior and in his accomplishments.
5. His fasting demonstrated one way of not cooperating.
6. He taught his people self-sufficiency in weaving cloth and making salt for themselves against British law.
7. Gandhi urged the tolerance of all religions.
8. Finally, the British granted freedom to India.

9. Some leaders in India questioned the freedom of religion.

10. Gandhi, the Indian prince of peace, was killed by an intolerant religious leader.

EXERCISE 4

Underline the subjects in the following sentences.

1. More than two hundred years ago, some tractors were powered by steam.

2. They could travel at about three miles per hour for about ten minutes.

3. (You) Consider that information in relation to the following material.

4. There was a great future ahead for these self-powered vehicles.

5. About a hundred years later, in 1897, Freelan O. Stanley and associates produced the Stanley steamer, the best-known steam automobile.

6. Around the same time, William Morrison built an electric car.

7. Without polluting the atmosphere, it could go twenty miles an hour.

8. After traveling for about fifty miles, its batteries had to be recharged.

9. Meanwhile in Germany, Gottlieb Daimler and Karl Benz were developing the internal-combustion engine.

10. In the 1890s, the first successful gasoline-powered automobiles took to the roads.

EXERCISE 5

In each sentence, underline the subject(s) and double-underline the verb(s). (See Answer Key for answers.)

1. (You) Read this exercise and learn how the Aztec ruled a huge empire in Mexico until the 1500s.

2. Their cities were as large as those in Europe at that time.

3. Government and religion were blended.

4. There was little difference between the two institutions.

5. They built huge temples to their gods and sacrificed human beings.

6. The religious ceremonies related mainly to their concerns about plentiful harvests.

7. Aztec society had nobles, commoners, serfs, and slaves.

8. The family included a husband, a wife, children, and some relatives of the husband.

9. At the age of ten, boys went to school, and girls either went to school or learned domestic skills at home.

10. The Aztec wore loose-fitting garments, they lived in adobe houses, and they ate tortillas.

11. Scholars in this culture developed a calendar of 365 days.

12. Huge Aztec calendars of stone are now preserved in museums.

13. Aztec language was similar to that of the Comanche and Pima Indians.

14. Aztec written language was pictographic and represented ideas and sounds.

15. Both religion and government required young men to pursue warfare.

16. By pursuing warfare, the soldiers could capture others for slaves and sacrifice, and enlarge the Aztec Empire.

17. In 1519, Hernando Cortez landed in what is now Mexico.

18. He was joined by Indians other than Aztec.

19. After first welcoming Cortez and his army, the Aztec then rebelled.

20. The Spaniards killed Emperor Montezuma II, and then they defeated the Aztec.

EXERCISE 6

In each sentence, underline the subject(s) and double-underline the verb(s).

1. Who are the Eskimos?

2. Where did they come from?

3. How do they live?

4. How has their way of life changed in the last century?

5. These questions are all important.

6. There may be different views on some of the answers.

7. They live in the Arctic from Russia east to Greenland.

8. Their ancestors came from Siberia in Northern Asia.

9. They have learned to live in a land of perpetual snow.

10. The word *Eskimo* means *eaters of raw meat* in a Native American language.

11. Their own name for themselves is *Inuit* or *Yuit,* meaning *people.*

12. For hundreds of years, their homes were made of blocks of ice or packed snow called *igloos.*

13. They ate the raw flesh of caribou, seals, whales, and fish.

14. During the 1800s, the whalers enlisted the Eskimos as helpers.

15. Later the traders came and bought furs from the Eskimos.

16. The traders and whalers brought guns, tools, technology, and disease to the Eskimos.

17. The Eskimos used their new harpoons and guns and killed more game.

18. Their simple, traditional way of life changed.

19. Now most Eskimos live in settlements.

20. Despite the many changes, Eskimos still treasure their ancient ways.

Chapter Checklist

The **subject** is what the sentence is about, and the **verb** indicates what the subject is doing or is being.

Verbs

Verbs show action or express being in relation to the subject.

1. **Action verbs** suggest movement or accomplishment in idea or deed.

   He *dropped* the book. (movement)

   He *read* the book. (accomplishment)

2. **Being verbs** indicate existence.

   They *were* concerned.

3. Verbs may occur as single words or phrases.

   He *led* the charge. (single word)

   She *is leading* the charge. (phrase)

4. Verbs that are joined by a coordinating conjunction such as *and* and *or* are called **compound verbs.**

   She *worked* for twenty-five years and *retired.*

5. Do not confuse verbs with **verbals;** verbals are verb-like words that function as other parts of speech.

   Singing (gerund acting as a noun subject) is fun.

   I want *to eat.* (infinitive acting as a noun object)

6. Do not confuse **adverbs** such as *never, not,* and *hardly* with verbs; they only modify verbs.

7. Do not overlook a part of the verb that is separated from another in a question.

   "Where *had* the defendant *gone* on that fateful night?"

Subjects

You can recognize the **simple subject** by asking Who? or What? causes the action or expresses the state of being found in the verb.

1. The **simple subject** and the **simple verb** can be single or compound.

   My *friend* and *I* have much in common.

   My friend *came* and *left* a present.

2. Although the subject usually occurs before the verb, it may follow the verb.

   There was *justice* in the verdict.

3. The command, or **imperative,** sentence has a "you" as the implied subject, and no stated subject.

   (*You* understood) Read the notes.

4. Be careful not to confuse subjects with **objects of prepositions.**

   The *foreman* (subject) of the *jury* (object of preposition) directs discussion.

Chapter Review

REVIEW 1

In each sentence, underline the subject(s) and double-underline the verb(s). (See Answer Key for answers.)

1. (You) Read this exercise carefully.

2. What causes earthquakes?

3. How much damage can they do?

4. As the name suggests, earthquakes shake the earth.

5. There is no simple answer to the question of cause.

6. The earth is covered by rock plates.

7. Instead of merely covering, they are in constant movement.

8. These plates bump into each other and then pass over each other.
9. The rocks get squeezed and stretched.
10. They pull apart or pile up and cause breaks in the earth's surface.
11. These breaks are called *faults.*
12. The formation of a fault is an earthquake.
13. During the breaking or shifting, a seismic wave travels across the earth's surface.
14. These quaking vibrations are especially destructive near the point of the breaking or shifting.
15. Their force is equal to as much as ten thousand times that of an atomic bomb.
16. For many years, scientists have tried to predict earthquakes.
17. There has been little success in their endeavors.
18. Earthquakes are identified only after they occur.
19. Some regions, such as California, experience more earthquakes than others.
20. Somewhere in the earth, a quake of some magnitude is almost certainly occurring as you read this sentence.

REVIEW 2

In each sentence, underline the subject(s) and double-underline the verb(s).

1. (You) Consider this information about Puerto Rico.
2. Just where is Puerto Rico?
3. What do the words *Puerto Rico* mean?
4. Are Puerto Ricans citizens?
5. How is Puerto Rico different from our states?
6. Will it ever become a state?
7. The Commonwealth of Puerto Rico is located southeast of Florida.
8. Puerto Rico means *rich port.*
9. Puerto Rico became a U.S. territory in 1898 after the Spanish-American War.

3

Sentence Problems

Sentence writing in college assignments is plagued with three recurring problems: the fragment, the comma splice, and the run-together. All three are structural problems that confuse the reader because they give false signals. If your readers encounter a false signal, they may be able to figure out what you intended to say, but they will have to expend extra effort in order to do so. They will have to work without the true signals that you should have given. A good sentence should not draw that unfavorable attention. It should be easy on the eye and easy on the mind.

Topics covered in this chapter:

Fragments

A correct sentence offers signals of completeness. The structure and punctuation provide those signals. For example, if I say to you, "She left in a hurry," you do not necessarily expect me to say anything else, but if I say, "In a hurry," you do. If I say, "Tomorrow I will give you a quiz on the reading assignment," and I leave the room, you will merely take note of my words. But if I say, "Tomorrow when I give you a quiz on the reading assignment," and leave the room, you will probably be annoyed, and you may even chase after me and ask me to finish my sentence. Those examples illustrate the difference between completeness and incompleteness. A fragment is punctuated as a sentence but is not a sentence.

In short, we can say that a sentence is a word or a group of words—usually with a subject and a verb—that makes sense. However, there are many one-word sentences and many arrangements of words that lack a subject and a verb but still make sense. You must then be able to distinguish between effective, or acceptable, fragments and the vague, unintentional fragments (usually phrases, incomplete structures, and dependent clauses) that do not make sense standing alone.

Among the commonly used acceptable fragments are the following:

- *Interjections:* Great! Hooray! Whoa!
- *Exclamations:* What a day! How terrible! What a bother!

- *Greetings:* Hello. Good morning. Good night. Good evening.
- *Questions:* What for? Why not? Where to?
- *Informal Conversation:* (What time is it?) Eight o'clock. Really.

You will notice that most of these acceptable fragments are conversational and would seldom appear in college writing. Other fragments that you may see in books are unconventional and are used for special effects.

Your main concern is with the unacceptable fragment, commonly called simply the fragment. A **fragment** is a word or group of words without either a subject or verb ("He going to town.") or without both ("Going to town."), or it is a group of words with a subject and verb that cannot stand alone ("When he left."). Although its punctuation signals a sentence, the structure of a fragment signals incompleteness. If you were to say it or write it to someone, that person would expect you to go on and finish the idea.

Other specific examples of common unacceptable fragments are these:

- *Dependent clause only:* When she came.
- *Phrase(s) only:* Waiting there for some help.
- *No subject in main clause:* Went to the library.
- *No verb in main clause:* She being the only person there.

The following exercises will give you an opportunity to work with each of the various types of unacceptable fragments.

Dependent Clauses as Fragments

Incorrect: They continued to dance. *While the ship was sinking.*

Correct: While the ship was sinking, they continued to dance.

Correct: The ship was sinking. They continued to dance.

Incorrect: I knew the senator. *Who led the fight for civil rights.*

Correct: I knew the senator who led the fight for civil rights.

Explanation

Although a dependent clause has a subject and verb, it cannot stand by itself because it begins with a subordinating word. The dependent clause as a fragment can be corrected by removing the subordinating word or by attaching the dependent clause to an independent clause. Some of the most common subordinating words are these:

Because (he left)

Although (he left)

That (he left)

When (he left)

After (he left)

Since (he left)

How (he left)

Till (he left) (a variation of *until*)

Unless (he left)

Before (he left)

He left is a sentence (an independent clause), but placing any one of these ten words before it turns it into a dependent clause and, by itself, a fragment. Note that the first letters of the words spell out BAT WASHTUB. Using that acronym to remember these common subordinating words, you will be able to spot many fragments easily.

EXERCISE 1

Underline and correct each fragment. (See Answer Key for answers.)

Because her handwriting was bad. She decided to type. Although she typed on an electric typewriter. Her typing was slow. Moreover, she still made many errors. It took her hours to complete her work. That she was frustrated is an understatement. When she bought a computer. She did so as a last resort. Because she had little money. She worked hard. During the two months since she purchased the computer. She has experienced both success and failure. How she might go wrong was a concern from the beginning. She was doing well. Until she bought some computer games. Then she became preoccupied with the games, and her school work suffered. She knew she would fail in school. Unless she learned to discipline herself. Before it was too late.

EXERCISE 2

Underline and correct each fragment.

Because Jack was a good citizen. He became concerned about voting. He was eighteen. Although he was not well informed. He, nevertheless, went to the city hall to register. When he was asked for his political party affiliation. He said he chose to be an Independent. Until he gained more knowledge. He said that soon he would be a voter. Who knew issues and candidates. After he had done some research on issues pertaining to the next election. He listened to some campaign speeches and political debates. He learned about the views, accomplishments, and reputations of the various candidates. On the second Tuesday in November, he voted in his first election. Unless he had somehow overlooked some critical information. He knew he was now well informed. He went to his neighborhood polling place. Where he exercised his right and performed his duty as a citizen.

EXERCISE 3

Change the following fragments into sentences. (See Answer Key for possible answers.)

1. Because he was the best driver.

    ___

2. Although he did not own the car.

    ___

3. That he was cool under pressure.

    ___

4. When he was challenged.

    ___

5. After the game had ended.

    ___

6. Since he moved to town.

    ___

7. How to make friends in a hurry.

    ___

8. Till he went for refreshments.

    ___

9. Unless he made the same mistake again.

    ___

10. Before he would do it.

    ___

EXERCISE 4

Change the following fragments into sentences.

1. Because she was not shy.

    ___

2. Although she had no automobile.

    ___

3. That he had not seen *Terminator II.*

4. When they left her house.

5. After they reached the theater.

6. Since she had asked for the date.

7. How to walk down the aisle.

8. Till he gained more confidence.

9. Unless he was hungry.

10. Before the show was over.

Phrases as Fragments

Verbal phrase

Incorrect: *Having studied hard all evening.* John decided to retire.

Correct: Having studied hard all evening, John decided to retire.

The italicized part of the incorrect example is a verbal phrase. A **verbal** is verb-like without being a verb in sentence structure. Verbals include verb parts of speech ending in *-ed* and *-ing.* They function as nouns (called **gerunds**) or adjectives and adverbs (called **participles**). They also include the infinitive, a construction made up of *to* and a verb—for example, *to leave.*

Prepositional phrase

Incorrect: *After the last snow.* The workers built the road.

Correct: After the last snow, the workers built the road.

Appositive phrase

Incorrect: He lived in the small town of Whitman. *A busy industrial center near Boston.*

Correct: He lived in the small town of Whitman, a busy industrial center near Boston.

In this example, the fragment is an appositive phrase—a group of words following a noun or pronoun and renaming it.

Explanation of How to Correct Phrases as Fragments

Although a phrase may carry an idea, it is fragmentary because it is incomplete in structure. It lacks a subject and verb. A phrase fragment can usually be corrected by connecting it to a complete sentence (independent clause). An appositive phrase is usually set off by a comma or commas. A verbal or prepositional phrase is usually set off by a comma when the phrase begins a sentence.

EXERCISE 5

Underline and correct each fragment. (See Answer Key for answers.)

The armadillo looks like a prehistoric animal. Wearing a suit of armor. The armadillo's shell is constructed. Of hard, bony plates. It is not suitable for a pet. Living in the wild. It is contented. Though having a fierce appearance. The armadillo is not a good fighter. Designed only for chewing. The armadillo's teeth are far back in its mouth. It uses its claws to burrow into soil for tunnels and nests. When it is attacked, it scurries for its tunnel or rolls up into a ball. A ball about the size of a basketball. The armadillo is common in Texas and Oklahoma. Two states with warm weather.

EXERCISE 6

Underline and correct each fragment.

As a subject of historical record. Dancing seems be a natural human act. Even prehistoric cave paintings depict dancing figures. Scrawled outlines of people in motion. Dancing takes many forms, but mainly it is a matter of moving rhythmically. In time to music. Most children jump up and down when they are excited and sway back and forth when they are contented. Having studied the behavior of many ethnic groups. Anthropologists confirm that dancing reveals much. About a group's culture. People dance for various reasons: to entertain others, to relax, to worship, to inspire others, and to celebrate life. One stylized form of dancing is the ballet. A story told with graceful rhythmic movement and music. Folk dances often

Fragments as Word Groups Without Subjects or Without Verbs

Incorrect: John studied many long hours. And received the highest grade in the class. (without subject)

Correct: John studied many long hours and received the highest grade in the class.

Incorrect: Few children living in that section of the country. (without verb)

Correct: Few children live in that section of the country.

Explanation

Each conventional sentence must have an independent clause, meaning a word or a group of words that contains a subject and a verb and that can stand alone. A command or direction sentence, such as "Think," has an understood subject of *you.*

EXERCISE 9

Underline and correct each fragment. (See Answer Key for answers.)

Fleas remarkable animals. Though they do not have wings, jump more than twelve inches. Fleas living on many kinds of animals. Suck blood from their victims. They often move from pets to human beings. They do not discriminate. They land on poets, politicians, physicians, and anyone else in close proximity. Carry germ-ridden blood and spread diseases. Fleas the main spreader of the bubonic plague. Rodents, including those infected with diseases, providing fleas with transportation and food. Nowadays one attacker is called the *human flea.* This creature in houses where it lays eggs on the carpet. Often bites human beings. Another kind of flea is the *chigoe.* Burrows under the skin and lays its eggs. For flea control, cleanliness and insecticide are important. Our pets, mainly our cats and dogs, among the main carriers of fleas in the typical household.

EXERCISE 10

Underline and correct each fragment.

Susan B. Anthony among the leaders in the early days of the women's rights movement. Her parents being Quakers who believed in the equality of the sexes. As a young woman, wanted to argue against alcohol abuse. Was not allowed to speak at rallies because she was a woman. Susan B. Anthony not to be silenced. She joined other women in fighting for women's rights in education, voting, and property ownership. Also fought for the abolition of slavery. When black men were given the right to vote in 1869, she was pleased. However, was disappointed that women did not receive the same consideration. For about sixty years, she was active in the National Woman Suffrage Movement. Died fourteen years before the 19th Amendment gave women the right to vote. In 1979, she was recognized for her civic contributions when the government placed her picture on a one-dollar coin.

EXERCISE 11

The following fragments lack either a subject or a verb. Correct them. (See Answer Key for possible answers.)

1. One of the two main industries in Florida which is tourism.
2. People going to Florida to visit Disney World.
3. Others who go to watch sporting events such as the Orange Bowl.
4. Tourists regarding the Everglades National Park as a national wonder.
5. St. Augustine having the oldest house in the United States.
6. Many major league baseball teams to Florida for spring training.
7. Can see a living coral reef formation at a state park.
8. Tours, demonstrations, and displays at the John F. Kennedy Space Center.
9. Some people who visit Florida for the pleasant weather and good beaches.
10. Circus World which offers opportunities for amateurs.

EXERCISE 12

The following fragments lack either a subject or a verb. Correct them.

1. Australia as the "down under" country because it is south of the equator.
2. It being colonized by the English.
3. The first English residents being convicts.
4. The aborigines moving away from their traditional lands.
5. Had lived there for many thousands of years.
6. The population of Australia now about twenty million.

7. Only about two hundred thousand aborigines.

8. Many people living in the southeastern part of the country.

9. The inner region as the "outback."

10. Australia being known for its unusual animals.

EXERCISE 13

Identify each of the following as a fragment (frag) or a complete sentence (OK). Correct the fragments. (They may be any of the kind you have studied in this chapter: dependent clause, phrase, or word group without a subject or without a verb.) Some fragments can be corrected with sentence combining.

_______ 1. Asia which developed much earlier than the West.

____

_______ 2. More than five thousand years ago, Asia had an advanced civilization.

____

_______ 3. People there who invented writing and created literature.

____

_______ 4. Involved in the development of science, agriculture, and religion.

____

_______ 5. The birthplace of the major religions of the world.

____

_______ 6. The most common religion in Asia being Hinduism.

____

_______ 7. The second most common religion is Islam.

____

_______ 8. Asia is the most populous continent.

____

_______ 9. With almost four billion people.

____

_______ 10. Hong Kong and Bangladesh which are among the most densely populated places in the world.

____

_______ 11. Asia having many ethnic groups.

____

_______ 12. Including the Chinese, the Indians, the Arabs, the Turks, and the Jews.

____

_______ 13. The Chinese have different groups.

____

_______ 14. Speaking many dialects.

____

_______ 15. Although they have different dialects.

____

_______ 16. There is a national language.

____

_______ 17. A language called Mandarin.

____

_______ 18. Cultural differences exist in Taiwan.

____

_______ 19. The main difference being between the Chinese from the mainland and the Taiwanese.

____

_______ 20. Despite the differences, all Chinese have much culture in common.

____

Comma Splices and Run-Togethers

The comma splice and the run-together are two other kinds of faulty "sentences" that give false signals to the reader. In each instance the punctuation suggests that there is only one sentence, but there is material for two.

The **comma splice** consists of two independent clauses with only a comma between them:

> *The weather was disappointing, we canceled the picnic.* (A comma by itself cannot join two independent clauses.)

The **run-together** differs from the comma splice in only one respect: it has no comma. Therefore, the run-together is two independent clauses with *nothing* between them:

The weather was disappointing we canceled the picnic. (Independent clauses must be connected by something.)

Because an independent clause can stand by itself as a sentence and because two independent clauses must be properly linked, you can use a simple technique to identify the comma splice and the run-together. If you see a sentence that you think may contain one of these two errors, ask yourself this question: "Can I insert a period at some place in the word group and still have a sentence on either side?" If the answer is yes and there is no coordinating conjunction, then you have a comma splice or a run-together to correct. In our previous examples of the comma splice and the run-together, we could insert a period after the word *disappointing* in each case, and we would still have an independent clause—therefore, a sentence—on either side.

EXERCISE 14

Identify each word group as a comma splice (CS), a run-together (RT), or a correct sentence (OK). (See Answer Key for answers.)

CS 1. The dragonfly is an aquatic insect it has been around in various forms for millions of years.

OK 2. The typical length now is about four inches, at one time some species had a wingspan of almost three feet.

OK 3. Their wings resemble gauze, and their bodies are slender.

RT 4. They can be green, blue, or brown, their eyes look like clear BBs.

CS 5. They can fly up to fifty miles an hour, their slender bodies and long, slender wings aid them in flight.

OK 6. They use their long legs to catch insects that they encounter in the air.

OK 7. They catch mosquitoes, therefore, they are helpful to people.

RT 8. Poets have written about them in imaginative language; people have given them colorful names.

RT 9. They have been called *snake doctors* they have also been called *devil's darning needles.*

CS 10. Dragonflies mate while flying the female often lays her eggs into the water without landing.

EXERCISE 15

Identify each word group as a comma splice (CS), a run-together (RT), or a correct sentence (OK).

CS 1. The Ramones were a highly influential punk band of the seventies and eighties, the band was from Forest Hills, New York.

OK 2. Although the Ramones reached their forties in the early '90s, they were still playing high-energy music.

OK 3. The Ramones had different last names, but they changed them for the sake of group identity.

RT 4. Their music was simple the Ramones relied on a fast beat, simple chords, and humorous lyrics.

RT 5. The group often poked fun at political figures one song was entitled "Bonzo Goes to Bitburg."

CS 6. The group was a favorite of the English punk scene of the 1970s, the Sex Pistols admired the Ramones.

RT 7. Their older fans were loyal at concerts by the Ramones the audience ranged in age.

RT 8. One reason they played simple songs was that they couldn't play complicated songs.

OK 9. They admitted that they were not talented musicians, however, their fans loved them anyway.

RT 10. In 1995 they released their last collection of songs, *Adios Amigos,* they took one more tour and retired.

Fixing the Comma Splice or the Run-Together

Once you identify a comma splice or a run-together in your writing, you need to correct it. There are four different ways to fix these common sentence problems.

First Way: Use a Comma and a Coordinating Conjunction

Incorrect: We canceled the picnic the weather was disappointing. (run-together)

Correct: We canceled the picnic, *for* the weather was disappointing. (Here we inserted a comma and the coordinating conjunction *for.*)

Knowing the seven coordinating conjunctions will help you in writing sentences and correcting sentence problems. The acronym FANBOYS should aid you in remembering them:

For

And

Nor

But

Or

Yet

So

EXERCISE 16

Identify each word group as a comma splice (CS), a run-together (RT), or a complete sentence (OK), and make needed corrections using commas and coordinating conjunctions. (See Answer Key for possible answers.)

Example: __CS__ He did the assignment, and his boss gave him a bonus.

______ 1. In 1846 a group of eighty-two settlers headed for California with much optimism, a hard road lay ahead.

______ 2. They had expected to cross the mountains before winter they were in good spirits.

______ 3. They would not arrive in California before winter, nor would some of them get there at all.

______ 4. When they encountered a heavy snowstorm, they stopped to spend the winter they still thought they would be safe.

______ 5. They made crude shelters of logs and branches some also used moss and earth.

______ 6. They had trouble managing they had not encountered such problems before.

______ 7. They ran out of regular food they ate roots, mice, shoe leather, and their horses.

______ 8. Thirty-five members of the Donner Party died that winter the survivors were so hungry that they ate the dead bodies.

______ 9. They were weak, sick, and depressed they did not give up.

______ 10. Fifteen people set out to get help seven survived and returned to rescue friends and relatives.

EXERCISE 17

Identify each word group as a comma splice (CS), a run-together (RT), or a complete sentence (OK), and make needed corrections using commas and coordinating conjunctions.

______ 1. John Dillinger was a troubled youth he dropped out of school when he was sixteen.

_______ 2. He held several jobs then he turned to crime.

_______ 3. He was arrested for armed robbery he spent nine years in prison.

_______ 4. He got out and formed a gang, they robbed eleven banks in 1933 and 1934.

_______ 5. He was twice captured by the police and imprisoned.

_______ 6. Each time he escaped by using clever schemes.

_______ 7. His bank jobs were well planned they often depended on deception.

_______ 8. On one occasion while he was robbing a bank, he explained to observers that he was making a gangster movie.

_______ 9. In 1934 he was shot dead when he came out of a movie.

_______ 10. He thought he was safe his date had made a deal with the FBI and wore a red dress as a signal.

Second Way: Make One of the Clauses Dependent

Incorrect: The weather was disappointing, we canceled the picnic.

Correct: *Because* the weather was disappointing, we canceled the picnic.

By inserting the subordinating conjunction *because,* you can transform the first independent clause into a dependent clause and correct the comma splice. Knowing the common subordinating conjunctions will help you in writing sentences and correcting sentence problems. Use the acronym BAT WASHTUB (introduced earlier in this chapter) to recall them:

Because

After

That

When

Although

Since

How

Till

Unless

Before

Other subordinating words include *if, besides, until, whereas, as, as if, whenever, wherever.*

EXERCISE 18

Identify each word group as a comma splice (CS), a run-together (RT), or a complete sentence (OK), and correct the errors by making a dependent clause. (See Answer Key for possible answers.)

_______ 1. Chris Evert was one of the most successful tennis players of the 1970s and 1980s she was not physically powerful.

_______ 2. She was intelligent and well coordinated, she became a top player.

_______ 3. She was still in her teens she won major championships.

_______ 4. She attracted much attention in 1974 she won fifty-five consecutive matches.

_______ 5. She reached the top she had much competition there.

_______ 6. Evonne Goolagong was Evert's main competition at first Martina Navratilova soon assumed that role.

_______ 7. Financially Chris Evert's career was notable she made more than six million dollars.

_______ 8. Chris Evert helped to make women's tennis what it is today, and she will not be forgotten.

_______ 9. She was called the "ice princess" she did not show her emotions.

_______ 10. She is regarded as one of the greatest athletes of the last thirty years.

EXERCISE 19

Identify each word group as a comma splice (CS), a run-together (RT), or a complete sentence (OK), and correct the errors by making a dependent clause.

_______ 1. Jesse Owens won four gold medals in the 1936 Olympics he became a famous person.

_______ 2. The 1936 Olympics were held in Nazi Germany Owens was placed at a disadvantage.

_______ 3. Hitler believed in the superiority of the Aryans, he thought Owens would lose.

_______ 4. Jesse Owens won Hitler showed his disappointment openly.

_______ 5. Owens broke a record for the 200-meter race that stood for thirty-six years.

_______ 6. Owens then jumped a foot farther than others in the long jump Hitler left the Stadium.

_______ 7. Before the day was at last over, Owens had also won gold medals in the 100-meter dash and the 400-meter relay.

_______ 8. Hitler's early departure was a snub at Owens, but Jesse did not care.

_______ 9. Owens returned to the United States, he engaged in numerous exhibitions, including racing against a horse.

_______ 10. In Owens' later years he became an official for the U.S. Olympic committee, he never received the recognition that many contemporary athletes do.

Third Way: Use a Semicolon

Incorrect: The weather was disappointing, we canceled the picnic.

Correct: The weather was disappointing; therefore, we canceled the picnic.

This comma splice was corrected by a semicolon. *Therefore,* the transitional connective, is optional. The most common transitional connectives are these:

However

Otherwise

Therefore

Similarly

Hence

On the other hand

Then

Consequently

Also

Thus

Did you pick out the phrase HOTSHOT CAT, made up of the first letter of each of these common transitional connectives? The acronym will help you remember them. Others include *in fact, for example, moreover,* and *nevertheless.*

EXERCISE 20

Identify each word group as a comma splice (CS), a run-together (RT), or a complete sentence (OK). Make corrections with a semicolon, and add a transitional connective if appropriate. (See Answer Key for possible answers.)

_______ 1. Madonna Louise Veronica Ciccone became one of the biggest pop stars in the 1980s, she is known to most people as Madonna.

_______ 2. Madonna was talented in dance she even won a dance scholarship to the University of Michigan in the mid-1970s.

_______ 3. She was not interested in staying in school, with a mere thirty-five dollars in her possession, she moved to New York City.

_______ 4. After working in several small bands, she finally made her first album in 1983.

_______ 5. When her first album became number one on the *Billboard* list in 1984, she immediately had new opportunities.

_______ 6. Madonna continues to be a very popular singer, she can also act.

_______ 7. She has performed well in the comedy movie *Desperately Seeking Susan* she was also a hit in the comic strip drama *Dick Tracy.*

_______ 8. Madonna is an expert at manipulating the media, she increases her popularity each time she changes her image.

_______ 9. Her show business career has prospered, she has had problems in her private life.

_______ 10. She continues to promote herself other people do too.

EXERCISE 21

Identify each word group as a comma splice (CS), a run-together (RT), or a complete sentence (OK). Make corrections with a semicolon, and add a transitional connective if appropriate.

_______ 1. Ants are highly social insects they live in colonies.

_______ 2. They work for the benefit of the group each individual is important.

_______ 3. Ants have different roles they will, in some species, have different sizes and shapes.

_______ 4. An ant will be either a queen, a worker, or a male there is not an identity problem among ants.

_______ 5. A worker may be a soldier whose job is to defend the nest that ant has large mandibles, or teeth.

_______ 6. The worker that is a janitor will have the job of cleaning the nest her head is big for pushing waste material through the tunnel.

_______ 7. The queen is very large because she must lay many eggs.

_______ 8. The workers are all female their job is to do all of the work.

_______ 9. The males have only one function, and that is to mate with the queen.

_______ 10. In some species, the workers may change roles in their work the males only mate and die young.

Fourth Way: Make Each Clause a Separate Sentence

Incorrect: The weather was disappointing, we canceled the picnic.

Correct: The weather was disappointing. We canceled the picnic.

To correct the comma splice, merely replace the comma with a period and begin the second sentence (clause) with a capital letter. After identifying a comma splice or run-together word group, this method is quite easy. You simply complete the procedure shown in the example. This method is at once the simplest and most common method of correcting comma-splice and run-together problems.

EXERCISE 22

Identify each word group as a comma splice (CS), a run-together (RT), or a complete sentence (OK), and make corrections with a period and a capital letter. (See Answer Key for possible answers.)

_______ 1. About a hundred and fifty years ago, the British soldiers wore a bright red coat, they also wore a black hat and white trousers.

_______ 2. The soldiers looked good in parades the queen was very proud.

_______ 3. On the battlefield, the situation was different, and the uniform was regarded differently.

_______ 4. The coat could be seen at a great distance enemies aimed at the red coats.

_______ 5. This had long been a problem, even in the days of the American Revolution.

_______ 6. No one in high position was willing to change the colors of the uniform, the soldiers decided to take action.

_______ 7. A solution was at hand, the soldiers would wear the red coats but change the colors.

_______ 8. At the time of their experiment, they were serving in India, they would use natural elements to solve their problem.

_______ 9. In the dry season, they would rub yellow-brown dust on their uniforms, and in the wet season they would use mud.

_______ 10. They liked the camouflage color so much they finally changed the color of their uniforms to the drab color they called it *khaki,* the Indian word for dust.

EXERCISE 23

Identify each word group as a comma splice (CS), a run-together (RT), or a complete sentence (OK), and make corrections with a period and a capital letter.

_______ 1. The phonograph was invented about a hundred years ago the inventor was Thomas Edison.

_______ 2. He calculated that sound vibrations could be recorded and that they could be played back.

_______ 3. He constructed an instrument with a mouthpiece, a speaker, a cylinder, a needle, and a crank he put tin foil around the cylinder.

_______ 4. He uttered the first words into the machine as he turned the crank the first words were "Mary had a little lamb."

_______ 5. Next he moved the needle back to its original position he turned the crank again and put his ear to the speaker.

_______ 6. The speaker looked like a large funnel Edison could hear scratchy sounds.

_______ 7. Then he heard his own voice his invention was a success.

_______ 8. The next step was to perfect his invention he worked to improve the sound and to simplify the process.

_______ 9. The quality of the needles was improved the cylinders were made of wax to improve the fidelity.

_______ 10. Soon it was possible for people all over the world to listen to great music and to hear the voices of famous people.

Techniques for Spotting Problem Sentences

1. For the fragment, ask yourself: "If someone were to say or write this to me, would I expect the person to add to the statement or rephrase it?"
2. For the comma splice or run-together, ask yourself: "Is there a point in this word group at which I can insert a period and create a sentence on either side, without there being a coordinating conjunction (FANBOYS) at that point?"
3. If you have much trouble with comma splices and run-togethers, be suspicious about these constructions as you revise:
   a. A comma preceded by a noun or pronoun followed by a noun or pronoun
   b. A sentence beginning with a subordinating conjunction (BAT WASHTUB)
   c. A sentence longer than fifteen words
4. If you have trouble with fragments, look for these clues:
   a. A word group with a single verb ending in *-ing*
   b. A word group without both a subject and verb
   c. A sentence shorter than six words

Chapter Checklist

Fragments

1. A correct sentence signals completeness; a **fragment** signals incompleteness—it doesn't make sense. You would expect the speaker or writer of a fragment to say or write more or to rephrase it.

2. A **dependent clause** cannot stand by itself because it begins with a subordinating word.

    Because he left.

    When she worked.

    Although they slept.

3. A **verbal phrase,** a **prepositional phrase,** and an **appositive phrase** may carry ideas, but each is incomplete because it lacks a subject and verb.

    verbal phrase: *having studied hard*
    sentence: Having studied hard, he expected to pass.

    prepositional phrase: *in the store*
    sentence: She worked in the store.

    appositive phrase: *a successful business*
    sentence: Marks Brothers, a successful business, sells clothing.

4. Each complete sentence must have an **independent clause,** meaning a word or a group of words that contains a subject and a verb that can stand alone.

    He enrolled for the fall semester.

Comma Splice and Run-Together

1. The **comma splice** (CS) consists of two independent clauses with only a comma between them.

    The weather was bad, we canceled the picnic. (A comma by itself cannot join two independent clauses.)

2. The **run-together** (RT) differs from the comma splice in only one respect: it has no comma between the independent clauses.

    The weather was bad we canceled the picnic. (Independent clauses must be properly connected.)

Correcting Comma Splices and Run-Togethers

1. Use a comma and a **coordinating conjunction** (for, and, nor, but, or, yet, so) to correct the CS or RT.

    The weather was bad, *and* we canceled the picnic.

2. Use a **subordinating conjunction** (such as because, after, that, when, although, since, how, till, unless, before) to make one clause dependent and correct the CS or RT.

    Because the weather was bad, we canceled the picnic.

3. Use a **semicolon** (with or without a transitional word such as however, otherwise, therefore, similarly, hence, on the other hand, then, consequently, also, thus) to correct the CS or RT.

    The weather was bad; *therefore,* we canceled the picnic.
    or The weather was bad; we canceled the picnic.

4. To correct the CS or RT, merely replace the comma with a period and add a capital letter (CS), or insert a period between the two independent clauses (RT) and add a capital letter.

    The weather was bad. We canceled the picnic.

Chapter Review

REVIEW 1

Correct each comma splice and run-together problem by using one of the preceding methods. In some instances, any one of the four will correct the problem structurally, but always select the one that you think is most effective for smoothness of expression and emphasis. You may find it helpful to read the material aloud as you work.

Dinosaurs were giant lizard-like animals, they lived more than a hundred million years ago. Some had legs like lizards and turtles, some had legs more like birds. The ones with legs like birds. Could walk easily with raised bodies. They varied in size, many were huge. The largest, the diplodocus, was about ninety feet long, equal to the distance between the bases in baseball. It weighed more than ten elephants. The smallest weighed no more than two pounds and was no bigger than a chicken. Some dinosaurs ate meat, almost certainly some dinosaurs ate other dinosaurs. Used their strong claws and fierce teeth to tear at their victims. Dinosaurs were different in design as well as size. They had horns, spikes, bills, armor-like plates, club-like tails, bony crests, and teeth in many sizes and shapes their heads were proportionately tiny or absurdly large. Their mouths varied. Depending on their eating habits.

REVIEW 2

Correct each fragment, comma splice, and run-together. Choose the methods of corrections that will promote smoothness of expression.

Deserts are often referred to as wastelands. It is true that not as many plants grow there as in a temperate zone, it is also true that animals do not live there in great numbers. But many plants and animals live and do quite well in the desert. Because of their adaptations.

Not all deserts have the same appearance. Many people think of the desert as a hot, sandy area. Actually sand covers only about twenty percent of the desert. Some deserts have mountains some others have snow.

Because deserts are dry for most of the year. Plants must conserve and store water. Several kinds of cacti can shrink during a dry season and swell during a rainy season. Some shrubs simply drop their leaves and use their green bark to manufacture chlorophyll. Seeds sometimes lying in the desert for several years before sprouting to take advantage of a rainfall.

Animals have quite effectively adjusted to the desert, some animals obtain moisture from the food they eat and require no water. One animal of the desert, the camel, produces fat. Which it stores in its hump. The fat allows the camel to reserve more body heat it needs little water. Still other animals feed only at night or are inactive for weeks or even months.

About fifteen percent of the land of the earth is covered by deserts. That area increasing every year. Because of overgrazing by livestock. Also because of the destruction of forests. Areas that were once green and fertile will now support little life and only a small population of human beings.

4

Types of Sentences

You may be pleased to discover that there are only four kinds of conventional sentences in English writing: simple, compound, complex, and compound-complex. The terms may be new to you, but the concepts are easy. If you can recognize subjects and verbs, distinguish between independent clauses and dependent clauses (covered in the previous chapter but discussed in more detail here), and count to four, you should be able to identify and write these forms with a little instruction and practice.

Of course, you have an advantage. You have been using these forms all along, perhaps without being aware of what you were doing technically. But after you have finished this chapter, you will be able to make conscious choices to vary your sentence patterns for emphasis and effectiveness of style.

Topics covered in this chapter:

Classifying Sentences

The following discussion will cover sentence types in detail according to the following principle: **On the basis of number and kinds of clauses, sentences may be classified as simple, compound, complex, and compound-complex.**

Clauses

A **clause** is a group of words with a subject and a verb that functions as a part or all of a complete sentence. There are two kinds of clauses: (1) independent (main) and (2) dependent (subordinate).

Independent clause: *I have the money.*

Dependent clause: *When you are ready*

An independent (main) clause is a group of words with a subject and verb that can stand alone and make sense. An independent clause expresses a complete thought by itself and can be written as a separate sentence.

A dependent clause, on the other hand, is a group of words with a subject and verb that depends on a main clause to give it meaning. The dependent clause functions in the common sentence patterns as a noun, adjective, or adverb.

that fell last night (no meaning alone)

The snow *that fell last night* is nearly gone. (has meaning with dependent adjective clause modifying the noun *snow*)

since Helen came home (no meaning alone)

Since Helen came home, her mother has been happy. (has meaning with dependent adverb clause answering the question *when* and modifying the verb *been*)

that he would win (no meaning alone)

That he would win seemed certain. (has meaning with dependent noun clause acting as the subject of the verb *seemed*)

Simple Sentences

A simple sentence consists of an independent clause and no dependent clauses. It may contain phrases and have more than one subject and/or verb.

The *lake looks* beautiful in the moonlight. (one subject and one verb)

The *Army, Navy,* and *Marines sent* troops to the disaster area. (three subjects and one verb)

We sang the old songs and *danced* happily at their wedding. (one subject and two verbs)

My *father, mother,* and *sister came* to the school play, *applauded* the performers, and *attended* the party afterwards. (three subjects and three verbs)

Compound Sentences

A compound sentence consists of two or more independent clauses with no dependent clauses.

He opened the door, and *he found the missing paper.*

He opened the door; he found the missing paper.

He opened the door; however, *he did not find the missing paper.*

Independent clauses in a compound sentence are usually connected by either a coordinating conjunction or a semicolon. Sometimes independent clauses are joined by conjunctions in pairs. At other times, independent clauses are joined by a semicolon and marked by one of the transitional connectives (conjunctive adverbs). The coordinating conjunctions are *for, and, nor, but, or, yet, so* (FANBOYS). Conjunctions in pairs include *either/or, neither/nor, not only/but also.* Among the most common transitional connectives are *however, otherwise, therefore, similarly, hence, on the other hand, then, consequently, also, thus* (HOTSHOT CAT).

Note the punctuation in these examples. Commas precede coordinating conjunctions; semicolons precede transitional connectives (except for *then, now, thus,* and *soon*) and commas follow them.

Neither is the battle over, *nor* the victory won.

He is not only the best athlete, *but* he is also the best student in our class.

We were late; *therefore,* we missed the first act.

We waited; *then* we left without him.

I am very tired, *and* I wish to rest for a few minutes.

John is a very able politician; he should win the election.

Complex Sentences

A complex sentence consists of one independent clause and one or more dependent clauses.

When lilacs are in bloom, we love to visit friends in the country. (one dependent clause and one independent clause)

Although it rained last night, we decided to take the path that led through the woods. (one independent clause and two dependent clauses)

At times, the complex sentence is written with a noun clause as subject, object, or complement (sentence completer).

That he continues to try is praiseworthy. (noun clause as subject)

I know *who will win.* (noun clause as object)

His difficulty was *how he should approach the matter.* (noun clause as complement)

Compound-Complex Sentences

A compound-complex sentence consists of two or more independent clauses and one or more dependent clauses.

Albert enlisted in the Army, and Robert, who was his older brother, joined him a day later.

Independent clauses: Albert enlisted in the Army; Robert joined him a day later.

Dependent clause: who was his older brother

Because Mr. Roberts was a talented teacher, he was voted teacher of the year, and his students prospered.

Independent clauses: he was voted teacher of the year; his students prospered

Dependent clause: Because Mr. Roberts was a talented teacher

Punctuation Tips

1. Use a comma before a coordinating conjunction (FANBOYS) between two independent clauses.

   The movie was good, but the tickets were expensive.

2. Use a comma after a dependent clause (usually beginning with a subordinating word from the BAT WASHTUB list) that occurs before the main clause.

   When the bus arrived, we quickly boarded.

3. Use a semicolon between two independent clauses in one sentence if there is no coordinating conjunction.

 The bus arrived; we quickly boarded.

4. Use a semicolon before and usually a comma after a transitional connective (HOTSHOT CAT) between two independent clauses. (No comma after *then, now, thus,* and *soon.*)

 The bus arrived; however, it was full of passengers.

EXERCISE 1

Label each sentence as S (simple), Cp (compound), Cx (complex), or CC (compound-complex). (See Answer Key for answers.)

_______ 1. The most popular sport in the world is soccer.

_______ 2. People in ancient China and Japan had a form of soccer, and even Rome had a game that resembled soccer.

_______ 3. The game as it is today got its start in England.

_______ 4. In the Middle Ages, whole towns played soccer on Shrove Tuesday.

_______ 5. Goals were set up at opposite ends of town, and hundreds of people who lived in those towns would play on each side.

_______ 6. Such games resembled full-scale brawls.

_______ 7. The first side to score a goal won and was declared village champion.

_______ 8. Then both sides tended to the wounded, and they didn't play again for a whole year.

_______ 9. The rules of the game as we know it today were drawn up in the late 1800s at British boarding schools.

_______ 10. Now nearly every European country has a national soccer team, and the teams participate in international tournaments.

EXERCISE 2

Label each sentence as S (simple), Cp (compound), Cx (complex), or CC (compound-complex).

_______ 1. For both rich and poor in Rome, public baths were a daily pleasure.

_______ 2. The baths were somewhat similar to modern health clubs, though they had little equipment for exercising.

_______ 3. Rome alone had 856 baths; most of them were private.

_______ 4. Citizens who struck it rich were expected to build baths for their fellow citizens, and many generously built huge marble facilities.

_______ 5. For the equivalent of about a quarter-penny, any Roman could be massaged, scrubbed, and soaked in a public bath.

_______ 6. First bathers might exercise, and then they went to a hot, dry room to sweat.

_______ 7. Next came a visit to a hot, steamy room, and the final stage was a plunge into ice-cold water.

_______ 8. After the citizens finished their baths, they would wrap themselves in towels and visit with friends or walk about the grounds.

_______ 9. The serious minded could browse through the bath's library.

_______ 10. They also sat around and played chess and checkers in game rooms.

EXERCISE 3

Label each sentence as S (simple), Cp (compound), Cx (complex), or CC (compound-complex). (See Answer Key for answers.)

_______ 1. In ancient Egypt 3,000 years ago, both men and women used cosmetics.

_______ 2. One concern was the matter of using beauty aids, but another was protection against the brilliant desert sun.

_______ 3. The three main colors of their makeup were green, black, and red.

_______ 4. These colors came from crushed rocks that were mixed with water or oil.

_______ 5. Lipstick was made from crushed iron ore and oil; it was applied with a brush that was made of animal hair and bristles.

_______ 6. They applied dark green and black makeup around their eyes by using small sticks.

_______ 7. They made perfume by crushing flowers and fragrant woods, and by mixing that substance with oil.

_______ 8. They put cones of this perfume into their hair where it melted slowly and gave off a fragrance.

_______ 9. Although they were apparently concerned about making themselves attractive to others, they quite effectively protected their skin, lips, and hair from the dry desert air.

_______ 10. Many containers of these cosmetics have been preserved in the pyramids.

EXERCISE 4

Label each sentence as S (simple), Cp (compound), Cx (complex), or CC (compound-complex).

_______ 1. Around 500 B.C., the Mayans began to create their civilization in the southern Gulf Coast region and present-day Guatemala.

_______ 2. The result was remarkable for its brilliant achievements.

_______ 3. Although they had no wheeled vehicles and no beasts of burden such as horses or oxen, they moved great pieces of stone to build their temples.

_______ 4. They had no iron tools; however, they shaped their stone blocks so skillfully that their pyramids still stand.

_______ 5. The pyramids were the center of Mayan religious ceremonies.

_______ 6. The Mayans built many city-states, and the ruins of at least eighty have been found.

_______ 7. The tallest pyramid was as high as a twenty-story building.

_______ 8. A small temple was constructed at the top where priests conducted ceremonies.

_______ 9. These pyramids were surrounded by plazas and avenues.

_______ 10. The Mayans were able to build complex structures and to invent an accurate calendar because they knew mathematics well.

Chapter Checklist

On the basis of number and kinds of clauses, sentences may be classified as simple, compound, complex, and compound-complex.

Clauses

1. A **clause** is a group of words with a subject and a verb that functions as a part or all of a complete sentence. There are two kinds of clauses: (1) independent (main) and (2) dependent (subordinate).
2. **An independent (main) clause is a group of words with a subject and verb that can stand alone and make sense.** An independent clause expresses a complete thought by itself and can be written as a separate sentence.

   I have the money.
3. **A dependent clause, on the other hand, is a group of words with a subject and verb that depends on a main clause to give it meaning.** The dependent clause functions in the common sentence patterns as a noun, adjective, or adverb.

   When you are ready

Types of Sentences

Type	Definition	Example
Simple	One independent clause	She did the work well.
Compound	Two or more independent clauses	She did the work well, and she was paid well.
Complex	One independent clause and one or more dependent clauses	*Because she did the work well,* she was paid well.
Compound-Complex	Two or more independent clauses and one or more dependent clauses	*Because she did the work well,* she was paid well, and she was satisfied.

Punctuation

1. Use a comma before a coordinating conjunction (FANBOYS) between two independent clauses.

   The movie was good, but the tickets were expensive.

2. Use a comma after a dependent clause (usually beginning with a subordinating word from the BAT WASHTUB list) that occurs before the main clause.

   When the bus arrived, we quickly boarded.

3. Use a semicolon between two independent clauses in one sentence if there is no coordinating conjunction.

   The bus arrived; we quickly boarded.

4. Use a semicolon before and usually a comma after a transitional connective (HOTSHOT CAT), between two independent clauses. (No comma after *then, now, thus,* and *soon.*)

   The bus arrived; however, it was full of passengers.

Chapter Review

REVIEW 1

Label each sentence as S (simple), Cp (compound), Cx (complex), or CC (compound-complex). (See Answer Key for answers.)

CP 1. Bastille Day is a holiday in France, for the French love freedom.

CP 2. The Bastille was a famous prison in Paris, and French people know its history.

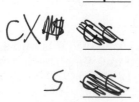

CX ______ 3. The Bastille will not be forgotten as a symbol in France and in other French-speaking countries.

S ______ 4. For hundreds of years, the Bastille was used to imprison those who offended the royalty, but on July 14, 1789, the common people stormed the gates.

8. ______________________________

____

9. ______________________________

____

10. ______________________________

____

REVIEW 5

Write ten complex sentences. The first five have been started for you.

1. Although he did the work quickly, ______________________________

____

2. ______________________________

because of the storm.

3. After you go to the party, ______________________________

____

4. That you are smart is ______________________________

____

5. When he turned to go, everyone ______________________________

____

6. ______________________________

____

7. ______________________________

____

8. ______________________________

____

9. ______________________________

____

10. ______________________________

____

REVIEW 6

Write ten compound-complex sentences. The first five have been started for you.

1. Because he was my friend, I had to defend him, and I ______________________________

 ____

2. Although he started late, he finished rapidly, and he ______________________________

 ____

3. That she was wealthy didn't interest me, nor did ______________________________

 ____

4. When the clock struck twelve, ______________________________

 ____

5. I have not eaten since ______________________________

 ____

6. ______________________________

 ____

7. ______________________________

 ____

8. ______________________________

 ____

9. ______________________________

 ____

10. ______________________________

 ____

5

Sentence Combining

The simple sentence, the most basic sentence in the English language, can be exceptionally useful and powerful. Some of the greatest statements in literature have been presented in this form. Its strength is in its singleness of purpose. However, a piece of writing made up of a long series of simple sentences is likely to be monotonous. Moreover, the form may suggest a separateness of ideas that does not serve your purpose well. If your ideas are closely related, some equal in importance and some not, you can work with patterns of sentence combining to show those relationships between ideas. These patterns are simply structures of coordination and subordination.

Coordination—The Compound Sentence

If you want to communicate two equally important and closely related ideas, you certainly will want to place them close together, probably in a **compound sentence.** Consider this arrangement.

> (1) Looking forward to the play-off games of the National League West, we find a few surprises. (2) The Los Angeles Dodgers have not played well in August. (3) The San Francisco Giants have now won ten games in a row. (4) These two teams are tied for the lead. (5) Atlanta and Cincinnati are only a few games back.

The paragraph contains five sentences. All are related, and the sequence of ideas is sound. But notice that the connection between ideas seems closer at two points. Sentences 2 and 3 stand in contrast. The writer can show that relationship by combining the sentences in either of two ways.

> The Los Angeles Dodgers have not played well in August, <u>but</u> the San Francisco Giants have now won ten games in a row.
>
> or
>
> The Los Angeles Dodgers have not played well in August; <u>however,</u> the San Francisco Giants have now won ten games in a row.

In each instance the period is dropped and the two sentences are combined into one. The first sentence uses a comma and the coordinating conjunction *but.* The second uses the transitional connective *however,* preceded by a semicolon and followed by a comma.

Sentences 4 and 5 have an almost identical contrasting relationship and can be similarly combined. The revised paragraph might look like this:

> Looking forward to the playoff games in the National League West, we find a few surprises. The favored Los Angeles Dodgers have not played well in August, but the San Francisco Giants have now won ten games in a row. These two teams are tired for the lead; however, Atlanta and Cincinnati are only a few games back.

Obviously, not all sentences can be or should be combined. Notice what happens when we combine sentences 3 and 4:

Illogical Combination: The San Francisco Giants have now won ten games in a row, and these two teams are tied for the lead.

Sentences 1 and 2 also could not be combined effectively.

You, the writer, must make the choice. These are the questions to ask yourself: Are the ideas closely and logically related? Are the ideas of somewhat equal importance?

Relevant Punctuation

When you combine two sentences by using a coordinating conjunction, drop the period, change the capital letter to a small letter, and insert a comma before the coordinating conjunction (one of the seven words, the first letters of which comprise the acronym FANBOYS).

independent clause	*, for* *, and* *, nor* *, but* *, or* *, yet* *, so*	independent clause

When you combine two sentences by using a semicolon, replace the period with a semicolon and change the capital letter to a small letter. If you wish to use a transitional connective, insert it after the semicolon and follow it with a comma. (Usually no comma follows *then, now, thus,* and *soon.*) The first letters of ten common transitional connectives comprise the acronym HOTSHOT CAT.

independent clause	*; however,* *; otherwise,* *; therefore,* *; similarly,* *; hence,* *; on the other hand,* *; then* *; consequently,* *; also,* *; thus*	independent clause

Other transitional connectives are *moreover, nevertheless,* and *in fact.*

7. The soldiers packed up their equipment. They left town.
8. No one knows why the heavy metal band Screaming Death has lost popularity. Some point to the illness of their pet python, Ziggy.
9. He believes in his own greatness. On his last birthday, he sent his parents a message of congratulations.
10. Pancake makeup poses no health threat to the user. Clowns and mimes use it liberally without worry.

EXERCISE 4

Combine the following pairs of sentences by changing the capital letter to a small letter, replacing the period with a semicolon, and inserting a transitional connective if appropriate. Consider the list of transitional connectives (HOTSHOT CAT and others) from the Relevant Punctuation section.

1. You are three hours late. I'll still go to the restaurant with you because I'm hungry.
2. The platypus is an ugly animal with a poisonous spine. It can be a good companion for someone who likes unattractive, dangerous pets.
3. Skip's '73 Gremlin belches smoke and grinds gears. I would still accompany him to the stock car races.
4. The gas-powered chainsaw is useful for my indoor projects. The Weed Wacker is my favorite tool.
5. I never complain about my new diet. I do grit my teeth when I am really hungry.
6. This fall's new fashions will feature sleek vinyl leggings and hats. Stores have ordered extra shipments.
7. Young buyers are likely to purchase many pairs of leggings. They will probably have less money left for entertainment.
8. Even people who organize monster tractor-pulling events anticipate the fad. They will be selling padded vinyl bumpers for pickups.
9. All pirates are required to give up personal hygiene. Only the most dedicated scoundrels can make that sacrifice.
10. The dentist said, "Jim, your teeth are about to fall out." Jim went shopping for toothpaste.

Subordination—The Complex Sentence

Whereas a compound sentence contains independent clauses that are equally important and closely related, a **complex sentence** combines ideas of unequal value in close relationship. The following two sentences can be combined as either a compound sentence or a complex sentence, depending on whether the writer thinks the ideas are of equal value.

My neighbors are considerate.

They never play loud music.

Combined as a compound sentence, suggesting that the ideas are of equal value, the new sentence looks like this:

My neighbors are considerate, and *they never play loud music.*

independent clause (main idea) — **independent clause (main idea)**

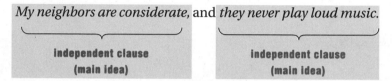

Here are the same two ideas combined as a complex sentence, suggesting that the ideas are of unequal value:

Because my neighbors are considerate, they never play loud music.

dependent clause (less-important idea) — **independent clause (main idea)**

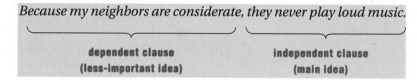

Although both of these forms, compound and complex, are correct, we are likely to believe that the complex form conveys the ideas more precisely in this sentence because one idea does seem to be more important—one idea depends on the other.

Thus if you have two sentences with closely related ideas and one is clearly more important than the other, you may want to consider combining them in a complex sentence. Compare these two paragraphs:

1. *Version 1* contains six simple sentences, implying that the ideas are of equal value:

   (1) I was very upset. (2) The Fourth of July fireworks were especially loud. (3) My dog ran away. (4) The animal control officer made his morning rounds. (5) He found my dog in another part of town. (6) I am relieved.

2. *Version 2,* on the other hand, consists of two simple sentences and two complex sentences, showing that some ideas are more important than others:

   (1) I was very upset. (2) Because the Fourth of July fireworks were especially loud, my dog ran away. (3) When the animal control officer made his morning rounds, he found my dog in another part of town. (4) I am relieved.

You will probably consider Version 2 superior to Version 1. Sentences 2 and 3 are closely related, but 3 is more important. And sentences 4 and 5 are closely related, but 5 is more important. The revision made each pair into a complex sentence.

Although you could combine sentences 1 and 2, the result would be illogical because the wrong idea would be conveyed:

Illogical Combination: I was upset because the Fourth of July fireworks were especially loud.

9. The ambulance drivers were taking a break. A man had a choking fit. The drivers came to his rescue.

10. The film was filled with scenes of violence. It included a charming love story. It became a tremendous hit.

EXERCISE 8

Combine each group of sentences into one compound-complex sentence. Use the rules of sentence combining and punctuation introduced in this chapter.

1. You are a good salesperson. You will make a big impact in our corporation. The rest will be marketing history.

2. The potato blight hit in Ireland in 1845. Many Irish people died. Many immigrated.

3. She was a member of the gender traditionally not associated with fish entrails and parts. She bought her own bait and tackle shop at Puddingstone Lake. She made a tremendous profit in the process.

4. Czar Ivan decided he didn't like beards. Men were told to shave. They could keep their beards and pay a tax.

5. The English controlled Ireland. They did not permit the Irish to own horses. The Irish could own donkeys.

6. The stray puppies moaned. They tried to run away. They did not know that a flea shampoo was a privilege.

7. People do not own as many horses as in the old days. Blacksmiths are not much in demand. Harness-making is a lost art.

8. The tourists watched. The waves broke at six to ten feet. Then a surfer grabbed her board and ran toward the water.

9. They reached the party. First they did the Twist. Then they did the Mashed Potato.

10. The bongo drums were too loud. The police arrived and impounded the instruments. The party was ruined.

Other Methods of Combining Ideas

In this chapter you have learned how to combine simple sentences into compound, complex, and compound-complex sentences that show the coordination and subordination of ideas. There are numerous other methods of combining ideas, too. Here are three you are likely to use in your own writing:

1. Use an appositive, a noun phrase that immediately follows a noun or pronoun and renames it.

   Susan is the leading scorer on the team. Susan is a quick and strong player.

   Susan, *a quick and strong player,* is the leading scorer on the team.

2. Use a prepositional phrase.

   Dolly Parton wrote a song about a coat. The coat had many colors.

   Dolly Parton wrote a song about a coat *of many colors.*

3. Drop the subject in a following sentence.

   Some items are too damaged for recycling. They must be disposed of.

   Some items are too damaged for recycling and must be disposed of.

Chapter Checklist

Coordination

If you want to communicate two equally important and closely related ideas, you certainly will want to place them close together, probably in a **compound sentence** (two or more independent clauses).

1. When you combine two sentences by using a **coordinating conjunction** (FANBOYS), drop the period, change the capital letter to a small letter, and insert a comma before the coordinating conjunction.

   I like your home, but I can visit for only three months.

2. When you combine two sentences by using a **semicolon,** replace the period with a semicolon and change the capital letter to a small letter. If you wish to use a transitional connective, insert it after the semicolon and usually follow it with a comma.

   I like your home. I can visit for only three months.

   I like your home; I can visit for only three months.

   I like your home; however, I can visit for only three months.

Subordination

If you have two ideas that are closely related, but one is secondary or dependent on the other, you may want to use a **complex sentence.**

My neighbors are considerate. They never play loud music.

Because my neighbors are considerate, they never play loud music.

1. If the dependent clause comes before the main clause, set it off with a **comma** (as is done in this sentence).

   Before you dive, be sure there is water in the pool.

2. If the dependent clause comes after the main clause, set it off with a comma only if you use the word *though* or *although,* or if the words are not necessary to convey the basic meaning in the sentence.

   Be sure there is water in the pool before you dive.

Coordination and Subordination

At times you may want to show the relationship of three or more ideas within one sentence. If that relationship involves two or more main ideas and one or more supporting ideas, the combination can be stated in a **compound-complex sentence** (two or more independent clauses and one or more dependent clauses).

> Before he learned how to operate a word-processor, he had trouble with his typewritten assignments, but now he produces clean, attractive material.

1. Use punctuation consistent with that of the compound and complex sentences.

Other Methods of Combining Ideas

1. Simple sentences can often be combined by using an **appositive** or a **prepositional phrase.**

   Dolly Parton wrote a song about a coat. The coat had many colors.

   Dolly Parton wrote a song about a coat, *a colored one* (appositive).

   Dolly Parton wrote a song about a coat *of many colors* (prepositional phrase).

2. Simple sentences can often be combined by dropping a repeated subject in the second sentence.

   Some items are too damaged for recycling. They must be disposed of.

   Some items are too damaged for recycling and must be disposed of.

Chapter Review

REVIEW 1

Combine two or more sentences from each group by using any pattern. (See Answer Key for possible answers.)

1. The Mercury Comet was judged the winner. It had imitation zebra-skin seat covers. It had an eight-ball shift knob.

2. Becky had a great plan to make some money. There was one problem. She had no money to develop her plan.

3. The mixture could not be discussed openly. Competitors were curious. Corporate spies were everywhere.
4. Nancy's bowling ball is special. It is red and green. It is decorated with her phone number in metal-flake.
5. The young bagpiper liked Scottish food. He enjoyed doing Scottish dances. Wearing a kilt in winter left him cold.
6. Ruby missed the alligator farm. She fondly remembered the hissing and snapping of the beasts as they scrambled for raw meat. Her neighbors were indifferent about the loss.
7. Many people are pleased to purchase items with food preservatives. Others are fearful. They think these chemicals may also preserve consumers.
8. Joanne loves her new in-line roller skates. They look and perform much like ice skates. They are not as safe as her conventional roller skates.
9. Fish sold at Discount Fish Market were not of the highest quality. Some of them had been dead for days without refrigeration. They were suitable only for bait.
10. Jerry wanted to impress his date. He splashed on six ounces of He-Man cologne. He put on his motorcycle leathers and a flying scarf.

REVIEW 2

Combine two or more sentences from each group by using any pattern.

1. The candidate had a unique platform. She wanted to use stray dogs to run treadmills in factories. She lost by a landslide.
2. Jack had a bold idea. He would establish a petting zoo. He would use the profits to send his daughter to beauty school.
3. The dinner was excellent. The frankfurters were done to a turn. The relish was fresh. The mustard had no "skin" on it.
4. The children were excited. They were going to the county fair. They would ride on the giant slide and motorized swings.

5. The visitors at the zoo were terrified. A young girl had climbed into the tiger cage. The tiger just licked the child and went back to sleep.
6. The new instructor was nervous. He told jokes. He made balloon animals for students.
7. Lucy O'Gallagher, tugboat captain, is her own boss. Sailors make sexist comments. She throws them into the drink.
8. The bankers were sporting chaps. They gave the Glasgows a choice. Either their home or their RV would be repossessed.
9. Mack and Betty are a happy long-haul driving team. Their sleeping cab has fine furniture. On the cab walls are velvet paintings of John Wayne.
10. The Witchdoctor is a professional wrestler. He occasionally has muscle pain. He enjoys his occupation immensely.

REVIEW 3

Use appropriate methods to combine sentences as needed. Add and delete words sparingly.

Muhammad Ali was arguably the most colorful heavyweight boxing champion ever. He won the title on four occasions. He was not one to hide from the press. He made up sayings and poems about himself and his opponents. He said he would "float like a butterfly and sting like a bee." He announced that he would win each fight. He even named the round. He became a Black Muslim. He refused induction into the armed services. He was convicted of a crime for having done so. As a result he lost his championship. Later the decision was reversed by the United States Supreme Court. He won back the championship by defeating George Foreman in 1974. In 1978 he lost to Leon Spinks. He won it back one more time the next year. He retired in 1980. He fought once more for the title. He quit for good.

Hot SHot Cat: However, otherwise, Therefor, Similarly, Hence
On the other hand, Then, Consequently, Also, Thus

6

Balance in Sentence Writing

We are surrounded by balance. Watch a high-performance jet plane as it streaks across the sky. If you draw an imaginary line from the nose to the tail of the aircraft, you will see the same parts on either side. This parallel arrangement, one that human beings also share, is called bilateral symmetry. If you were to replace one of the streamlined wings of the jet with the straight and long wing of a glider, the plane would never fly. This same lack of balance can also cause a sentence to crash.

Consider these statements:

> "*To be* or not *to be*—that is the question." (dash added)
> This line from Hamlet's soliloquy by Shakespeare is one of the most famous in literature. Compare it to the jet in full flight. It looks good and it "flies" well.
>
> "*To be* or *not being*—that is the question."
> It still vaguely resembles the sleek aircraft, but now a phrase dips like a wing tip. Lurching, the line begins to lose altitude.
>
> "*To be* or *death is the other alternative*—that is the question."
> The wings of rehtoric shear off, and the fuselage plummets to earth at Mach 2.3. The writer and the line slam into the ground with a deafening boom, scattering words across the landscape.

Topics covered in this chapter:

In summation, the first sentence is forceful and easy to read. The second is more difficult to follow. The third is almost impossible to understand. We understand it only because we know what it should look like from having read the original. The point is that perceptive readers will probably be as critical of sentences as pilots are of airplanes.

EXERCISE 5

Fill in the blanks in the following sentences with parallel elements. (See Answer Key for possible answers.)

1. The animated Disney classic concerns a little girl who follows a white rabbit to a land of wonder, ______________, and ______________.
2. In this exciting and ______________ family adventure, Benji is adopted by a loving family.
3. When the two children are kidnapped, Benji is the only one who knows where they are and ________________. *(Benji)*
4. A daring family decides to move to Alaska and ______________ completely apart from society. *(The Alaska Wilderness Adventure)*
5. This film takes us into the forest to share the excitement, ______________, and ______________ of a little deer. *(Bambi)*
6. The caped-crusader and his faithful boy-wonder fight for ______________, ______________, and ______________. *(Batman)*
7. Acme Co.'s best customer uses his entire arsenal, but Road Runner ______________ and ______________.
8. Coldheart has captured children and made them his slaves, and the Care Bears must outwit him with ______________ and ______________. *(The Care Bears in a Land Without Feeling)*
9. Van Dyke is delightful as a man whose old automobile suddenly develops the ability to ______________ and ______________. *(Chitty-Chitty Bang-Bang)*
10. The mistreated stepdaughter is transformed by her fairy godmother, who ______________ her and ______________ her to the royal ball. *(Cinderella)*

EXERCISE 6

Fill in the blanks in the following sentences with parallel elements. (See Answer Key for possible answers.)

1. Schwarzenegger plays a ______________, ______________ killing machine.
2. Nothing can stop him from his mission to find and ______________ an innocent woman. *(The Terminator)*

3. His dreams lead him to Mars in search of certain danger, his old ______________, and a mysterious ______________. *(Total Recall)*

4. A spaceship crash-lands on an unknown planet, and the three astronauts ______________.

5. There, the apes are the rulers, and the ______________________. *(Planet of the Apes)*

6. Ultimately the alien grows to be an enormous size and ______________ killing everyone on board. *(Alien)*

7. When unsuspecting guests check in to a hotel, they are surprised to find vicious ants who appear and ______________ them with a vengeance. *(Ants)*

8. A futuristic ex-cop is drawn out of retirement to seek and ______________ a group of renegade robots. *(Bladerunner)*

9. This is a touching and sometimes comical adventure of an ______________ but ______________ alien. *(E.T.)*

10. Max's somewhat cloudy origin is brought to light as the "creation" of an ______________ and ______________ computer-generated talk show host. *(Max Headroom—The Original Story)*

Combination Signal Words

The words *and* and *but* are the most common individual signal words used with parallel constructions. Sometimes, however, **combination words** signal the need for parallelism or balance. The following are the most common combination conjunctions used in making comparisons: *either/or, neither/nor, not only/but also, both/and, whether/or.* Now consider this faulty sentence and two possible corrections:

Nonparallel: *Either* we will win this game *or* go out fighting.
After *either* we have a clause; after *or* we have a verb.

Parallel: We will *either* win this game *or* go out fighting.
The correction is made by moving the word *either,* thereby balancing a verb *(win)* with a verb *(go).*

Parallel: *Either* we will win this game, *or* we will go out fighting.
The correction is made by inserting a comma and the words *we will,* thereby balancing a clause with a clause.

EXERCISE 9

Underline the parallel elements—words, phrases, or clauses—and double-underline the combination signal words in the following sentences. If the elements are not parallel (and most are not), change them to achieve balance.

1. James Bond protects the U.S. gold reserve both with some wonderfully ingenious gadgets and a few unusually lovely ladies. *(Goldfinger)*
2. Two convicts decide that either they must escape from Devil's Island or die. *(Papillon)*
3. These prehistoric people are not only competing in a quest for fire but also in a struggle for dominance.
4. Whether one side won or the other, humans beings would benefit. *(Quest for Fire)*
5. Neither his poor physical condition nor his reputation would discourage Rocky Balboa. *(Rocky)*
6. Both Al Capone and Bugs Moran neglected to pass out Valentine's Day cards in 1934. *(The St. Valentine's Day Massacre)*
7. It was neither a bird nor was it a plane; it was Superman. *(Superman—The Movie)*
8. The pilot loved both the experience of flying jets and to be around a certain beautiful astrophysicist. *(Top Gun)*
9. A computer whiz-kid manages not only to get himself hooked into a top-secret military computer but also finds the fate of the world in his hands. *(Wargames)*
10. Only one person would walk away from this friendship; it would be either the drug smuggler or it would be the cop. *(Tequila Sunrise)*

Chapter Checklist

1. Parallelism is a balancing of one structure with another of the same kind—nouns with nouns, verbs with verbs, adjectives with adjectives, phrases with phrases, clauses with clauses.

   Men, women, and *children* (nouns) *enjoy* the show and *return* (verbs) each year.

   She fell *in love* and *out of love* (phrases) in a few seconds.

   She fell in love with him, and *he fell in love with her* (clauses).

2. Faulty parallel structure is awkward and draws unfavorable attention to what is being said.

   To talk with his buddies and *eating* fast foods were his favorite pastimes (should be *Talking . . . and eating* or *To talk . . . and to eat*).

3. Some words signal parallel structure. All coordinating conjunctions (FANBOYS: for, and, nor, but, or, yet, so) can give such signals.

   The weather is hot *and* humid. He purchased a Dodger Dog, *but* I chose Stadium Peanuts.

4. Combination words also signal the need for parallelism or balance. The most common ones are *either/or, neither/nor, not only/but also, both/and, whether/or.*

   We will *either* win this game *or* go out fighting (verb following each of the combination words).

Chapter Review

REVIEW 1

Eliminate awkwardness in the following passage by using parallel structure.

Ken Kesey wrote *One Flew Over the Cuckoo's Nest* as a novel. It was later made into a stage play and a film. The title was taken from a children's folk rhyme: "One flew east, one flew west, / One flew over the cuckoo's nest."

The narrator in the novel is Chief Bromden, the central character is Randle McMurphy, and Nurse Ratched is the villain. Bromden sees and can hear but does not speak. He is a camera with a conscience. McMurphy is both an outcast and serves as a leader, and he speaks out for freedom and as an individual. Nurse Ratched is the voice of repression. She is the main representative of what Bromden calls the "Combine." She organizes, directs, controls, and, if necessary to her purposes, will destroy.

The setting is a mental institution where McMurphy has gone to avoid doing more rigorous time in the nearby prison. Discovering what the inmates are going through, he seeks to liberate them from their affliction and freeing them from Nurse Ratched's domination.

A battle of wills ensues, and the reader wonders who will win. The nurse has the whole system behind her, one that prevents the inmates from regaining self-esteem. McMurphy is a colorful, irreverent, expressive person and who appeals to the men's deepest need for self-respect and to be sane. She offers her therapy; his is also offered. She gives them drugs. She also gives them group therapy, which is tightly controlled by her to produce humiliation. McMurphy provides recreation in the form of first a fishing trip and then sex (for some).

McMurphy is eventually defeated by the system. Neither his energy was enough nor his intelligence when the Combine moves in. McMurphy is given a lobotomy and reduced to a mere body without a mind. Out of profound respect and deeply loving, Bromden destroys McMurphy's body, and then escapes.

REVIEW 2

Complete each of the following sentences by adding a construction that is parallel to the underlined construction.

1. We went to the zoo not only for fun but also for ______________________________

____

2. He attended Utah State University for the good education and ______________

____

3. For a college major, she was considering English, history, and ______________
4. Mr. Ramos was a good neighbor and ______________________________
5. My diet for breakfast that week consisted of a slice of bread, a glass of low-fat milk, and ______________________________

6. She decided that she must choose between a social life and ______________________

____

7. Either she would make the choice, or ______________________

____

8. Because we are mutually supportive, either we will all have a good time, or

____

9. Like the Three Musketeers, our motto is "All for one, and ______________________

____

10. My intention was to work for a year, save my money, and ______________________

____

REVIEW 3

Use each of these signal words or combined signal words in a sentence of ten or more words.

1. and

____

____

2. but

____

____

3. so

____

____

4. either/or

____

____

5. both/and

____

____

7

Verbs

This chapter covers the use of standard verbs. To some, the word *standard* implies "correct." A more precise meaning is "that which is appropriate among educated people." Therefore, a standard verb is the right choice in most school assignments, most published writing, and most important public speaking situations. We all change our language when we move from these formal occasions to informal ones: we don't talk to our families in the same way we would speak at a large gathering in public; we don't write letters to friends the same way we write a history report. But even with informal language we would seldom change from standard to nonstandard usage.

Topics covered in this chapter:

Community Dialects and Standard Usage

The "nonstandard" may be part of what we call a community dialect, one that serves a person well within a given community of speakers. However, outside that community it may bring unfavorable attention to itself.

Consider this hypothetical situation. I am your teacher. At our first class meeting, I say to you, "I be your educational leader in here." At that moment, the English department head bursts into the room and shouts, "Don't listen to him. He don't know his verbs, and he ain't qualified to learn you." Chances are, you would rightly question the quality of teaching in that department. The problem would not be one of understanding—you would know what the speakers meant. The problem would instead be the appropriate use of language. Both the chairperson and I would be using verbs that are not customarily used by people in our roles and situations. Even if *you* sometimes use some of those words in those ways, you might be bothered and disappointed by *our* doing so.

If, however, in a certain community of speakers, one person says, "He don't look good today," and that person's companion says, "She don't either," then there is no problem, because there the word *don't,* used with the third-person-singular subject, draws no unfavorable attention and understanding is clear.

Community dialects may be highly expressive and colorful. Popular songs and many television programs often use them well. Some people who use only a community dialect are much more gifted in communicating—explaining things, telling a story, getting to the point—than those who use only the standard dialect. And some people can use either the standard or the community dialect with equal skill. Those people are, in a limited sense, bilingual.

That said, we turn to our concern in this book, the standard use of language—and specifically in this chapter, the standard use of verbs. Standard usage is advantageous because it is appropriate for the kind of writing and speaking you are likely to do in pursuing your college work and future career.

Verbs can be divided into categories labeled *regular* and *irregular,* depending on their forms. The **regular verbs** use an *-ed* ending to indicate past tense (meaning time). For example, you would say, "I *need* this instruction now," for present tense and "I *needed* this instruction last year" for past tense. In **irregular verbs,** the past tense forms vary widely. The following patterns will show the difference between a community dialect and the standard dialect for a regular verb *(walk)* and three irregular verbs (*do, be,* and *have*).

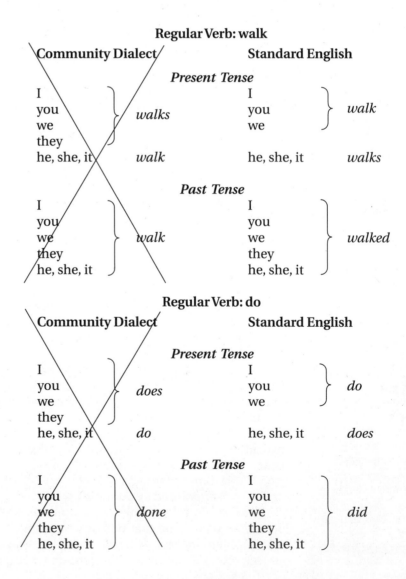

Regular Verb: walk

Community Dialect		Standard English	
Present Tense			
I, you, we, they	*walks*	I, you, we	*walk*
he, she, it	*walk*	he, she, it	*walks*
Past Tense			
I, you, we, they, he, she, it	*walk*	I, you, we, they, he, she, it	*walked*

Regular Verb: do

Community Dialect		Standard English	
Present Tense			
I, you, we, they	*does*	I, you, we	*do*
he, she, it	*do*	he, she, it	*does*
Past Tense			
I, you, we, they, he, she, it	*done*	I, you, we, they, he, she, it	*did*

Irregular Verb: be

Community Dialect		Standard English	
Present Tense			
I, you, we, they, he, she, it	*be, is,* or no verb	I	*am*
		you, we, they	*are*
		he, she, it	is
Past Tense			
I, he, she, it	*were*	I, he, she, it	*was*
we, you, they	*was*	we, you, they	*were*

Irregular Verb: have

Community Dialect		Standard English	
Present Tense			
I, you, we, they	*has*	I, you, we	*have*
he, she, it	*have*	he, she, it	*has*
Past Tense			
I, you, we, they, he, she, it	*have* or *has*	I, you, we, they, he, she, it	*had*

EXERCISE 1

Underline the standard English verb form. (See Answer Key for answers.)

1. I (talk, talks) fast at times. He (talk, talks) fast all the time.
2. I (talked, talks) to her on the phone. She (talked, talk) back.
3. We (talks, talked) about our secrets. We (talks, talked) softly.
4. We (walks, walked) home in the dark. I (walks, walked) in front.
5. I (walks, walk) fast when I am scared. She (walk, walks) fast all the time.
6. She (be, is) my best friend. I (be, am) her best friend.
7. We (be, is, are) very close. We (was, were) strangers last year.

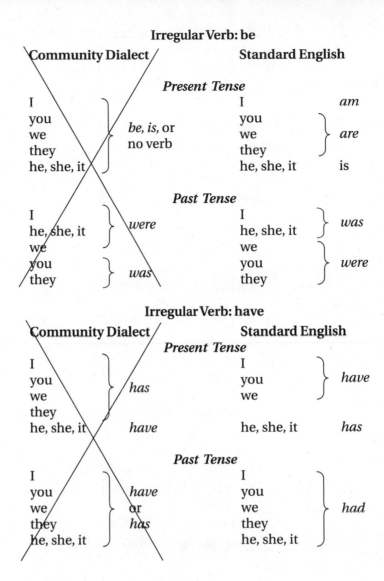

8. At school I (does, do) my work, and she (do, does) hers.

9. In the neighborhood, we (have, has) a close relationship. I (has, have) no need of other friends.

10. She (does, do) her school work each day. I (does, do) mine almost every day.

EXERCISE 2

Underline the standard English verb form.

1. My school mascot (be, is) a Mountaineer. He (is, be) a funny little figure of a man with a coonskin cap.

2. We (calls, call) him Mountie. I (like, likes) him very much.

3. He (be, is) no sex symbol. He (be, is) just a symbol of someone struggling to reach the top of a mountain.

4. He (don't, doesn't) have any pretensions. He always (have, has) a smile.

5. The Mountie logo (appears, appear) on many items. My favorite logo items (are, be, is) caps and t-shirts.

6. The Mountie (walks, walk) to the top of the mountain in education. The Mountie (play, plays) sports at the top of the league.

7. An hour ago, at the Mountie Grill, I (order, ordered) two Mountie Burgers and (paid, pay) good money for them.

8. They (be, are) a bargain at any price. I (washed, wash) them down with a thick Mountie Shake.

9. I soon (has, had) a Mountie stomach. It (be, was) full of Mountie gas.

10. I (walk, walked) to the Mountie Health Office. Where (be, is) a Mountie aspirin when you (need, needs) one?

EXERCISE 3

Underline the standard English verb forms.

I (has, have) learned that language usage (is, be) much like wearing clothes. When I (talk, talks) to my friend, who (use, uses) a community dialect, I may (use, uses) his words. He (don't, doesn't) commonly use standard English. That circumstance (don't, doesn't) bother me. He (be, is) an intelligent person, who (express, expresses) himself well. Many popular songs use the same language he (do, does). On other occasions when I (be, am) at work or school, I am very careful about using standard English. If I (talks, talk) in community dialect, I will be understood, but the way I (speak, speaks) may draw unfavorable attention, and some people might (discredit, discredits) what I have to say. Many of the great thinkers and leaders (grew, grow) up speaking a community dialect, but they (used, use) standard English in their famous speeches and written statements. We (dresses, dress) differently and (speak, speaks) differently for different occasions.

Regular and Irregular Verbs

Whereas regular verbs are predictable—having an *-ed* ending for past and past-participle forms—irregular verbs, as we have seen and as the term suggests, follow no definite pattern. Some similar-sounding irregular verbs pattern differently.

shake	shook	shaken
make	made	made
ring	rang	rung
swing	swung	swung
bring	brought	brought

The lists on pages 116–118 give you the basic forms for both regular and irregular verbs. We suggest that you go through the list of irregular verbs systematically and discover which ones you do not know; then master them. The words *be, is, am, are, were, have, has,* and *had* were covered in the preceding section.

The **present tense** form of most regular and irregular verbs fits *I, you,* and *they* as it is. For *he, she,* and *it,* add an *-s,* an *-es,* or if the present tense form ends in *-y,* drop the *-y* and add *-ies.*

I *drink* a gallon of Koolaid each day.

She *drinks* two gallons of Koolaid each day.

The **past tense** of regular verbs is formed by adding *-ed* to the base or by dropping the ending *-y* and adding *-ied* to a verb like *marry.* Past-tense forms of irregular verbs vary.

We *drank* Koolaid at the pool.

The **past participle** form is used with a helping verb or verbs such as *has, have, had,* or *will have.*

He has drunk Koolaid since he was three.

The **present participle** form is simply the present-tense form plus *-ing.* It must be used with helping verbs such as *is, am, are, was,* or *were.*

I *am drinking* Koolaid while I write this sentence.

Because this form presents no significant problems for most writers, it is not included in the list. You should note, however, that the present participle used as a verb without a helping verb will make a fragment, not a sentence. No word ending in *-ing* can be a verb all by itself.

He *going* to town. (fragment)

He *is going* to town. (correct)

Regular Verbs

Present Tense	Past Tense	Past Participle
For *he, she,* and *it,* add an -*s* or an -*es.* For some words ending in -*y,* drop the -*y* and add -*ies.* This base form can also be used with the words *do, does, did, may, shall, will, could, might, should, would,* and *must.*	Add -*ed* to the base form, or if the word ends in -*y* preceded by a consonant, drop the -*y* and add -*ied.*	Use the past tense form with helping words such as *have, has,* or *had.*
ask	asked	asked
answer	answered	answered
compare	compared	compared
cry	cried	cried
decide	decided	decided
delight	delighted	delighted
display	displayed	displayed
encourage	encouraged	encouraged
enjoy	enjoyed	enjoyed
extract	extracted	extracted
fill	filled	filled
finish	finished	finished
force	forced	forced
glow	glowed	glowed
happen	happened	happened
head	headed	headed
hire	hired	hired
introduce	introduced	introduced
jump	jumped	jumped
laugh	laughed	laughed
learn	learned	learned
lick	licked	licked
like	liked	liked
love	loved	loved
lust	lusted	lusted
need	needed	needed
nod	nodded	nodded
open	opened	opened

Irregular Verbs

Present Tense	Past Tense	Past Participle
For *he, she,* and *it,* add an *-s* or an *-es.* For some words ending in *-y,* drop the *-y* and add *-ies.* This base form can also be used with the words *do, does, did, may, shall, will, could, might, should, would,* and *must.*	Use the form shown in the table.	Use the form shown in the table with helping words such as *have, has,* or *had.*
arise	arose	arisen
awake	awoke, awaked	awaked, awoken
become	became	become
begin	began	begun
bend	bent	bent
blow	blew	blown
break	broke	broken
bring	brought	brought
buy	bought	bought
catch	caught	caught
choose	chose	chosen
cling	clung	clung
come	came	come
creep	crept	crept
deal	dealt	dealt
dive	dived, dove	dived
drink	drank	drunk
drive	drove	driven
eat	ate	eaten
feel	felt	felt
fight	fought	fought
fling	flung	flung
flow	flowed	flowed
fly	flew	flown
forget	forgot	forgotten, forgot
freeze	froze	frozen
get	got	got, gotten
go	went	gone
grow	grew	grown
kneel	knelt	knelt
know	knew	known
lead	led	led
leave	left	left

Irregular Verbs (continued)

Present Tense	Past Tense	Past Participle
lose	lost	lost
mean	meant	meant
read	read	read
ride	rode	ridden
ring	rang	rung
seek	sought	sought
shine	shone	shone
shoot	shot	shot
show	showed	shown, showed
shrink	shrank, shrunk	shrunk, shrunken
sing	sang	sung
sink	sank	sunk
slay	slew	slain
sleep	slept	slept
slink	slunk	slunk
speak	spoke	spoken
spend	spent	spent
spring	sprang, sprung	sprung
steal	stole	stolen
stink	stank, stunk	stunk
strike	struck	struck, stricken
sweep	swept	swept
swim	swam	swum
swing	swung	swung
take	took	taken
teach	taught	taught
tear	tore	torn
think	thought	thought
throw	threw	thrown
weep	wept	wept
wring	wrung	wrung
write	wrote	written

The Twelve Verb Tenses

Some languages, such as Chinese and Navajo, have no verb tenses to indicate time, but English has a fairly complicated system of tenses. Most verbs are either present or past tense. In your paragraphs and essays you will strive to maintain overall consistency in one of those tenses; however, within almost any lengthy passage, numerous time periods will be indicated by verb forms. Altogether there are twelve tenses. The following four charts present those tenses in sentences, and then place each verb on a time line. The charts also explain what the different tenses mean and show you how each verb is composed.

SIMPLE TENSES

TENSE	TIME LINE	TIME	VERB FORM
Present I drive to work. She drives to work.	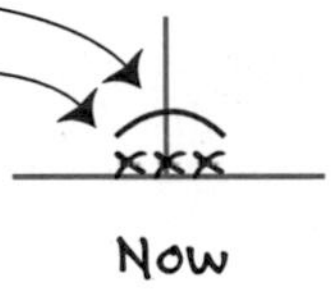	Present, may imply a continuation from past to future	Present drive drives
Past I drove to work.		Past	Past drove
Future I will drive to work.		Future	Present preceded by will will drive

PERFECT TENSES

TENSE	TIME LINE	TIME	VERB FORM
Present Perfect I have driven to work.		Completed recently in past, may continue to present	Past participle preceded by have or has have driven
Past Perfect I had driven to work before I moved to the city.	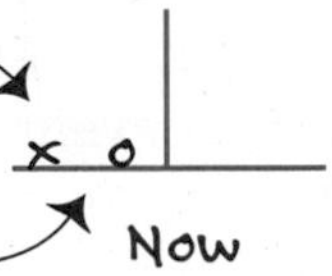	Prior to a specific time in the past	Past participle preceded by had had driven
Future Perfect I will have driven to work thousands of times by Christmas.	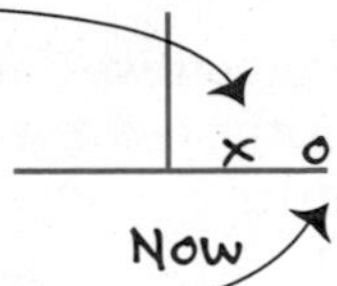	At a time prior to a specific time in the future	Past participle preceded by will have will have driven

PROGRESSIVE TENSES

TENSE	TIME LINE	TIME	VERB FORM
Present Progressive I am driving to work.		In progress now	Progressive (-ing ending) preceded by is, am, or are am driving
Past Progressive I was driving to work.		In progress in the past	Progressive (-ing ending) preceded by was or were was driving
Future Progressive I will be driving to work.		In progress in the future	Progressive (-ing ending) preceded by will be will be driving

PROGRESSIVE PERFECT TENSES

TENSE	TIME LINE	TIME	VERB FORM
Present Perfect Progressive I have been driving to work.		In progress before now or up to now	Progressive (-ing ending) preceded by have been or has been have been driving
Past Perfect Progressive I had been driving when I began ride-sharing.		In progress before another event in the past	Progressive (-ing ending) preceded by had I had been driving
Future Perfect Progressive By May 1 (event), I will have been driving to work for six years.	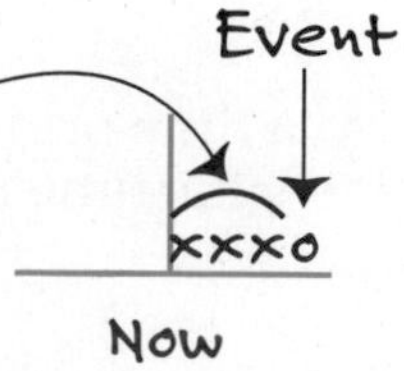	In progress before another event in the future	Progressive (-ing ending) preceded by will have been will have been driving

This is a more direct presentation of the twelve verb tenses. You can work with the patterns of any verb forms by simply replacing, for example, the word *drive* and its forms with another verb and its forms.

Simple Tenses

Present Tense

I, we, you, they *drive.*
He, she, it *drives.*

Past Tense

I, we, you, he, she, it, they *drove.*

Future Tense

I, we, you, he, she, it, they *will drive.*

Perfect Tenses

Present Perfect Tense

I, we, you, they *have driven.*
He, she, it *has driven.*

Past Perfect Tense

I, we, you, he, she, it, they *had driven.*

Future Perfect Tense

I, we, you, he, she, it, they *will have driven.*

Progressive Tenses

Present Progressive

I *am driving.*
He, she, it *is driving.*
You, they *are driving.*

Past Progressive

I, he, she, it *was driving.*
You, they *were driving.*

Future Progressive

I, you, he, she, it, they *will be driving.*

Perfect Progressive Tenses

Present Perfect Progressive

I, you, they *have been driving.*
He, she, it *has been driving.*

Past Perfect Progressive

I, you, he, she, it, they *had been driving.*

Future Perfect Progressive

I, you, he, she, it, they *will have been driving.*

EXERCISE 4

Underline the correct verb form. (See Answer Key for answers.)

1. Jason (received, had received) his appointment before he graduated.
2. She (worked, had worked) in sales for two years before she was promoted.
3. After parking their car, they (walk, walked) to the beach.
4. I (have, had) never encountered a genius until I met her.
5. I hoped that we (could have gone, went) to the big game.
6. They knew that they (will complete, will have completed) the job before the first snow.
7. We (are considering, consider) the proposal.
8. He told us of the many interesting adventures he (has had, had).
9. We went to the desert to see the cabin they (built, had built).
10. Tomorrow I (will go, go) to the supermarket for party items.

EXERCISE 5

Underline the correct verb form.

1. The scholars (worked, had worked) for many hours before they solved the problem.
2. The shipping clerks said they (had sent, sent) the package.
3. We (study, are studying) the issue now.
4. We (decide, will decide) on the winner tomorrow.
5. They reminded us that we (made, had made) the same promise before.
6. Jill (had believed, believed) in his guilt until she saw the complete evidence.
7. Jake (had been napping, napped), when the alarm sounded.

8. By the time he finished talking, he realized that he (said, had said) too much.

9. At the end of the semester, the course grade (depends, will depend) on your ability to write well.

10. After he retired, I realized how much I (had learned, learned) by working with him.

EXERCISE 6

Underline the correct verb form.

1. This story is about Bill "Chick" Walker, who (lossed, lost) all he owned at the Wagon Wheel Saloon in Las Vegas.

2. Chick had (laid, layed) one thousand dollars on the red 21 at the roulette table.

3. For that spin, he (done, did) an amazing thing—he (won, wins).

4. But after a while, Chick (became, becomed) stupid, and his luck (ran, run) out.

5. Before he had (ate, eaten) breakfast, he accepted free drinks from the charming Trixie, who (served, serve) cocktails.

6. His judgment was soon (spoiled, spoilt) by the drinks, and he (put, putted) all his money on one spin.

7. That wager (cost, costed) Chick everything, and he couldn't (raise, rise) any more money.

8. Moreover, Trixie would not (sit, set) with him because she (like, liked) only winners.

9. Chick drained his glass, (rose, raised) from his red tufted vinyl barstool, and (head, headed) for the parking lot.

10. There he (known, knew) Bonnie Lou, who suffered from low self-esteem, would be waiting for him because she (lust, lusted) for losers.

EXERCISE 7

Underline the correct verb form.

1. This morning I (saw, seen) an intriguing new product on an infomercial.

2. As I (pause, paused) at Channel 17, my interest (grew, growed).

3. The Sandwich Demon was the name of the product, and I (knew, knowed) I wanted one.

4. Judy, the spokesperson, (extracted, extract) a piping hot, toasted cheese sandwich from the Demon's steaming jaws.

5. Then a hungry member of the audience (jumped, jumpt) up and (eat, ate) the sandwich in one gulp.

6. Judy (force, forced) a laugh and (accepted, accept) the audience's applause.

7. She then (nodded, nod) to two stage hands who (dragged, drug) the man back up to center stage.

8. While smiling serenely at the camera, Judy (thrust, thrusted) the man's hand into the Sandwich Demon, at which he (flung, fling) his body convulsively like a hooked fish.

9. After the man pulled free from the Demon, Judy (rose, raised) his hand and (displayed, display) it to the audience.

10. Amazingly the hand (didn't, doesn't) look much different from the toasted cheese sandwich!

EXERCISE 8

Underline the correct verb form.

1. Recycling is very important; almost nothing should be (throwed, thrown) away.

2. For instance, ties that are worn-out can (become, became) tails for kites or leashes for dogs.

3. Engine grease can be (spreaded, spread) on wounds to prevent infection.

4. I personally (raised, rose) vacation money by recycling lard for candles.

5. (Sitting, Setting) used plutonium fuel pellets on patio furniture will (help, helped) people deal with insects.

6. The plutonium will (make, made) the insects large so they can be (hit, hitted) with recycled tennis rackets.

7. The plutonium will also make insects (glow, glowed) in the dark so they can be easily (saw, seen).

8. This textbook can be (used, use) to wrap fish.

9. Strapped to the chest, it can (stop, stopped) small caliber bullets.

10. When (dropped, dropt) from sufficient height, a single copy has been (known, knowed) to kill small rodents.

"Problem" Verbs

The following pairs of verbs are especially troublesome and confusing: *lie* and *lay, sit* and *set,* and *rise* and *raise.* One way to tell them apart is to remember that the words *lay, set,* and *raise* take objects and the others do not. In the examples, the italicized words are objects.

Present Tense	Meaning	Past Tense	Past Participle
lie	to rest	lay	lain
lay	to place something	laid	laid
Examples:	I lay down to rest.		
	I laid the *book* on the table.		
sit	to rest	sat	sat
set	to place something	set	set
Examples:	I sat in the chair.		
	I set the *basket* on the floor.		
rise	to go up	rose	risen
raise	to lift	raised	raised
Examples:	The smoke rose quickly.		
	She raised the *question.*		

EXERCISE 9

Underline the correct verb form.

1. Young Hubert has answered too many questions without (rising, raising) his hand.
2. Pugsy, the bully of the class, runs across the room and (sits, sets) on Hubert.
3. The teacher (lies, lays) a heavy hand on Pugsy's head.
4. He then tells the two boys to (lie, lay) down and cool off.
5. They (raise, rise) themselves and retire to opposite corners of the classroom.
6. Both of them have (lain, laid) there for several minutes before the class comes to order.
7. The teacher decides to use them to (sit, set) an example.
8. Looking at Hubert, the teacher says, "What if everyone answered without a (risen, raised) hand?"

9. "What if we solved all our problems by (sitting, setting) on those we disagree with?" he continues, trying to (sit, set) Pugsy straight.

10. "We would all be (lying, laying) over here in the corner," says Pugsy, without (rising, raising) his hand, and all of his fellow students run over to (set, sit) on him.

Subject-Verb Agreement

In this section we are concerned with **number agreement** between subjects and verbs. The previous section showed how subjects and verbs agreed in terms of person: verbs also change in the present tense, depending on whether the subject is first person (I, we), second person (you), or third person (*he, she, it, they*). The helping words and irregular verbs *be, is, are, am, was, were, have,* and *has* have also been discussed.

The basic principle of subject-verb agreement of number is that if the subject is singular, the verb should be singular, and if the subject is plural, the verb should be plural. There are ten major problem areas. In the following examples, the true subjects and verbs are italicized.

1. **Do not let words that come between the subject and verb affect agreement.**
   a. Modifying phrases and clauses frequently come between the subject and verb.

      The various *types* of drama *were* not *discussed.*

      Henry, who is hitting third, *is* the best player.

      The *price* of those shoes *is* too high.

   b. Certain unfamiliar prepositions cause trouble. The following words are prepositions, not conjunctions: *along with, as well as, besides, in addition to, including, together with.* The words that function as objects of prepositions cannot also be subjects of the sentence.

      The *coach,* along with the players, *protests* the decision.

   c. In compound subjects in which one subject is positive and one subject is negative, the verb agrees with the positive subject.

      Phillip, not the other boys, *was* the culprit.

2. **Do not let inversions (verb precedes subject, not the normal order) affect the agreement of subject and verb.**
   a. Verbs and other words may come before the subject. Do not let them affect the agreement. To understand subject-verb relationships, recast the sentence in normal word order.

      Are Juan and his *sister* at home? (question form)

      Juan and his *sister are* at home. (normal order)

   b. A sentence filler is a word that is grammatically independent of other words in the sentence. The most common fillers are *there* and *here.* Even though the filler precedes the verb, it should not be treated as the subject.

      There *are* many *reasons* for his poor work.

   Using *is* as a verb in this sentence would have been faulty subject-verb agreement.

3. A singular verb agrees with a singular indefinite pronoun.

a. Most indefinite pronouns are singular.

Each of the women *is* ready at this time.

Neither of the women *is* ready at this time.

One of the children *is* not paying attention.

b. Certain indefinite pronouns do not clearly express either a singular or plural number. Agreement, therefore, depends on the meaning of the sentence. These pronouns are *all, any, none,* and *some.*

All of the melon *was* good.

All of the melons *were* good.

None of the pie *is* acceptable.

None of the pies *are* acceptable.

4. Two or more subjects joined by *and* usually take a plural verb.

The *captain* and the *sailors were* happy to be ashore.

The *trees* and *shrubs* need more care.

a. If the parts of a compound subject mean one and the same person or thing, the verb is singular.

One: The *secretary* and *treasurer is* not present.

More than one: The *secretary* and the *treasurer are* not present.

b. When *each* or *every* modify singular subjects joined by *and,* the verb is singular.

Each *boy* and each *girl brings* a donation.

Every *woman* and *man has asked* the same questions.

5. Alternate subjects—that is, subjects joined by *or, nor, either/or, neither/nor, not only/but also*—should be handled in the following manner:

a. If the subjects are both singular, the verb is singular.

Rosa or *Alicia* is responsible.

b. If the subjects are plural, the verb is plural.

Neither the *students* nor the *teachers were* impressed.

c. If one of the subjects is singular and the other subject is plural, the verb agrees with the nearer subject.

Either the Garcia *boys* or their *father goes* to the hospital each day.

6. Collective nouns—*team, family, group, crew, gang, class,* and the like—take a singular verb if the verb is considered a unit, a plural verb if the group is considered as a number of individuals.

The *jury are voting* on a verdict.

(Here the individuals are acting not as a unit but separately. If you don't like the way this sounds, substitute "The members of the jury are voting on a verdict.")

7. Titles of books, essays, short stories, and plays, a word spoken of as a word, and the names of businesses take a singular verb.

Canterbury Tales was written by Geoffrey Chaucer.

Markle Brothers has a sale this week.

8. **Sums of money, distances, and measurements are followed by a singular verb when a unit is meant, a plural verb when the individual elements are considered separately.**

   Three dollars was the price. (unit)

   Three dollars were lying there. (individual)

   Five years is a long time. (unit)

   The *first five years were* difficult ones.

9. **Be careful of agreement with nouns ending in *-s*. Several nouns ending in *-s* take a singular verb—for example, *aeronautics, civics, economics, ethics, measles, mumps.***

   Mumps is an extremely unpleasant disease.

   Economics is my major field of study.

10. **Some nouns have only a plural form and so take only a plural verb—for example, *clothes, fireworks, headquarters, scissors, trousers.***

    His *trousers are* badly wrinkled.

    Marv's *clothes were* stylish and expensive.

EXERCISE 10

Underline the verb that agrees in number with the subject. (See Answer Key for answers.)

1. Most of my friends (are, is) going to celebrate the Feast of Lupercal.
2. The feast, which occasionally lasts for several days, (were, was) most commonly celebrated in ancient Rome.
3. One of my friends (celebrate, celebrates) this noble holiday by constructing fancy sculptural busts of Roman emperors in Spam.
4. Every person who attends these holiday feasts (becomes, become) a celebrity in my town.
5. Young Ruthina and her girlfriend (have, has) a problem.
6. Their dates, who love beef stew, (is, are) coming over for a home-cooked dinner.
7. The problem is that neither Ruthina nor her friend (know, knows) how to cook beef stew.
8. Cleverly, they simply (fill, fills) the crockpot with Beefy Chunks dog food.
9. The Beefy Chunks dinner (is, are) so wholesome and attractive that both dates wolf it down and beg for more.
10. Although we have made several calls to corporate headquarters to verify this story, Beefy Chunks, Inc., still (refuse, refuses) to comment.

EXERCISE 11

Underline the verb that agrees in number with the subject.

1. Pennys (is, are) my favorite department store.
2. My scissors (is, are) dull.
3. To mature men, mumps (is, are) a serious disease.
4. Ethics (is, are) my favorite subject.
5. *Current Affairs* (is, are) an exciting program.
6. Sears (is, are) having a sale.
7. Fireworks (is, are) dangerous.
8. Six years (is, are) too long to wait.
9. The team (is, are) trying on their uniforms.
10. The manager and the coach (is, are) leaving the stadium.

EXERCISE 12

Underline the verb that agrees in number with the subject.

1. Who (is, are) more skillful, the mime or the magician?
2. The mime is one of the fascinating people who (are, is) involved in projects to help the needy.
3. Mimes, among all the performers on the street, (is, are) important because they let us take a look at the absurdities of life.
4. Yet, some people, out of pure discomfort, (flee, flees) when they see a mime approaching.
5. *Famous Mimes* (is, are) a best-selling book in Hollywood.
6. In the circus, mimes, according to tradition, (is, are) called clowns.
7. Circus entertainments (are, is) clearly among the best ever devised.
8. However, the life of circus people (is, are) not all fun and games; circus performers (is, are) responsible for many mundane tasks.
9. For instance, the ringmaster and the strong men (helps, help) roll up the big-top tent.
10. Not only that, the magician and his lovely assistant (feed, feeds) the two-headed cow after each show.

Consistency in Tense

Consider this statement:

> We went (1) downtown, and then we watch (2) a movie. Later we met (3) some friends from school, and we all go (4) to the mall. For most of the evening, we play (5) video games in arcades. It was (6) a typical but rather uneventful summer day.

Does the shifting verb tense bother you (to say nothing about the lack of development of ideas)? It should! The writer makes several unnecessary changes. Verbs 1, 3, and 6 are in the past tense and verbs 2, 4, and 5 are in the present tense. Changing all verbs to past tense makes the statement much smoother.

> We went downtown, and then we watched a movie. Later we met some friends from school, and we all went to the mall. For most of the evening, we played video games in arcades. It was a typical but rather uneventful summer day.

In other instances you might want to maintain a consistent present tense. There are no inflexible rules about selecting a tense for a certain kind of writing, but you should be consistent, changing tense only for a good reason.

It is worth noting that the present tense will usually serve you best in writing about literature, even if the literature was written long in the past:

> *Moby Dick is* a novel about Captain Ahab's obsession with a great white whale. He *sets* sail with a full crew of sailors who *think* they *are going* on merely another whaling voyage. Most of the crew *are* experienced seamen.

The past tense is likely to serve you best in writing about your personal experiences and about historical events (though the present tense can often be used effectively to establish the feeling of intimacy and immediacy):

> In the summer of 1991, Hurricane Bob *hit* the Atlantic coast region. It *came* ashore near Cape Hatteras and *moved* north. The winds *reached* a speed of more than ninety miles per hour on Cape Cod, but then *slackened* by the time Bob reached Maine.

EXERCISE 13

Change the verbs in the following paragraphs as necessary to maintain a mostly consistent present tense. Three verbs should be changed to past tense. (See Answer Key for the answers.)

The hottest game show in TV-Land was called "Guess My Shoe Size." At the beginning of each show, the renowned quiz show host, Vic Binkly, introduces a guest whose feet were concealed in enormous clown shoes. Guest-celebrity panelists, whose identities are also disguised with masks, then asked the mystery guest questions for five minutes. At this point, the guest revealed his or her shoe size, and then the audience responded to the proceedings with questions. In one program, the audience is stunned because they thought the guest wears a $6\frac{1}{2}$D when in reality she wears a $5\frac{1}{2}$EE. If the guest stumps the celebrity panel, he or she received a year's supply of fine footwear. The critics have proclaimed this show a winner. And, of course, the Vic Binkly fans were pleased that their hero has another show after his "Guess My Hat Size" show failed when the audience cannot hear the contestants talking through the paper bags on their heads.

EXERCISE 14

Correct verbs as needed in the following paragraph to achieve verb-tense consistency. Most verbs will be present tense.

A trip to the dentist should not be a terrible experience—unless one goes to Dr. Litterfloss, credit dentist. Although he graduated *magna cum lately* from Ed's School of Dentistry, he had a reputation for being one of the dirtiest and most careless dentists in the state. He don't even know about germs. He never used Novocain. He just spins the chair until his patients lost consciousness. Then he shot them with his x-ray gun from behind a lead wall. Sometimes he missed, and now his dental technician glows in the dark, so he don't need a light as he worked. While drilling with one hand, he snacked on Vienna sausages with the other. Stray alley cats and mangy curs fights around his feet for food scraps, so he don't need a cleaning service. He seldom washed his Black and Decker drill or Craftsman chisel, and he squirts tobacco juice into his spit sink. I recommended him only with strong reservation.

EXERCISE 15

Revise these sentences for verb-tense consistency by making all verbs past tense.

Judy had a weird hobby. A few years ago, she start to collect shreds of automobile tires in the street. She goes home and put them into interesting patterns on her mother's carpet. Then she takes a big can of industrial-strength glue and glued them together. Her mother is not amused by this tire-shred mosaic. Sometimes the glue stuck to the carpet. On those occasions, Judy's mother shook her fists and chases Judy around the house. Then one day, an art critic walks through the neighborhood in search of folk art. The critic saw Judy's tire-shred mosaic and buys it for a thousand dollars. Judy's mother smiles. She was very proud of her artistic daughter.

Active and Passive Voice

Which of these sentences sounds better to you?:

Don Mattingly slammed a home run.

A home run was slammed by Don Mattingly.

They both carry the same message, but the first expresses it more effectively. The subject *(Don Mattingly)* is the actor. The verb *(slammed)* is the action. The direct object *(home run)* is the receiver of the action. The second sentence lacks the vitality of the first because the receiver of the action is the subject and the doer is embedded in the prepositional phrase at the end of the sentence.

The first sentence demonstrates the **active voice.** It has an active verb (one that accepts a direct object), and the action moves from the beginning to the end of the sentence. The second exhibits the **passive voice** (with the action reflecting back on the subject). When given a choice, you should usually employ the active voice. It promotes energy and directness.

1. Though not usually the preferred form, the passive voice does have its uses, as in these two instances:
   a. When the doer of the action is unknown or unimportant

      My car was stolen. (The doer, a thief, is unknown.)

   b. When the receiver of the action is more important than the doer

      My neighbor was permanently disabled by an irresponsible drunk driver. (The neighbor's suffering is the focus, not the drunk driver.)

2. As you can see, the passive construction places the doer at the end of a prepositional phrase (as in the second example) or does not include the doer in the statement at all (as in the first example). Instead, passive voice places the receiver of the action in the subject position, and presents the verb in its past-tense form preceded by a *to be* helper. The transformation is a simple one.

   She read the book. (active)

   The book was read by her. (passive)

Because most voice-related problems involve the unnecessary and ineffective use of the passive form, the exercises below will concentrate on identifying passive voice and changing it to active.

EXERCISE 16

Identify each sentence as either active voice (A) or passive voice (P). If a sentence with the passive form would be more effective in the active voice, rewrite it. (See Answer Key for answers.)

_______ 1. The pit bull was named Homicide by the young lad.

_______ 2. The convict, despite his surly comportment, was given his last request, an audience with Dick Clark.

_______ 3. The warden was questioned by reporters as he left the scene of the execution.

_______ 4. The noisy rappers were sentenced by the solemn judge to listen to a hundred waltz records.

_______ 5. The picnic was interrupted by hungry bears.

_______ 6. As the picnickers scattered, the food was grabbed by the bears.

_______ 7. Your last warning has been given by me to you; the next time you leave a mess in your room, I will yodel for the rest of the day.

_______ 8. Rip Van Winkle was known by his friends for his long sleeping spells.

_______ 9. For the party, we hired a Dixieland jazz band.

_______ 10. The souffle should be eaten by you before it hardens into the processed cheese spread that it once was.

EXERCISE 17

Identify each sentence as either active voice (A) or passive voice (P). If a sentence with the passive form would be more effective in the active voice, rewrite it.

_______ 1. Listen and a story will be told to you by me.

_______ 2. A terrible thing happened to a local ventriloquist the other day.

_______ 3. While hundreds of his fans were being delighted by him at a local county fair performance, his dummy suddenly burst into flames.

_______ 4. Some are now speculating that the tragedy was caused by spontaneous combustion.

_______ 5. Others believe that the fire was produced by a system of cleverly placed mirrors engineered by the ventriloquist to increase his notoriety.

_______ 6. The story was covered by all three major television networks.

_______ 7. The scene of the mysterious combustion was viewed by thousands of curious folk.

_______ 8. The ventriloquist has been made a rich man by the publicity.

_______ 9. In fact, he has been given several offers to appear on television talk shows to discuss the event.

_______ 10. He is happy in his new wealth, but he will never forget how his little wooden friend and their friendship went up in smoke.

Strong Predication

As we have pointed out, the verb is an extremely important part of any sentence. Therefore, the verb (often called the predicate) should be chosen with care. Some of the most widely used verbs are the "being" verbs: *is, was, were, are, am.* We couldn't get along in English without them, but because of their commonness, writers often use them when more forceful and effective words are available. Revising and editing for better verbs is sometimes called "strengthening predication."

Consider these examples:

Weak predication: He is the leader of the people.

Strong predication: He leads the people.

Weak predication: She was the first to finish.

Strong predication: She finished first.

EXERCISE 18

Change the verbs for stronger predication. Delete unnecessary words to make the sentence even more concise if you can. (See Answer Key for answers.)

1. My watch is running slowly.
2. My computer is quite inexpensive.
3. The horse was a fast runner.
4. They were writers who wrote well.
5. The dog is sleeping on the bed.
6. Mr. Hawkins is a real estate salesperson.
7. Jose is in attendance at Rancho Santiago College.
8. This assignment is something I like.
9. We are the successful students here.
10. She is in the process of combing her hair.

EXERCISE 19

Change the verbs for stronger predication. Delete unnecessary words to make the sentence even more concise if you can.

1. William Shakespeare was the writer of many great plays.
2. The students were the recipients of praise.
3. A big, red apple is my desire.
4. I was the writer of that article.
5. Jannell is the leader of the study group in the library.
6. Baseball is something I like to play.
7. She was in a state of excitement over her high grade.
8. The Dodgers will be winners next year.

9. They were in tears after the defeat.

10. The fire in the hills was in a condition of subsidence.

Subjunctive Mood

Mood refers to the intention of the verb. Three moods are relevant to our study.

The indicative mood expresses a statement of fact.

I was tired.

The imperative mood expresses a command (and has a *you* understood subject).

Go to the store.

The subjunctive mood expresses a statement as contrary to fact, conditional, desirable, possible, necessary, or doubtful. In current English the subjunctive form is distinguishable only in two forms: The verb *to be* uses *be* throughout the present tense and *were* throughout the past tense.

He requires that we *be* (instead of *are*) on time.

If she *were* (instead of *was*) the candidate, she would win.

In other verbs, the final *s* is dropped in the third person singular (he, she, it) of the present tense to make all forms the same in any one tense.

I request that he *report* (instead of *reports*) today.

Here are examples of the common forms:

If I *were* (instead of *was*) you, I wouldn't do that. (contrary to fact)

She behaves as if she *were* (instead of *was*) not certain. (doubt)

I wish I *were* (instead of *was*) in Texas. (wish)

EXERCISE 20

Underline the subjunctive verbs.

1. If I (was, were) going to work, I would give you a ride.

2. I wish I (were, was) on the beach.

3. I hope she (will be, is) there.

4. They act as if they (are, were) rich.

5. I require that my workers (are, be) on time.

6. You may wish you (are, were) an adult, but you must show your ID.

7. You talk as if your winning (was, were) possible.

8. My manager insists that I (be, am) on time.

9. Suppose, for sake of argument, your statement (was, were) true.

10. Sometimes I wish I (were, was) of the younger generation.

Chapter Checklist

1. **Standard usage** is advantageous because it is appropriate for the kind of writing and speaking you are likely to do in pursuing your college work and future career.
2. Whereas **regular verbs** are predictable—having an *-ed* ending for past and past-participle forms—*irregular verbs,* as the term suggests, follow no definite pattern.

   raise, raised, raised (regular); *see, saw, seen* (irregular)

3. Certain verbs (present tense here) can be troublesome and should be studied with care (page 125).

   lie, lay; sit, set; rise, raise

4. If the subject is singular, the verb should be singular; if the subject is plural, the verb should be plural.

   The *price* of the shoes *is* high.

   The *advantages* of that shoe *are* obvious.

5. There are no inflexible rules about selecting a **tense** for certain kinds of writing, but you should be consistent, changing tense only for a good reason.
6. Usually you should select the present tense to write about literature.

   Moby Dick *is* a famous white whale.

   Select the past tense to write about yourself or something historical.

   I *was* eighteen when I *decided* I *was* ready for independence.

7. English has twelve verb tenses. (See charts on pp. 119–120 for names, examples, functions, and forms.)
8. The **active voice** expression (subject, active verb, and object) is usually preferred over the **passive voice** expression (subject as the receiver of action, with doer unstated or at the end of a prepositional phrase).

   She read the book. (active)

   The book was read by her. (passive)

9. Revising and editing verbs for better verbs, sometimes called **"strengthening predication,"** is an extremely important part of your writing.

   She *was* the first to finish. (weak verb)

   She *finished* first. (strong verb)

10. The **subjunctive mood** expresses a statement contrary to fact, conditional, desirable, possible, necessary, or doubtful. *Be* is used throughout the present tense and *were* throughout the past.

    He requires that we *be* (not *are*) on time.

    I wish I *were* (not *was*) home.

    In other verbs, the final *s* is dropped in the third person singular (he, she, it) of the present tense.

    I request that he *report* (instead of *reports*) today.

With the bones still tied to the skiff, the exhausted old man returned to shore. Other fishermen and tourists marvel at the eighteen-foot skeleton of the fish, as the old man lays asleep. The young boy knew he has much to learn from the old man and is determined to go fishing with him again.

REVIEW 6

Change the verbs for stronger predication. Delete unnecessary words to make the sentence even more concise if you can.

1. She is in the process of breaking the horse.
2. She is a person who is capable of leading our group.
3. Walter was the scorer of the last touchdown.
4. Maria is a worker at the department store.
5. Jonathan is one who won the race.
6. Lauren has a smile that is sweet.
7. Shane is waiting for the next train.
8. Jarrett is a swift runner.
9. Jannell was the second to finish the race.
10. This review is something that makes me think.

8

Pronouns

Do you say, "Between you and *I*" or "Between you and *me*"? What about "Let's you and *I* do this" or "Let's you and *me* do that"? Are you confused about when to use *who* and *whom?* Is it "Everyone should wear *their* coat, or *his* coat, or *his or her* coat"? Is there anything wrong with saying, "When *you* walk down the streets of Laredo"?

Chances are, you are not absolutely certain about which of those examples are correct. After all, you quite naturally have learned language mostly from listening, and you have heard people use all of those variations. In fact, you may have heard one individual alternate choices, sometimes saying "between you and *I*" and sometimes "between you and *me*." Regardless of the choice, you have understood the speakers. So, you may ask, who cares? Try these for answers: (1) someone for whom you are writing, (2) someone who is offering a job you want, (3) someone who might buy the product you have for sale, (4) someone who might be interested in dating you or developing a relationship—is that enough? Of course, poor pronoun usage may be more of an irritation factor than a determining factor for these people; nevertheless, in some situations a "wrong" pronoun can stand out like a shred of spinach on a front tooth. Again, as with verbs, the difference is between substandard and standard. If you use a substandard pronoun in addressing an audience that expects a standard choice, you will draw unfavorable attention to your language.

The examples in the first paragraph represent the most common problems. But even if you were unsure about your choices, you can take heart in the knowledge that by the time you are finished with this chapter, you will be able to identify the standard forms and know why they are correct. The result is expertise and confidence.

All that you have studied so far in grammar and sentence structure will help you to work on the problems of pronoun case, pronoun-antecedent agreement, and pronoun reference.

Pronoun Case

Case is the form a pronoun takes as it fills a position in a sentence. Words such as *you* and *it* do not change, but others do, and they change in predictable ways. For example, *I* is a subject word and *me* is an object word. As you refer to yourself, you will select a pronoun that fits a certain part of sentence structure. You say, "*I* will write the paper," not "*Me* will write the paper" because *I* is in the subject position. But you say, "She will give the apple to *me*," not "She will give the apple to *I*" because *me* is in the object position. These are pronouns that do change:

Subject	Object
I	me
he	him
she	her
we	us
they	them
who	whom

Subjective Case

Person	Singular	Plural
1st	I	we
2nd	you	you
3rd	he she it	they
	who	

Subjective pronouns can fill two positions in a sentence.

1. Pronouns in the subjective case may fill subject positions.

   a. Some will be easy to identify because they are at the beginning of the sentence.

      I dance in the park.

      He dances in the park.

      She dances in the park.

      We dance in the park.

      They dance in the park.

      Who is dancing in the park?

   b. Others will be more difficult to identify because they are not at the beginning of a sentence and may not appear to be part of a clause. The words *than* and *as* are signals for these special arrangements, which can be called incompletely stated clauses.

He is taller than *I* (am).

She is faster than *we* (are).

We work as hard as *they* (do).

The words *am, are,* and *do,* which by understanding complete the clauses, have been omitted. We are actually saying, "He is taller than *I am,*" "She is faster than *we are,*" and "We work as hard as *they do.*" The italicized pronouns are subjects of "understood" verbs.

2. Pronouns in the subjective case may refer back to the subject.
   a. They may follow a form of the verb *to be,* such as *was, were, are, am,* and *is.*

      I believe it is *he.*

      It was *she* who spoke.

      The victims were *they.*

   b. Some appositives will not refer back through a verb.

      The leading candidates—Juan, Darnelle, Steve, Kimlieu, and *I*—made speeches.

Objective Case

	Singular	Plural
Person		
1st	me	us
2nd	you	you
3rd	him her it	them
	whom	

Objective pronouns can also fill two positions in sentences.

1. Pronouns in the objective case may fill object positions.
   a. They may be objects after the verb.

      I gave *him* the message. (indirect object)

      We saw *her* in the library. (direct object)

   b. They may be objects after prepositions.

      The problem was clear to both of *us.*

      I offered the opportunity to *him.*

2. Appositives may refer back to object words.

   They gave the results to us—Steve and *me.* (referring back to an object of preposition)

9. He said that Mantle, who had just hit his five hundredth home run, wanted to meet my brother and (I, me).

10. After the game, we met (he, him), and he gave (we, us) each an autographed bat.

EXERCISE 3

Underline the correct pronoun. (See Answer Key for answers.)

1. (We, Us) are going to the flea circus tonight.

2. There are those (who, whom) think flea circuses are inhumane.

3. Between you and (I, me), I think their performance for (us, we) higher order creatures is their only redeeming quality.

4. People (who, whom) don't like flea circuses should talk to thinking people like (I, me).

5. Tomorrow you and (I, me) can go to the 'gator synchronized swimming show.

6. These animal friends from the swamps can teach you and (I, me) much about water travel.

7. My sister said (her, she) would like to go with (we, us).

8. Either you or (me, I) should pick up fireworks at Crazy Charley's stand.

9. No one sells bigger, cheaper, and more dangerous fireworks than (he, him).

10. (They, Them) (who, whom) have not been to Crazy Charley's have missed some high-class fun.

EXERCISE 4

Underline the correct pronoun.

1. (She, Her) and (I, me) are going to the museum of dental instruments.

2. (We, Us) young people are fascinated by rusty drills, saws, and heavy-duty pliers.

3. I would rather go to the museum with you than with (she, her).

4. There are those (who, whom) would say early dentistry was barbaric.

5. Before anesthesia was developed, the patient (who, whom) passed out was lucky.

6. In 1844, laughing gas, nitrous oxide, was used on Horace Wells, (who, whom) had developed it.

7. My boss said that his wife and (he, him) wanted an unusual gift.

8. I gave (they, them) a puppy.

9. Just between you and (me, I), the pup is half coyote and half hyena.

10. They gave it back because it howled and laughed at (whoever, whomever) came to visit.

EXERCISE 5

Underline the correct pronoun. (See Answer Key for answers.)

1. (Who, Whom) are you taking to the monster truck rodeo?

2. I am not sure (who, whom) I will be taking.

3. The person with (whom, who) I witness the event must love loud engines as much as (I, me).

4. To (who, whom) will you give your whoopee cushion?

5. Some people (who, whom) are wealthy never shop for themselves.

6. Fisherfolk (who, whom) admire floating stink bait will love our new floating sandwich spread.

7. It is designed for clumsy fisherfolk (who, whom) sometimes drop their food into the water.

8. (Whom, Who) will you invite to your Christmas party?

9. May I suggest someone (who, whom) looks like Bob Cratchit?

10. (Whom, Who) may I say is calling so late at night?

EXERCISE 6

Underline the correct pronoun.

1. I know some people (who, whom) fear technology.

2. They are afraid that those (who, whom) own super computers will control (us, we) (who, whom) own dinky computers.

3. Homer asked Becky, "(Who, Whom) are you asking to the Sadie Hawkins dance?"

4. Looking into his eyes tenderly, she answered, "(Whom, Who) do you think, you silly dunderhead?"

5. The ancient philosopher asked the age-old question, "(Who, Whom) wrote the book of love?"

6. His life's companion said, "Someone (who, whom) was very young."

7. The child asked her father, "(Whom, Who) makes babies?"

8. Her father, (who, whom) didn't expect that question, said, "Your mother will tell you (who, whom) does."

9. (Who, Whom) will receive the award?

10. The person (who, whom) does will get a free school lunch.

Pronoun-Antecedent Agreement

A pronoun agrees with its antecedent in person, number, and gender. Person—first, second, or third—indicates perspective. **Number** indicates singular or plural. **Gender** indicates sex: masculine, feminine, or neuter.

Subject Words			Object Words		
Person	**Singular**	**Plural**	**Person**	**Singular**	**Plural**
First	I	we	First	me	us
Second	you	you	Second	you	you
Third	he, she, it	they	Third	him, her, it	them

Agreement in Person

Avoid needless shifting in person, which means shifting of point of view. The following paragraph is an example of an inconsistent point of view. See if you can tell where the shifts occur.

Inconsistent: The wedding did not go well. It was a disaster. *You* could see the trouble develop when the caterers started serving drinks before the ceremony. Then the bride started arguing with her future mother-in-law. *I* was ready to leave right away. Then the sound system went out and the band canceled. *You* wished *you* hadn't come, but *you* had to stay. *I* will never forget that day.

The word *you* is second person; the word *I* is first person. When the writer switches back and forth, the result is reader confusion and annoyance. The following revision corrects the problem by making the point of view consistently first person.

Consistent: The wedding did not go well. It was a disaster. *I* could see the trouble develop when the caterers started serving drinks before the ceremony. Then the bride started arguing with her future mother-in-law. *I* was ready to leave right away. After that, the sound system went out and the band canceled. *I* wished *I* hadn't come, but *I* had to stay. *I* will never forget that day.

EXERCISE 7

Each of the following sentences has one or more needless changes in pronoun person. Correct each problem by crossing out the inconsistent pronoun and substituting a consistent one. Change verb forms also, if necessary. (See Answer Key for answers.)

1. When tourists play with wild animals, you often get more than you bargain for.
2. I told her you shouldn't take feral children away from their parents.
3. I tried, but you couldn't persuade her not to adopt little Napoo, son of wolves.
4. The Cave Bear priest told his warriors that you should watch the sky for omens.
5. An individual should not lend money unless you are willing to use muscle to get it back.
6. The nature guide told us that you should not pet the Tasmanian devil unless you were wearing full body armor.
7. People may think they will never receive a Chia Pet, but you never know until Christmas Day.
8. Tourists love Venice, especially when you walk on the beach.
9. Every beauty contestant knew that you shouldn't wear fishnet stockings during the talent part of the program.
10. The kick boxer was taught that you should look an opponent in the feet.

EXERCISE 8

Correct the problems in pronoun person.

1. When a person buys tickets from scalpers at sporting events, they should know what to do.
2. As a youngster, I discovered that you should learn how to buy tickets at Dodger Stadium.
3. Scalpers sell tickets to anyone who has money, but you can't always trust those people.
4. I always bring a drawing of the ballpark with me because you needs to know seat locations.

5. Scalpers may sell counterfeit tickets, so you should know which tickets are genuine.
6. The typical scalper isn't dishonest; they just want to make a little extra money from selling unwanted tickets.
7. If you wait until you hear the national anthem, you can get better ticket prices.
8. Any scalper will lower their prices after the game starts.
9. A scalper is more likely to lie about the seat location than they are to sell counterfeit tickets.
10. If several scalpers are competing and game time is near, you can get tickets at a good price.

Agreement in Number

Most problems with pronoun-antecedent agreement involve number. The principles are simple: If the antecedent (the word the pronoun refers back to) is singular, use a singular pronoun. If the antecedent is plural, use a plural pronoun.

1. A singular antecedent requires a singular pronoun.

   Jim forgot *his* notebook.

2. A plural antecedent requires a plural pronoun.

   Many *students* cast *their* votes today.

3. A singular indefinite pronoun as an antecedent takes a singular pronoun.

   Each of the girls brought *her* book.

4. A plural indefinite pronoun as an antecedent takes a plural pronoun.

   Few knew *their* assignments.

5. Two or more antecedents, singular or plural, take a plural pronoun. Such antecedents are usually joined together by *and* or by commas and *and.*

   Howard and his *parents* bought *their* presents early.

6. Alternate antecedents—that is, antecedents joined by *or, nor, whether/or, either/or, neither/nor, not only/but also*—require a pronoun that agrees with the nearer antecedent.

   Neither John nor his *friends* lost *their* way.

   Neither his friends nor *John* lost *his* way.

7. In sentence constructions with the expressions *one of,* the antecedent is usually the plural noun immediately before it.

   He is one of those *people who* want *their* money now.

8. In sentence constructions with the expression *only one of,* the antecedent is usually the singular word *one.*

   She is the only *one* of the members *who* wants *her* money now.

9. Collective nouns such as *team, jury, committee,* and *band* used as an antecedent will take a singular pronoun if they are considered as units.

   The *jury* is doing *its* best (not *their*).

   Collective nouns with meaning suggesting individual behavior would usually take a plural form.

   The *jury* are putting on *their* coats.

10. The words *each, every,* and *many a(n)* preceding and modifying nouns make them singular.

    Each child and *adult* was *his or her* own authority. *Each* and *every person* doubted *himself* or *herself. Many a person* is capable of knowing *himself* or *herself.*

EXERCISE 9

Underline the correct pronoun. (See Answer Key for answers.)

1. The team is doing (its, their) best to win.
2. Each and every person should be prepared for work or (they, he or she) will waste a lot of time.
3. Each student should try (their, his or her) best.
4. If the family doesn't stick together now, (it, they) may never be functional.
5. Each of those Moroccan Palace Guards has (their, his) own fez-pressing machine.
6. Mathilda and Jake have (their, his or her) sights set on chinchilla ranching.
7. Someone has left (his or her, their) fingerprints on my velvet painting.
8. Either Bryant or one of his friends offered to bring (his, their) fresh Tater Tots.
9. She is one of those free spirits who insist on having (their, her) wedding in a tree.
10. Every gorilla picks fleas from (its, their) closest associates.

EXERCISE 10

Underline the correct pronoun.

1. Many a Viking raiding party allowed (its, their) terrified captives to decide between slavery and death.
2. The team of Knute Grunson, arctic explorer, and his trusted malamute, Thor, made (their, its) way through a snowstorm.

3. The famous heavy-metal band, Hemorrhage, will travel in (its, their) bright red bus.

4. Young Freda was the only one of the schoolgirls to wear (her, their) raincoat today.

5. Neither dogs nor birds can hold (their, its) own with pigs in intelligence tests.

6. One of the children left (his or her, their) pet muskrats on the schoolbus.

7. The snake-handling troupe brought (their, its) defanged rattlesnakes to show the curious children.

8. In one day, a hummingbird can eat (its, their) weight in nectar.

9. Each member of the Boffo Brothers acrobatic troupe can balance a lawn chair on (his, their) nose.

10. Those wacky acrobats will expand (its, their) act to table balancing next year.

Agreement in Gender

The pronoun should agree with its antecedent in gender, if the gender of the antecedent is specific. Masculine and feminine pronouns are gender specific: *he, him, she, her.* Others are neuter: *I, we, me, us, it, they, them, who, whom, that, which.* The words *who* and *whom* refer to people. *That* can refer to ideas, things, and people, but usually not to people. *Which* refers to ideas and things, but never to people.

My *girlfriend* gave me *her* best advice. (feminine)

Mighty *Casey* tried *his* best. (masculine)

The *people whom* I work with are loud. (neuter)

Indefinite singular pronouns used as antecedents require, of course, singular pronouns. Handling the gender of these singular pronouns is not as obvious; opinion is divided.

1. Traditionally, writers have used the masculine form of pronouns to refer to the indefinite singular pronouns when the gender is unknown.

   Everyone should work until *he* drops.

2. In order to avoid a perceived sex bias, most writers prefer to use *he or she* or *his or her* instead of just *he* or *his.*

   Everyone should work until *he or she* drops.

3. Although option 1 is more direct, it is illogical to many listeners and readers and Option 2 used several times in a short passage can be awkward. To avoid those possible problems, writers often use plural forms.

   Option 1: Everyone should mind his own business.

   Option 2: Everyone should mind his or her own business.

   Option 3: Everyone should mind their own business.

In any case, avoid using a plural pronoun with a singular indefinite pronoun; such usage violates the basic principle of number agreement.

Everyone should do *their* best. (incorrect)

EXERCISE 11

Underline the pronoun that agrees with the subject in gender and number. (See Answer Key for answers.)

1. The fry cooks at Campus Kitchen have developed a new chocolate cookie that (they, he or she) will try to sell to (us, we) students.
2. The cookies taste terrible, but an official EPA test proved that (they, it) are biodegradable and will not harm the environment.
3. Weather forecasters were especially pleased when (their, his or her) prediction for tornadoes was accurate.
4. Commuters driving home in (their, his or her) cars can learn to swear in several tongues by listening to foreign language tapes.
5. My neighbors avoid harmful radiation by wearing (his or her, their) lead suits.
6. If all class members would work together, (they, he or she) might accomplish much, especially on tests.
7. Each child in this population of young people should do vigorous exercises during (his or her, their) television viewing.
8. Whether children want to or not, (they, he or she) will be required to walk rapidly to and from the refrigerator.
9. Joe, the blacksmith, finally had to close down (his, their) business.
10. Almost no one needed to furnish (his or her, their) home or business with hand-wrought ironware.

EXERCISE 12

Correct the faulty pronouns for problems in gender and number.

1. The teacher which helped me most is now retired.
2. Everyone interested in improving their vocabulary should purchase a dictionary and use it.

3. A person who can make their vocation and avocation the same will find contentment.
4. The storyteller was the first person which was responsible for maintaining tradition.
5. The tribal storyteller, who is also the historian, should take their task seriously.
6. Almost every person has their own definition of romantic love.
7. A person which cannot resist counting objects is called *compulsive.*
8. According to legend, a groundhog that ventures forth from their den in early February can forecast weather.
9. If the groundhog sees their shadow, it goes back inside its cave and warm weather will be late in coming.
10. The blacksmith which specialized in ironware for camping prospered.

Pronoun Reference

A pronoun must refer clearly to its antecedent. Because a pronoun is a substitute word, it can express meaning clearly and definitely only if its antecedent is easily identified.

In some sentence constructions, gender and number make the reference clear.

> Thomas and Jane discussed *his* absences and *her* good attendance. (gender)
>
> If the three older boys in the *club* carry out those plans, *it* will break up. (number)

Word order can also make reference clear. A pronoun should be placed as close to its antecedent as possible. An antecedent is preferably the first noun or indefinite pronoun before the pronoun.

The following are additional guidelines for making pronoun reference clear in your writing.

1. When using a pronoun to refer to a general idea, make sure that the reference is clear. The pronouns used frequently in this way are *this, that, which,* and *it.* The best solution may be to recast the sentence to omit the pronoun in question.

Unclear: She whistled the same tune, *which* irritated me.

Clear: She whistled the same tune, a *habit* that irritated me.

Recast: Her whistling the same tune irritated me.

Unclear: They treated him like a thief, and *that* angered him.

Clear: They treated him like a thief, and *that kind* of treatment angered him.

Recast: Their treating him like a thief angered him.

Confusion caused by vague reference of a pronoun to its antecedent can be eliminated by repeating the word intended as the antecedent or by using a synonym for the word. Confusion may also be eliminated by rephrasing the sentence.

Unclear: You could defend his position, but *it* would be weak.

Clear: You could defend his position, but *your defense* would be weak.

Recast: Your defense of his position would be weak.

2. Avoid ambiguous reference. The following sentences illustrate the kind of confusion that results from structuring sentences with more than one possible antecedent for the pronoun.

Unclear: John gave David *his* money and clothes.

Clear: John gave his own money and clothes to David.

Unclear: Mary told her sister that *her* car has a flat tire.

Clear: Mary said to her sister, "Your car has a flat tire."

3. Avoid implied reference. Implied reference occurs when the antecedent is not stated; it may be a related word, a modifier, or a possessive form.

Vague: We put mosquito netting over the opening, but *some* of *them* still got into the tent. (a modifier)

Clear: We put mosquito netting over the opening, but some of the mosquitoes still got into the tent.

Vague: This is my brother's boat, *whom* you met yesterday. (possessive)

Clear: This boat belongs to my brother, whom you met yesterday.

4. Usually avoid the indefinite use of *it, they,* and *you.*

Vague: They say the Republican party needs new leadership.

Clear: The editor of the Los Angeles *Times* says the Republican party needs new leadership.

Vague: In the army, you make few decisions.

Clear: In the army, privates make few decisions.

Indefinite forms have their place, however, and are part of well-established expression.

Examples: It is cool today.

It is a certainty that he will lose.

It is late.

EXERCISE 13

Label each sentence as OK if it is clear or V for vague pronoun reference. (See Answer Key for answers.)

1. (a) _______ Pickled eggs were served on paper plates at the wedding which was really tacky.

   (b) _______ At the wedding pickled eggs were served on paper plates, a practice that was really tacky.

2. (a) _______ I took my defective mustache-straightening compound back to the drugstore and told the salesperson to give me my money back.

   (b) _______ I took my defective mustache-straightening compound back to the drugstore and told them to give me my money back.

3. (a) _______ The druggist was eating a double cheeseburger and wiping the grease from his fingers onto his grubby old smock, which didn't give me much confidence.

   (b) _______ The druggist was eating a double cheeseburger and wiping the grease from his fingers onto his grubby old smock, and that situation didn't give me much confidence.

4. (a) _______ Young Douglas told his father that he was having trouble in school.

   (b) _______ Young Douglas told his father, "I am having trouble in school."

5. (a) _______ His father replied to Douglas that it was time for him to study.

   (b) _______ His father replied that it was time for Douglas to study.

6. (a) _______ Bert has bought a 1975 Gremlin and customized it with bumper stickers and chrome mud flaps, which has made him the envy of all the kids at the high school.

   (b) _______ Bert has bought a 1975 Gremlin and customized it with bumper stickers and chrome mud flaps, and the project has made him the envy of all the kids at the high school.

7. (a) _______ The little girl told her mother, "I have a craving to watch reruns of 1950s family sitcoms."

   (b) _______ The little girl told her mother that she had a craving to watch reruns of 1950s family sitcoms.

8. (a) _______ After hearing the offer on a television commercial, I rushed to the doctor's office and asked them for my free snake-bite kit.

   (b) _______ After hearing the offer on a television commercial, I rushed to the doctor's office and asked the receptionist for my free snake-bite kit.

9. (a) ______ The astronaut told his commanding officer that he was a sorry specimen of a human being.

   (b) ______ The astronaut told his commanding officer, "You are a sorry specimen of a human being."

10. (a) ______ The gypsies traveled in a whimsically painted wagon and told fortunes, all of which impressed the townsfolk greatly.

   (b) ______ The gypsies traveled in a whimsically painted wagon and told fortunes, which impressed the townsfolk greatly.

EXERCISE 14

Identify and correct the problems with pronoun reference and agreement.

1. They say the Yankees aren't what they used to be.
2. In London they say that Americans talk funny.
3. When you walk down the streets of Laredo, a person should look out for traffic.
4. When he drove his car into the swimming pool, it was damaged.
5. We sprayed Microbe Eradicator everywhere, but some of them still got in.
6. Maria told her friend that she cherished her cool date.
7. When a student signs up for English 1A, you had better be ready for dedication.
8. Toni told Mae that she had an attitude problem.
9. In a hidden message in this book, it says you should learn your grammar or die.
10. He was always showing off his big vocabulary, which aroused, riled, inflamed, irritated, infuriated, and enraged me.

Chapter Checklist

1. **Case** is the form a pronoun takes as it fills a position in a sentence.
2. **Subjective pronouns** are *I, he,* and *she* (singular); and *we* and *they* (plural). *Who* can be either singular or plural.
   Subject case pronouns can fill subject positions.

   We dance in the park.

   It was *she* who spoke. (referring back to and meaning the same as the subject)

3. **Objective case pronouns** are *me, him,* and *her* (singular); and *us* and *them* (plural). *Whom* can be either singular or plural.

REVIEW 2

Each one of the following sentences has one or more needless changes in pronoun person. Correct each problem. Change verb form, also, if necessary.

1. Everyone knows that you should carry an emergency kit while backpacking.
2. I want to know if a man's man eats possum stew before you go on a date.
3. Our scoutmaster said, "Boys, one can never have too many dry socks."
4. It was the best wrestling match I had ever seen; you could almost feel the agony of Hawkman as he was slammed by Global Savage.
5. A man may think that his date wants you to provide fancy wining and dining for every occasion.
6. In fact, every man should know that his date may want you to plan something simple.
7. She may even prefer a man who would take you to something simple like an amateur hog-calling contest.
8. She might even prefer a man who would let you share equally in planning the date.
9. I thought you couldn't mix weasels with ferrets, but I was wrong.
10. Let's write a public service commercial that tells drivers how you can improve gas mileage.

REVIEW 3

Some of the following sentences have a problem with pronoun-antecedent number agreement. If a sentence is correct, label it C. If not, correct it.

_______ 1. Young Rudy and his brothers chased their shadows through the streets.

_______ 2. The dance company pranced for the pleasure of their audience.

_______ 3. The singing cowboy and his horse, Bright Star, left his fans in shock when they disappeared from the world of entertainment.

_______ 4. Nothing would dissuade Roger from pursuing their chosen career of toothpick sculpting.

_______ 5. Not only Robin but also Batman wore his sleek and elegant crime-prevention bat boots.

______ 6. Few of the clowns ever took off his or her exploding slap shoes.

______ 7. The jackals and the coyotes sneaked out of its cage and began gobbling up dropped popcorn.

______ 8. The throng of spectators stood up from its seats as the contortionist bent his leg behind his head and then licked his big toe.

______ 9. Slick Veekel, tractor-pulling champion, and his lovely wife and mechanic, Thelma, were a team that did their best.

______ 10. The crew members of the Russian freighter wanted to pilot its boat to Disneyworld.

REVIEW 4

Correct the faulty pronoun-antecedent gender agreement in the following sentences. Rewrite sentences as necessary.

1. The person who does not attend to their personal hygiene will not be welcomed at social activities.
2. A person needs to know that, or they may be lonely.
3. Of course, people with poor hygiene can have his or her own stinking parties.
4. Rupert Schlagel, one of several famed accordion virtuosos, made their debut with the Galloping Polka Minstrels.
5. The fly fisherfolk wore their rubber waders around the house to simulate the outdoor feeling for which he or she tragically yearned.
6. Many an anonymous Halloween prankster used their cans of Wacky String to decorate fellow revelers.
7. Any one of the assembled baseball fans would have exchanged all their baseball cards for one of young Babe Ruth.
8. The members of the ski team left their boots and skis by the hot tub.
9. Each of the firewalkers is available to exhibit their talents at bar mitzvahs and weddings.
10. Each and every wrestler must supply their own tights and intimidation mask.

REVIEW 5

Correct the pronoun reference problems.

1. His boss had a rule for all situations, and that made Tom uncomfortable.
2. Joanne gave Mabel her paycheck.
3. They say that we can be sure of only two things: death and taxes.
4. They say he's so lazy his paycheck should be gift-wrapped.
5. Shana told Louanne that she bought the dress for a low price.
6. We put some mothballs in the closet, but some of them still got in.
7. In the army, you have few choices.
8. The doctor told Samantha that she needed some little, round pills.
9. They say that "love conquers all."
10. Some of us procrastinate habitually and that interferes with our productivity.

REVIEW 6

Write a sentence using each of the following words. Do not use the word as the first one in the sentence. One sentence should contain the word between *before a pronoun such as "between you and ______________".*

1. she

____

____

____

2. her

____

____

____

3. him

____

____

____

4. us

5. who

6. whom

7. me

8. I

9. they

10. then

9

Modifiers

What would be on your list of things you can't do without? your cassette/CD collection? your car? your companion? that new pair of shoes? your pager? your dog? tickets to the __________ concert? weekends? The Simpsons? Madonna? Michael Jordan? vacation? Christmas? your Chia Pet? Mr. Potato Head? Saran Wrap?

A tough question? Certainly it is, but let's consider two really important things that may not have made your can't-do-without list—adjectives and adverbs.

That's right, adjectives and adverbs.

Try reading this sentence with the adjectives and adverbs left out: Communication would be __________ ________ __________ _____ ________. (ineffective without adjectives and adverbs)

> *Without adjectives and adverbs,* (adv phrase) *even* (adv) John Steinbeck, the *famous* (adj)
>
> *Nobel Prize–winning* (adj) author, *surely* (adv) could *not* (adv) have described the
>
> *crafty* (adj) octopus *very* (adv) *well.* (adv)

Topics covered in this chapter:

EXERCISE 1

The following excerpt is from Steinbeck's novel Cannery Row. *Only some of the adjectives and adverbs have been omitted. Try filling in some words before looking at Steinbeck's choices in the margin.*

(1) __________ the (2) __________ murderer, the octopus, steals (3) __________, (4) __________, (5) __________, moving like a (6)

Answers:
1. Then
2. creeping
3. out
4. slowly
5. softly
6. gray
7. now
8. now
9. now
10. decaying
11. evil
12. coldly
13. feeding
14. yellow
15. rosy
16. pulsing
17. Then
18. suddenly
19. lightly
20. ferociously
21. charging
22. savagely
23. black
24. struggling
25. sepia

__________ mist, pretending (7) __________ to be a bit of weed, (8) __________ a rock, (9) __________ a lump of (10) __________ meat while its (11) __________ eyes watch (12) __________. It oozes and flows toward a (13) __________ crab, and as it comes close its (14) __________ eyes burn and its body turns (15) __________ with the (16) __________ color of anticipation and rage. (17) __________ (18) __________ it runs (19) __________ on the tips of its arms, as (20) __________ as a (21) __________ cat. It leaps (22) __________ on the crab, there is a puff of (23) __________ fluid, and the (24) __________ mass is obscured in the (25) __________ cloud while the octopus murders the crab.

Of course, Steinbeck conveys much through his skillful choice of nouns such as *murderer* and *rage*, and of verbs such as *steals, oozes, flows, burn, runs,* and *leaps,* but the absence of adjectives and adverbs eliminates a whole dimension of expression.

Definitions: Adjectives and Adverbs

Adjectives modify (describe) nouns and pronouns and answer the questions *Which one?, What kind?,* and *How many?* They may be words, phrases, or clauses.

Which one?: The *new car* is mine.
adj n

What kind?: *Mexican food* is my favorite.
adj n

How many?: A *few friends* are all one needs.
adj n

Adverbs modify verbs, adjectives, or other adverbs and answer the questions *Where?, When?, Why?,* and *How?* They may be words, phrases, or clauses. Most words ending in *-ly* are adverbs.

Where?: The cuckoo *flew south.*
v adv

When?: The cuckoo *flew yesterday.*
v adv

Why?: The cuckoo *flew because of the cold weather.*
v adv phrase

How?: The cuckoo *flew swiftly.*
v adv

We have two concerns regarding the use of adjectives and adverbs in writing. One is a matter of diction, or word choice—in this case, selecting adjectives and adverbs that will strengthen the writing. The other is common problems with modifiers—how to identify and correct them.

Selecting Adjectives and Adverbs

If you want to finish the sentence "She danced ________," you have quite a list of adverbs to select from, including these:

bewitchingly	angelically	quaintly	zestfully
gracefully	grotesquely	carnally	smoothly
divinely	picturesquely	serenely	unevenly
exquisitely	seductively	mirthfully	happily
vivaciously	gleefully	skillfully	obediently
solemnly	weirdly	awkwardly	

If you want to finish the sentence "She was a(n) ________ speaker," you have another large list, this time one of adjectives such as the following:

distinguished	dependable	effective	sly
influential	impressive	polished	astute
adequate	boring	abrasive	humorous
fluent	eloquent	finished	funny
brilliant	scared	handicapped	witty
liberal	hardy	unintelligible	satirical
adroit	flippant	scintillating	aggressive
inspiring	principal	crafty	deft

Adjectives and adverbs can often be used to enhance communication. If you have a thought, you know what it is, but when you deliver that thought to someone else in the form of words, you may not say or write what you mean. Your thought may be eloquent and your word choice weak. Keep in mind that no two words mean exactly the same thing. Further, some words are very vague and general. If you use a common word such as *good* or a slang word such as *neat* to characterize something that you like, you will be limiting your communication. Of course, those who know you most intimately will understand fairly well; after all, certain people who are really close may be able to convey ideas using only grunts and gestures.

But what if you want to write to someone you hardly know and explain how you feel about an important issue? Then the more precise the word, the better the communication. By using modifiers you may be able to add significant information about the words being modified—the nouns, pronouns, adjectives, adverbs, and verbs. Keep in mind that anything can be overdone; therefore, use adjectives and adverbs wisely and economically.

Your first resource in searching for more effective adjectives should be your own vocabulary storehouse. Just stop and reflect, especially during the drafting and editing stages of writing. Still another resource is a good thesaurus (book of synonyms). Finally, you may want to work with others in collaborative learning and share word knowledge and insight.

Supply the appropriate modifiers in the following exercises, using the resources designated by your instructor.

EXERCISE 2

Provide at least ten adjectives to modify these nouns. Use only single words, not adjective phrases.

1. A(n) ____________________ dog
2. A(n) ____________________ comedian
3. A(n) ____________________ voice
4. A(n) ____________________ neighbor
5. A(n) ____________________ ball player
6. A(n) ____________________ party
7. A(n) ____________________ singer
8. A(n) ____________________ date
9. A(n) ____________________ car
10. A(n) ____________________ job

EXERCISE 3

Provide at least ten adverbs to modify these verbs. Use only single words, not adverb phrases.

1. to sleep ____________________
2. to run ____________________
3. to talk ____________________
4. to walk ____________________
5. to kiss ____________________
6. to smile ____________________
7. to drive ____________________
8. to leave ____________________
9. to laugh ____________________
10. to eat ____________________

EXERCISE 4

Add adjectives and adverbs to this passage from "Flight" by John Steinbeck. (Steinbeck's choices are in the margin.)

Answers:
1. sane
2. puffed
3. angry
4. black
5. Automatically
6. big
7. black
8. sharp
9. proud
10. green
11. Instantly
12. gray
13. deep
14. exactly
15. waterless
16. desolate
17. heavy
18. sharp
19. thinly
20. brushed
21. starving
22. littered
23. broken
24. giant
25. granite

When the dawn came, Pepe pulled himself up. His eyes were (1) ____________ again. He drew his great (2) ____________ arm in front of him and looked at the (3) ____________ wound. The (4) ____________ line ran up from his wrist to his armpit. (5) ____________ he reached in his pocket for the (6) ____________ (7) ____________ knife, but it was not there. His eyes searched the ground. He picked up a (8) ____________ blade of stone and scraped at the wound, sawed at the (9) ____________ flesh and then squeezed the (10) ____________ juice out in big drops. (11) ____________ he threw back his head and whined like a dog. His whole right side shuddered at the pain, but the pain cleared his head.

In the (12) ____________ light he struggled up the last slope in the ridge and sprawled over and lay down behind a line of rocks. Below him lay a (13) ____________ canyon (14) ____________ like the last, (15) ____________ and (16) ____________. There was no flat, no oak trees, not even (17) ____________ brush in the bottom of it. And on the other side a (18) ____________ ridge stood up, (19) ____________ (20) ____________ with (21) ____________ sage, (22) ____________ with (23) ____________ granite. Strewn over the hill there were (24) ____________ outcroppings, and on the top the (25) ____________ teeth stood out against the sky.

Identifying and Correcting Common Problems with Adjectives and Adverbs

Comparative and Superlative Forms

The form of certain adjectives and adverbs will change according to the meaning of the statement, depending on which one out of how many are being modified.

Adjectives

1. The following chart shows how some adjectives change following a regular pattern:

Positive (one)	Comparative (two)	Superlative (three or more)
nice	nicer	nicest
rich	richer	richest
big	bigger	biggest
tall	taller	tallest
lonely	lonelier	loneliest
terrible	more terrible	most terrible
beautiful	more beautiful	most beautiful

These are usually the rules:

a. Add an *-er* to short adjectives (one or two syllables) to rank units of two:

Julian is *nicer* than Sam.

b. Add an *-est* to short adjectives (three or more syllables) to rank units of three or more:

Of the fifty people I know, Julian is the *nicest.*

c. Add the word *more* to long adjectives to rank units of two.

My hometown is *more beautiful* than yours.

d. Add the word *most* to long adjectives to rank units of three or more.

My hometown is the *most beautiful* in all America.

2. Some adjectives are irregular in the way they change to show comparison.

Positive (one)	Comparative (two)	Superlative (three or more)
good	better	best
bad	worse	worst

Adverbs

1. For most adverbs, use the word *more* before the comparative form (two) and the word *most* before the superlative form (three or more).

Joan performed *skillfully.*

Jim performed *more skillfully* than Joan.

But Tom performed *most skillfully* of all.

2. Avoid double negatives. Words such as *no, not, none, nothing, never, hardly, barely,* and *scarcely* should not be combined.

Double negative: I do *not* have *no* time for recreation. (incorrect)

Single negative: I have *no* time for recreation. (correct)

Double negative: I've *hardly never* lied. (incorrect)

Single negative: I've *hardly* ever lied. (correct)

3. Do not confuse adjectives with adverbs. Among the most commonly confused adjectives and adverbs are *good/well, bad/badly,* and *real/really.* The words *good, bad,* and *real* are always adjectives. *Well* is sometimes an adjective. The words *badly* and *really* are always adverbs. *Well* is usually an adverb.

In order to distinguish these words, consider what is being modified. Remember that adjectives modify nouns and pronouns and that adverbs modify verbs, adjectives, and other adverbs.

Wrong: I feel *badly* today. (We're concerned with the condition of *I.*)

Right: I feel *bad* today. (The adjective *bad* modifies the pronoun *I.*)

Wrong: I feel *well* about that choice.

Right: I feel *good* about that choice. (We're concerned with the condition of *I.* But if the context is different, and we are concerned with the health of an individual, it is right to say, "I feel well" because we are saying "well person.")

Wrong: He did *real* well. (Here adjective *real* modifies the adverb *well,* but adjectives should not modify adverbs.)

Right: He did *really* well. (The adverb *really* modifies the adverb *well.*)

4. Do not use an adverb such as *very, more,* or *most* before absolute forms of adjectives such as *perfect, round, unique, square,* and *straight.*

Wrong: It is more round.

Right: It is round.

Right: It is more nearly round.

EXERCISE 5

Underline the correct word or words. (See Answer Key for answers.)

1. Skip did (real, really) (well, good) on his alchemy exam.
2. Trixie was the (more, most) talented of all the performers in the go-go club.
3. Beowulf, King of Geats, was (bigger, biggest) among all the warriors in the northern kingdoms.
4. The kind old man did not have (no, any) trinkets to give the children.
5. After drinking two bottles of Volt Cola, the moviegoer felt much (worse, worst).
6. Sadie is (friendliest, friendlier) than her twin, Veronica.
7. Except for locking my keys in my car, I am doing pretty (good, well) today.
8. Evelyn was (more, most) sophisticated than the other girls at the boarding school.
9. Ivan was (more, most) terrible than the other cruel despots of his time.
10. After being sick with jungle rot for two years, I am finally (good, well) again.

EXERCISE 6

Underline the correct word or words, or cross out the improper word or words.

1. Bud Sneagle, a famed sky writer, was the (most, more) successful stunt pilot in the world.
2. The producers knew that they had a (real, really) hit on their hands.
3. After being hit by the snowplow, my car looked rather (badly, bad).
4. I was (not hardly, hardly) ready to play ball when a big linebacker tackled me.
5. After sighting Elvis buying some peanut butter cups at the mini-market, Thelma Lou was the (more, most) happy person in Fayetteville.
6. I am afraid that I did (bad, badly) on my Sanskrit exam today.
7. The Tyrannosaurus rex was the (more, most) hideous predator of the age of dinosaurs.
8. The dinosaurs were (not hardly, hardly) intelligent.
9. Because I won the bake-off, I can now tell people that I am a (real, really) fine cook.
10. The (best, better) thing about my cooking is that it is the (best, better) tasting in the whole world.

EXERCISE 7

Correct problems with adjectives and adverbs in the following sentences. (See Answer Key for answers.)

1. The chili cook-off event was a real big success.
2. People did not have no complaints about the food.
3. After being sucked through the turbo fan engine of a 737 airliner, the stuntman was a little worst for the wear.
4. When the old bloodhound was near death, he was never no lonelier.
5. Rudy Vingstadt, Olympic ski jumper, looked well during practice runs.
6. The fourth-grader was real proud after completing her project.
7. I never saw a woman more perfect than Sharon Stone.
8. Calf roping is not never an easy thing to learn.

9. I remember the real big explosion of the nacho machine at the convenience store; a horribler sight I have never seen.
10. It was the most nastiest scene of cheesy destruction in the store's history.

EXERCISE 8

Correct problems with adjectives and adverbs in the following sentences. Some sentences might have no errors.

1. Howard Hughes was one of the most richest men in American history.
2. The actor read bad for the part of Whimsey, Prince of the Leprechauns.
3. There has never been anyone quicker with a six shooter than old Dead-Eye Pete.
4. She drew a more round figure.
5. I know of no one who would make a best executioner than you.
6. I don't feel so well today.
7. That milk turned sourly.
8. They did their work bad.
9. He spoke quieter than the others.
10. She was the better of the three candidates.

Dangling and Misplaced Modifiers

Modifiers should clearly relate to the word or words they modify.

1. A modifier that gives information but fails to make clear which word or group of words it refers to is called a **dangling modifier.**

   Dangling: *Walking down the street,* a snake startled me. (The snake was not walking.)

   Correct: *Walking down the street, I* was startled by a snake.

   Correct: As I walked down the street, I was startled by a snake.

   Dangling: *At the age of six,* my uncle died. (The uncle was not six.)

   Correct: *When I was six,* my uncle died.

2. A modifier that is placed so that it modifies the wrong word or words is called a **misplaced modifier.** The term also applies to words that are positioned so as to unnecessarily divide closely related parts of sentences such as infinitives or subjects and verbs.

   Misplaced: The sick man went to a doctor *with a high fever.*

   Correct: The sick man *with a high fever* went to a doctor.

   Misplaced: I saw a great movie *sitting in my pickup.*

   Correct: *Sitting in my pickup,* I saw a great movie.

Misplaced: I saw many new graves *walking through the cemetery.*

Correct: *Walking through the cemetery,* I saw many new graves.

Misplaced: I forgot all about my sick dog *kissing my girlfriend.*

Correct: *Kissing my girlfriend,* I forgot all about my sick dog.

Misplaced: I tried to *earnestly and sincerely* complete the task. (splitting of the infinitive *to complete*)

Correct: I tried *earnestly and sincerely* to complete the task.

Misplaced: My neighbor, *while walking to the store,* was mugged. (unnecessarily dividing the subject and verb)

Correct: *While walking to the store,* my neighbor was mugged.

3. Try this procedure in working with the following exercises.
   a. Circle the modifier.
   b. Draw an arrow from the modifier to the word or words it modifies.
   c. If the modifier does not relate directly to anything in the sentence, it is dangling, and you must recast the sentence.
   d. If the modifier does not modify the nearest word or words, or if it interrupts related sentence parts, it is misplaced and you need to reposition it.

EXERCISE 9

Each of the following sentences has a dangling (D) or a misplaced (M) modifier. Identify the problems and correct them by rewriting the sentences in the space provided. (See Answer Key for answers.)

______ 1. Driving through the field, the wild jackrabbits were excited.

____

______ 2. The delivery truck drove past the library carrying fresh meat.

____

______ 3. Walking through the meadow, the satisfied wolverines slept deeply after gorging on the road kill.

____

______ 4. He went for a walk with his cute puppy hoping to meet an available female.

____

______ 5. I saw a slimy monster watching a television program.

____

______ 6. The lass ran home to her parents nursing a head wound inflicted by crazed weasels.

____

_______ 7. I began to fearfully unwrap the ticking package from my loved one.

____

_______ 8. Trailing smoke and flames, I watched the plane.

____

_______ 9. Soaked to the bone, I saw the men remove their boots at the front door.

____

_______ 10. Understanding the need for medical attention, the galley slaves were allowed ten minutes to dip their wounds in salt water.

____

EXERCISE 10

Each of the following sentences has either a dangling (D) or a misplaced (M) modifier. Identify the problems and correct them by rewriting the sentences.

_______ 1. Exploding noisily, I watched the fireworks.

____

_______ 2. Count von Swerdlow started to merrily whistle his favorite themes from the *Elvis Gold* album.

____

_______ 3. Running in front of the car, my sister tried to catch up with her dog.

____

_______ 4. The crusty old sailor went to the fortune teller with bad luck.

____

_______ 5. Burning out of control, the firemen did their best in attacking the fire.

____

_______ 6. I felt inadequate in the shopping mall without credit cards.

____

_______ 7. Wearing striped suits and chains, the guards watched the convicts.

____

_______ 8. I wanted to desperately obtain the recipe for the molded Jello dessert.

____

_______ 9. Lounging in my hammock, the crime took place before my very eyes.

____

_______ 10. I decided to foolishly purchase the solar-powered electric blanket.

____

EXERCISE 11

Each of the following sentences has either a dangling (D) or a misplaced (M) modifier. Identify the problems and correct them by rewriting the sentences.

_______ 1. The ball players kissed their wives covered with dirt and sweat.

____

_______ 2. The young lady began to abruptly dump mustard and relish over her boyfriend's head.

____

_______ 3. The alleged burglar addressed the judge on his knees.

____

_______ 4. Wearing gaudy makeup and silly polka-dot pants, we watched the clowns.

____

_______ 5. The anguished pet owner went to the veterinarian with a sick iguana.

____

_______ 6. I saw a snail, a lizard, and a turtle on the way to church.

____

_______ 7. Trying to succeed in school, my teacher was my greatest source of information and inspiration.

____

_______ 8. By watching my diet, a long, healthy life is possible.

____

_______ 9. Wearing a pink taffeta gown, Josh fell in love with his date.

____

_______ 10. Dripping with tomato sauce, I began eating huge portions of my mother's special Mexican casserole.

____

Chapter Checklist

1. **Adjectives** modify (describe) nouns and pronouns and answer the questions *Which one?*, *What kind?*, and *How many?* They may be words, phrases, or clauses.
2. **Adverbs** modify verbs, adjectives, or other adverbs and answer the questions *Where?*, *When?*, *Why?*, and *How?* They may be words, phrases, or clauses. Most words ending in *-ly* are adverbs.
3. If you settle for a common word such as *good* or a slang word such as *neat* to characterize something you like, you will be limiting your communication. The more **precise** the word, the better the communication. Keep in mind that anything can be overdone; therefore, use adjectives and adverbs wisely and economically.
4. The form of certain **comparative** and **superlative adjectives** and **adverbs** changes according to the meaning of the statement, depending on how many units are being ranked.
   a. Adjectives
      1. Add an *-er* to short adjectives (one or two syllables) to rank units of two.

         Julian is *kinder* than Sam.

      2. Add an *-est* to short adjectives (one or two syllables) to rank units of more than two.

         Of the fifty people I know, Julian is the *kindest.*

      3. Add the word *more* to long adjectives to rank units of two.

         My hometown is *more beautiful* than yours.

      4. Add the word *most* to long adjectives to rank units of three or more.

         My hometown is the *most beautiful* in all America.

      5. Some adjectives are irregular in the way they change to show comparison.

         good, better, best; bad, worse, worst

   b. Adverbs

      For most adverbs, use the word *more* before the comparative form (two) and the word *most* before the superlative form (three or more).

      Jim performed *skillfully.* (modifier)

      Joan performed *more skillfully* (comparative modifier) than Joan.

      But Susan performed *most skillfully* (superlative modifier) of all.

5. **Avoid double negatives.** Words such as *not, nothing, never, hardly, barely,* and *scarcely* should not be combined.

   I've *hardly never* lied. (incorrect)

   I've hardly ever lied. (correct)

6. Do not confuse an adjective (*bad*) with an adverb (*badly*).
7. A modifier that gives information but fails to make clear which word or group of words it refers to is called a **dangling modifier.**

   Walking down the street, a snake startled me. (dangling)

   Walking down the street, I was startled by a snake. (correct)

8. A modifier that is placed so that it modifies the wrong word or words is called a **misplaced modifier.**

The sick man went to a doctor *with a high fever.* (misplaced)

The sick man with a high fever went to a doctor. (correct)

Chapter Review

REVIEW 1

Correct problems with modifiers.

Old-time cowboys are among the better known figures in American folklore. Of course, they were versatiler than the word *cowboy* suggests. They did whatever work was needed on ranches, and they were able to do it real good. They mended fences, built sheds, took care of ranch equipment, and branded calves. They rounded up cattle, riding on their horses. Many times the roundups, as they were called, took in hundreds of square miles of range. After the cattle were rounded up, some were taken as trail herds to places such as Dodge City, Kansas, to be sold. Often barren and dry; cowboys were the lonesomest fellows in the world on the trail. At night they would sing soft to the cattle, and life seemed more perfect than ever. No doubt most of them sang very bad, but the animals were soothed remarkable by the simple melodies and bellowed, bawled, and mooed in response. Sometimes the cattle stampeded, and, the cowboys had to depend mighty on their horses to control the animals wearing practical saddles. The horses often saved the cowboys from death. When the trail herds reached their rail head destinations, the cowboys usual went to town for refresh-ments and entertainment in saloons. Some of these cowboys developed differences of opinions with other cowboys, and because they couldn't think critical to settle their problems in discussion groups, they ended up in places such as Boot Hill, a cemetery where men who died violent with their boots on were buried that way.

REVIEW 2

Write sentences using each of the words in parentheses.

1. (good, better, best)

2. (good, well)

3. (more, most)

4. (bad, badly)

10

Punctuation and Capitalization

Why are punctuation and capitalization so important? Read this (or try to) and find out for yourself:

> still i was amused one day when my small four year old neighbor looked at me as i was hoeing in my garden and said you arent a real indian are you scotty is little talkative likable finally i said im a real indian he looked at me for a moment and then said squinting into the sun then wheres your horse and feathers the child was simply a smaller whiter version of my own ignorant self years before wed both seen too much tv thats all he was not to be blamed and so in a way the moronic man on the beach today is blameless we come full circle to realize other people are like ourselves as discomfiting as that may be sometimes

Frustrating, isn't it? And why? No punctuation or capitalization. The passage you just struggled with is a paragraph in a piece by Lewis Sawaquat. Take a look at the original:

> Still, I was amused one day when my small, four-year-old neighbor looked at me as I was hoeing in my garden and said, "You aren't a real Indian, are you?" Scotty is little, talkative, likable. Finally I said, "I'm a real Indian." He looked at me for a moment and then said, squinting into the sun, "Then where's your horse and feathers?" The child was simply a smaller, whiter version of my own ignorant self years before. We'd both seen too much TV, that's all. He was not to be blamed. And so, in a way, the moronic man on the beach today is blameless. We come full circle to realize other people are like ourselves, as discomfiting as that may be sometimes.

Of course, the author, Lewis Sawaquat, could probably have read the passage as it is, with ease, because it came from his mind, and our ideas are usually fairly clear in our minds, even without punctuation marks and capital letters. And if I were to read it aloud to you, it would be clear because we do vocalize punctuation. But

Topics covered in this chapter:

faced as you are with a passage without punctuation and capitalization, you are rightly irritated because you are deprived of the signals that show you how to read the words. It would be of no comfort to know that the author himself didn't need other symbols in order to read his own writing.

The inescapable fact is that punctuation and capitalization are necessary, and that your knowing how to use those tools well will help you to communicate better.

Understanding punctuation usage will also give you the knowledge of how to use patterns of written expression not available to the uninformed. If you aren't sure of how to punctuate a compound or compound-complex sentence, then you probably will not write one. If you don't know how to show that some of the words you use come from other sources, you may mislead your reader. And if you misuse punctuation, you will force your readers to struggle, and thereby invite unfavorable opinions of your work; worse, your readers may not get your message.

End Punctuation

Periods

1. Place a period after a statement.

   The weather is beautiful today.

   Leave your coat in the hall.

2. Place a period after common abbreviations.

   Dr. Mr. Mrs. Dec. B.C. A.M.

   Exceptions: FBI UN NAACP FHA NATO

3. Use an ellipsis—three periods within a sentence and four periods at the end of a sentence—to indicate that words have been omitted from quoted material.

   He stopped walking and the buildings . . . rose up out of the misty courtroom. . . . (James Thurber, "The Secret Life of Walter Mitty")

Question Marks

1. Place a question mark at the end of a direct question.

   Will you go to the country tomorrow?

2. Use a single question mark in sentence constructions that contain a double question—that is, a quoted question following a question.

   Did he say, "Are you going?"

3. Do *not* use a question mark after an indirect question.

   She asked me what caused the slide.

Exclamation Points

1. Place an exclamation point after a word or a group of words that express strong feeling.

   Oh! What a night! Help! Gadzooks!

2. Do not overwork the exclamation point. Do not use double exclamation points. Use the period or comma for mild exclamatory words, phrases, or sentences.

   Oh, we can leave now.

EXERCISE 1

Add end punctuation. (See Answer Key for answers.)

1. The exhausted sponge divers asked their skipper whether they could have shore leave so they could get more tattoos of mermaids and anchors
2. Your car is on fire
3. I wonder if my boyfriend will like my new mohawk
4. Junior, put down that water balloon and get away from your sister this minute
5. Holy cow, I've just won the lottery
6. Now I can buy that pink '59 Coupe de Ville I've always wanted
7. "Have a nice day," the clerk said with a leer
8. Hmmm, I wonder how my neighbor would react if I trimmed his Saint Bernard's coat French-poodle style
9. All right, who *is* responsible for writing "The Book of Love"
10. Let us stop and give thanks to the king, Elvis, for his moving performance in *Viva Las Vegas*

EXERCISE 2

Add end punctuation.

1. It is very hard to find time to study when so much excellent television programming is available
2. As a good American, I know that I must watch at least four or five hours of television each day
3. When I don't watch at least three hours of television, I wonder if I'm somehow not a good citizen
4. Would you like to spend a few hours watching game shows with me this morning
5. The sky is falling
6. If we are to get the children of this great country away from television, we must encourage them to read and exercise

7. The knave asked if he could have another bowl of gruel

8. Would you like some gruel

9. It is made from old potato skins, cabbage water, and bits of chicken fat

10. "Help," she screamed, "my otter has escaped"

Commas

The comma is the most frequently used punctuation mark. It is used essentially to separate and to set off sentence elements.

Commas to Separate

1. Use a comma to separate main clauses joined by one of the coordinating conjunctions—*for, and, nor, but, or, yet, so.* The comma may be omitted if the clauses are brief and parallel.

   We traveled many miles to see the game, but it was canceled.

   Mary left and I remained. (brief and parallel clauses)

2. Use a comma after introductory dependent clauses and long introductory phrases (generally, four or more words is considered long).

   Before the arrival of the shipment, the boss had written a letter protesting the delay. (two prepositional phrases)

   If you don't hear from me, assume that I am lost. (introductory clause, an adverbial modifier)

   In winter we skate on the river. (short modifier, no comma)

3. Use a comma to separate words, phrases, and clauses in a series.

   Red, white, and *blue* were her favorite colors. (words)

   He ran *down the street, across the park,* and *into the arms of his father.* (phrases)

   When John was asleep, when Mary was at work, and *when Bob was studying,* Mother had time to relax. (clauses)

4. However, when coordinating conjunctions connect all the elements in a series, the commas are omitted.

   He bought apples and pears and grapes.

5. When words, phrases, and clauses make up a series without a conjunction, use a comma between all series elements.

   He bought us *paper, pencils, crayons, books.* (words)

   She went west *by car, by train, by ship.* (phrases)

   Lupe is a person *who is fair, who is honest, who is sincere.* (clauses)

6. Use a comma to separate coordinate adjectives not joined by *and* that modify the same noun.

   I need a *sturdy, reliable* truck.

7. Do not use the comma to separate adjectives that are not coordinate. Use this technique to determine whether the adjectives are coordinate: Put *and* between the adjectives. If it fits naturally, the adjectives are coordinate; if it does not, they are not, and you do not need a comma.

   She is a kind, beautiful person.

   kind *and* beautiful (natural, hence the comma)

   I built a red brick wall.

   red *and* brick wall (not natural, no comma)

8. Use a comma to separate sentence elements that might be misread.

   Inside the dog scratched his fleas.

   Inside, the dog scratched his fleas.

   Without benefit of the comma, the reader might initially misunderstand the relationship among the first three words.

EXERCISE 3

Insert commas where needed. (See Answer Key for answers.)

1. The professional wrestlers circled each other like caged wild beasts and the crowd loved the spectacle.
2. According to official records California has more tanning booths per capita than any other state.
3. If you know what is good for you you will eat a big hearty breakfast of tofu and wheat germ every day.
4. Buffy Nifton, sports reporter, ran up to the football coach grabbed his hand shook it enthusiastically and congratulated him on his successful weight-loss program.
5. The cheerful young waitress helped the squirming screaming toddler into the highchair.
6. Figure skating star Henri Tartuffe executed a death-defying leap into the snack stand adjacent to the skating rink and the fans gasped.
7. Without the invention of the hot dog baseball would be a dreary dismal affair to some.
8. The teenager proudly displayed his bright shiny pickup to his admiring friends.

9. Contrary to popular belief the chameleon can be an attractive amusing alternative to a boyfriend.
10. Beef jerky tarot cards and Flemish paintings were the passions of Mugsie O'Flannigan's life.

EXERCISE 4

Insert commas where needed.

1. Until the introduction of the whoopee cushion office parties and meetings were exquisitely dull.
2. The Campfire Girls gave an excellent demonstration of the uses of tourniquets but their musical tribute to the Heimlich maneuver was the favorite of the audience.
3. Bink Barkley, sports reporter, was hit in the forehead with a slapshot puck but he was filling up on refreshments at the pretzel line within a matter of minutes.
4. Upside down on the jungle gym the youngsters slurped juice boxes.
5. The young farmer said he needed a hearty strong wife who would stand up to field toil and motherhood.
6. The eager, confident, and ambitious salesperson smiled as she cheerfully demonstrated the many handy uses of the new Lint-O-Matic lint- and fur-removal kit.
7. During the demonstration the salesperson accidentally sucked the toupee off her startled customer's head with the Lint-O-Matic's powerful fur-removal wand.
8. In desperation and embarrassment the salesperson tried to extricate the bedraggled hair piece from the stainless steel jaws of the machine.
9. If you would like a home demonstration of this remarkable new piece of technology just let me know.
10. Oh by the way not only is the Lint-O-Matic a fine machine but it is also sleek elegant and practical.

EXERCISE 5

Insert commas where needed. (See Answer Key for answers.)

1. Many people have criticized spinach in recent years and I would like to offer a rebuttal.
2. First of all spinach comes in an interesting attractive shade of green.
3. It is also inexpensive nutritious and delicious.
4. I have recently purchased a young perky toy poodle named Maxine.
5. Maxine and I take walks each day but we are often cursed by the unwanted advances of amorous bachelor dogs vying for the affection of my beautiful pampered beast.
6. These would-be suitors will never win the love of Maxine for her affections are directed to the handsome clever Pierre a standard poodle.
7. Zeke Rimkin defense attorney will be representing me next week and I hope he can get my case dismissed.
8. He is a bright articulate person, and he will do almost anything to win a case for his clients.
9. According to his commercials on television he is the only local attorney who specializes in skateboard litigation.
10. When the jury members see Zeke Rimkin skate into court they will be impressed.

Commas to Set Off

1. Use commas to set off (enclose) adjectives in pairs that follow a noun.

    The scouts, *tired and hungry,* marched back to camp.

2. Use commas to set off nonessential (unnecessary for meaning of the sentence) words, phrases, and clauses.

    My brother, *a student at Ohio University,* is visiting me. (If you drop the phrase, the basic meaning of the sentence remains intact.)

    Marla, *who studied hard,* will pass. (The clause is not essential to the basic meaning of the sentence.)

All students *who studied hard* will pass. (Here the clause *is* essential. If you remove it, you would have *All students will pass,* which is not necessarily true.)

I shall not stop searching *until I find the treasure.* (A dependent clause at the end of a sentence is usually not set off with a comma. However, a clause beginning with the word *though* or *although* will be set off regardless of where it is located.)

I felt unsatisfied, *though we had won the game.*

3. Use commas to set off parenthetical elements such as mild interjections (*oh, well, yes, no,* and others), transitional connectives (*however, otherwise, therefore, similarly, hence, on the other hand, then, consequently, also, thus*) quotation indicators, and special abbreviations (*etc., i.e., e.g.,* and others)

    Oh, what a silly question! (mild interjection)

    It is necessary, *of course,* to leave now. (transitional connective)

    "When I was in school," *he said,* "I read widely." (quotation indicators)

    Books, paper, pens, *etc.,* were scattered on the floor. (This abbreviation, however, should be used sparingly.)

4. Use commas to set off nouns used as direct address.

    Play it again, Sam.

    Jane, I didn't hear your answer.

5. Use commas to separate the numbers in a date.

    June 4, 1965, is a day I will remember.

6. Do not use commas if the day of the month is not specified, or if the day is given before the month.

    June was my favorite time.

    One day I will never forget is 4 June 1965.

7. Use commas to separate the city from the state. No comma is used between the state and the ZIP code.

    Walnut, California 91789

8. Use a comma following the salutation and the complementary closing in a letter.

    Dear John,

    Sincerely,

9. Use a comma in numbers to set off groups of three digits. However, omit the comma in dates, serial numbers, page numbers, years, and street numbers.

    The total assets were $2,000,000.

    I look forward to the year 2000.

EXERCISE 6

Insert commas where needed. (See Answer Key for answers.)

1. After long consideration I decided that I would be grand marshal for the recycled products parade.
2. The cowpokes tired and hungry settled down to a satisfying meal of beans and hardtack.
3. Contrary to popular belief hardtack can be quite palatable if one soaks it in bacon fat and slurps it down with a cup of scalding coffee.
4. Barstow California is the gateway to the Mojave and the last major gas stop before Las Vegas Nevada.
5. I have decided therefore to move there because I like open spaces.
6. Debbi Winthrop inventor of the waterproof match retired in Cleveland Ohio.
7. The fifth grade class gobbled up hundreds of marshmallows Eskimo Pies and hot dogs at the party.
8. The woman who swallowed small live fish at the fair for a living became an instant celebrity.
9. The motorcycle gang rowdy and bored drew happy faces on all the road signs in the tri-state area.
10. He knew of course that winning the Nobel Prize for inventing a new kind of instant pudding was a long shot at best.

EXERCISE 7

Insert commas where needed.

1. The wood-burning kit a source of many household fires in the fifties and sixties was one of my favorite childhood toys.
2. The young, energetic campaign workers offered free promotional hamsters to the harried distracted commuters.
3. They responded of course with looks of deep appreciation.

4. The kind generous government agents gave packages of astronaut ice cream to the aliens from outer space.
5. The alto-sax player "Space" Jackson was renowned for his ability to chew gum talk and play his instrument at the same time.
6. I however think that there must be some sort of trick involved with Jackson's act.
7. You sir are the biggest cad and bounder in Fullerton California.
8. Alexander Dumas author of *The Three Musketeers* curiously enough never handled a sword in his life.
9. He was however renowned for his skill in handling a fondue fork.
10. August 19 1961 was certainly one of the greatest days in history.

Semicolons

The semicolon indicates a longer pause and stronger emphasis than the comma. It is used principally to separate main clauses within a sentence.

1. Use a semicolon to separate main clauses not joined by a coordinating conjunction.

   You must buy that car today; tomorrow will be too late.

2. Use a semicolon between two main clauses joined by a transitional connective such as one of the HOTSHOT CAT words (*however, otherwise, therefore, similarly, hence, on the other hand, then, consequently, accordingly, thus*).

   It was very late; therefore, I remained at the hotel.

3. Use a semicolon to separate main clauses joined by a coordinating conjunction if one or both of these clauses contain distracting commas.

   Byron, the famous English poet, was buried in Greece; and Shelley, who was his friend and fellow poet, was buried in Italy.

4. Use a semicolon in a series between items that contain commas.

   He has lived in Covina, California; Reno, Nevada; Tribbey, Oklahoma; and Bangor, Maine.

5. Do *not* use the semicolon to separate elements of unequal grammatical rank, before a direct quotation, before a listing, or in place of a dash in a list.

   Wrong: If I were sure of the answer; I would raise my hand. (unequal grammatical rank)

   Right: If I were sure of the answer, I would raise my hand.

   Wrong: He said; "I will go home now." (direct quotation)

   Right: He said, "I will go home now."

Wrong: We bought the following supplies; sugar, flour, bread, butter, and eggs. (listing)

Right: We bought the following supplies: sugar, flour, bread, butter, and eggs.

EXERCISE 8

Insert semicolons and commas where needed. (See Answer Key for answers.)

1. Jeb had a hobby he liked to draw pictures.
2. Wherever he went he drew pictures.
3. He drew on napkins, tablecloths, and sidewalks sometimes he drew on pieces of paper.
4. When he went to restaurants he left drawings for tips.
5. He gave drawings to his relatives for Christmas presents moreover he was equally generous with his loving friends.
6. One day he took time out from drawing to read a matchbook cover that advertised the Acme Art School in Shawnee Oklahoma.
7. He discovered that if he could draw a tree, a rock, and a cloud with great skill he could win a scholarship.
8. For years he practiced drawing trees, rocks, and clouds he became quite proficient in depicting those objects.
9. He traveled to Santa Ana California Grants Pass Oregon and Kelso Washington.
10. He became something of a legend he was known as the Johnny Appleseed of the art world.

EXERCISE 9

Insert semicolons and commas where needed.

1. Jeb's relatives grew very weary of receiving so many tree, rock, and cloud pictures waiters and waitresses would no longer serve him and his friends were no longer loving.

2. Jeb knew that he had gone as far as possible in this stage of his quest therefore he drew one tree, one rock, and one cloud and sent the drawings to the Acme Art School.
3. In only a few months Jeb had the opportunity of his lifetime he was offered a full scholarship at Acme.
4. He packed up his portfolio of tree, rock, and cloud pictures he tearfully said goodbye to his surly relatives, the disgruntled waiters and waitresses, and his alienated friends.
5. He traveled through Phoenix Arizona Roswell New Mexico and Amarillo Texas.
6. Finally he reached his destination he was on the campus of the Acme Art School of Shawnee Oklahoma.
7. He was eagerly greeted by the faculty and students they all had admired the tree, rock, and cloud drawings he had submitted.
8. He took a course in drawing the human figure he looked at the models and drew and drew and drew.
9. Unfortunately his drawings did not look like human beings instead his drawings looked very much like trees, rocks, and clouds.
10. His art instructors were very disappointed he did not make friends and waiters and waitresses scorned him.

EXERCISE 10

Insert semicolons and commas where needed.

1. In despair Jeb moved to Venice California to live among other artists.
2. Artists were everywhere they were on lawns, on sidewalks, and on the beach.
3. They accepted him into their community for he was friendly and hardworking.
4. He also posed no threat to the artists' professional territory there were no tree, rock, and cloud depictors even among the tattooists.

5. He began painting designs on bodies for food tourists appreciated his fine work and low prices.
6. Jeb had developed one novel approach at the Acme Art School he had learned how to draw tree, rock, and cloud people.
7. One day a Hollywood producer of fantasy films visited Venice he intended merely to enjoy the colorful sights.
8. There he saw Jeb working with his paints and at that moment a legend was born.
9. The Hollywood producer was just out for a lark however he knew a good cinematic idea when he saw one.
10. He would produce a series of tree, rock, and cloud animated fantasy films with Jeb as the illustrator in no time at all Jeb became rich and famous.

Quotation Marks

Quotation marks are used principally to set off direct quotations. A direct quotation consists of material taken from the written work or the direct speech of others; it is set off by double quotation marks. Single quotation marks are used to set off a quotation within a quotation.

> Double quotation marks: He said, "I don't remember."
>
> Single quotation marks: He said, "I don't remember if she said, 'Wait for me.'"

1. Use double quotation marks to set off direct quotations.

> John said, "Give me the book."
>
> Socrates said, "Know thyself."
>
> As Edward McNeil writes of the Greek achievement: "To an extent never before realized, mind was supreme over faith, logic and science over superstition."

2. Use double quotation marks to set off titles of shorter pieces of writing such as magazine articles, essays, short stories, short poems, one-act plays, chapters in books, songs, and separate pieces of writing published as part of a larger work.

> The book *Literature: Structure, Sound, and Sense* contains a deeply moving poem entitled "On Wenlock Edge."
>
> Poe's story "The Tell-Tale Heart" is about an insane narrator.
>
> My favorite Elvis song is "Don't Be Cruel."

3. Use double quotation marks to set off slang, technical terms, and special words.

   There are many aristocrats, but Elvis is the only true "King." (special word)

   The "platoon system" changed the game of football. (technical term)

   Everyone knows that Michael Jackson is "bad." (slang)

4. Use double quotation marks in writing dialogue (conversation). Write each speech unit as a separate paragraph and set it off with double quotation marks.

   "Will you go with me?" he asked.

   "Yes," she replied. "Are you ready now?"

   "Of course. How about you?"

   "Certainly," she answered. "When do we leave?"

5. Use single quotation marks to set off a quotation within a quotation.

   Professor Baxter said, "You should remember Shakespeare's words, 'All the world's a stage.'"

6. Do *not* use quotation marks for indirect quotations.

   Wrong: He said that "he would bring the supplies."

   Right: He said that he would bring the supplies.

   Right: He said, "I will bring the supplies."

7. Do *not* use quotation marks for the title of your own written work as you use it as a title.

   Wrong: "Struggling with Math"

   Right: Struggling with Math

Punctuation with Quotation Marks

1. A period or comma is always placed *inside* the quotation marks.

   Our assignment for Monday was to read Poe's "The Raven."

   "I will read you the poem," he said. "It is a good one."

2. A semicolon or colon is always placed outside the quotation marks.

   He read Robert Frost's poem "Design"; then he gave the examination.

3. A question mark, exclamation point, or dash is placed *outside* the quotation marks when it applies to the entire sentence and *inside* the quotation marks when it applies to the material in quotation marks.

   He asked, "Am I responsible for everything?" (quoted question within a statement)

   Did you hear him say, "I have the answer"? (statement within a question)

   Did she say, "Are you ready?" (question within a question)

   She shouted, "Impossible!" (exclamation)

   "I hope—that is, I—" he began. (dash)

Italics

Italics (slanting type) are used to call special attention to certain words or groups of words. In handwriting or typing, such words are underlined.

1. Italicize (underline) foreign words and phrases that are still listed in the dictionary as foreign.

   nouveau riche *Weltschmerz*

2. Italicize (underline) titles of books (except the Bible), long poems, plays, magazines, motion pictures, musical compositions, newspapers, and works of art.

   I think Hemingway's best novel is *A Farewell to Arms.*

   His source material was taken from *Time, Newsweek,* and the Los Angeles *Times.* (Sometimes the name of the city in titles of newspapers is italicized—for example, *The New York Times*)

   The *Mona Lisa* is my favorite painting.

3. Italicize (underline) the names of ships, airplanes, spacecraft, and trains.

   Ships: *Queen Mary* *Lurline* *Stockholm*

   Spacecraft: *Challenger* *Voyager 2*

4. Italicize (underline) to differentiate letters, figures, and words when they refer to themselves rather than to the ideas or things they usually represent.

   Do not leave the *o* out of *sophomore.*

   Your *3*'s look like *5*'s.

EXERCISE 11

Insert quotation marks and italics (underlining) as needed. (See Answer Key for answers.)

1. Professor Jones said, Now we will read from The Complete Works of Edgar Allan Poe.
2. The enthusiastic students shouted, We like Poe! We like Poe!
3. The professor lectured for fifty-seven minutes before he finally said, In conclusion, Poe was an unappreciated writer during his lifetime.
4. The next speaker said, I believe that Poe said, A short story should be short enough so that a person can read it in one sitting.
5. Then, while students squirmed, he read The Fall of the House of Usher in sixty-eight minutes.
6. Now we will do some reading in unison, said Professor Jones.
7. Each student opened a copy of The Complete Works of Edgar Allan Poe.

8. Turn to page 72, said Professor Jones.
9. What parts do we read? asked a student.
10. You read the words, or maybe I should say word, of the raven, said the professor.

EXERCISE 12

Insert quotation marks and italics (underlining) as needed.

1. The students were not pleased with their small part in the group reading of The Raven.
2. They made several derogatory comments about Professor Jones, even though he had written a learned textbook entitled A Short, Brief, and Concise Study of English Rhetoric and the Art of Using English Effectively, Correctly, and Well.
3. As Professor Jones lit candles around a sculpted art work, one student yelled, The poem says bust of Pallas, and that is not Pallas.
4. Professor Jones retorted archly, We didn't have a bust of Pallas in the department, so I brought a bust of Elvis from the chairperson's office.
5. Another student nodded approval and whispered to his enthralled companion, That prof is cool, real cool.
6. His companion, an English minor with a keen knowledge of grammar, whispered good-naturedly, Really cool is what you mean.
7. Yes, he said, that's what I mean. Sometimes I leave out my ly's and use the wrong words, and people think I'm a gashead.
8. The professor reached into his bag of props and took out a dark, feathered object and said, I have brought a stuffed raven.
9. That's not a raven. That's a crow, said a student who was majoring in ornithology.
10. The professor waggled his finger playfully at his audience and said, I believe Coleridge once observed, Art sometimes requires the willing suspension of disbelief.

Dashes

The dash is used when a stronger pause than the comma indicates is desired. The dash is typed as two hyphens with no space before or after them (--).

1. Use a dash to indicate a sudden change in sentence construction or an abrupt break in thought.

    Here is the true reason for his failing—but maybe you don't care.

2. Use a dash after an introductory list. The words *these, those, all,* and occasionally *such* introduce the summarizing statement.

    English, French, history—these are the subjects I like.

    Dodgers, Giants, Yankees—such names bring back memories of exciting World Series games.

3. Use a dash to set off material that interrupts the flow of an idea, sets off material for emphasis, or restates an idea as an appositive.

    You are—I am certain—not serious. (interrupting)

    Our next decision is—how much money did we raise? (emphasis)

    Dione has one talent—playing the kazoo. (restatement)

4. Use a dash to indicate an unfinished statement or word, or an interruption. Such interruptions usually occur in dialogue.

    Susan said, "Shall we—" (no period)

    "I only wanted—" Jason remarked. (no comma)

5. Do *not* use a dash in places in which other marks of punctuation would be more appropriate.

    Wrong: Lupe found the store—and she shopped.

    Right: Lupe found the store, and she shopped.

    Wrong: I think it is too early to go—

    Right: I think it is too early to go.

Colons

The colon is a formal mark of punctuation used chiefly to introduce something that is to follow, such as a list, a quotation, or an explanation.

1. Use a colon after a main clause to introduce a formal list, an emphatic or long restatement (appositive), an explanation, an emphatic statement, or a summary.

    The following automobiles were in the General Motors show: Cadillac, Chevrolet, Buick, Oldsmobile, and Pontiac. (list)

    He worked toward one objective: a degree. (restatement or appositive)

    Let me emphasize one point: I do not accept late papers. (emphatic statement)

2. Use a colon to introduce a formal quotation or a formal question.

    Shakespeare's Polonius said: "Neither a borrower nor a lender be." (formal quotation)

    The question is this: Shall we surrender? (formal question)

3. Use a colon in the following conventional ways: to separate a title and subtitle, a chapter and verse in the Bible, and hours and minutes; after the salutation in a formal business letter; and between the act and the scene of a play.

    Title and subtitle: *Korea: A Country Divided*

    Chapter and verse: Genesis 4:12

    Hour and minutes: 8:25 P.M.

    Salutation: Dear Members: Dear Ms. Johnson:

    Act and scene: *Hamlet* III:ii

Parentheses

Parentheses are used to set off material that is of relatively little importance to the main thought of the sentence. Such material—numbers, parenthetical material, figures, supplementary material, and sometimes explanatory details—merely amplifies the main thought.

1. Use parentheses to set off material that is not part of the main sentence but is too relevant to omit altogether. In this category are numbers that designate items in a series, amplifying references, explanations, directions, and qualifications.

    He offered two reasons for his losing: (1) he was tired; (2) he was out of condition. (numbers)

    Review the chapters on the Civil War (6, 7, and 8) for the next class meeting. (references)

    Her husband (she had been married about a year) died last week. (explanation)

2. In business writing, parentheses are often employed to enclose a numerical figure that repeats and confirms a spelled-out number.

    I paid twenty dollars ($20) for the book.

3. Correctly punctuate sentences with parentheses. Use the comma, semicolon, and colon after the parentheses when the sentence punctuation requires their use. Use the period, question mark, and exclamation points in positions depending on whether they go with the material within the parentheses or with the entire sentence.

    The greatest English poet of the seventeenth century was John Milton (1608–1674).

Brackets

Brackets are used within a quotation to set off editorial additions or corrections made by the person who is quoting.

Churchill said: "It [the Yalta agreement] contained many mistakes."

EXERCISE 13

Insert dashes, colons, parentheses, brackets, and quotation marks as needed. (See Answer Key for answers.)

1. Ben Jonson 1573–1637 wrote these poems "On My First Son" and "Though I Am Young and Cannot Tell."
2. William Blake 1757–1827 he is my favorite poet wrote The Tyger.
3. In that famous poem, he included the following words Tyger, Tyger, the spelling of his time burning bright/In the forests of the night.
4. Rudyard Kipling 1865–1936 wrote in several forms short stories, poems, and novels.
5. Robert Frost 1874–1963 he is probably America's best-loved poet lived in New England for most of his life.
6. He wrote about many subjects in his environment trees, walls, spiders, and ants.
7. Poet, philosopher, speaker Frost had many talents.
8. Dylan Thomas 1914–1953 was a great poet and a flamboyant individual.
9. Thomas acquired a reputation some say he didn't deserve it for being a drunk.
10. One of Thomas's most moving poems, "Fern Hill," begins with this line Now I was young and easy under the apple boughs.

EXERCISE 14

Insert dashes, colons, parentheses, brackets, and quotation marks as needed.

1. Anne Sexton 1928–1970 began writing poetry seriously as therapy for her mental illness.
2. Many of her poems were about those she knew well her children, her parents, herself.
3. Her style was colorful and imaginative, and her subjects some say she was too confessional often related directly to her life experiences.
4. Articulate, engaging, and intense she was popular on her poetry-reading tours.

5. After years of struggling with her emotional problems, she did what friends had long feared she would do she committed suicide.
6. John Keats 1795–1821 is an English poet who suffered from the most dreaded disease of his time tuberculosis.
7. Keats wrote extraordinary poems abut the "big" topics truth, beauty, love, death.
8. He went to Italy to live in a warmer climate he knew he was about to die and to visit his friends.
9. Alfred, Lord Tennyson wrote these words I Ulysses cannot rest from travel.
10. Ulysses restless, curious, and imaginative was bored with life on Ithaca.

Capitalization

In English, there are many conventions concerning the use of capital letters. However, because style and use of capital letters may vary, certain established rules for capitalization will prove helpful to you.

1. Capitalize the first word of a sentence.
2. Capitalize proper nouns and adjectives derived from proper nouns.

Names of persons:
Edward Jones

Adjectives derived from proper nouns:
a Shakespearean sonnet, a Miltonic sonnet

Countries, nationalities, races, languages:
Germany, English, Spanish, Chinese

States, regions, localities, other geographical divisions:
California, the Far East, the South

Oceans, lakes, mountains, deserts, streets, parks:
Lake Superior, Fifth Avenue, Sahara Desert

Educational institutions, schools, courses:
Rancho Santiago College, Spanish 3, Joe Hill School, Rowland High School

Organizations and their members:
Boston Red Sox, Boy Scouts, Audubon Society

Corporations, governmental agencies or departments, trade names:
U.S. Steel Corporation, Treasury Department, White Memorial Library

Calendar references such as holidays, days of the week, months:
Easter, Tuesday, January

Historic eras, periods, documents, laws:
Declaration of Independence, Geneva Convention, First Crusade, Romantic Age

3. Capitalize words denoting family relationships when they are used before a name or substituted for a name.

    He walked with his nephew and Aunt Grace.
    but
    He walked with his nephew and his aunt.

    Grandmother and Mother are away on vacation.
    but
    My grandmother and my mother are away on vacation.

4. Capitalize abbreviations after names.

    Henry White, Jr.

    William Green, M.D.

5. Capitalize titles of themes, books, plays, movies, poems, magazines, newspapers, musical compositions, songs, and works of art. Do not capitalize short conjunctions and prepositions unless they come at the beginning of the title.

    Desire Under the Elms

    Last of the Mohicans

    "Blueberry Hill"

    Terminator

    Of Mice and Men

6. Capitalize any title preceding a name or used as a substitute for a name. Do not capitalize a title following a name.

Judge Stone	Alfred Stone, a judge
General Clark	Raymond Clark, a general
Professor Fuentes	Harry Jones, the former president

Apostrophes

The apostrophe is used with nouns and indefinite pronouns to show possession, to show the omission of letters and figures in contractions, and to form the plurals of letters, figures, and words referred to as words.

1. Use an apostrophe and *-s* to form the possessive of a noun, singular or plural, that does not end in *-s*.

    man's coat

    women's suits

    child's toy

2. Use an apostrophe alone to form the possessive of a plural noun ending in *-s*.

    girls' clothes

    dogs' food

    the Browns' house

3. Use an apostrophe and *-s* or the apostrophe alone to form the possessive of singular nouns ending in *-s*. Use the apostrophe and *-s* only when you would pronounce the *s*.

    James' hat or (if you would pronounce the *s*) James's hat

4. Use an apostrophe and *-s* to form the possessive of certain indefinite pronouns.

    everybody's

    one's

    another's

5. Use an apostrophe to indicate that letters or figures have been omitted.

    I can't stop now.

    six o'clock

    in the '80s

6. Use an apostrophe to indicate the plural of letters, figures, and words used as words.

    five *8*'s

    and's

    Dot your *i*'s.

7. Use an apostrophe with pronouns only when you are making a contraction. Problems in understanding this rule account for a large percentage of errors in mechanics.

    Wrong: The dog bit it's tail. (not a contraction)

    Right: The dog bit its tail.

    Wrong: The problem is your's. (not a contraction)

    Right: The problem is yours.

    Wrong: The problem is also their's. (not a contraction)

    Right: The problem is also theirs.

    Wrong: Whose the leader now?

    Right: Who's the leader now? (a contraction of *who is*)

    Wrong: Its a big problem.

    Right: It's a big problem. (a contraction of *it is*)

Hyphens

The hyphen is used for the purpose of bringing two or more words together into a single compound word. Hyphenation, therefore, is essentially a spelling problem rather than one of punctuation. Because the hyphen is not used with any high degree of consistency, it is advisable to consult your dictionary to learn current usage. Study the following uses as a beginning guide.

1. Use a hyphen to separate the parts of many compound words.

    brother-in-law

    go-between

    about-face

2. Use a hyphen between prefixes and suffixes and proper names.

    all-American

    neo-Nazi

    mid-Atlantic

3. Use a hyphen with spelled-out compound numbers up to ninety-nine, and with fractions.

    twenty-six

    one hundred eighty-one

    two-thirds

4. Use a hyphen to join two or more words used as a single adjective modifier before a noun.

    bluish-gray eyes

    first-class service

    hard-fought game

    sad-looking mother

EXERCISE 15

Write in capital letters and insert hyphens, apostrophes, and quotation marks as needed. (See Answer Key for answers.)

1. Ive heard that you intend to move to el paso, texas, my brother in law said.
2. My date of departure on united airlines is july 11, I said.
3. Then youve only thirty three days remaining in california, he said.
4. My mother gave me some samsonite luggage, and dad gave me a ronson razor.
5. Jennifer does not know i am leaving for the university of texas at el paso.
6. Jennifer, my mothers dog, is one quarter poodle and three quarters cocker spaniel.
7. That dogs immediate concern is almost always food rather than sentimentality.
8. I wouldnt have received my scholarship without the straight As from my elective classes.
9. I am quite indebted to professor jackson, a first rate teacher of english and several courses in speech.
10. I wasnt surprised when grandma gave me a box of stationery and a note asking me to write mother each friday.

EXERCISE 16

Write in capital letters and insert hyphens, apostrophes, and quotation marks as needed.

1. Susan James likes to brag about her first new bicycle, a schwinn orange krate.
2. She bought it when she was in the eighth grade for ninety three dollars from her sister in law, who owned a bike store.
3. She said, my bike had factory installed shock absorbers and a battery-powered horn.
4. I named it the *Peeler,* she said. I used it on my paper route with the *Daily tribune.*
5. Her thirty three customers' needs were well served by her bike.
6. With her earnings, she purchased chrome bike fenders made by Acme manufacturing.
7. Later, she installed a mirror purchased at the midland bike barn.
8. I quit riding it when I entered high school, she said.
9. She said that owning the bike helped her build self esteem as a youth.
10. Now the bike is on display at the Amarillo museum of mid century pop art, which Susans family visited once during a recent summer vacation.

EXERCISE 17

Insert all capitalization and marks of punctuation as needed.

will rogers 1879–1935 was a famous movie star newspaper writer and lecturer. A part cherokee indian he was born in what was then indian territory before oklahoma became a state. He is especially known for his humor and social and political criticism. He said, my ancestors may not have come over on the *mayflower,* but they met em at the boat. When many oklahomans moved to california in the early 1930s he said that the average IQ increased in both states. In his early years, he was a first rate performer in rodeos, circuses, and variety shows. When he performed variety shows, he often twirled a rope. He usually began his presentations by saying, all I know is what I read in the papers. Continuing to be close to his oklahoma roots he appeared in fifty one silent movies and twenty one talking movies. At the age of fifty six he was killed in an airplane crash near Point Barrow Alaska. He was so popular and influential that his statue now stands in washington d.c. On another statue of him in Claremore Oklahoma is inscribed one of his most famous sayings I never met a man I didn't like.

Chapter Checklist

1. Three marks of end punctuation need be mastered.
   a. Periods
      Place a period after a statement.
      Place a period after common abbreviations.
   b. Question Marks
      Place a question mark at the end of a direct question.
      Use a single question mark in sentence constructions that contain a double question—that is, a quoted question following a question.

      Did he say, "Are we going?"

      Do not use a question mark after an indirect question.

      She asked me what caused the slide.

   c. Exclamation Points
      Place an exclamation point after a word or group of words that express strong feeling.
      Do not overwork the exclamation point. Do not use double exclamation points.
2. The **comma** is used essentially to separate and to set off sentence elements.
   a. Use a comma to separate main clauses joined by one of the coordinating conjunctions—*for, and, nor, but, or, yet, so.*

      We went to the game, but it was canceled.

   b. Use a comma after long introductory modifiers. The modifiers may be phrases or dependent clauses.

      Before she and I arrived, the meeting was called to order.

   c. Use a comma to separate words, phrases, and clauses in a series.

      He ran down the street, across the park, and into the forest.

d. Use a comma to separate coordinate adjectives not joined by *and* that modify the same noun.

I need a sturdy, reliable truck.

e. Use a comma to separate sentence elements that might be misread.

Inside, the dog scratched his fleas.

f. Use commas to set off nonessential (unnecessary for meaning of the sentence) words, phrases, and clauses.

Maria, who studied hard, will pass.

g. Use commas to set off nouns used as direct address.

Play it again, Sam.

h. Use commas to separate the numbers in a date.

June 4, 1965, is a day I will remember.

i. Use commas to separate the city from the state. No comma is used between the state and the ZIP code.

3. The semicolon indicates a longer pause and stronger emphasis than the comma. It is used principally to separate main clauses within a sentence.

a. Use a semicolon to separate main clauses not joined by a coordinating conjunction.

You must buy that car today; tomorrow will be too late.

b. Use a semicolon between two main clauses joined by a transitional connective (such as *however, otherwise, therefore, similarly, hence, on the other hand, then, consequently, accordingly, thus*).

It was very late; therefore, I remained at the hotel.

4. Quotation marks bring special attention to words.

a. Quotation marks are used principally to set off direct quotations. A direct quotation consists of material taken from the written work or the direct speech of others; it is set off by double quotation marks. Single quotation marks are used to set off a quotation within a quotation.

He said, "I don't remember if she said, 'Wait for me.' "

b. Use double quotation marks to set off slang, technical terms, and special words.

The "platoon system" changed the game of football. (technical term)

Dead or alive, Elvis is "cool." (slang)

5. Italics (slanting type) are also used to call special attention to certain words or groups of words. In handwriting or typing, such words are underlined.

a. Italicize (underline) foreign words and phrases that are still listed in the dictionary as foreign.

nouveau riche   *Weltschmerz*

b. Italicize titles of books, long poems, plays, magazines, motion pictures, musical compositions, newspapers, works of art, names of aircraft, ships, and letters, figures, and words referred to by their own name.

War and Peace   *Apollo 12*   leaving *o* out of *sophomore*

6. The dash is used when a stronger pause than the comma is needed. It can also be used to indicate a break in the flow of thought and to emphasize words (less formal than the colon in this situation).
7. The colon is a formal mark of punctuation used chiefly to introduce something that is to follow, such as a list, a quotation, or an explanation.

   These cars are my favorites: Cadillac, Chevrolet, Buick, Oldsmobile, and Pontiac.

8. Parentheses are used to set off material that is of relatively little importance to the main thought of the sentence. Such material—numbers, parenthetical material, figures, supplementary material, and sometimes explanatory details—merely amplifies the main thought.

   The years of the era (1961–1973) were full of action.

   I paid twenty dollars ($20) for the item.

9. Brackets are used within a quotation to set off editorial additions or corrections made by the person who is quoting.

   "It [the Yalta Agreement] contained many mistakes."

10. In English, there are many conventions concerning the use of capital letters. Although style and use of capital letters may vary, certain rules for capitalization are well established.
    a. Capitalize the first word of a sentence.
    b. Capitalize proper nouns and adjectives derived from proper nouns such as the names of persons, countries, nationalities, dances, days of the week, months, and titles of books.
    c. Capitalize words denoting family relationships when they are used before a name or substituted for a name.

       He walked with his nephew and Aunt Grace.

11. The apostrophe is used with nouns and indefinite pronouns to show possession, to show the omission of letters and figures in contractions, and to form the plurals of letters, figures, and words referred to as words. Examples: man's coat, girls' clothes, can't, five *and*'s, it's (contraction).
12. The hyphen is used for the purpose of bringing two or more words together into a single compound word. Hyphenation, therefore, is essentially a spelling problem rather than one of punctuation. Because the hyphen is not used with any degree of consistency, it is advisable to consult your dictionary to learn current usage.
    a. Use a hyphen to separate the parts of many compound words.

       about-face, go-between

    b. Use a hyphen between prefixes and suffixes and proper names.

       all-American, neo-Nazi

    c. Use a hyphen with spelled-out compound numbers up to ninety-nine, and with fractions.

       twenty-six, one hundred, eighty-one

    d. Use a hyphen to join two or more words used as a single adjective modifier before a noun.

       first-class service, hard-fought game, sad-looking mother

Quotation Marks **(4, a–b)**

5. To set off a quotation (words taken from the written work or the speech of others)

____

Italics (underlining) **(5, a–b)**

6. Word or letter referred to by its name

____

7. Title of a book

____

Hyphen **(2, a–d)**

8. Numbers

____

9. Two-word modifiers

____

Colon **(7)**

10. To introduce a list

____

Apostrophe **(11)**

11. A contraction

____

12. Possession of a singular or plural noun

____

PART TWO

Writing Paragraphs and Beyond

11

Filling the Blank Sheet: Prewriting, Stage One

The Blank-Paper Blues

Let us begin at the beginning, with a blank sheet of paper. All writers have been terrified by that monster of pulp and bleach that seems to reflect raw fear and panic.

> *Flashback: You are in a classroom, taking an essay test, confronting a blank sheet of paper. The person to your right is on page two, scribbling away in perpetual motion. The person to your left is on page three, pencil moving along lines like the Roadrunner on desert highways. You envy (hate on a really rotten day) those persons, and your Acme Writing School Strategies are not working. You've got a bad case of the blank-paper blues, and you need help.*

Have you been there? Done that? We all have. But you need sing that sad song no longer. This book is designed to address the problem of the blank-paper blues and to make you a skillful performer.

Determination is the key to your success, and practice is essential. However, practice without using good techniques will not eliminate bad habits. If you're using only two fingers while you try to play the piano, you can practice for twenty years and never get a concert gig. You'll just be stuck tossing coins to someone who can. You'll never be able to express yourself well musically. The same goes for writing.

Chapters 11 through 14 of this book will give you those good techniques. They will help you find workable topics, read for ideas to write about, organize, write correctly, revise, and produce a final version you can be proud of. But first there is the blank sheet of paper—worse than a song without words—and the assignment. What *can* you do?

The Blank Sheet of Opportunity

Certain strategies commonly grouped under the heading "prewriting" can help you get started. Actually, these strategies—**freewriting, brainstorming,** and **clustering**—are very much a part of writing because writing is a process extending from need to communication, not something that drops onto a paper. The understandable desire to skip to the finished statement is what causes the most common student-writer grief, that of not filling the blank sheet or of filling it but not significantly improving upon the blankness. These beginning strategies will help you attack the blank sheet constructively with imaginative thought, analysis, and experimentation. They can lead to clear, effective communication.

Although these strategies can work very well, not all are used in all writing assignments. Learn them now, and later use them as needed. Think of this approach as carrying a box of tools and selecting the ones that do the job.

Freewriting

One strategy is **freewriting,** an exercise that its originator, Peter Elbow, has called "babbling in print." In freewriting, you write without stopping, letting your ideas tumble forth. You do not concern yourself with the fundamentals of writing, such as punctuation and spelling. Freewriting is an adventure into your memory and imagination. It is concerned with discovery, invention, and exploration. If you are at a loss for words on your subject, write in a comment such as "I don't know what is coming next" or "blah, blah, blah," and continue when relevant words come. Of course, freewriting immediately eliminates the blank page and thereby helps you break through an emotional barrier, but that is not the only benefit. The words that you sort through in that idea kit will include some you can use. You can then underline or circle those words, and even add notes on the side so that the freewriting continues to grow even after its initial spontaneous expression.

The way in which you proceed depends on the type of assignment:

working with a topic of your choice,

working from a restricted list of topics, or

working with a prescribed topic.

The *topic of your choice* affords you the greatest freedom of exploration. You would probably select a subject that interests you and freewrite about it, allowing your mind to wander among its many parts, perhaps mixing fact and fantasy, direct experience, and hearsay. A freewriting about music might uncover areas of special interest and knowledge, such as jazz or folk rock, that you would want to pursue further in freewriting or other prewriting strategies.

Working from a *restricted list* would require a more focused freewriting. With the list, you can, of course, experiment with several topics to discover what is most suitable for you. If, for example, "career choice," "career preparation," "career guidance," and "career prospects" are on the restricted list, you would probably select one and freewrite about it. If it works well for you, you would probably proceed with the next step of your prewriting. If you are not satisfied with what you uncover in freewriting, you would explore another item from the restricted list.

Working with the *prescribed topic,* you would focus on a particular topic and try to restrict your freewriting to its boundaries. If your topic specifies a division of a subject area such as "political involvement of your generation," then you would tie those key words to your own information, critical thinking, and imaginative responses. If the topic is restricted to, let's say, a particular reading selection such as your own reactions to a poem, then that poem would give you the framework for your free associations with your own experiences, creations, and opinions.

You should learn to use freewriting because it will often serve you well, but you need not use it every time you write.

- Some very short writing assignments do not call for freewriting.
- An in-class assignment when time is exceedingly limited may not permit freewriting.
- An assignment such as a summary or outline of a reading does not require freewriting.
- An assignment on a topic that you know very well might not necessitate freewriting.

Nevertheless, freewriting is often a useful strategy in your toolbox of techniques. It can help you get words on paper

to break emotional barriers,

to generate topics,

to discover ideas, and

to explore ideas.

Freewriting can also lead to other stages of prewriting and writing, and it can provide content for details and insights as you develop your topic.

In the following example of freewriting, student Alta Hawkins has freewritten on "zoos," a topic taken from a restricted list. Had she been working with a prescribed topic, she might have been directed to concentrate on only one aspect of zoos, such as the historical development of zoos, the different kinds of zoos, or the arguments for and against having zoos. But she had no such limitation and, therefore, covered zoos broadly.

There are lots of zoos. People have been interested in animals for a long time but people don't have time and money to go all over to see them. Even in ancient times back with the Egyptians people liked zoos. Now every large city in the United States has a zoo and some of them are famous. I have been to zoos in San Diego and Los Angeles and in Oklahoma city when I was a kid. I think they serve a good purpose. I have almost always thought of them as a kind of entertainment, maybe as recreation. It's a place where you go and look at animals that you otherwise would not have a chance to see anywhere. Such as elephants and tigers and lions and girafes. When you go to a zoo you see animals in cages usually but some of them in the larger zoos live in places that are like what they would have lived in their native countries. And so on and on and on. I think there are many benifits to
1 zoos. For example, the animals--some of the animals are very rare, in fact they are endangered and they might be killed or die off if they were in the wild and some of them get good care from vetenarians here in the zoo.

possible topic: rare animals saved

breeding

2 Blah, blah, blah. They also breed animals in the zoo too
and do scientific work and sometimes the animals that are
born in the zoo are shipped back to where their parents
came from. I've heard about the White Rhino and the Orix
or something like that and both have multiplied in the
zoo. The bigger zoos have more money to do that kind of
thing than the small zoos. When lots of people go and
spend money the profit can be used to help animals even
more. Some of the people who go are children in classes

education

3 and they see the animals and develop good ideas about the
importance of animals and how we should save them. I
don't know what comes next I think I am running out of
what to say. The people that think zoos are cruel because
some still have cages are not looking at the whole picture. They may not be all wrong, but they're more wrong
than right.

anti-zoo people
limited

After doing this freewriting, Alta Hawkins went back through her work looking for ideas that might be developed in a paper.

Observe how Alta returned to her freewriting and examined it for possible ideas to develop for a writing assignment. As she recognized those ideas, she underlined key words and phrases and made a few notes in the margins. By reading only the underlined words, you can obtain a basic understanding of what is important to her; it is not necessary to underline entire sentences.

In addition to putting some words on that dreaded blank sheet of paper, she discovered that she had quite a lot of information about zoos and that she had selected a favorable topic to develop. The entire process took no more than seven minutes. Had she found few or no promising ideas, she might have freewritten about another topic. Although in going back through her work she saw some errors in writing, she did not correct them because the purpose of freewriting is discovery, not editing. She was confident that she could then continue with the process of writing a paper.

EXERCISE 1

Freewrite for five minutes on one of these topics. After you finish your freewriting, take about two minutes to mark the key words and phrases. Then make a few notations if you find some promising topic ideas.

AIDS

a place that was important to you in your youth

a concert, a movie, or a television program

someone who influenced you

your first job

a date

gangs

drugs

your biggest mistake last year

your best decision last year

Brainstorming

This strategy features key words and phrases that relate in various ways to the subject area or to the specific topic you are concerned with. One effective way to address your subject area is with the "Big Six Questions": Who? What? Where? When? Why? and How? Let your mind run free as you jot down answers to these six questions in single entries or lists. Some questions may not fit, and some may be more important than others, depending on the purpose of your writing. For example, if you are writing about the causes of a situation, the Why? question could be more important than the others; if you are concerned with how to do something, the How? question would predominate. If you are writing in response to a reading selection (as you will be doing frequently in assignments in Part Three of this book), confine your thinking to questions appropriately related to that content.

Whatever your focus for the questions is, the result is likely to be a long list of ideas that will provide information for continued exploration and development of your topic. Thus, your pool of information for writing grows.

Student Alta Hawkins continued with her topic of "zoos," but now the topic focused on particular areas. Although she could have listed some words from her underlining and annotating, she used the "Big Six Questions" for her framework.

Who? animals in zoos, wild animals, endangered animals, people who take care of the animals, people who are against zoos

What? zoos, animals, idea of zoos being good or bad, zoos as labs, zoos as freak shows featuring animals

Where? in zoos all over, but mainly in the Western world, in Los Angeles, San Diego, Oklahoma City

When? right now, maybe a bit of history on early zoos, mainly about what zoos have done, zoos when my parents were children and now

Why? zoos are bad; show animals as creatures for entertainment; zoos are good because they educate people, preserve threatened species, and study animal diseases; zoos bring money to cities and maybe support themselves

How? zoos as business, as school, as laboratory, as natural environment, as entertainment, as exploitation

(This listing could have been extended. For example, an item such as "endangered animals" could have become a list. After all, in this strategy, you merely pick out one aspect of your topic and allow your brain to create a storm of thought.)

EXERCISE 2

Continue with the topic you selected in Exercise 1 or select another and brainstorm. Begin with the Big Six Questions and continue with other lists if appropriate.

Clustering

Still another technique of prewriting is clustering (also called *mapping*). Start by "double bubbling" your topic (writing it down and drawing a double circle around it). Then, in response to the question, What comes to mind?, single-bubble other ideas on spokes radiating out from the hub that contains the topic. Any bubble can lead to another bubble or numerous bubbles in the same fashion. This strategy is sometimes used instead of an outline.

The more specific your topic inside the double bubble, the fewer the number of spokes that will radiate with their single bubbles. For example, a topic such as "high school dropouts" would have more spokes than "reasons for dropping out of high school."

Student Alta Hawkins continued with her topic of zoos. (See cluster diagram; page 219.)

Notice that after completing her basic cluster, she went back and made broken circles around subclusters that offer encouraging areas for focus. Some subclusters, usually with further clustering to provide details, are regarded as equal to the outline in offering structure and content for development. "Benefits," for example, could be developed into a well-organized piece of writing.

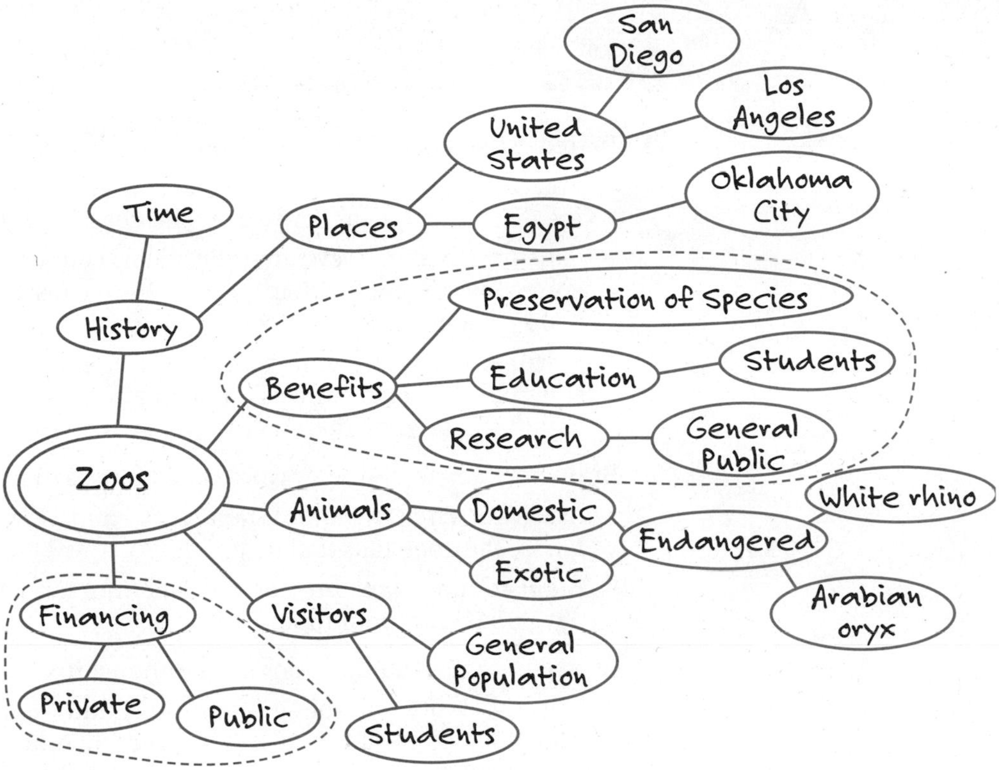

EXERCISE 3

Using a continuing topic or another from the list in Exercise 1, complete a cluster. After you finish, draw broken circles around subclusters that have potential for concentrated writing.

Chapter Checklist

1. In **freewriting,** you write without stopping, letting your ideas tumble forth.
   a. Freewriting is concerned with breaking emotional barriers, generating topics, discovering ideas, and exploring ideas.
   b. Your approach to freewriting will depend on whether you work on a topic of your choice (great freedom), a topic from a restricted list (more focused), or a topic that is prescribed (concentration on one idea).
   c. You need to use freewriting for all writing experiences (probably not on very short assignments, in-class assignments with limited time, outline and summary assignments, and assignments on well-known topics).
2. **Brainstorming** features key words and phrases that relate to your topic.
   a. Ask Who? What? Where? When? Why? and How? questions of your topic. Ignore the questions that do not fit.
   b. Brainstorming will provide information for continued exploration and development of your topic.
3. **Clustering** shows connections and relationships.
   a. Start by "double-bubbling" your topic, and then, in response to the question, What comes to mind?, single-bubble other ideas on spokes radiating out from the hub, which contains the topic.
   b. Clustering is sometimes used with the outline, sometimes in place of.

Chapter Review

Complete one of the following items.

1. Select another topic from Exercise 1 and freewrite, brainstorm, and cluster to generate prewriting ideas about the topic.
2. Prewrite about the idea that "writing has not always been easy, but now that I have learned these techniques of prewriting, I will perform much better." You will be discussing the benefits and properties of freewriting, brainstorming, and clustering at the same time that you are using the three techniques.
3. Select a topic from another class that you are taking and freewrite, brainstorm, and cluster to generate prewriting ideas about it.

12

Paragraphs: Prewriting, Stage Two

Defining the Paragraph

Defining the word *paragraph* is no easy task because there are different kinds of paragraphs, each one having a different purpose:

Introductory: Usually the first paragraph in an essay, it gives the necessary background and indicates the main idea, called the thesis.

Transitional: A very brief paragraph, it merely directs the reader from one point in the essay to another.

Concluding: Usually the last paragraph in an essay, it makes the final comment on whatever has been developed.

Developmental: A unit of several sentences, it expands on an idea. This book features the writing of developmental paragraphs.

The following paragraph is both a definition and an example of the developmental paragraph.

> *The developmental paragraph contains three parts: the subject, the topic sentence, and the support.* The **subject** is what you will write about. It is likely to be broad and must be focused or qualified for specific treatment. The **topic sentence** contains both the subject and the treatment—what you will do with the subject. It carries the central idea to which everything else in the paragraph is subordinated. For example, the first sentence of this paragraph is a topic sentence. Even when not stated, the topic sentence as an underlying idea unifies the paragraph. The **support** is the evidence and/or reasoning by which a topic sentence is developed. It comes in several basic patterns and serves any of the four forms of expression:

narration	(What happened?);
description	(What does it look like?);
exposition	(What does it mean?); and
argumentation	(What should we believe?).

These forms, which are usually combined in writing, will be presented with both student and professional examples in the following chapters. *The developmental paragraph, therefore, is a group of sentences, each with the function of stating or supporting a single, controlling idea that is contained in the topic sentence.*

Patterns

The most important point about writing a paragraph is that one should state an idea and support it. The support, or development, can take several forms, all of which you already use. It can:

1. give an account (tell a story).
2. describe people, things, or events.
3. explain by analyzing, giving examples, comparing, defining, showing how to do something, or showing causes.
4. argue that something should be done or resisted, that something is true or untrue, or that something is good or bad.

(All of the forms of expression are discussed with examples in Chapters 16 through 22.) You will not find it difficult to write solid paragraphs once you understand that good writing requires the support of main ideas so that your reader can understand how you have arrived at your main conclusions, or generalizations.

Usually the developmental paragraph will be indented only one time; however, you will note in your reading that some writers, especially journalists, break a paragraph into parts and indent more than once in developing a single idea. That arrangement, called a *paragraph unit,* is fairly common in magazine and newspaper articles (frequently with each sentence indented) but less so in college writing. Two effective patterns of conventional paragraph structure are shown in Figure 12.1. Form A merely states the controlling idea, the topic sentence, and develops it; Form B adds a restatement following the development.

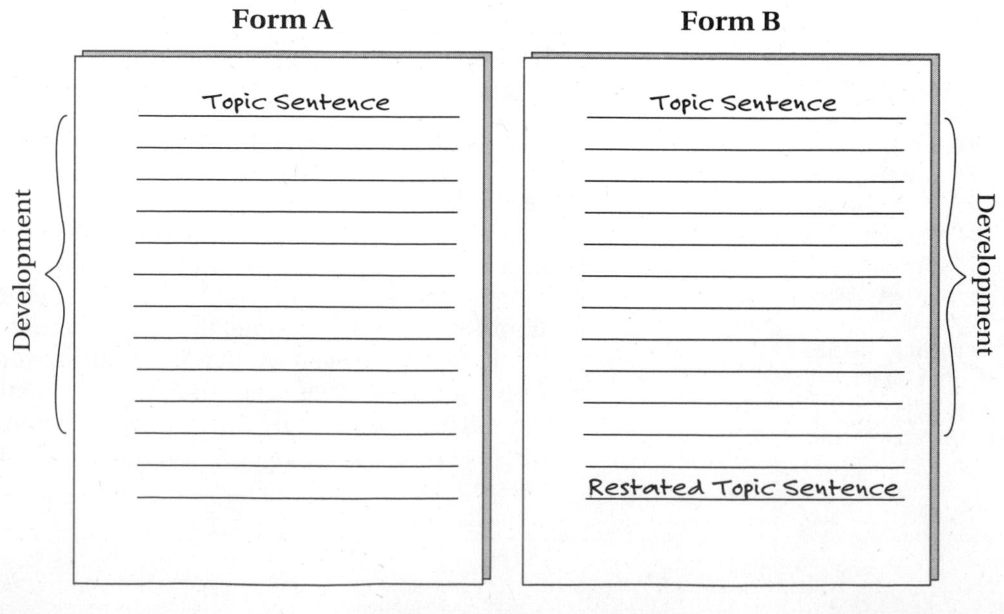

Figure 12.1
Paragraph Patterns

Prewriting, Stage Two

Topic Sentence

The topic sentence is the most important sentence in your prewriting and also in your paragraph. It includes two parts: the subject and the treatment, what you will do with your subject. Consider, for example, this topic sentence:

> <u>Zoos</u> <u>are beneficial because they make important contributions</u>.
> **subject** (Zoos) — **treatment** (are beneficial because they make important contributions)

It is an effective topic sentence because it limits the subject and indicates treatment that can be developed in additional sentences. Another sound version is the following, which includes divisions for the treatment.

> <u>Zoos</u> <u>are beneficial because they promote scientific research, education, and conservation of species</u>.
> **subject** (Zoos) — **treatment** (are beneficial because they promote scientific research, education, and conservation of species)

Ineffective topic sentences are often too broad or too narrow.

Ineffective: Too broad or vague

Zoos are great.

The San Diego Zoo is fun.

The San Diego Zoo is interesting.

Ineffective: Too narrow

The San Diego Zoo was established in 1903.

The San Diego Zoo contains 5205 animal species.

The San Diego Zoo is located in Southern California.

EXERCISE 1

Mark the following statements for subject (S) and treatment (T) and label each as E (effective) or I (ineffective). The effective ones are those that you can easily relate to supporting evidence. About those you can say, "This statement is true because . . . [often for several reasons]." This ineffective statements are too broad, too vague, or too narrowly factual.

_______ 1. The two teams in the Rose Bowl have similar records.

_______ 2. Michigan State is in the Rose Bowl.

_______ 3. Columbus is located in Ohio.

_______ 4. Columbus is a fabulous city.

_______ 5. Columbus has dealt thoroughly with its housing problems.

_______ 6. A monkey is a primate.

_______ 7. Monkeys are fun.

_______ 8. In clinical studies monkeys have demonstrated a remarkable ability to reason.

_______ 9. More than a million cats are born in California each year.

_______ 10. A simple observation of a domesticated cat in the pursuit of game will show that it has not lost its instinct for survival.

EXERCISE 2

Complete the following entries by making each into a solid topic sentence. Only a subject and part of the treatment are provided. The missing part may be more than a single word.

Example: Car salespersons behave differently depending on <u>the car they are selling and the kind of customer they are serving</u>.

1. Television commercials are often _______________.
2. Rap music promotes _______________.
3. My part-time job taught me _______________.
4. I promote environmental conservation by _______________.
5. The clothing that a person wears often reveals _______________.
6. My close friend is preoccupied with _______________.
7. Racial discrimination is not always _______________.
8. Country music appeals to our most basic _______________.
9. Friendship depends on _______________.
10. A good salesperson should _______________.

EXERCISE 3

Make each of the following subjects into a topic sentence.

1. Computer literacy

2. My taste in music

3. Bus transportation

4. The fear of crime

5. An excellent basketball player

6. Doing well in college English classes

7. Violence on television

8. Day care centers

9. Good Samaritans

10. Teenage voters

Outlines

The outline is a pattern for showing the relationship of ideas. Use it to demonstrate the framework of a reading passage or to show the organization of a reading selection. In writing about a reading selection, both uses may merge.

The two main outline forms are the *sentence outline* (each entry is a complete sentence) and the *topic outline* (each entry is a key word or phrase). The topic outline is more common in writing both paragraphs and essays.

Indentation, number and letter sequences, punctuation, and the placement of words are important to clear communication in an outline. The outline is not a creative effort. We do not read it expecting to be surprised by form and content, as we do a poem. We go to the outline for information, and we expect to find ideas easily. Unconventional marks (circles, squares, half-parentheses) and items out of order are distracting and, therefore, undesirable in an outline. The standard form is as easily mastered as a nonstandard form, and it is worth your time to learn it. Outlining is not difficult: the pattern is flexible and can have any number of levels and parts. Here is the pattern:

Main idea (will usually be the topic sentence for the paragraph or the thesis for the essay)

I. Major support
  A. Minor support
    1. Details (specific information of various kinds)
    2. Details
  B. Minor support
    1. Details
    2. Details

II. Major support
  A. Minor support
  B. Minor support
    1. Details
    2. Details
    3. Details

Here is an outline with content:

Topic Sentence: Zoos are beneficial because they promote scientific research, education, and conservation of species.

I. Scientific research (major)
 A. To promote animal well-being (minor)
 B. To help us understand human beings (minor)

II. Education (major)
 A. General public (minor)
  1. Signs and diagrams with regular displays (details)
  2. Special programs on grounds and on television (details)
 B. School system (minor)
  1. Sleepovers (detail)
  2. Field trips (detail)

III. Conservation of species (major)
 A. Breeding (minor)
  1. White rhino (detail)
  2. Great panda (detail)
 B. Breeding and reintroduction to native areas (minor)
  1. American bison (detail)
  2. Arabian oryx (detail)

EXERCISE 4

Organize the following ideas into an outline. Fill in the number of each idea on the outline form that follows to show whether it is a topic idea, major idea, minor idea, or detail.

1. Highly effective shooter
2. Averages more than twenty points per game
3. Voted captain by teammates
4. Scores lay-ups frequently
5. Good on defense
6. Quick reflexes that help him intercept passes
7. Jumping ability helps him block shots
8. The acknowledged team leader
9. Shoots free throws well
10. Excellent three-point shooter
11. Often is given ball with the game on the line
12. Intimidating physique
13. Tall, with long arms
14. Strong, muscular body
15. Michael Jordan is a great, all-around basketball player.

Main idea: __________

I. ______

A. ______

B. ______

C. ______

D. ______

II. ______

A. ______

B. ______

C. ______

1. ______

2. ______

III. ______

A. ______

B. ______

The foundation of a good outline and hence a good paragraph is a strong topic sentence, which means one with a specific subject and well-defined treatment. After writing a good topic sentence, the next step is to divide the treatment into parts. Just what the parts are will depend on what you are trying to do in the treatment. Just think of the thought process involved. What sections of material would be appropriate in your discussion to support or explain that topic sentence?

Among the most common forms of division are these:

Divisions of time or incident to tell a story

I. Situation and problem
II. Struggle
III. Result

Divisions of example or examples

I. First example
II. Second example
III. Third example

Divisions of causes or effects

I. Cause (or effect) one
II. Cause (or effect) two
III. Cause (or effect) three

Division of a unit into parts (such as a pencil into eraser, wooden barrel, and lead)
I. Part one
II. Part two
III. Part three

Divisions of how to do something or how something was done
I. Preparations
II. Steps
  A. Step 1
  B. Step 2
  C. Step 3

EXERCISE 5

Fill in the missing parts. Considering whether you are dealing with time, examples, causes, effects, parts, or steps may be useful. The answers will vary depending on individual experiences and views.

1. Too many of us are preoccupied with material things.
   I. Clothing
   II. Cars
   III.
2. Television sit-coms may vary, but every successful show has certain components.
   I. Good acting
   II.
   III. Good situations
   IV.
3. A female who is trying to discourage unwanted sexual advances should take several measures.
   I.
   II. Set clear boundaries
   III. Avoid compromising situations
4. Concentrating during reading involves various techniques.
   I. Preview material
   II. Pose questions
   III.
5. Crime has some bad effects on a nearby neighborhood.
   I. People fearful
      A. Don't go out at night
      B.
   II. People without love for neighborhood
      A.
      B. Put houses up for sale
   III. People as victims
      A. Loss of possessions
      B.

6. Exercising can improve the qualities of one's life.
   I. Looks better
      A. Skin
      B.
   II. Feels better
      A.
      B. Body
   III. Performs better
      A. Work
      B.
7. Shoppers in department stores can be grouped according to needs.
   I.
   II. Special-needs shoppers
   III. Bargain-hunters
8. There are different kinds of intelligence based on situations.
   I. Street-smart
   II. Common sense
   III.
9. Smoking should be discouraged.
   I. Harm to smokers
      A.
      B. Cancer prone
   II. Harm to those around smokers
      A.
      B. Fellow workers
   III. Cost
      A. Industry—production and absenteeism
      B.
10. An excellent police officer must have six qualities.
   I.
   II. Knowledge of law
   III.
   IV. Emotional soundness
   V. Skill in using weapons
   VI.

Chapter Checklist

1. The **developmental paragraph** contains three parts: the subject, the topic sentence, and the support.
2. The developmental paragraph is a group of sentences, each with the function of stating or supporting a single controlling idea that is contained in the **topic sentence.**

3. The two main patterns of the developmental paragraph are these:

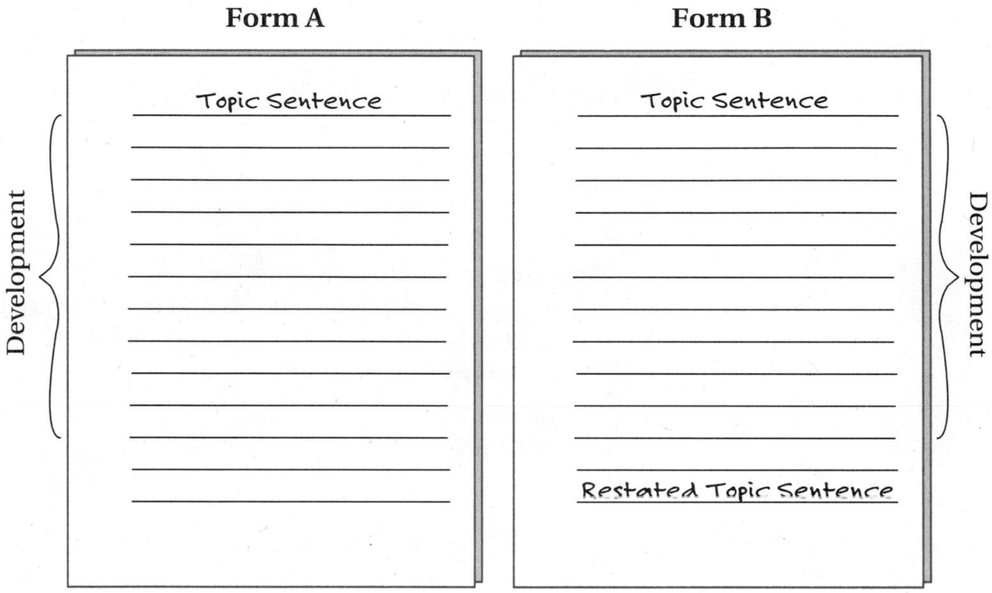

4. The **topic sentence** includes what you are writing about—the **subject**—and what you intend to do with that subject—the **treatment.**

> Zoos (**subject**) are beneficial because they promote scientific research, education, and conservation of species (**treatment**).

5. The **outline** is a pattern for showing the relationship of ideas.

6. The outline can be used in revealing the structure and content of something you read and in showing the structure and content of something you intend to write.

   Main idea (will usually be the topic sentence for the paragraph or the thesis for the essay)

   I. Major support
      A. Minor support
         1. Details (specific information of various kinds)
         2. Details
      B. Minor support
         1. Details
         2. Details

II. Major support
   A. Minor support
   B. Minor support
      1. Details
      2. Details
      3. Details

Chapter Review

Complete one of the following:

1. Write a topic sentence and a topic outline on a problem (at home, work, or school, or in the community) and how it should be dealt with (replace something, change something, or ignore the problem). In your outline, the problem and the solution might be represented by two Roman numerals. Label the subject and treatment parts of the topic sentence. Include at least fifteen lines (entries, points) in your outline.
2. Continue with a topic you worked on in the previous chapter by completing a topic sentence and a topical outline. Label the subject and treatment parts of the topic sentence. Include at least fifteen lines (entries, points) in your outline.

13

Writing, Revising, and Editing

The First Draft

Once you have completed your topic sentence and outline (or list or cluster, as directed by your instructor), you are ready to begin writing your paragraph. The initial writing is called the first, or rough, draft. Your topic sentence is likely to be at or near the beginning of your paragraph and will be followed by your support as ordered by your outline.

Paying close attention to your outline for basic organization, you should proceed without being preoccupied with the refinements of writing. After you have finished that first draft, take a close look at it, beginning with the most important part of your writing—the revision. If your topic sentence is sound and your outline has served you well, you now have a basic discussion. You have made a statement and supported it. Immediately you see that you can express yourself more effectively by using this process.

Don't be embarrassed by the roughness of the work. You should be embarrassed only if you leave it that way. You are seeing the reason why a first draft is called "rough." Famous authors have said publicly that they wouldn't show their rough drafts even to their closest, most forgiving friends.

Topics covered in this chapter:

Revision

The problem for many struggling writers is that they do not know how to make the rough draft smooth and effective through a process of revision. They simply change the spelling and punctuation and send the writing on its way. Unfortunately for them, revision is much more than making simple changes.

Here are six words to consider when transforming the rough draft into an effective piece of writing. To aid you in remembering what to cover in revising, the first letter of each word forms the acronym **CLUESS.** You need not complete these parts in any order or even work on them one at a time, but each one is important. You will be able to use all of these ideas immediately to a significant degree, and as you work your way through this book, you will become more competent in dealing with them.

Coherence

Coherence is the flow of ideas, with each idea leading logically and smoothly to the next. It is achieved by numbering parts or otherwise indicating time (*first, second, third, then, next, soon,* and so on), giving directions (according to space, as in "To the right is a map, and to the left of that map is a bulletin board"), using transitional words (*however, otherwise, therefore, similarly, hence, on the other hand, then, consequently, accordingly, thus*), using demonstrative pronouns (*this, that, those*), and moving in a clear order (from the least important to the most important or from the most important to the least important).

Language

Language here means using words that are suitable for what you are writing and for your audience. In college writing that means you will usually avoid slang and clichés such as "a barrel of laughs," "happy as a clam," and "six of one and a half dozen of another." Your writing will contain standard grammar and usage (the main concerns of Chapters 1–10 of this book).

Unity

Unity begins with a good topic sentence. Everything in your passage should be related and subordinated to your topic sentence. Repetition of a key word or phrase can make the unity even stronger.

Emphasis

Emphasize important ideas by using *position* (the most emphatic parts of a work are the beginning and the end), *repetition* (repeat key words and phrases), and *isolation* (a short, direct sentence among longer ones will usually command attention).

Support

Support is the material that backs up, justifies, or proves your topic sentence or thesis. Work carefully with the material from your outline (or list or cluster) to make sure that your ideas are well supported. If your paragraph is skimpy and your ideas slender, you are probably generalizing and not explaining how you arrived at your conclusions. Avoid repetition that does not add to the content; use details and examples; indicate parts and discuss relationships; explain why your generalizations are true, logical, and accurate. Your reader can't accept your ideas unless he or she knows by what reasoning or use of evidence you developed them.

Sentences

Be sure your sentences are complete (not fragments) and that you have not incorrectly combined word groups that could be sentences (comma splices and run-togethers). Consider using different types of sentences and different sentence beginnings.

Write as many drafts as necessary, revising as you go for all the aspects of effective writing. Don't confuse revising with editing (the final stage of the writing process) and get bogged down in fixing such things as spelling and punctuation.

Editing

This final stage of the writing process involves a careful examination of your work. Look for basic problems such as capitalization, omissions, punctuation, and spelling (COPS). These points are addressed in detail in other chapters of this book.

Before you submit your writing to your instructor, do what almost all professional writers do before sending their material along: read it aloud, to yourself or to a willing accomplice. Reading material aloud will help you catch awkwardness of expression, omission and misplacement of words, and other problems that are easily overlooked by the author.

As you can see, writing is a process and is not a matter of just sitting down and "banging out" a statement. The parts of the process from prewriting to revision to editing are connected and your movement is ultimately forward, but this process allows you to go back and forth in what is called a *recursive* manner. If your outline is not working out, perhaps the flaw is in your topic sentence, and then you will need to go back and fix it. If one paragraph of your development is skimpy, perhaps you will have to go back and reconsider a pertinent section of your outline or clustering. There you might find more details or alter a statement so that you can move into more fertile areas of thought.

Despite all these movements you make in working and reworking your material, the approach presented in this book is systematic. If you would like further guidance and even forms to follow in using this system, see DCODE in the Appendix, p. A-37. An acronym representing Delve, Concentrate, Organize, Draft, and Edit, DCODE offers a steady yet flexible guide to writing and is an abbreviated version of Chapters 11, 12, and 13. The Appendix includes an example of a paragraph developed with all the stages of DCODE, and a blank tear-out worksheet suitable for college writing assignments.

Student Alma Hawkins wrote this first draft, marked for revision, and then completed the final draft. For simplification, only two drafts are included here, though a typical writing might include several. Editing is also done along with the marking for revision on the rough draft, though it is often a separate phase of the writing process.

Rough Draft Marked for Revision and Editing

An "A+" for Zoos

~~Most large American cities have zoos~~. Zoos ~~They~~ are usually thought of as part of recreational programs. and ~~s~~ome people have criticized them on that basis, charging animal exploitation. But they offer ~~Zoos are~~ much more than recreation ~~that~~. ~~I had always taken zoos for granted. Because to me they were neat and I had never thought about such questions. So I decided to check out the situation. My conclusion is that~~ Specifically zoos are ben~~i~~eficial because they promote scientific research, education, and conservation of species. ~~I didn't know about the research that zoos have~~

s

~~done. I discovered that~~ ~~s~~cientists working in zoos have

how i

discovered ~~ways~~ to treat animal d~~e~~seases, and these meth-

and medicines field. By watching

ods^can be used in the^~~wild. They watched~~ animals in

scientists also

zoos, ~~they~~ have^learned just how dependent certain crea-

n have used that information

tures are on their enviro^ment, and ~~know how~~ to help rein-

their native habitat.

troduce creatures such as the American condor ~~back~~ to ~~the~~^

~~wild. I have seen them in the Los Angeles County Zoo.~~

another e

Education is ~~an~~ important ben~~i~~fit of zoos. The general

s by observing them in zoos and by reading educational signs

public learn~~ing more~~ about animals^ School children

learn both on field trips and on sleepover visits for

third

special study. The conservation of species is a^big

e in zoos

ben~~i~~fit of zoos. The breeding of threatened species^has

been very successful. The great panda~~, my favorite zoo~~

one that the population of

~~animal~~, is ~~the~~ subject of ~~much~~ work now, and^the white

in zoos in the last decade, possibly saving it from extinction

rhino ~~population~~ has increased dramatically^ Some for-

merly threatened animals such as the American bison and

the Arabian oryx have been bred in zoos and reintroduced

ir native habitats. in an ideal world

back to the^~~wild.~~ Although ~~it would be great if~~ all ani-

would free, current

mals ~~could~~ live ~~in their natural surroundings~~ conditions

e

make it necessary to have zoos, and their ben~~i~~fits far

outweigh problems of captivity.

Final Draft

An "A+" for Zoos

Zoos are usually thought of as part of recreational programs, and some people have criticized them on that basis, charging animal exploitation. But they offer much more than recreation. Specifically, zoos are highly beneficial because they promote scientific research, education, and conservation of species. Scientists working in zoos have discovered how to treat animal diseases, and these methods and medicines can now be used in the field. By watching animals in zoos, scientists have also learned just how dependent certain creatures are on their environment, and have used that information to help reintroduce creatures such as the American condor to their native habitat. Education is another important benefit of zoos. The general public learns much about animals by observing them in zoos and by reading educational signs. School children learn both on field trips and on sleep-over visits for special study. The conservation of species is a third big benefit of zoos. The breeding of threatened species in zoos has been very successful. The great panda is one focus of that work now, and the population of the white rhino has increased dramatically in zoos over the last decade, possibly saving it from extinction. Some formerly threatened animals such as the American bison and the Arabian oryx have been bred in zoos and reintroduced to their native habitats. Although in an ideal world all animals would live free, current conditions make it necessary to have zoos, and their benefits far outweigh problems of captivity.

Chapter Checklist

1. **Revision.** Here are the main points of CLUESS expressed as simple questions:

   Coherence: Does the material flow smoothly with each idea leading logically and smoothly to the next?

   Language: Are the words appropriate for the message, occasion, and audience?

   Unity: Are all ideas related and subordinate to the topic sentence?

   Emphasis: Have you used techniques such as repetition and placement of ideas to emphasize your main point(s)?

   Support: Have you presented material to back up, justify, or prove your topic sentence?

   Sentences: Have you used some variety of structure and avoided fragments, comma splices, and run-togethers?

2. **Editing.** This final stage of the process involves a careful examination of your work. Look for basic problems such as capitalization, omissions, punctuation, and spelling (COPS). These points are addressed in detail in other chapters of this book.

Chapter Review

REVIEW 1

Mark this rough draft for coherence, language, unity, emphasis, support, and sentence structure; then edit, correcting fundamentals such as capital letters, omissions, punctuation, and spelling.

High school dress codes don't make any sense to me. I've heard all the reasons. Too many kids wear gang clothes and some get attacked or even killed. Parents have to put up too much money and even then the kids without parents with deep pockets can't compete. And then there are those that say kids behave bad if they dress in a free spirit way. Let's take them one at a time. As for the gang stuff, it's mainly how you act, not how you look, and if the gang stuff is still a problem, then just ban certain items of clothing. You don't have to go to the extreames of uniforms, just change the attitude, not the clothes. Then comes the money angle. Let the kid get a part-time job if they want better clothes. The behavior number is not what I can relate to. I mean, you go to class and learn, and you do it the school way, but the way you dress should have something to do with how you want to express yourself. Do they want to turn out a bunch of little robots that think the same way, behave the same way, and yes with the dress code even look the same way. Get real! If they'll cut us some slack with how we dress, they'll get happier campers in the classroom. Later better-citizens in society.

REVIEW 2

Mark this rough draft for coherence, language, unity, emphasis, support, and sentence structure; then edit it, correcting fundamentals such as capital letters, omissions, punctuation, and spelling.

Young voters are not voting the way they should. The latest figures show that only 20 percent are going to the poles. The next older generation is, the so-called baby boomers, they are going to the poles at about twice that rate. Since I'm part of the young group, I'm concerned, but the answers to why we usually don't bother to vote are as obvious as the nose on your face. For one thing younger people don't think that voting changes anything. The political parties are all about the same and the candidates look and talk alike, even though they seem angry with each other. For another a lot of young voters don't have parents that voted or even talked about politics when they were growing up, they don't either. Still another thing is that the issues going around don't move young people that much. The politicians talk about the national debt and social security and health care and we're concerned about jobs and the high cost of education. If they could get people we could believe in and they would talk about issue that matter to us, then maybe they'd see more of us at the polls.

REVIEW 3

Using your topic from the previous chapter(s), write a rough draft and a final draft. Use points in the "Chapter Checklist" for revising and editing.

14

Writing the Short Essay

The essay is as difficult to define as the paragraph, but the paragraph definition gives us a framework. Consider the definition from Chapter 12, p. 222:

> The developmental paragraph . . . is a group of sentences, each with the function of stating or supporting a single, controlling idea that is contained in the topic sentence.

The main parts of the developmental paragraph are the topic sentence (subject and treatment), support (evidence and reasoning), and, often, the restated topic sentence at the end. Now let's use that framework for the essay:

> The essay is a group of paragraphs, each with the function of stating or supporting a controlling idea called the thesis.

The main parts of the essay are:

Introduction: carries the thesis, which states the controlling idea—much like the topic sentence for a paragraph but on a larger scale.

Development: evidence and reasoning—the support.

Transition: points out divisions of the essay (seldom used in the short essay).

Conclusion: an appropriate ending—often a restatement of or reflection on the thesis.

Thus, considered structurally, the paragraph is often an essay in miniature. That does not mean that all paragraphs can grow up to be essays or that all essays can shrink to become paragraphs. For college writing, however, a good understanding of the parallel between well-organized paragraphs and well-organized essays is useful. As you learn the properties of effective paragraphs—those with strong topic sentences and strong support—you also learn how to organize an essay, if you just magnify the procedure.

The following diagram illustrates the parallel parts of outlines, paragraphs, and essays:

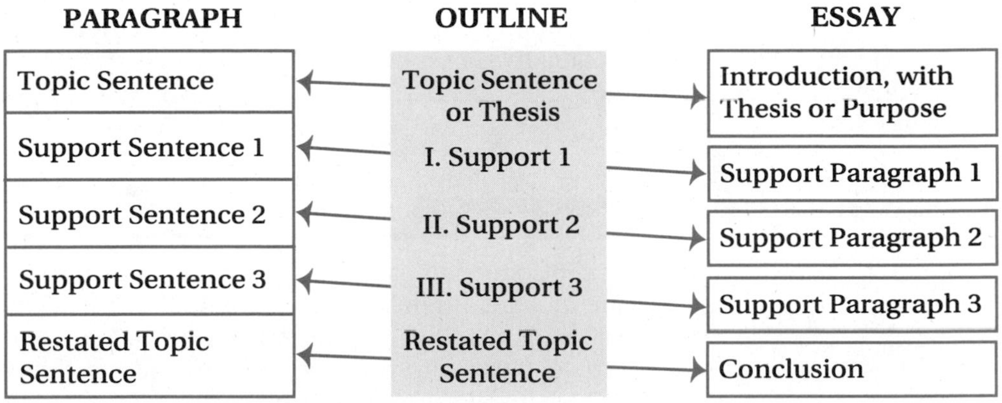

Of course, the parallel components are not exactly the same in the two writing forms—the paragraph and the essay. The paragraph is shorter and requires much less development, and some paragraph topics simply couldn't be developed much more extensively to their advantage. But let's consider the ones that can. What happens? How do we proceed?

Introductory Paragraph

The topic sentence idea is expanded to the introductory paragraph through elaboration. It may be enhanced through the use of explanation, historical background, anecdote, quotation, or stress on the significance of an idea. In most instances the introduction will be about three to six sentences long. If you say too much, your paper will be top-heavy. If you don't say enough, your readers will be confused. But a solid opening paragraph should

- introduce the subject through the thesis or controlling idea (either an assertion, which must be supported, or a clear indication of content).
- gain reader interest.
- move the reader into the middle paragraphs. You should avoid any statement of apology about your topic or your writing and avoid beginning with a statement like "I am writing an essay about. . . ."

Middle Paragraphs

The middle paragraphs are similar to what you have been writing in the previous chapter. Each one will have its own unity based on the topic sentence, will move logically and coherently, and will have adequate and appropriate development. The topic sentence will usually be at the beginning of the paragraph in a college essay, regardless of the form. Although some essays will be an expansion of a particular form of discourse and, therefore, will use basically the same pattern for each paragraph, many essays will combine the forms. For example, you might have one middle paragraph that gives examples, one that defines, and one that classifies.

And you may have combinations within paragraphs. Nevertheless, the paragraphs will always be related to the central idea and presented in a logical arrangement. The coherence of these paragraphs can often be improved by the use of the same principles that you have applied to individual paragraphs: using sequence words such as *first, second,* and *third;* using transitional words such as *therefore, moreover,* and *for example;* and arranging material in chronological order, spatial order, or order of relative importance.

Concluding Paragraph

Like the introduction paragraph, the concluding paragraph is a special unit with a specific function. In this paragraph, probably one of about three to six sentences, you will end on a note of finality. The way that you end will depend on what you want to do. If you can't decide on how to end, try going back to your introduction and see what you said there. If you posed a question, the answer should be in the conclusion. If you laid out the framework for an exploration of the topic, then perhaps you would want to bring your discussion together with a summary statement. Or perhaps a quotation, an anecdote, or a restatement of the thesis in slightly different words would be effective. Do not end with a complaint, an apology, or the introduction of a new topic or new support. And do not begin your conclusion with the words such as "last but not least" or "in conclusion."

Here are examples of a developmental paragraph and an essay, both on the topic of drunk driving. Notice how each is developed.

Get Them Off the Road

Topic Sentence Drunk driving has become such a severe problem in California that something must be done. The only solution is to do what Sweden did long ago: lower the blood-alcohol content level to .04 for drunk driving arrests. **I. Support** Driving is not a right; it is a privilege, and that privilege should not be extended to the person who drinks to the extent that his or her physical and mental abilities are significantly impaired. **II. Support** Alcohol, working as a depressant, does affect our entire system according to numerous sources cited in The Police Officers Source Book. As a result of this impairment, "50% of all fatal traffic accidents" involve intoxicated drivers, according to The National Highway Traffic Safety Administration. Cavenaugh and Associates, research specialists, say that 119,000 people were killed in the five-year period from 1990 through 1993. **III. Support** They go on to say that intoxicated drivers cost us somewhere between eleven and twenty-four billion dollars each year. **Restated Topic Sentence** It is time to give drunk drivers a message: "Stay off the road. You are costing us pain, injury, and death, and no one has the right to do that."

Daniel Humphreys

Get Them Off the Road

The state of California, along with the rest of the nation, has a problem with society involving drinking and driving. Prohibition is not the answer, as history has **Intro.** demonstrated. But there is a practical answer to be found in a law. I believe that the legal BAC (blood-alcohol **Thesis** concentration) while driving should be lowered from .08% to .04% for three strong reasons.

First, driving in California is a privilege, not a **Topic Sentence** right, and a person impaired by alcohol should not be allowed that privilege. Statutory law states that when stopped by a police officer who suspects drunk driving, one must submit to a BAC test. The level of **I. Dev. Support ¶** impairment is an individual trait because of the elapsed time of consumption, body size, and tolerance, but alcohol is a depressant to all of us. It affects our nervous system and slows our muscular reactions. As a result of extensive scientific study, the nation of Sweden determined that .04% BAC was the level of significant impairment, and therefore, it passed a federal law to enforce drunk driving at that point. Penalties there are extreme.

We, like the people in Sweden, are concerned about **Topic Sentence** the dangers of drunk driving. The National Highway Traffic Safety Administration has stated that "50 percent of all fatal accidents" involve intoxicated drivers and that 75 percent of the drivers have a BAC of .10 or greater. Cavenaugh and Associates, a California **II. Dev. Support ¶** think tank, reports that in the five-year period between 1990 and 1993, 215,000 people were injured and 43,000 were killed in alcohol-related accidents in the state of California.

Even if we are among the fortunate few who are not **Topic Sentence** touched directly by the problems of drunk driving in a lifetime, there are other effects. One is money. There is the loss of production, cost of insurance, costs due to delays in traffic, cost of medical care for those who **III. Dev. Support ¶** have no insurance, and many other sources. Cavenaugh and Associates say that drunken drivers cost us somewhere between $11 billion and $24 billion dollars a year.

Police officers report that drinking people are quick to say, "I'm okay to drive," but in one year alone we **Concl.** lose more lives than we lost in the entire Vietnam War. To lower the legal BAC limit to .04% would mean saving **Restated Thesis** lives, property, and money.

Daniel Humphreys

Some essays are very short. On a test an instructor may ask for an essay response and prefer an essay—complete with an introduction, development, and conclusion—rather than a long paragraph. In some instances the difference between the long paragraph and the short essay is only a matter of indenting. The change of a paragraph to a short essay is easy if you have written a clear topic sentence, strong support, and a final statement.

EXERCISE 1

The following paragraph could easily be developed into an essay. Mark it with lines and the paragraph symbol (¶) to show where the divisions would be for an introduction, paragraphs of development, support and conclusion if you wanted to expand the ideas.

What Is a Gang?

The word *gang* is often used loosely to mean "a group of people who go around together," but that does not satisfy the concerns of law enforcement people and sociologists. For these professionals, the definition of gang has five parts. These five parts combine to form a unit. First a gang has to have a name. Some well-known gang names are Bloods, Crips, Hell's Angels, and Mexican Mafia. The second part of the definition is clothing or other identifying items such as tattoos. The clothing may be of specific brands or colors, such as blue for Crips and red for Bloods. Members of the Aryan Brotherhood often have blue thunderbolt tattoos. A third component is rituals. They may involve such things as the use of handshakes, other body language or signing, and graffiti. A fourth is binding membership. A gang member is part of an organization, a kind of family, with obligations and codes of behavior to follow. Finally, a gang will be involved in some criminal behavior, something such as prostitution, drugs, thievery, or burglary. There are many different kinds of gangs--ethnic, regional, behavioral--but they all have these five characteristics.

Kimberly James

You should not think that one should set out to write an essay by first writing a paragraph. But the organization for the paragraph and the essay is often the same, and the writing process is also the same. You still proceed from prewriting to topic, to outline, to draft, to revision, to editing, to final paper. The difference is often only a matter of development and indentation.

Topics for Short Essays

Many topics for paragraph assignments in this book will serve well for short-essay assignments. The essay "Get Them Off the Road" is organized as an argument, with the support forming the middle part of the work. Other essays, both those that combine forms of discourse and those that follow mainly one form, will have divisions that are appropriate for their treatment of subject material. The one-form approach for organization will take the same organizational pattern shown for paragraphs. For example, a narrative account might be divided into paragraphs of time units; an essay of exemplification might have three examples; classification would show three or four classes in the three or four middle paragraphs; cause-and-effect essays would have separate paragraphs of causes or effects; and comparison-and-contrast papers would present one paragraph for each point in the point-by-point method. These guidelines may seem very mechanical, but keep in mind that they are only the framework. Once the bones are fleshed out with discussion, your essay can flow very naturally.

Chapter Checklist

1. The well-designed **paragraph** and the well-designed **essay** often have the same form.
   a. The **introduction** carries the thesis, which states the controlling idea—much like the topic sentence for a paragraph but on a larger scale.
   b. The **development,** or middle part, supplies evidence and reasoning—the support.
   c. The **conclusion** provides an appropriate ending—often a restatement of, or reflection on, the thesis.
2. These are the important relationships:

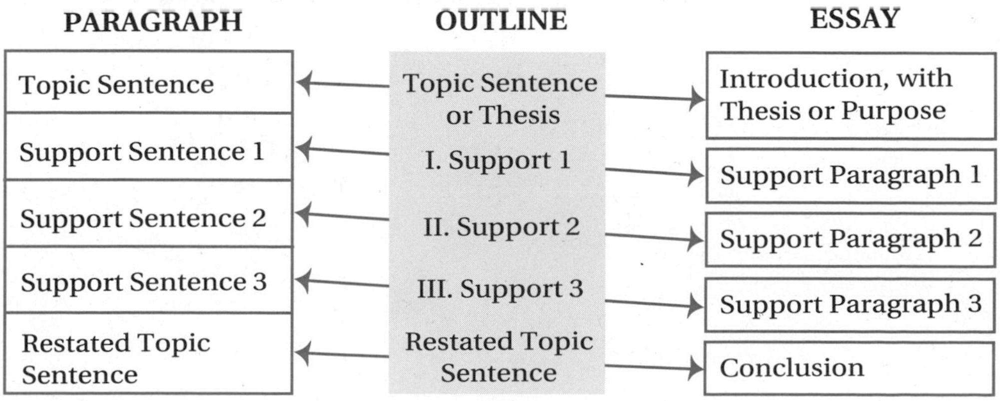

Chapter Review

REVIEW 1

At 202 words the following paragraph is well-developed as a short independent statement. It is perhaps a bit on the long side if it were a part of an essay. If you wanted to divide the parts into sections for a five-paragraph essay, where would you make the divisions for an introduction, three developmental paragraphs, and a concluding paragraph?

1. Insert lines to show those parts.
2. By writing in the margins, indicate paragraphs that need more development.
3. If you are familiar with Madonna, add information for that development.

Madonna the Magnificent

What makes Madonna such a popular entertainer? Could it be her music, her ability to perform on stage, or just the fact that she is so controversial? Actually, these three factors together are what does it. Madonna's musical talent is incredible. Her voice combined with the background music and moving lyrics is what made her produce numerous platinum and gold records. Next, Madonna's concerts continue to amaze her fans. Sure, people attend Madonna's concerts to hear her sing, but since she lip-syncs on stage, that leads me to believe that the majority of the people attending are there to see a show, not hear music they could listen to on tape. The choreography, along with the dancing ability, makes the show worth seeing. Furthermore, Madonna's consistent use of sexuality on stage draws even more fans. This also brings us to another reason for her popularity, and that is Madonna's controversiality. Everything she wears, doesn't wear, says, or does offends someone. This behavior probably makes her one of the, if not *the,* most controversial performers today. These reasons have caused Madonna to attract fans as well as disgust others, but if nothing else, they have made her a very popular performer.

Brian Vanderhoof

REVIEW 2

Use a topic you have developed as a paragraph in one of the previous three chapters and write an essay of three paragraphs or more.

PART Three

The Reading Connection

15

Writing About Reading Selections

Much of your college writing will require you to evaluate and to reflect on what you read, rather than write only about personal experience. You will be expected to read, think, and write. The writing in these circumstances is commonly called reading-related writing. It includes:

- effective reading (which may include underlining, annotation, and outlining);
- writing the *summary* (main ideas in your own words);
- writing the *reaction* (usually meaning how it relates specifically to you, your experiences and attitudes, but also often the critique, involving the worth and logic of a piece); and
- writing the *spin-off* (a smaller form of the reaction, in that it takes one aspect of the reading and develops a parallel experience, or simply one that has an interesting connection to the piece of writing).

These kinds of writing have certain points in common; they all:

- originate as a response to something you have read;
- indicate, to some degree, content from that piece; and
- demonstrate a knowledge of the piece of writing.

Topics covered in this chapter:

Reading for Writing

Good reading begins with desire; and concentration, or focus, is the first product of desire. *Focus is no problem if you have a strong purpose in reading.* If you go to a cookbook to find a recipe for enchiladas, you will probably find the recipe, read it, and refer back to it periodically while you prepare the dish. It is unlikely that you will put the book aside and say, "I wanted to read about making enchiladas, but I just couldn't concentrate." Surely if you can capture that sense of concentration and apply it to all of your reading experiences, you will become a stronger reader.

Of course, a desire that naturally emerges from a situation is different from a need that occurs because, let's say, a teacher has assigned three chapters in a history book. In the latter case, you may be motivated and you may not be. If not, you will want to manufacture that concentration somehow.

Underlining

One way to build concentration is to develop a relationship with the reading material. Imagine you are reading a chapter of several pages, and you decide to underline and write in the margins. Immediately, the underlining takes you out of the passive television-watching frame of mind. You are involved. You are participating. It is now necessary for you to discriminate, to distinguish more important from less important ideas. Perhaps you have thought of underlining as a method designed only to help you with your review. That is, when you study the material the next time, you won't have to read all the material; instead, you can deal only with the most important, underlined parts. But even while you are underlining, you are benefiting from an imposed concentration, because this procedure forces you to think, to focus. Consider these guides for underlining:

1. Underline the main ideas in paragraphs. The most important statement, the topic sentence, is likely to be at the beginning of the paragraph.
2. Underline the support for those main ideas.
3. Underline answers to questions that you bring to the reading assignment. These questions may have come from the end of the chapter, from subheadings that you turn into questions, or from your independent concern for the topic.
4. Underline only the key words. You would seldom underline all the words in a sentence and almost never a whole paragraph.

Does that fit your approach to underlining? Possibly not. Most students, in their enthusiasm to do a good job, overdo underlining.

Maybe you have had this experience: You start reading about something you have not encountered before. The idea seems important. You highlight it. The next idea is equally fresh and significant. You highlight it. A minute or two later, you have changed the color of the page from white to orange, but you haven't accomplished anything.

The trick is how to figure out what to underline. You would seldom underline more than about 30 percent of a passage, though the amount would depend on your purpose and the nature of the material. Following the preceding four rules will be useful. Learning more about the principles of sentence, paragraph, and essay organization will also be helpful. These principles are presented in Chapters 12 through 14.

Consider this passage with effective underlining.

The Pharaoh in Ancient Egypt

Egyptians believed that their pharaoh ruled even after his death. He had an eternal spirit, or *ka* (kah), that continued to take part in the governing of Egypt.

In the Egyptian's mind, the ka remained much like a living pharaoh in its needs and pleasures. To provide for the pharaoh's eternal comfort, artists decorated the walls of his burial chamber with pictures of whatever he might need or like. A picture of many fat geese, for instance, would assure him of endless sumptuous meals. Images of loved ones and devoted servants would keep him company and see that his commands were carried out. The burial chamber was also stocked with such luxuries as fine jewelry, game boards covered with precious stones, and rich clothing. Inscriptions on the tomb walls recounted the pharaoh's achievements.

Even though the ka was a spiritual being, it needed to refresh itself occasionally by entering its human body. Thus, the Egyptians preserved the pharaoh's body by making it a mummy. Scholars still accept Herodotus's description of the process of mummification:

> *First, they draw out the brains through the nostrils with an iron hook... Then with a sharp stone they make an incision in the side, and take out all the bowels... Then, having filled the belly with pure myrrh, cassia, and other perfumes, they sew it up again; and when they have done this they steep it in natron [a mineral salt], leaving it under for 70 days... At the end of 70 days, they wash the corpse, and wrap the whole body in bandages of waxen cloth.*

Since pharaohs expected to reign forever, their tombs were even more important than their palaces. For the pharaohs of the Old Kingdom, home after death was an immense structure called a **pyramid**. The Old Kingdom was the great age of pyramid building in ancient Egypt.

Janzten, Kreiger, and Neill, *World History*

EXERCISE 1

Apply the four underlining rules to this passage. (See Answer Key for possible answers. Keep in mind that it is unlikely that any two readers will underline precisely the same words.)

The Leadership of Martin Luther King, Jr.

1 On December 1, 1955, in Montgomery, Alabama, a black woman named Rosa Parks was arrested for refusing to give up her bus seat to a white man. In protest, Montgomery blacks organized a year-long bus boycott. The boycott forced white city leaders to recognize the blacks' determination and economic power.

2 One of the organizers of the bus boycott was a Baptist minister, the Reverend Martin Luther King, Jr. King soon became a national leader in the growing civil rights movement. With stirring speeches and personal courage, he urged blacks to demand their rights. At the same time, he was completely committed to nonviolence. Like Gandhi, . . . he believed that justice could triumph through moral force.

3 In April 1963, King began a drive to end segregation in Birmingham, Alabama. He and his followers boycotted segregated businesses and held peaceful marches and demonstrations. Against them, the Birmingham police used electric cattle prods, attack dogs, clubs, and fire hoses to break up marches.

4 Television cameras brought those scenes into the living rooms of millions of Americans, who were shocked by what they saw. On May 10, Birmingham's city leaders gave in. A committee of blacks and whites oversaw the gradual desegregation of the city and tried to open more jobs for blacks. The victory was later marred by grief, however, when a bomb exploded at a Birmingham church, killing four black children.

—Jantzen *et al., World History: Perspectives on the Past*

Writing in Margins—Annotating

A practice related to underlining is writing in the margins, sometimes called *annotation.* You can do it independently, though it usually appears in conjunction with underlining to mark the understanding and to extend the involvement.

Writing in the margins represents intense involvement because it makes the reader a writer. If you read material and write something in the margin as a reaction to it, then in a way you have had a conversation with the author. The author has made a statement and you have responded. In fact, you may have added something to the text; therefore, for your purposes you have become a co-author or collaborator. The comments you make in the margin are of your own choosing according to your interests and the purpose you bring to the reading assignment. Your response in the margin may merely echo the author's ideas, it may question them critically, it may relate them to something else, or it may add to them.

In the following example you can see how the reader has reinforced the underlining by placing numbers in the text and by commenting in the margin.

Salem witchcraft—broad interest

The Salem witchcraft crisis of 1692–1693, in which a small number of adolescent girls and young women accused hundreds of older women (and a few men) of having bewitched them, has fascinated Americans ever since. It has provided material for innumerable books, plays, movies, and television productions. To twentieth-century Americans, the belief in witchcraft in the seventeenth-century colonies is difficult to explain or understand; perhaps that is why the Salem episode has attracted so much attention. For those interested in studying women's experiences, of course, witchcraft incidents are particularly intriguing. The vast majority of suspected witches were female, and so, too, were many of their accusers. Although colonial women rarely played a role on the public stage, in witchcraft cases they were the primary actors. What accounts for their prominence under these peculiar circumstances?

Why mostly women?

To answer that question, the Salem crisis must be placed into its proper historical and cultural context. People in the early modern world believed in witchcraft because it offered a rationale for events that otherwise seemed random and unfathomable. In the absence of modern scientific knowledge about such natural phenomena as storms and diseases, and clear explanations for accidents of various sorts, the evil actions of a witch could provide a ready answer to a person or community inquiring about the causes of a disaster.

Historical/cultural background

Without modern science

Therefore, witchcraft accusations—and some large-scale "witch hunts"—were not uncommon in Europe between the early fourteenth and late seventeenth centuries (1300 to 1700). In short, the immigrants to the colonies came from a culture in which belief in witchcraft was widespread and in which accusations could result in formal prosecutions and executions. Recent research has demonstrated that the Salem incident, though the largest and most important witch hunt in New England, was just one of a number of such episodes in the American colonies.

Witch hunts in Europe—the extent

Question—repeated

Answers: 1 2 3

But why were witches women? Admittedly, historians have not yet answered that question entirely satisfactorily. Certain observations can be made: women gave birth to new life and seemed to have the potential to take life away. In Western culture, women were seen as less rational than men, more linked to the "natural" world, in which magic held sway. Men, who dominated European society, defined the characteristics of a "proper woman," who was submissive and accepted a subordinate position. The stereotypical witch, usually described as an aggressive and threatening older woman, represented the antithesis of that image. These broad categories need further refinement, and historians are currently looking closely at the women who were accused of practicing witchcraft in order to identify the crucial characteristics that set them apart from their contemporaries and made them a target for accusations.

—Norton, *Major Problems in American Women's History*

EXERCISE 2

Mark the following paragraphs with underlining and annotation. Compare your marks with those of your fellow students.

Buddhism Taught Nonviolence

Buddha gave his first sermon to the five wisdom seekers who had been his companions. That sermon was a landmark in the history of world religions. Buddha taught the four main ideas that had come to him in his enlightenment, calling them the Four Noble Truths.

First Noble Truth Everything in life is suffering and sorrow.

Second Noble Truth The cause of all this pain is people's self-centered cravings and desires. People seek pleasure that cannot last and leads only to rebirth and more suffering.

Third Noble Truth The way to end all pain is to end all desires.

Fourth Noble Truth People can overcome their desires and attain enlightenment by following the Eightfold Path.

The Eightfold Path was like a staircase. According to Buddha, those who sought enlightenment had to master one step at a time. The steps of the Eightfold Path were right knowledge, right purpose, right speech, right action, right living, right effort, right mindfulness, and right meditation. By following the Eightfold Path, anyone could attain *nirvana* (nur-VAHN-uh), Buddha's word for release from pain and selfishness.

Buddha taught his followers to treat all living things (humans, animals, and even insects) with loving kindness. A devout Buddhist was not even supposed to swat a mosquito.

Buddhists and Hindus both sought to escape from the woes of this world, but their paths of escape were very different. Unlike traditional Hinduism, Buddhism did not require complex rituals. Moreover, Buddha taught in everyday language, not in the ancient Sanskrit language of the Vedas and the Upanishads, which most Indians in 500 B.C. could no longer understand. Buddha's religion was also unique in its concern for all human beings—women as well as men, lowborn as well as highborn.

Forms of Writing

Among the forms of writing that will be suggested as assignments in most of these chapters are Outlines, Summaries, and Reading-Related Paragraphs. In some instances you might be asked to use all three forms after reading a passage. The three forms are also tied to reading and critical thinking, in that they contribute to reading comprehension and utilize systematic and analytical thought.

In order to show how the same reading subject material can be dealt with by all three forms, the next three writing examples will be based on the following brief passage.

The Roman Toga

Practicality has never been a requirement of fashion. The Roman toga was an uncomfortable garment. It was hot in summer, cold in winter, and clumsy for just about any activity but standing still. The toga was, however, practical in one way: It was easy to make, since it involved no sewing. Not even a buttonhole was needed. An adult's toga was basically a large wool blanket, measuring about 18 by 7 feet. It was draped around the body in a variety of ways, without the use of buttons or pins.

In the early days of the Roman republic, both women and men wore togas. Women eventually wore more dresslike garments, called *stolas,* with separate shawls. For men, however, the toga remained in fashion with very little change.

Soon after the republic was formed, the toga became a symbol of Roman citizenship. Different styles of togas indicated a male citizen's place in society. For example, a young boy would wear a white toga with a narrow purple band along the border. When his family decided he was ready for adult responsibilities, he would don a pure white toga. On that day, usually when he was about 16, his family would take him to the Forum, where he would register as a full citizen. For the rest of his life, he would wear a toga at the theater, in court, for religious ceremonies, and on any formal occasion. At his funeral his body would be wrapped in a toga to mark him, even in death, as a Roman citizen.

—Jantzen *et al.*, *World History: Perspectives on the Past*

Outlining

Following is a topic outline by student Leon Batista. Note parallel structure.

I. Practicality
  A. Not practical
    1. Hot in summer
    2. Cold in winter
    3. Clumsy
  B. Practical
    1. Easy to make
    2. Easy to put on and take off

II. Fashion in Roman republic
  A. Worn by men and women
    1. Changes little with men
    2. Alternates with stolas and shaws for women
  B. Symbol of citizenship
    1. One style for young male
    2. Another style for adult male
      a. Presented at point of adulthood
      b. Worn on all occasions

EXERCISE 3

Use the outline form to organize these sentences on College English into an outline.

1. It can help you express yourself more effectively in speaking and writing.
2. It can help you with your reading.
3. It will present the difference between fact and opinion.
4. It will help you to recognize and avoid logical fallacies.
5. It will offer complex courses in the interpretation of literature.
6. It will teach that a fact is something that can be verified.
7. It will offer courses in reading skills.
8. It will teach that an opinion is a subjective view.
9. It will offer courses in composition.
10. It will offer instruction in inductive and deductive thinking.
11. It will offer courses that involve discussion.
12. It can help you think critically.
13. College English can benefit you in many ways.
14. It will help you understand causes and effects.

Main idea: ___________

I. ______

A. ______

B. ______

II. ______

A. ______

B. ______

III. ______

A. ______

1. ______

2. ______

B. ______

C. ______

D. ______

Summarizing

A **summary** is a rewritten, shortened version of a piece of writing in which you use your own wording to express the main ideas. Learning to summarize effectively will help you in many ways. Summary writing reinforces comprehension skills in reading. It requires you to discriminate among the ideas in the target reading passage. Summaries are usually written in the form of a well-designed paragraph or paragraph unit. Frequently, they are used in collecting material for research papers and in writing conclusions to essays.

The rules below will guide you in writing effective summaries. The summary:

- is usually shorter than the original by about two-thirds, though the exact reduction will vary depending on the content of the original.
- concentrates on the main ideas and includes details only infrequently.
- changes the wording without changing the idea.
- does not evaluate the content or give an opinion in any way (even if you see an error in logic or fact).
- does not add ideas (even if you have an abundance of related information).
- does not include any personal comments by the author of the summary (therefore, no use of "I" referring to self).
- seldom uses quotations (but if you do, only with quotation marks).

- begins with the main idea (as you usually do in middle paragraphs) and proceeds to cover the main points in an organized fashion while using complete sentences.

The following is a summary of "The Roman Toga," written by the same student who prepared the sample outline. The writing process used by Leon Batista was direct and systematic. When first reading the material, he had underlined key parts and written comments and echo phrases in the margin. Then he wrote his outline. Finally, referring to both the marked passage and the outline, he wrote this summary. Had he not been assigned to write the outline, he would have done so, anyway, as preparation for his summary.

Summary of "The Roman Toga"

For citizens of the Roman republic, the toga was the main form of dress, despite its being too hot in the summer, too cold in the winter, and clumsy to wear. Perhaps the Romans appreciated the simplicity of wearing a piece of woolen cloth about eighteen by seven feet without buttons or pins. The women also wore another garment similar to a dress called the "stola," but Roman male citizens were likely to wear only the toga—white with a purple edge for the young and solid white for the adult. These were worn from childhood to death.

EXERCISE 4

Underline the parts of this passage that violate the rules of good summary writing. Compare this summary with the original passage and with the student summary preceding.

Summary About One of My Favorite Garments

For citizens of the Roman republic, the toga was the main form of dress, despite its being too hot in the summer, too cold in the winter, and clumsy to wear. Frankly, I don't see why a bright bunch of people like the Romans couldn't have come up with a better design. Perhaps the Romans appreciated the simplicity of wearing a piece of woolen cloth about eighteen by seven feet without buttons or pins: But I've read elsewhere that the togas were sometimes stolen at the public baths. The women also wore another garment similar to a dress called the "stola," but the Roman male citizen was likely to wear only the toga—white with a purple edge for the young and solid white for the adult. For the rest of his life, he would wear a toga at the theater, in court, for religious ceremonies, and on any formal occasion. At his funeral, his body would be wrapped in a toga to mark him, even in death, as a Roman citizen.

Reading-Related Writing

The following three paragraphs are examples of simple reaction, critical reaction, and spin-off writing.

The Simple Reaction

This reading-related writing takes the subject material of the original passage and relates it to modern times. Using specific examples, it incorporates ideas from the original passage, relating them to twentieth-century society.

The Idea of the Toga

The idea of the toga as a garment for men and women in Western society has been almost completely abandoned, but it is not forgotten. . . . About ten years ago, toga parties were very popular. Animal House, a film about a raunchy, crude, party-loving fraternity, did much to popularize the toga party, as well as the toga itself. Young people, especially college students, draped themselves in bed sheets and had parties that were well known for the consumption of huge quantities of beer and food. The toga was usually not nearly as large as the eighteen-by-seven-foot Roman item and was usually fastened with safety pins. Often the wearer of the toga also wore a wreath and sandals. Existing primarily as a novelty item, the toga has not recently been very important as a fashion influence. About thirty years ago, the film Cleopatra with Elizabeth Taylor and Richard Burton inspired the fashion industry to come up with some loose-fitting gowns that resembled togas and stolas. But that style did not last. The toga, along with its related forms, has remained essentially in its historical setting, which we study about in history and occasionally see represented in films.

The Critical Reaction

This reading-related writing analyzes, evaluates, and interprets the original passage. Then the writer applies her insights to human behavior as she knows it.

Witches Are for Scapegoating

The "witchcraft crisis of 1692–1693" is not so surprising to some of us who look back after three hundred years. Most of the people charged were "uppity" older women who didn't know their places. The charges came mainly from adolescent girls and young women, but the power structure was adult men. Out of ignorance, the men were looking around to find reasons for the misfortunes—bad weather, diseases, and accidents—that their society faced. It is a fact that if people are crazy enough to look for witches, they are crazy enough to find them. And they did: they found mainly a few old women who didn't know their place, individuals of a gender associated with the emotions. If these women had been meek and mild, if they had been properly submissive to the menfolk, and if they had still been young and sexy, they would not have been vulnerable. But they were what they were—mature and relatively independent women, who seemed to be different—and that made them witches to those who were said not to be emotionally based—the men.

The Spin-Off

In this reading-related writing, the author takes a basic idea from the original and finds parallels. She could have written about one parallel situation or condition—personal or historical.

Sticks and Stones

Reading "Women and Witchcraft" reminded me of a long line of indignities against women. If something goes wrong, and women can be blamed, they are. For centuries if a woman didn't have babies, it was said *she* couldn't, though the man was just as likely as the woman to be the cause of her childlessness. If, heaven forbid, the woman kept having female babies, that woman, it was said, couldn't produce a male. Yet we know now that it is the male who determines the sex of the child. If the child was not bright, as recently as a hundred years ago some doctors said it was because the woman was reading during pregnancy and took away the brain power from the fetus. As a result many women were not allowed to open a book during pregnancy. Of course, because it was believed that women were so weak, husbands were allowed to beat their wives, but according to English law, the stick could be no thicker than the man's thumb, hence "the rule of thumb." Even voting was argued against by some who said that the typical woman, controlled by emotions, would allow her husband to tell her how to vote, and each married man would then have two votes. It's no wonder that three hundred years ago men looked around and, finding many misfortunes, decided that women were the culprits and should be punished. Sticks were not enough. It was time for stones.

Writing a Journal

Your journal entries are likely to be concerned primarily with the relationship between the reading material and you—your life experiences, your views, your imagination. The reading material will give you something of substance to write about, but you will be writing especially for yourself, developing confidence and ease in writing, so that writing becomes a comfortable part of your everyday activities, as speaking already is.

These journal entries will, in a sense, be part of your intellectual diary, recording what you are thinking about a certain issue. They will be of use in helping you understand the reading material, in helping you develop your writing skills, in uncovering ideas that can be used on other assignments, and in helping you think more clearly and imaginatively. Because these entries are of a more spontaneous nature than the more structured writing assignments, organization and editing are likely to be of less concern.

Each journal entry should be clearly dated and, if reading related, should specify the title and author of the subject piece.

Even if your instructor wants you to concentrate on what you read for your journal writing, he or she might not want you to be restricted to the material in this text. Fortunately, you are surrounded by reading material in newspapers, magazines, and, of course, textbooks from other courses. These topics can serve you well.

Chapter Checklist

1. **Underlining** will help you to prepare for review and to concentrate when reading.
   a. Underline the main idea in paragraphs.
   b. Underline the support for those main ideas.
   c. Underline answers to questions.
   d. Underline only key words; almost never underline entire sentences.
2. **Annotating** along with underlining will make you an engaged, active reader.
3. **Outlining** reading selections will show main and supporting ideas.
4. **Summarizing** will help you concentrate on main ideas; this is helpful in both reading and writing. (See pages 259–260 for specific rules.)
5. Reading-related writing can take several forms:
   a. The **simple reaction** in reading-related writing explains the reading and discusses relevance.
   b. The **critical reaction** in reading-related writing analyzes, evaluates, and interprets the passage.
   c. The **spin-off** in reading-related writing takes the basic idea from the original and shows parallels, either of a personal or historical nature.
6. **Journal writing** offers frequent practice in writing, especially about what you read.

Chapter Review

Write an outline, a summary, and a paragraph response (evaluation or reaction) to the following passage. In your response, consider relating this passage to your own family or to another you are familiar with.

Pointers on Staying Strong

Here are some of the recommendations that have grown out of research on healthy families:

1 • Understand that family conflict is inevitable. "Any time you get two people together in a physical space with limited resources and work that they have to share, conflict will develop," said Ohio State University psychologist Andrew Schwebel.

2 • When confronted with family problems or crises, try to search for new alternatives. Reframe the problem in a way you've never considered before. Ask for help from all family members. Even if they don't come up with the solution, they will feel that they have contributed.

3 • Imagine your family life as a drama on stage. Try to look at it objectively. "You can see family defense mechanisms that you may be using," said Schwebel.

4 • Don't forget the couple part of a family. Studies at the University of California at Berkeley found that new parents fared best in adjusting to their babies when they continued to make time for themselves. The most helpful solution was an intervention group where new parents could share their experiences. A year and half after the birth of their first child, none of the couples in the intervention group had divorced. During the same time, 12.5 percent of a comparison group of couples who were also new parents had separated or divorced.

5 • Hold family meetings. Be sure that every family member gets involved in the discussion. It doesn't matter whether these meetings are regularly scheduled or occur on the spur of the moment. "They work just as well either way," Schwebel said.

6 • Spend time together as a family. Strong families make time for each other. "More often than not that means quality time in great quantities," said University of Nebraska psychologist John DeFrain. "I don't think we do families a service by trying to look for a happy time on the cheap."

—Sally Squires

16

Growing Pains and Pleasures (Narration)

Even under the best of conditions, growing up is not a smooth progression. It is actually a hobbling and sprinting back and forth with some jogging to the sides and, usually, movement forward and up.

Because of the unevenness of this journey, we can all reflect on particular experiences during which we have relocated ourselves in a personal sense as if we were dealing with geography: have reached a plateau, climbed a mountain, fallen into a canyon, been stranded on an island, been lost in a desert, stumbled into paradise. These experiences may be events—special occasions, holidays, ceremonies, celebrations, graduations, special recognition. They may be traumatic events—accidents, injuries, illnesses, deaths, betrayals, escapes, entrapments. They may be struggles—for recognition, acceptance, self-identity, respect. They may involve relationships—love (in its many forms), changes in family makeup, establishing and reestablishing friendships as a result of moving or changing. They may be seemingly small acts of kindness, insults to the spirit, tokens of love.

Whatever they are, they are key experiences, as indelible on our memories as dark ink on white linen. Against these key experiences we measure the more ordinary ones and chart our progress or lack of it toward where we are today. We don't bury these experiences; from time to time they pop up on our mind screens like CD-ROM images as reminders of who we are and how we got that way. If we made time lines for our lives, these experiences would be the listed items, on a personal scale equal to the great wars, developments, discoveries, creations, and inventions of world history. They will always be with us for pain or pleasure.

Like life itself, this chapter is full of variety. Karen Bradley finds her "Moment in the Sun" as a sports hero, surprising even herself. Regina Ochoa explores the shock, embarrassment, pain, and anger of being falsely accused and "Busted for No Good Reason." In "Liked for Myself," Maya Angelou is rescued from muteness by a loving grandmother and a neighbor. In "A Girlhood Among Ghosts," Maxine Hong Kingston recalls the time when she, a lonely girl in a crowded society, covered the colorful pictures of her childhood with black paint.

Ponder Questions

1. What events or persons have had the greatest influence on you?
2. Does one learn more from joyful or painful experiences?
3. Does "growing" ever end?
4. What experience do you recall most vividly? Why?
5. To what extent is growth sometimes reversible?

These kinds of experiences take the form of writing called *narration.*

Narration

In our everyday lives, we tell stories and invite other people to do so by asking questions such as "What happened at work today?" and "What did you do last weekend?" We are disappointed when the answer is "Nothing much." We may be equally disappointed when a person doesn't give us enough details—or maybe gives us too many and spoils the effect. After all, we are interested in people's stories and in the people who tell them. We like the narrative.

What is the narrative? *The narrative is an account of an incident or a series of incidents that make up a complete and significant action.* Each narrative has five properties:

- ***setup,*** which may be quite brief or even implied, but always gives the necessary setting or situation for the action ("It was a Saturday afternoon in the park.");
- ***conflict,*** which is at the heart of each story ("when this mugger came up and grabbed my purse.");
- ***struggle,*** which adds action to the conflict, though it need not be physical engagement ("He yanked and I yanked back, and then I kicked him in the groin.");
- ***outcome,*** which is merely the result of the struggle ("He ran away, and I smirked."); and
- ***meaning,*** which is the significance and may be deeply philosophical or simple, stated or implied ("Don't mess with me!").

These components are present in some way in all of the many forms of the narrative. They are enhanced by the use of various techniques and devices. They include:

- *description* (with specific details to advance action and images, as relevant, to make your readers see, smell, taste, hear, and touch):

  > Hearing running footsteps on the wet pavement, I turned to see him. He was wearing a ski mask, and I could feel his hot tobacco breath in my face as his raspy voice gave the mugger's traditional demand.

- *dialogue* (exact words of speakers enclosed in quotation marks):

  > "Your purse or your life," he snarled.

- *transitional words* (words that move a story forward, for the narratives are presented in chronological order):

  > next, soon, after, next, later, then, finally, when, following

Keep in mind that most narratives written as college assignments will have an expository purpose (that is, serve to explain a specified idea). Often the narrative will be merely an extended example. Therefore, the *meaning* part of the five properties is exceedingly important and should be emphasized in the account through statement and repetition.

Writer's Checklist for Narration

Use this as a checklist so that you will be sure you have a complete narrative:

- Setup (situation at beginning)
- Conflict
- Struggle
- Outcome
- Meaning

Use these techniques or devices as appropriate:

- Images (see, smell, taste, hear, touch) and other details to advance action
- Dialogue
- Transitional devices (such as next, soon, after, next, later, then, finally, when, following) to enhance chronological order

Topics for Narration

For this short writing assignment, concentrate on the event, which may take only a few minutes or less, rather than what went on before or after it. Make the story the main framework of your account, one that features the five properties in the Checklist for Narration.

- Write a narrative paragraph about a personal experience which you characterize as

  > the most—amusing, sad, terrifying, satisfying, ironic, stupid, rewarding, self-centered, generous, stingy, loving, thoughtful, cruel, regrettable, educational, corrupting, sinful, virtuous, disgusting—thing I have ever experienced/done/witnessed.

- Write a paragraph about a recent event you have heard about, read about in any source, or learned about through radio or television. The subject could concern an incident in a ballgame (any athletic contest); an event (emphasizing a single incident that occurred in a short time period) in the entertainment field illustrating the success or failure of a celebrity figure; a local, state, national, or international news event; or a historical event you have studied in a history class.

A Moment in the Sun

STUDENT PARAGRAPH by Karen Bradley

Often the difference between a star player and an ordinary player is that the star player frequently plays very well and an ordinary player only occasionally plays well. In this narrative, student Karen Bradley tells of that one moment when she was a star.

Topic sentence One event in my childhood stands out clearly in my memory and becomes even stronger as I grow older. When I was eleven years old, I wanted to be a great softball player. Unfortunately for me and my ambition, I was only a bit above average in ability and was smaller than my peers. That didn't keep me from becoming catcher on a **Situation** Lassie League team called the Ripping Rodents. Like me our team was only average in competition. As we approached the last game of the season, I was batting seventh, and we were fourth in a league of seven teams. **Conflict** The team we were playing, the much-dreaded Hotshot Hornets, needed this win to take the league championship. Their players were cocky and boastful before the game. They even made rodent jokes. Then they walked by our dugout after taking infield practice and acted as if we were not there. Finally they posed for some pictures a parent was taking; they even had a little sign saying "2A Lassie League Champions." For the first time all year we were angry—at them, at ourselves. And then we went on to surprise ourselves. In the last inning with them at bat, we were leading by one run. After their first two batters made outs, the next one, a speedy, little second baseman **Struggle** named Toni, walked. Everyone knew she would try to steal second. She was the fastest player in the league and had never been thrown out. On the first pitch she took off. The ball was shoulder-high to me. I grabbed it out of my glove and threw it as hard as I could in the direction of second base. To my surprise, and even more so to Toni's, the ball went on a line right to our shortstop, knee- **Outcome** high. Toni slid, but she was out by three feet. The game was over, and the Ripping Rodents were all over me. It was as if we had won the championship. It was my only **Meaning** moment of stardom in softball, but it will do.

Discussion and Critical Thinking

1. How does the writer's being an ordinary player on an ordinary team make this paragraph more dramatic?
2. Why does the writer remember the incident so well?
3. How important is it for people to have these special moments?
4. How much does the author reveal about herself?

Reading-Related Writing

1. Write about a time when you exceeded expectations in sports or in other endeavors such as work, family life, school, or social situations.
2. Discuss the properties of this long paragraph about Karen's special moment. What factors made this special? Refer directly to the selection as you analyze it.
3. Write about this incident from the point of view of Toni (the speedster who was thrown out).

Busted for No Good Reason

STUDENT ESSAY by Regina Ochoa

Quite a few people shoplift, some of them get caught, and occasionally a person who is innocent gets "detained." Being charged with something one has not done, in a public place and in the presence of a parent and an older sibling, is not an incident one will ever forget. Second-year college student Regina Ochoa looks back on her experience with a keen memory.

Thesis I will never forget the time I was wrongfully accused of shoplifting. It was another one of those days when I was dragged out shopping with my mom and oldest sister. After we had a satisfying lunch at the food park, Mom decided to make a last stop at a nearby department store.

Situation I decided to amuse myself by browsing around alone. I kept my eye out looking for my mom and sister, hoping they would come looking for me to tell me it was time to leave. As I turned fixtures of colorful earrings around and around, I played with the spare change in my pocket, hearing the chiming, clinking sound.

After a few minutes, which seemed like hours, had passed, I decided to go find my mom and sister. "There you are, Regina," my mom said impatiently as I came upon them. "Are you ready to go?"

She didn't even wait for my answer, but I thought to myself, "Of course, I am."

Conflict As we were leaving the store, two men came running out after us. "Excuse me, miss," one said directly to me, "but we'd like you to come back inside for a moment." Bewildered and very confused, we all walked back into the store while the men cautiously followed behind us. It was as if they expected me to run away and hide out in the mall.

"What's wrong?" my mom asked them. "What did she do?"

"You'll see," they answered simultaneously, as if one answering wasn't emphatic enough.

Inside the elevator, one man pushed the button, taking us all the way down to the basement level. Suddenly it hit me, and I knew I was being wrongfully accused of something I did not do.

Struggle I turned to my mom and desperately said, "I swear I didn't take anything."

"I hope so, Regina, because if you did this will be pretty embarrassing," she said, offering a bit less comfort than I wanted.

The elevator seemed to be taking forever. It was as if the walls were caving in, and the men just stared right through me as if I were a mug shot.

Finally the elevator door opened, and they took me to a small room where I watched myself on television.

There I was on the screen, browsing through earring fixtures, and my hand appeared to be stuffing something in my pocket. One couldn't quite tell because of the way the camera was positioned.

"There's nothing in my pocket but loose change," I screamed out angrily. I was already in tears. Embarrassment was all over my face. My sister reached over to help me empty my pocket, and sure enough, there was nothing but about a dozen coins.

"I was just putting my hand into my pocket to play with the change," I said to the men. This time I was the accuser.

Outcome "You owe my daughter an apology," my mom said to the man who seemed to be in charge.

"Sorry," he said. He barely whispered it. I knew he felt foolish, but at that moment I couldn't feel much pity for him.

Meaning As we all left the store in silence, I vowed to myself never to accuse anyone of anything without being absolutely certain—no, without being doubly absolutely certain.

Discussion and Critical Thinking

1. What conditions (her frame of mind, her clothing, her possessions) made the writer behave in a way that would seem suspicious to the store detectives?
2. After she was detained, what factors made the following sequence of events more dramatic?
3. Is Regina's mother appropriately concerned about her daughter's behavior? Discuss.
4. Should Regina's mother require more than an apology? Is the mumbled apology enough?
5. What would you have done under those conditions?
6. What does this essay imply about the differences between fact and opinion?

Reading-Related Writing

1. Write about a memorable time when you were falsely accused (work, game playing, relationship, school).
2. Write about this incident from the point of view of one of the detectives.
3. Write about a time when you thought someone else did something wrong, only to discover later that the person was innocent.
4. Discuss this essay in terms of the confusion about facts and opinions.

Liked for Myself

Maya Angelou

As a child, Marguerite Johnson, the central character in the autobiographical book I Know Why the Caged Bird Sings, *was raped by a friend of her mother. In this excerpt she has only recently come to live in her grandmother's home in rural Arkansas. There, psychologically wounded by her experience, she does not speak. She is desperate for self-confidence. She needs to be liked for the person she is.*

1 For nearly a year, I sopped around the house, the Store, the school and the church, like an old biscuit, dirty and inedible. Then I met, or rather got to know, the lady who threw me my first life line.

2 Mrs. Bertha Flowers was the aristocrat of Black Stamps. She had the grace of control to appear warm in the coldest weather, and on the Arkansas summer days it seemed she had a private breeze which swirled around, cooling her. She was thin without the taut look of wiry people, and her printed voile dresses and flowered hats were as right for her as denim overalls for a farmer. She was our side's answer to the richest white woman in town.

3 Her skin was a rich black that would have peeled like a plum if snagged, but then no one would have thought of getting close enough to Mrs. Flowers to ruffle her dress, let alone snag her skin. She didn't encourage familiarity. She wore gloves too.

4 I don't think I ever saw Mrs. Flowers laugh, but she smiled often. A slow widening of her thin black lips to show even, small white teeth, then the slow effortless closing. When she chose to smile on me, I always wanted to thank her. The action was so graceful and inclusively benign.

5 She was one of the few gentlewomen I have ever known, and has remained throughout my life the measure of what a human being can be. . . .

6 One summer afternoon, sweet-milk fresh in my memory, she stopped at the Store to buy provisions. Another Negro woman of her health and age would have been expected to carry the paper sacks home in one hand, but Momma said, "Sister Flowers, I'll send Bailey up to your house with these things."

7 She smiled that slow dragging smile, "Thank you, Mrs. Henderson. I'd prefer Marguerite, though." My name was beautiful when she said it. "I've been meaning to talk to her, anyway." They gave each other age-group looks. . . .

8 There was a little path beside the rocky road, and Mrs. Flowers walked in front swinging her arms and picking her way over the stones.

9 She said, without turning her head, to me, "I hear you're doing very good school work, Marguerite, but that it's all written. The teachers report that they have trouble getting you to talk in class." We passed the triangular farm on our left and the path widened to allow us to walk together. I hung back in the separate unasked and unanswerable questions.

10 "Come and walk along with me, Marguerite." I couldn't have refused even if I wanted to. She pronounced my name so nicely. Or more correctly, she spoke each word with such clarity that I was certain a foreigner who didn't understand English could have understood her.

11 "Now no one is going to make you talk—possibly no one can. But bear in mind, language is man's way of communicating with his fellow man and it is language alone which separates him from the lower animals." That was a totally new idea to me, and I would need time to think about it.

12 "Your grandmother says you read a lot. Every chance you get. That's good, but not good enough. Words mean more than what is set down on paper. It takes the human voice to infuse them with the shades of deeper meaning."

13 I memorized the part about the human voice infusing words. It seemed so valid and poetic.

14 She said she was going to give me some books and that I not only must read them, I must read them aloud. She suggested that I try to make a sentence sound in as many different ways as possible.

15 "I'll accept no excuse if you return a book to me that has been badly handled." My imagination boggled at the punishment I would deserve if in fact I did abuse a book of Mrs. Flowers'. Death would be too kind and brief.

16 The odors in the house surprised me. Somehow I had never connected Mrs. Flowers with food or eating or any other common experience of common people. There must have been an outhouse, too, but my mind never recorded it.

17 The sweet scent of vanilla had met us as she opened the door.

18 "I made tea cookies this morning. You see, I had planned to invite you for cookies and lemonade so we could have this little chat. The lemonade is in the icebox."

19 It followed that Mrs. Flowers would have ice on an ordinary day, when most families in our town bought ice late on Saturdays only a few times during the summer to be used in the wooden ice-cream freezers.

20 She took the bags from me and disappeared through the kitchen door. I looked around the room that I had never in my wildest fantasies imagined I would see. Browned photographs leered or threatened from the walls and the white, freshly done curtains pushed against themselves and against the wind. I wanted to gobble up the room entire and take it to Bailey, who would help me analyze and enjoy it.

21 "Have a seat, Marguerite. Over there by the table." She carried a platter covered with a tea towel. Although she warned that she hadn't tried her hand at baking sweets for some time, I was certain that like everything else about her the cookies would be perfect.

22 They were flat round wafers, slightly browned on the edges and butter-yellow in the center. With the cold lemonade they were sufficient for childhood's lifelong diet. Remembering my manners, I took nice little lady-like bites off the edges. She said she had made them expressly for me and that she had a few in the kitchen that I could take home to my brother. So I jammed one whole cake in my mouth and the rough crumbs scratched the insides of my jaws, and if I hadn't had to swallow, it would have been a dream come true.

23 As I ate she began the first of what we later called "my lessons in living." She said that I must always be intolerant of ignorance but understanding of illiteracy. That some people, unable to go to school, were more educated and even more intelligent than college professors. She encouraged me to listen carefully to what country people called mother wit. That in those homely sayings was couched the collective wisdom of generations.

24 When I finished the cookies she brushed off the table and brought a thick, small book from the bookcase. I had read *A Tale of Two Cities* and found it up to my standards as a romantic novel. She opened the first page and I heard poetry for the first time in my life.

25 "It was the best of times and the worst of times. . . ." Her voice slid in and curved down through and over the words. She was nearly singing. I wanted to look at the pages. Were they the same that I had read? Or were there notes, music, lined on the pages, as in a hymn book? Her sounds began cascading gently. I knew from listening to a thousand preachers that she was nearing the end of her reading, and I hadn't really heard, heard to understand, a single word.

26 "How do you like that?"

27 It occurred to me that she expected a response. The sweet vanilla flavor was still on my tongue and her reading was a wonder in my ears. I had to speak.

28 I said, "Yes, ma'am." It was the least I could do, but it was the most also.

29 "There's one more thing. Take this book of poems and memorize one for me. Next time you pay me a visit, I want you to recite."

30 I have tried often to search behind the sophistication of years for the enchantment I so easily found in those gifts. The essence escapes but its aura remains. To be allowed, no, invited, into the private lives of strangers, and to share their joys and fears, was a chance to exchange the Southern bitter wormwood for a cup of mead with Beowulf or a hot cup of tea and milk with Oliver Twist. When I said aloud, "It is a far, far better thing that I do, than I have ever done . . ." tears of love filled my eyes at my selfishness.

31 On that first day, I ran down the hill and into the road (few cars ever came along it) and had the good sense to stop running before I reached the Store.

32 I was liked, and what a difference it made. I was respected not as Mrs. Henderson's grandchild or Bailey's sister but for just being Marguerite Johnson.

33 Childhood's logic never asks to be proved (all conclusions are absolute). I didn't question why Mrs. Flowers had singled me out for attention, nor did it occur to me that Momma might have asked her to give me a little talking to. All I cared about was that she had made tea cookies for *me* and read to *me* from her favorite book. It was enough to prove that she liked me.

Vocabulary Highlights*

taut (2)

voile (2)

benign (4)

infuse (12)

valid (13)

leered (20)

cascading (25)

sophistication (30)

essence (30)

aura (30)

*Number in parentheses indicates paragraph number in which vocabulary word appears.

Discussion and Critical Thinking

1. The narrator refers to Mrs. Bertha Flowers as an aristocrat and the blacks' "answer to the richest white woman in town." In what ways does she deserve that characterization? Is she rich?
2. What techniques does Mrs. Flowers use to encourage Marguerite to speak?
3. What does Mrs. Flowers mean by the word *educated*?
4. What does the narrator mean by "childhood's logic" (33)?
5. What are "lessons in living" (23)? In what way can this episode be called such a lesson?

Reading-Related Writing

1. Write a paragraph about someone in your neighborhood (or in your household) who in his or her own way can be called an "aristocrat"—someone who has true class.
2. Write a paragraph that defines the term *aristocrat* as the narrator does. Consider these aspects: how the person looks, how the person acts, what the person says, and how others react to the person. You may use Mrs. Flowers as an example or you can write about someone you know, someone you have read about, or someone you have discovered through the media.
3. Write a detailed account of how someone helped you at a time when your self-esteem was low.
4. Assume the role of either the grandmother or Mrs. Flowers and give a report of the progress of your relationship with Marguerite.
5. If you have helped or are now helping someone through a time of hardship, write an account of your involvement and the results.
6. Analyze this narrative account by discussing the factors (such as readiness and need by the narrator and compassion, understanding, and personal stature by Mrs. Flowers) that made the narrator's change possible.

A Girlhood Among Ghosts

Maxine Hong Kingston

Growing up is difficult for everyone. Growing up as a Chinese female in America adds two more dimensions to the problem. Now a celebrated writer of The Woman Warrior: Memories of a Girlhood Among Ghosts, China Men, *and* Tripmaster Monkey, *Maxine Hong Kingston was once so deficient in English speech that she flunked kindergarten. Here she tells of her early struggles as a frightened, silent girl caught between two cultures. In her native culture she lives among people, but in her new culture she is surrounded by "ghosts."*

1 When I went to kindergarten and had to speak English for the first time, I became silent. A dumbness—a shame—still cracks my voice in two, even when I want to say "hello" casually, or ask an easy question in front of the check-out counter, or ask directions of a bus driver. I stand frozen, or I hold up the line with the complete, grammatical sentence that comes squeaking out at impossible length. "What did you say?" says the cab driver, or "Speak up," so I have to perform again, only weaker the second time. A telephone

call makes my throat bleed and takes up that day's courage. It spoils my day with self-disgust when I hear my broken voice come skittering out into the open. It makes people wince to hear it. I'm getting better, though. Recently I asked the postman for special-issue stamps; I've waited since childhood for postmen to give me some of their own accord. I am making progress, a little every day.

2 My silence was thickest—total—during the three years that I covered my school paintings with black paint. I painted layers of black over houses and flowers and suns, and when I drew on the blackboard, I put a layer of chalk on top. I was making a stage curtain, and it was the moment before the curtain parted or rose. The teachers called my parents to school, and I saw they had been saving my pictures, curling and cracking, all alike and black. The teachers pointed to the pictures and looked serious, talked seriously too, but my parents did not understand English. ("The parents and teachers of criminals were executed," said my father.) My parents took the pictures home. I spread them out (so black and full of possibilities) and pretended the curtains were swinging open, flying up, one after another, sunlight underneath, mighty operas.

3 During the first silent year I spoke to no one at school, did not ask before going to the lavatory, and flunked kindergarten. My sister also said nothing for three years, silent in the playground and silent at lunch. There were other quiet Chinese girls not of our family, but most of them got over it sooner than we did. I enjoyed the silence. At first it did not occur to me I was supposed to talk or to pass kindergarten. I talked at home and to one or two of the Chinese kids in class. I made motions and even made some jokes. I drank out of a toy saucer when the water spilled out of the cup, and everybody laughed, pointing at me, so I did it some more. I didn't know that Americans don't drink out of saucers.

4 I liked the Negro students (Black Ghosts) best because they laughed the loudest and talked to me as if I were a daring talker too. One of the Negro girls had her mother coil braids over her ears Shanghai-style like mine; we were Shanghai twins except that she was covered with black like my paintings. Two Negro kids enrolled in Chinese school, and the teachers gave them Chinese names. Some Negro kids walked me to school and home, protecting me from the Japanese kids, who hit me and chased me and stuck gum in my ears. The Japanese kids were noisy and tough. They appeared one day in kindergarten, released from concentration camp, which was a tic-tac-toe mark, like barbed wire, on the map.

5 It was when I found out I had to talk that school became a misery, that the silence became a misery. I did not speak and felt bad each time that I did not speak. I read aloud in first grade, though, and heard the barest whisper with little squeaks come out of my throat. "Louder," said the teacher, who scared the voice away again. The other Chinese girls did not talk either, so I knew the silence had to do with being a Chinese girl.

6 Reading out loud was easier than speaking because we did not have to make up what to say, but I stopped often, and the teacher would think I'd gone quiet again. I could not understand "I." The Chinese "I" had seven strokes, intricacies. How could the American "I," assuredly wearing a hat like the Chinese, have only three strokes, the middle so straight? Was it out of politeness that this writer left off strokes the way a Chinese has to write her own name small and crooked? No, it was not politeness; "I" is a capital

and "you" is lower-case. I stared at that middle line and waited so long for its black center to resolve into tight strokes and dots that I forgot to pronounce it. The other troublesome word was "here," no strong consonant to hang on to, and so flat, when "here" is two mountainous ideographs. The teacher, who had already told me every day how to read "I" and "here," put me in the low corner under the stairs again, where the noisy boys usually sat.

7 When my second grade class did a play, the whole class went to the auditorium except the Chinese girls. The teacher, lovely and Hawaiian, should have understood about us, but instead left us behind in the classroom. Our voices were too soft or nonexistent, and our parents never signed the permission slips anyway. They never signed anything unnecessary. We opened the door a crack and peeked out, but closed it again quickly. One of us (not me) won every spelling bee, though.

8 I remember telling the Hawaiian teacher, "We Chinese can't sing 'land where our fathers died.' " She argued with me about politics, while I meant because of curses. But how can I have that memory when I couldn't talk? My mother says that we, like the ghosts, have no memories.

9 After American school, we picked up our cigar boxes, in which we had arranged books, brushes, and an inkbox neatly, and went to Chinese school, from 5:00 to 7:30 P.M. There we chanted together, voices rising and falling, loud and soft, some boys shouting, everybody reading together, reciting together and not alone with one voice. When we had a memorization test, the teacher let each of us come to his desk and say the lesson to him privately, while the rest of the class practiced copying or tracing. Most of the teachers were men. The boys who were so well behaved in the American school played tricks on them and talked back to them. The girls were not mute. They screamed and yelled during recess, when there were no rules; they had fistfights. Nobody was afraid of children hurting themselves or of children hurting school property. The glass doors to the red and green balconies with the gold joy symbols were left wide open so that we could run out and climb the fire escapes. We played capture-the-flag in the auditorium, where Sun Yat-sen and Chiang Kai-shek's pictures hung at the back of the stage, the Chinese flag on their left and the American flag on their right. We climbed the teak ceremonial chairs and made flying leaps off the stage. One flag headquarters was behind the glass door and the other on stage right. Our feet drummed on the hollow stage. During recess the teachers locked themselves up in their office with the shelves of books, copy-books, inks from China. They drank tea and warmed their hands at a stove. There was no play supervision. At recess we had the school to ourselves, and also we could roam as far as we could go—downtown, Chinatown stores, home—as long as we returned before the bell rang.

10 At exactly 7:30 the teacher again picked up the brass bell that sat on his desk and swung it over our heads, while we charged down the stairs, our cheering magnified in the stairwell. Nobody had to line up.

11 Not all of the children who were silent at American school found voice at Chinese school. One new teacher said each of us had to get up and recite in front of the class, who was to listen. My sister and I had memorized the lesson perfectly. We said it to each other at home, one chanting, one listening. The teacher called on my sister to recite first. It was the first time a teacher had called on the second-born to go first. My sister was scared. She glanced at me and looked away; I looked down at my desk. I hoped that she could do

it because if she could, then I would have to. She opened her mouth and a voice came out that wasn't a whisper, but it wasn't a proper voice either. I hoped that she would not cry, fear breaking up her voice like twigs underfoot. She sounded as if she were trying to sing through weeping and strangling. She did not pause to stop to end the embarrassment. She kept going until she said the last word, and then she sat down. When it was my turn, the same voice came out, a crippled animal running on broken legs. You could hear splinters in my voice, bones rubbing jagged against one another. I was loud, though. I was glad I didn't whisper.

12 How strange that the emigrant villagers are shouters, hollering face to face. My father asks, "Why is it I can hear Chinese from blocks away? Is it that I understand the language? Or is it they talk loud?" They turn the radio up full blast to hear the operas, which do not seem to hurt their ears. And they yell over the singers that wail over the drums, everybody talking at once, big arm gestures, spit flying. You can see the disgust on American faces looking at women like that. It isn't just the loudness. It is the way Chinese sounds, ching-chong ugly, to American ears, not beautiful like Japanese sayonara words with the consonants and vowels as regular as Italian. We make guttural peasant noise and have Ton Duc Thang names you can't remember. And the Chinese can't hear Americans at all; the language is too soft and western music unhearable. I've watched a Chinese audience laugh, visit, talk-story, and holler during a piano recital, as if the musician could not hear them. A Chinese-American, somebody's son, was playing Chopin, which has no punctuation, no cymbals, no gongs. Chinese piano music is five black keys. Normal Chinese women's voices are strong and bossy. We American-Chinese girls had to whisper to make ourselves American-feminine. Apparently we whispered even more softly than the Americans. Once a year the teachers referred my sister and me to speech therapy, but our voices would straighten out, unpredictably normal, for the therapists. Some of us gave up, shook our heads, and said nothing, not one word. Some of us could not even shake our heads. At times shaking my head no is more self-assertion than I can manage. Most of us eventually found some voice, however faltering. We invented an American-feminine speaking personality.

Vocabulary Highlights

skittering (1)

ideographs (6)

emigrant (12)

sayonara (12)

guttural (12)

Discussion and Critical Thinking

1. When she was a child, how were Kingston's drawing and painting similar to her speaking?
2. Why did she initially enjoy her silence?
3. Why did the author like the black students best?
4. How does Kingston explain her silence? Why does this make sense to her logically?
5. What do the author's thoughts about writing *I* reveal about her native culture?

6. Why were the children so noisy and boisterous at the Chinese school?
7. What is Kingston's view of the female in American society? Why was her invention of an "American-feminine speaking personality" a reasonable choice to her?

Reading-Related Writing

1. Assume the role of Kingston's kindergarten teacher and write a description of the narrator and her behavior.
2. Write a paragraph about the relationship between the narrator's silence and her artwork.
3. Write a paragraph about a childhood experience when you felt self-consciously outside your culture or social class.
4. Discuss in a paragraph the submissive, subordinate role often assumed by immigrants and females.
5. Assume the role of a childhood peer of the narrator and react to her behavior.
6. Pretend that you were once a primary-school classmate of the silent narrator. Now that you have read what was going on in her mind when she was a shy, young child, write a paragraph in which you reflect on what you thought then and know now.
7. If you are not an immigrant, interview some people who are and write about their struggles in school resulting from feeling out of place culturally.

Connections

1. In a paragraph or short essay, discuss how the young people in "Liked for Myself" and "A Girlhood Among Ghosts" have problems that are similar and problems that are different. Explain how the problems are solved. Consider these questions in your statement:

   What gave confidence and comfort to each?

   Could each have learned from the other?

   What is the importance of community for each?

   Is community more important in one than the other?

   What kind of influence is present in one and absent in the other?

17

Prized and Despised Possessions (Description)

We all own things we couldn't do without, maybe things we expect to be buried with. Some of our loved ones might like to bury the things first—it sometimes happens. And, of course, there are the things that we'd like to get rid of, but we can't.

This section features these prized and despised possessions. Janice Hill once carried a latchkey that she said in winter was "icicle cold as it dangled against my skinny chest." Herman Velasco wore a pair of athletic gloves that smelled so bad his coaches made him "place them in a plastic bag until just before a game." Gary Soto's object was a jacket. It was the primary item of clothing in his most formative years. He holds the wretched garment responsible for his major discomfort and failures. Having hoped for a studly motorcycle jacket, he instead received a vinyl jacket the color of "day-old guacamole." His account is one of his somehow outlasting that coat. Maria Varela owned something worse than a car that was a lemon; hers was a banana.

These descriptive accounts of possessions will remind you of your own loves and loathings of the inanimate objects to which you perhaps attach much more meaning than they warrant.

A well-loved possession might be an old pair of blue jeans, a sweater, a stuffed toy, a tattered book, a piece of jewelry, a pocket knife, a pair of shoes, a picture album, a record, a thimble, a coin, or a piece of sports equipment. You may turn to them in times of stress as talismans the same way that some people who are having trouble will eat "comfort" foods related to the happier, simpler times of childhood.

Other objects may inspire hatred, and they may be identical to the items above. In fact, any item can move from the loved to hated category. A hated item might be a tool (associated with the chores you disliked), an instrument (perhaps musical such as an accordion, a violin, a piano), an alarm clock, a lunch pail, a latchkey, and an identification bracelet.

Ponder Questions

1. What is your most despised possession? Why?
2. What is your most prized possession? Why?
3. Can some prized objects become even more valuable after they are lost or destroyed? Explain.
4. Would some people be better off if prized objects (the ones that serve as security items) were to disappear?

A main concern in contemplating any of these objects is description: What are they like? Only after you have properly described your possession will your reader really understand why you despise it or prize it.

Description

Description means the use of words to represent the appearance or nature of something. Often called a word picture, description attempts to present its subject for the mind's eye. In doing so, it does not merely become an indifferent camera; instead, it selects details that will convey a good depiction. Just what details the descriptive writer selects will depend on several factors, especially the type of description and the dominant impression in the passage.

Types of Description

On the basis of treatment of subject material, description is customarily divided into two types: objective and subjective.

Effective objective description presents the subject clearly and directly as it exists outside the realm of feelings. If you are explaining the function of the heart, the characteristics of a computer chip, or the renovation of a manufacturing facility, your description would probably feature specific, impersonal details. Most technical and scientific writing is objective in that sense. It is likely to be practical and utilitarian, making little use of speculation and poetic technique.

Effective subjective description is also concerned with clarity and it may be direct, but it conveys a feeling about the subject and sets a mood while making a point. Because most expression involves personal views, even when it explains by analysis, subjective description (often called "emotional description") has a broader range of uses than objective description.

Descriptive passages can have a combination of objective and subjective description; only the larger context of the passage will reveal the main intent.

Imagery

In order to convey your main concern effectively to readers, you will have to give some sensory impressions. These sensory impressions, collectively called *imagery,* refer to that which can be experienced by the senses—what we can see, smell, taste, hear, and touch.

Subjective description is likely to make more use of images and words rich in associations than does objective description. But just as a fine line cannot always be drawn between the objective and the subjective, a fine line cannot always be drawn between word choice in one and in the other. However, we can say with certainty that whatever the type of description, careful word choice will always be important. Consider these points about precise diction:

General and Specific Words/Abstract and Concrete Words

To move from the general to the specific is to move from the whole class or body to the individual(s); for example:

General	*Specific*	*More Specific*
food	hamburger	Hefty Burger
mess	grease	oil slicks on table
drink	soda	mug of root beer
odor	smell from grill	smell of frying onions

Words are classified as abstract or concrete depending on what they refer to. *Abstract words* refer to qualities or ideas: *good, ordinary, ultimate, truth, beauty, maturity, love. Concrete words* refer to a substance or things; they have reality: *onions, grease, buns, tables, food.* The specific concrete words, sometimes called *concrete particulars,* often support generalizations effectively and convince the reader of the accuracy of the account.

Dominant Impression

Never try to give all of the details in description; instead, be selective, picking only those that you need to project a dominant impression, always taking into account the knowledge and attitudes of your readers. Remember, description is not photographic. If you wish to describe a person, select the traits that will project your intended dominant impression. If you wish to describe a landscape, do not give all the details that you might find in a picture; on the contrary, pick the details that support your intended dominant impression. That extremely important dominant impression is directly linked to your purpose and is created by the judicious choice and arrangement of images, figurative language, and revealing details.

Order: Time and Space

All of these details must have some order. Time and space are the main controlling factors here.

If you are describing something that is not changing, such as a room, you would be concerned with space and give directions to the reader such as

> *next to, below, under, above, behind, in front of, beyond, in the foreground, in the background, to the left,* or *to the right.*

If you are describing something small that is changing and you are mainly concerned with the change such as the metamorphosis of a butterfly, you would be concerned mainly with time and use transitional words such as

> *first, second, then, soon, finally, while, after, next, later, now,* and *before.*

If you are walking through an area that is changing, you would use both time and space for order.

Useful Procedure for Writing Description

What is your subject? (school campus during summer vacation)

What is the dominant impression? (deserted)

What is the situation? (You are walking across the campus in early August.)

What is the order of details? (time and place)

What details support the dominant impression?

1. (smell of flowers and cut grass rather than food and smoke and perfume)
2. (dust accumulated on white porcelain drinking fountain)
3. (sound of the wind, wildlife, and silence rather than people)
4. (crunch of dead leaves underfoot)
5. (echo of footsteps)

Writer's Checklist for Description

- In an objective description, use direct, practical language, and usually appeal mainly to the sense of sight.
- In emotional description, appeal to the reader's feelings, especially through the use of figurative language and images of sight, sound, smell, taste, and touch.
- Use specific and concrete words if appropriate.
- Consider this procedure:

  What is the subject?

  What is the dominant impression?

  What is the situation?

  What is the order of details?

  What details support the dominant impression?

Topics for Writing Description

Objective Description

Give your topic some kind of frame. As you develop your purpose, consider the knowledge and attitudes of your readers. You might be describing a lung for a biology instructor, a geode for a geology instructor, a painting for an art instructor, or a comet for an astronomy instructor. Or maybe you could pose as the seller of an object such as a desk, a table, or a bicycle. Try the following topics:

1. A simple object, such as a pencil, a pair of scissors, a cup, a sock, a dollar bill, a coin, ring, notebook.
2. A human organ, such as a heart, liver, lung, or kidney.
3. A visible part of your body, such as a toe, a finger, an ear, a nose, an eye.
4. A construction, such as a room, a desk, a chair, a commode, a table.
5. A mechanism, such as a bicycle, a tricycle, a wagon, a car, a motorcycle, a can opener, a stapler.

Subjective Description

The following topics should also be presented in the context of a purpose other than writing a description. Your intent can be as simple as giving a subjective reaction to your subject. But unless you are dealing with one of those topics that you can present reflectively or a topic interesting in itself, you will usually need some kind of situation. The narrative frame (something happening) is especially useful in providing order and vitality to writing. Here are three possibilities for you to consider:

1. Personalize a trip to a supermarket, a stadium, an airport, an unusual house, a mall, the beach, a court, a church, a club, a business, the library, or the police station. Deal with a simple conflict in one of those places, while emphasizing descriptive details.
2. Pick a high point in any event, and describe it as it lasts for only a few seconds. Think about how a scene can be captured by a video camera, and then give focus by applying the dominant impression principle, using the images of sight, sound, taste, touch, and smell that are relevant. The event might be a ball game, a graduation ceremony, a wedding ceremony, a funeral, a dance, a concert, a family gathering, a class meeting, a rally, a riot, a robbery, a fight, a proposal, or a meal. Focus on a body of subject material that you can cover effectively in the passage you write.
3. Pick a moment when you were angry, sad, happy, confused, lost, rattled, afraid, courageous, meek, depressed, or elated. Describe how the total context of the situation contributed to your feeling.

Latchkey

STUDENT PARAGRAPH by Janice Hill

Janice Hill had no trouble identifying the possession she most despised. It's a key she carried around her neck, first on a thong, then a chain. It seemed to take on a life of its own as it hung there. She probably would have preferred a millstone or even an albatross.

Topic sentence The thing I hated most when I was growing up was a metal object about two inches long. The top part was of an oval shape turned on the side, with a hole at the top middle. Down from the oval was a flat shaft, which was **Sight images** straight on one side, notched irregularly on the other, grooved in a straight line near the middle on each flat side, and pointed at the end. At the top, near the middle of the inch-long oval was the word *Master*. Oddly that's what it was to me—my master. It was my latchkey. When I went to school, it went everywhere I did. One day I took it off at school and misplaced it. My mother was very angry. I said I hated the leather thong from which it **Smell** hung because it was ugly and smelled of sweat. She replaced that with a silver chain, and said I should never take the key off. Each day I would wear that chain and key, always inside my sweater, shirt, or blouse. In **Touch** the winter it was icicle cold as it dangled against my skinny chest. In the summer it was hot against my sweaty skin, sticking like a clammy leech. Because I was forbidden to take it off by myself, even upon coming home, I always bent forward when I inserted it into the lock, my

Sight sad, sometimes scared, face reflecting with weird distortions in the brass door knob. I inserted the key, **Sound** turned it with a click, and removed it. After three years of my life with the detested key, I had to bend way over to turn it in the lock, my head pressed against the solid wood door. By that time the key and the chain had worn **Sight** smooth in places, and the crisscross pattern around the name had darkened. I always feared what lurked inside **Restated topic idea** that house. Though I had a neighbor I could call if I needed help, that key always represented loneliness and fear. I was glad when my mother got a new job with shorter hours, and I was no longer a latchkey kid.

Discussion and Critical Thinking

1. Without looking back at the paragraph, can you picture the object Hill describes? What are its sight, touch, smell, and sound features?
2. What two brief experiences does Hill relate?

Reading-Related Writing

1. Write a descriptive paragraph from the key's point of view.
2. Write a descriptive paragraph from the mother's point of view.
3. Use this paragraph as a model to write one of your own about something you prized or despised, such as braces for teeth or a cast for a broken bone.

Magical Stinky Gloves

STUDENT ESSAY by Herman Velasco

Objects that are prized by one person may be despised by others, and sometimes these objects "disappear." The qualities of the gloves that made them special to student Herman Velasco also made them subjects of a locker-room hit list.

When I was a sophomore in high school, I had the privilege of playing varsity football. Football was a big thing in my school. Most of all, my friends were playing junior varsity, so I didn't personally know anybody on the team. My first day at practice was a hellish experience. I played on the line, so I had to go up against really big opponents. All the veteran players would try to hurt all the newcomers. I remember my hands being cut up, bruised, and bloody. We had a star lineman by the name of Eric Winter. He saw my hands and gave me his brand new gloves. Those gloves were state of the art. **Sight** They featured black cowhide leather stitched with white thread, padded with wool fiber, and topped at the wrist **Thesis** with a velcro strap. Receiving a gift like this from a player like him made me feel special, and for almost three years the gloves were extremely important to me.

I wore those gloves throughout most of my high school **Touch** football career. By the time I was a senior, they were **Sight** all crusty with the salt from sweat, the blood from **Smell** wounds, and the dirt and fertilizer from dozens of playing fields. Their smell was somewhere between that of roadkill and a barnyard, but I still cherished them. They fit my hands perfectly. I had to tape them up with gray **Sight** duct tape because the padding was coming out. They were no longer black. They were now a sort of mustard brown with green around the palm, from algae, I think. If there were an athletes' hand disease, I would have had it. A **Smell** few games into that season, they smelled so bad that my coaches made me place them in a plastic bag until just before I took the field. Feeding on the moisture trapped in that bag, the gloves turned a deeper shade of green.

I enjoyed having those gloves and the reputation that went along with them. They gave me the confidence and the identification I needed on the field. If the opposing team started "talking trash," I would place them on the face of a downed opponent as a form of torture or punishment. Everyone who went up against me hated those gloves. One day not long before my last game, someone stole them. Only my so-called friends and the coaches had access to them, but I never found out who it was.

Playing gloveless in that game, I suffered a serious knee injury. Later I was told I could never play football again. Sometimes I think of those gloves and wonder if I would have been injured if I had been wearing my magical, stinky gloves. Maybe I would have gone on to a fine career on the gridiron. Then maybe I wouldn't and would instead be sitting here wearing those obnoxious gloves as I write this essay. What a wonderful essay I could write, if only I had those gloves!

Discussion and Critical Thinking

1. Would you say this essay is mainly narration (a story) or mainly a description or both?
2. Do you think Velasco kept the gloves in spite of their disgusting qualities or because of their disgusting qualities? Why?
3. In the last few sentences, the writer speculates about how well he would write if he only had those gloves. Usually, it's better not to make that kind of aside in an essay, but does it work here?

Reading-Related Writing

1. Write about the gloves from their point of view (and from wherever they are now).
2. Write about the gloves from a coach's or a teammate's perspective.
3. Using this as a model, write about an item of clothing that you liked better as it became older and more decrepit. Consider items such as shoes, a shirt, trousers, a belt, a purse, sweats, or socks. Be sure to relate the possession to different phases and events in your life.
4. Write about the power of a so-called "good-luck" object to install confidence in the carrier. Describe one or more such objects owned by you, someone you know, or someone you have read about.

The Jacket

Gary Soto

A writer and university professor, Gary Soto well remembers the self-consciousness of growing up. On one occasion he was all set to be cool with a fine new jacket; then his mother bought the wrong one—one that was "the color of day-old guacamole" and was "the ugly brother who tagged along everywhere [he] went." Soto's best-known book is *Living Up the Street.*

1 My clothes have failed me. I remember the green coat that I wore in fifth and sixth grades when you either danced like a champ or pressed yourself against a greasy wall, bitter as a penny toward the happy couples.

2 When I needed a new jacket and my mother asked what kind I wanted, I described something like bikers wear: black leather and silver studs with enough belts to hold down a small town. We were in the kitchen, steam on the windows from her cooking. She listened so long while stirring dinner that I thought she understood for sure the kind I wanted. The next day when I got home from school, I discovered draped on my bedpost a jacket the color of day-old guacamole. I threw my books on the bed and approached the jacket slowly, as if it were a stranger whose hand I had to shake. I touched the vinyl sleeve, the collar, and peeked at the mustard-colored lining.

3 From the kitchen mother yelled that my jacket was in the closet. I closed the door to her voice and pulled at the rack of clothes in the closet, hoping the jacket on the bedpost wasn't for me but my mean brother. No luck. I gave up. From my bed, I stared at the jacket. I wanted to cry because it was so ugly and so big that I knew I'd have to wear it a long time. I was a small kid, thin as a young tree, and it would be years before I'd have a new one. I stared at the jacket, like an enemy, thinking bad things before I took off my old jacket whose sleeves climbed halfway to my elbow.

4 I put the big jacket on. I zipped it up and down several times, and rolled the cuffs up so they didn't cover my hands. I put my hands in the pockets and flapped the jacket like a bird's wings. I stood in front of the mirror, full face, then profile, and then looked over my shoulder as if someone had called me. I sat on the bed, stood against the bed, and combed my hair to see what I would look like doing something natural. I looked ugly. I threw

it on my brother's bed and looked at it for a long time before I slipped it on and went out to the backyard, smiling a "thank you" to my mom as I passed her in the kitchen. With my hands in my pockets I kicked a ball against the fence, and then climbed it to sit looking into the alley. I hurled orange peels at the mouth of an open garbage can and when the peels were gone I watched the white puffs of my breath thin to nothing.

5 I jumped down, hands in my pockets, and in the backyard on my knees I teased my dog, Brownie, by swooping my arms while making bird calls. He jumped at me and missed. He jumped again and again, until a tooth sunk deep, ripping an L-shaped tear on my left sleeve. I pushed Brownie away to study the tear as I would a cut on my arm. There was no blood, only a few loose pieces of fuzz. Damn dog, I thought, and pushed him away hard when he tried to bite again. I got up from my knees and went to my bedroom to sit with my jacket on my lap, with the lights out.

6 That was the first afternoon with my new jacket. The next day I wore it to sixth grade and got a D on a math quiz. During the morning recess Frankie T., the playground terrorist, pushed me to the ground and told me to stay there until recess was over. My best friend, Steve Negrete, ate an apple while looking at me, and the girls turned away to whisper on the monkey bars. The teachers were no help: they looked my way and talked about how foolish I looked in my new jacket. I saw their heads bob with laughter, their hands half-covering their mouths.

7 Even though it was cold, I took off the jacket during lunch and played kickball in a thin shirt, my arms feeling like braille from goose bumps. But when I returned to class I slipped the jacket on and shivered until I was warm. I sat on my hands, heating them up, while my teeth chattered like a cup of crooked dice. Finally warm, I slid out of the jacket but a few minutes later put it back on when the fire bell rang. We paraded out into the yard where we, the sixth graders, walked past all the other grades to stand against the back fence. Everybody saw me. Although they didn't say out loud, "Man, that's ugly," I heard the buzz-buzz of gossip and even laughter that I knew was meant for me.

8 And so I went, in my guacamole jacket. So embarrassed, so hurt, I couldn't even do my homework. I received Cs on quizzes, and forgot the state capitals and the rivers of South America, our friendly neighbor. Even the girls who had been friendly blew away like loose flowers to follow the boys in neat jackets.

9 I wore that thing for three years until the sleeves grew short and my forearms stuck out like the necks of turtles. All during that time no love came to me—no little dark girl in a Sunday dress she wore on Monday. At lunchtime I stayed with the ugly boys who leaned against the chainlink fence and looked around with propellers of grass spinning in our mouths. We saw girls walk by alone, saw couples, hand in hand, their heads like bookends pressing air together. We saw them and spun our propellers so fast our faces were blurs.

10 I blame that jacket for those bad years. I blame my mother for her bad taste and her cheap ways. It was a sad time for the heart. With a friend I spent my sixth-grade year in a tree in the alley waiting for something good to happen to me in that jacket, which had become the ugly brother who tagged along wherever I went. And it was about that time that I began to grow. My chest puffed up with muscle and, strangely, a few more ribs. Even

my hands, those fleshy hammers, showed bravely through the cuffs, the fingers already hardening for the coming fights. But that L-shaped rip on the left sleeve got bigger; bits of stuffing coughed out from its wound after a hard day of play. I finally Scotch-taped it closed, but in rain or cold weather the tape peeled off like a scab and more stuffing fell out until that sleeve shriveled into a palsied arm. That winter the elbows began to crack and whole chunks of green began to fall off. I showed the cracks to my mother, who always seemed to be at the stove with steamed-up glasses, and she said that there were children in Mexico who would love that jacket. I told her that this was America and yelled that Debbie, my sister, didn't have a jacket like mine. I ran outside, ready to cry, and climbed the tree by the alley to think bad thoughts and watch my breath puff white and disappear.

11 But whole pieces still casually flew off my jacket when I played hard, read quietly, or took vicious spelling tests at school. When it became so spotted that my brother began to call me "camouflage," I flung it over the fence into the alley. Later, however, I swiped the jacket off the ground and went inside to drape it across my lap and mope.

12 I was called to dinner: steam silvered my mother's glasses as she said grace; my brother and sister with their heads bowed made ugly faces at their glasses of powdered milk. I gagged too, but eagerly ate big rips of buttered tortilla that held scooped up beans. Finished, I went outside with my jacket across my arm. It was a cold sky. The faces of clouds were piled up, hurting. I climbed the fence, jumping down with a grunt. I started up the alley and soon slipped into my jacket, that green ugly brother who breathed over my shoulder that day and ever since.

Discussion and Critical Thinking

1. Why is the jacket more of a disappointment than it would have been if his mother had given it to him as a surprise?
2. What kind of jacket did Soto request?
3. How is the jacket like a person and an evil force?
4. What are some of the failures Soto attributes to his jacket?
5. Why doesn't he lose it or throw it away?
6. What does he do to make this essay funny?
7. Is this mainly a description or a narration, or is it a combination with purposes nicely integrated?
8. One might think that Soto had an unhappy, or even twisted, childhood. Do you think so? Explain.

Reading-Related Writing

1. Write about the jacket from the point of view of Soto's mother.
2. Write about the jacket from the jacket's point of view.
3. Write about an embarrassing article of clothing you wore as a child, an article that you thought at the time had an influence on how others felt about you and certainly how you felt about yourself.
4. Write about an article of clothing you wore with pride as a child or one that you now wear with pride.

My Banana Car

STUDENT ESSAY by Maria Varela

To an American youngster, a first car is something to be anticipated, celebrated, and remembered. It should be the apple of one's eye, but it may be a different fruit. It could be a lemon. Even worse, as was the case for student Maria Varela, it was a "banana car." Recreated here for you, the experience is probably funnier to read about than it was to live through.

I remember how excited I was right after my sixteenth birthday. My dad was going to buy me a car! I imagined it would be a nice little red car with chrome rims (not hubcaps). It would have a tan interior, a sunroof, and a great stereo system that could be heard blocks away. All my friends would envy me. The good-looking boys would notice me with favor. I would be so popular. After all, the cooler the car, the cooler the car owner.

I could not believe what was parked in my driveway when I came home from school that Monday afternoon. It was a 1974 Chevy Monte Carlo, the kind that has the great big front end. The car was huge. It could seat forty people if it were a dinner table. To top it off, it was yellow like a banana. As a matter of fact it looked like a banana. I held my breath as I walked slowly toward the car, hoping that it belonged to someone who was visiting. At that moment my father ran out of the house with a big smile on his face. "Well, what do you think?" he said. "Nice, huh?"

I looked at my dad, managed to break a smile, and said weakly, "Yeah, Dad. Thanks."

I spent the rest of the afternoon trying to find a good quality on the car. First I looked at the outside. It had ugly hubcaps, the kind you find at Pick-a-Part for ten dollars a set. Worst of all, it had a sticker of a horse's head stuck right on the paint near the trunk. I knew that if I tried to remove it, the paint would come off and leave the outline of a horse's head in another color.

I opened the driver's door slowly as if something like a weasel might pop out at me from inside. The interior was light brown with dark brown stripes. It smelled like Old Spice. I got an image of the previous owner. He must have been a tall, heavy man who wore cheap cologne and liked horses. I plopped down in the driver's seat and grabbed the steering wheel with both hands. "Great!" My feet barely reached the pedals, and my nose was at the same level as the top of the steering wheel. I was a short girl, but at that moment I felt even shorter. I got a fat cushion from the house. I would have to sit on this cushion every time I drove this car. I just hoped that no one noticed I was sitting on a cushion. "Maria's so short, she can't even reach the pedals on her car." "Can you see over the dashboard, Maria?" I could already hear them tease.

As I drove my banana car to school the next day, I saw people staring at me. I knew what they were whispering. "How could she drive that ugly car?" and "I would rather walk," and, this one with much laughter, "I can't wait till she peels out of here."

To make matters worse, the car was expensive to drive and prone to breakage. It would take over thirteen dollars in gas to fill up, and that would last me only four days. One day as I was driving down the street, the muffler came off and started dragging on the ground. It made a horrible noise and sparks were flying everywhere. I knew what they were saying: "The sparkling banana car!" I was a legend. Another time I tried to open the window, but it just plopped down, never to be seen again. I could not keep anything valuable in the car for fear that it would be stolen. But, of course, I did not fear that the car would be stolen. After all, who would want it!

Because my banana car was so large, it was very hard to maneuver. Twice I knocked over our mailbox that was located at the side of the driveway. I would break into a sweat whenever I was forced to parallel park. The most embarrassing situation occurred that night when my friend Monica and I went out to Tommy's. Tommy's is a popular restaurant where all the popular people from our school hang out. Monica and I decided to chance the drive-through, but as I tried to maneuver the large car up the narrow passageway, it got stuck right in the middle. There was no room to move backward or forward. I could feel my ears getting hot from embarrassment. Like the window, Monica sank down out of sight. The people behind me started honking. I could see the people inside the restaurant looking out to see what the commotion was all about. I was ready to cry, but at that moment Danny Gurrero, one of the cutest boys from our school, came over and asked if I needed help. "Yes, please," I blurted out. He jumped into the car and managed to maneuver it out of that tight spot. Before he left, he advised me not to take the drive-through anymore. I accepted his advice.

Every morning as I walked out of my house, I hoped the car would be gone, but my banana car was always there waiting for me to drive it to school. I got a part-time job at Togo's Eatery. I wanted to save money for a new car, but after two years, I still did not have enough for the down payment. One day at dinner, my father announced that since I was so responsible with my Monte Carlo, he would help me buy a new car. I jumped out of my seat and wrapped my arms around him. Then, remembering my last expectation, I backed off. "Can I pick the car?" "Yes," he said. Goodbye, banana car.

Discussion and Critical Thinking

1. What is the effect of the first paragraph?
2. While at home, how does Varela manage to conceal her dislike for the car during those three years? How does that self-control measure her love and respect for her father?
3. In what way was she optimistic after she saw the car?
4. How does she characterize the previous banana car owner?
5. Is there any moment of niceness connected with the banana car?

Reading-Related Writing

1. Write about your first (or any other) car, one that you came to prize or despise. Include detailed description along with discussion about the car and your life at that particular time.
2. Interview someone and write about that person's first car.
3. Write about your first bicycle or other vehicle.
4. Rewrite the essay, this time from the car's point of view.
5. Rewrite the essay, this time from the point of view of the ghost of the first owner.

Connections

1. In "The Jacket" and "My Banana Car" the authors discuss what they dislike about their possessions. In a paragraph or short essay, discuss why they dislike and how they regard what was bought for them. Consider these questions:

   What is the importance of peer pressure—how others will regard them?

   What is the importance of the quality of the possession?

   Why is it important that they did not immediately reveal their disappointment?

   With the passage of time, do these authors look back with some amusement and even pleasure? Why or why not?

2. Write about an imaginary date between Soto and Varela, during which he wears his "guacamole jacket" and she drives her "banana car." Write from the point of view of either person or describe it from the view of an observer.

18

Heroes: Who Are They? (Exemplification and Functional Analysis)

Once a person said, "Pity the nation that has no heroes." It is a statement worthy of our consideration, especially since it is often said that we have no heroes today or that a hero is only good for about fifteen minutes, because, with media scrutiny, we're likely to know of any prominent person's flaws soon after the applause has died. That, of course, brings up the question of just how much we should expect from our heroes. Naturally our heroes should be more than ordinary, but should they be bigger than life? We need a definition, one that fits a special word often used loosely. Are famous athletes and other celebrities "heroes," or even role models? Some pretend to be and disappoint us. Some "big names" don't want to be known as either a hero or role model. The irascible Charles Barkley said, "Raise your own kids. I'm a basketball player."

Ponchitta Pierce offers a comprehensive view in "Who Are Our Heroes?," a collection of interviews about the definition of *hero* with eight well-known people. Some define heroes on a grand scale; others do not. Student writers in this section reflect that range. Can an ordinary person be heroic? Nancy Samuels, in her paragraph "More Than Ordinary," describes her strong, self-sacrificing mother as heroic. Then Susan Miller presents an example of an extraordinary person from history, "Susan B. Anthony: Hero in Bloomers," a political leader of noble stature who helped shape our nation.

One thing we know for sure: it was a wise writer who said, "Tell me who your heroes are, and I'll tell you what kind of person you are."

Ponder Questions

1. The preceding section began with the quotation, by Berthold Brecht: "Pity the nation that has no heroes." Soon after he first said that, another writer responded with the statement "Pity the nation that needs heroes." What does that opinion mean and what is your reaction to it?

2. How do you define *hero*?
3. Who are your heroes?
4. What is the difference between the terms *hero* and *role model*?

The readings in this chapter follow two forms of writing: exemplification and functional analysis. Exemplification is no more than using an example or examples to explain. Functional analysis shows how something works as a unit by discussing its parts. In this chapter, the subject is heroes. The reading selections use examples of heroes and discuss their traits. Grouping these two forms is an acknowledgment that a piece of writing is almost never made up of one single form of writing.

Exemplification

Sources of Examples

For the personal essay, the best source of examples is your own knowledge. If you know your subject well, from either reading or experience, you will be able to recall many examples through your writing strategies of freewriting, brainstorming, and clustering. Good examples are likely to come from something you know well. If you have worked in a fast-food restaurant, you probably have dozens of stories about activities there. Some of these stories might be appropriate for illustrating a topic on human behavior. Even if a reader has not shared an experience with a writer, he or she will almost certainly be able to judge and appreciate its authenticity. Professional writers working outside their specialties often interview (and sometimes pay) ordinary individuals in order to obtain concrete particulars to color and enliven their work. Television crime show writers, for instance, regularly collect information from police officers.

A more academic topic, such as one on a novel, might be researched by scrutinizing the book itself for incidents, statements, or descriptions. A history topic might be researched in a textbook or in library sources.

Connecting Examples with Purpose

Examples, by their very definition, are functional. They are representative of something, or they illustrate something. In purpose, they may explain, convince, or amuse. The connection between this purpose and the example must be clear. If your example is striking, yet later your reader can remember the example but not the point being illustrated, then you have failed in your basic task. Writing good exemplification begins with a good topic sentence or thesis.

Broad: People seeking plastic surgery have various motives.

Subject / **Treatment**

Focused: Some people seeking plastic surgery are driven by irrational emotional needs that can never be met.

In the following paragraph on essentially that focused idea, the author uses an example effectively by stating the purpose (topic sentence), connecting it with the example, and restating the purpose while relating it, in turn, directly to the example.

topic sentence Leigh Lachman, a plastic surgeon in Manhattan, notes that "some patients are never satisfied." One of his clients, a 45-year-old woman, came to him for a facelift, then a nose job, and then a

extended example breast reduction. She now insists that her breasts are too small and

restatement of topic sentence

she wants them augmented. Then she plans to get an eye-lift. She started bringing in friends to see Lachman. "Her attitude seems to be that she's bringing me business, so I should continue to operate on her," Lachman says. "These kinds of patients can be very difficult to help, because it becomes obvious that they want more than a surgical correction can provide."

Holly Hall, "Scalpel Slaves"

Writer's Checklist for Exemplification

- Write a strong thesis or statement of purpose.
- Select an example or examples that are both typical and representative while also being interesting.
- Repeat key words from the topic sentence to maintain a clear relationship between supporting examples and the main idea.
- Don't overlook personal experience as a source of good examples.
- Consider how your audience will react to your examples.
- If you use several examples, present them in an orderly manner such as by time, space, or relative importance.
- Be specific. When appropriate, use names, dates, and locations.

Topics for Exemplification

- Begin with a familiar saying and use one or more examples (from your personal experience, if possible) to illustrate its truth. Here are some ideas:

  Never give advice to a friend.
  If it isn't broken, don't fix it.
  Every person has a price.
  It isn't *what* you know; it's *whom* you know.
  You get what you pay for.
  What goes around, comes around.
  A fool and his (or her) money are soon parted.
  Haste makes waste.
  Pretty is as pretty does.
  He (or she) has hooey on top and phooey on bottom.
  Virtue is its own reward.
  The saddest word is *if.*
  If you can't do the time, don't do the crime.
  Don't look a gift horse in the mouth.
  Beware of people bearing gifts.

- Make a judgmental statement about a social issue you believe in strongly and then discuss a specific instance that will illustrate your point. These are some possible topics:

  The price of groceries is too high.
  Professional athletes are paid too much.
  A person buying a new car may get a lemon.
  Drivers sometimes openly ignore the laws on a selective basis.
  Politicians should be watched.
  Working and going to school is tough.
  Working, parenting, and going to school is tough.

Functional Analysis

If you need to explain how something works or exists as a unit, you will write a *functional analysis*. You will break down your subject into its parts and explain how each part functions in relation to the operation or existence of the whole.

Moving from Subject, to Principle, to Division, to Relationship

Almost anything can be analyzed for function—for example, how the parts of the ear work in hearing, how the parts of the eye work in seeing, or how the parts of the heart work in pumping blood throughout the body. Subjects such as these are all approached with the same systematic procedure.

Step 1. Begin with something that is a unit.

Step 2. State the principle by which that unit functions.

Step 3. Divide the unit into parts according to that principle.

Step 4. Discuss each of those parts in relation to the unit.

This is the way you might apply that procedure to a boss.

Unit	Manager
Principle of function	Effective as a leader
Parts based on the principle	Fair, intelligent, stable, competent in field
Discussion	Consider each part in relation to person being effective as a manager.

Writer's Checklist for Functional Analysis

- Follow the procedure discussed above: from (1) unit to (2) principle to (3) parts to (4) discussion.
- Write a strong statement of focus to unify your writing.
- Repeat key words in order to promote emphasis and unity.
- Present the parts in an order that will promote coherence.
- Emphasize how the parts function in relation to the operation of the whole thing.

Topics for Functional Analysis

- Discuss the qualities that make something or someone successful or praiseworthy. Consider these:

  A specific performer (a singer, dancer, actor, or musician)
  A team, a company, a school, a class, an organization

  A movie, a television program, a music video, a video game
  A family, a marriage, a relationship, a club

- Discuss how a physical object works, perhaps a part of the body (heart, ear, lungs, skin), part of a car (carburetor, water pump), a tape player, a stapler, a pencil sharpener, or a hair dryer.

More Than Ordinary

STUDENT PARAGRAPH by Nancy Samuels

Faced with writing on the topic of "an example of a hero with a discussion of the hero's traits," Nancy Samuels didn't have to go to the library. Right in her household she found her subject—her mother. She writes of an ordinary person who faced a difficult challenge and succeeded, in a situation in which others gave up too easily.

Topic sentence My mother is the best example of a hero I can think of. No one will read about her in a book about heroes, but in her small circle of friends, no one doubts her heroism. Certainly my younger brother doesn't. He is the special beneficiary of her heroism. He was in an accident when he was five years old, and the doctor told us that he would never walk. My mother listened respectfully, but she didn't believe him. **Trait** She had optimism. She went to another doctor and then another. Finally she found one who prescribed exercises. She worked with my brother for three years. **Trait** Day after dismal day, she persevered. It wasn't just her working with him that helped my brother. It was her raw courage in the face of failure. My brother worked with her. **Trait** They both were courageous. We other family members weren't. To us my brother and mother were acting like a couple of blind fools. We thought my mother especially, the leader, was in prolonged denial. But in three years my brother was walking. He won't be an athlete; nevertheless, he gets around. We're proud of him, but we know—and he knows—that without Mother he would never have walked. Of course, she's not a miracle worker. Most of the time, doctors are right, and some injured people can never walk. But the ones, like my brother, who somewhere have that hidden ability, need that special someone like my mother. She's more than ordinary. She's a hero.

Discussion and Critical Thinking

1. What are the main traits of Samuels' heroic mother?
2. Is she a miracle worker?
3. Will her kind of strength always succeed?
4. Would she have been heroic if she had not succeeded?

Reading-Related Writing

1. Write about an ordinary person who has struggled mightily and deserves the title *hero*. Structure your piece around the person's achievements and traits, especially the traits.

Susan B. Anthony: Hero in Bloomers

STUDENT ESSAY by Susan Miller

In reading history, we often discover our heroes. They include those who established the institutions and the basic freedoms that we so often take for granted. In elementary school, student Susan Miller discovered Susan B. Anthony. She remembered so well that for this essay she hardly needed to review the facts about one of the women responsible for women gaining the right to vote.

When I first read about Susan B. Anthony, I ran to my mother and asked if I was named after her. The answer was no. I was named Susan because it is a pretty name. So when I think of her, I will not think of the idea of namesake, but I will think of the idea of hero. In fact, she is the best example I know of. Against all odds she was a hero, displaying the qualities any hero needs, in my definition. **Thesis** As a hero she was courageous, persistent, and willing to sacrifice self.

Those qualities are not easily separated in discussing **Trait** Anthony. Certainly she was courageous, because she acted as an individual equal to any others in her strong stands against slavery and alcohol. When she was thirty-two years old, she attended a temperance movement meeting and wanted to speak against the sale of alcohol, which she saw as destructive of the family, especially among the poor. Although she was not allowed to speak because she was a woman, she argued individually and was widely criticized and scorned by the men in attendance.

Trait Nothing would dissuade her as she persisted in her views. The more she argued about slavery and temperance, the more it became apparent that women were treated unfairly. They did not have equal opportunity in education, social relationships, and politics. She began writing and speaking on all those issues. When she was told that women should stay in their place under their dresses, she began wearing bloomers, loose-fitting trousers that were regarded as scandalous clothing by the male-dominated society.

After the Civil War, she rejoiced as black men were given the right to vote. It was a right she had long upheld. But she was disappointed because women, all women, were denied that right. For the remainder of her life, women's suffrage was her passion. In 1872 she dressed as a man and voted, although she was breaking a federal law in doing so. But she believed that the right for women to vote was so fundamental that she put herself at risk. **Trait**

Susan B. Anthony would not be around when women were given the right to vote in 1919. She had died fourteen years earlier. But her name and reputation remain. Because of heroes like her, women now have opportunities hardly thought of at the beginning of her life.

Discussion and Critical Thinking

1. What were Susan B. Anthony's main traits?
2. Are courage and self-sacrifice almost the same? Explain.
3. If Susan B. Anthony were around today, what do you think she would be involved in?

Reading-Related Writing

1. Write about some notable person from history (any culture, any field) who could be called heroic. Your writing will define the idea of hero by discussing the achievements and traits of your exemplary person. Use this essay as a basic model, whether you write a paragraph or a short essay.

Who Are Our Heroes?

Ponchitta Pierce

In this essay, some prominent Americans share their ideas on heroism and tell whom they admire. Their definitions are different, but each is supported with examples, and several include the traits of the heroes.

What is a hero? Today the term is applied to everyone from the founding fathers to movie stars to classical composers. We asked prominent Americans in many fields, some of whom are seen as heroes themselves, to give their views. They don't always agree, but all have strong opinions on whom we should admire—and why.

1 Daniel Boorstin, 80—a historian, Pulitzer Prize-winning author and former Librarian of Congress—finds heroes in the past. "Read history, read books," he said, "not just newspapers and magazines. The temptation to make your contemporaries into heroes is the temptation to see them as divine. That is what happened with Hitler."

2 Today's world may have heroes, he added, but they are now overshadowed by celebrities. "The hero is known for achievements," Boorstin explained, "the celebrity for well-knownness. The hero reveals the possibilities of human nature. The celebrity reveals the possibilities of the press and media. Celebrities are people who make news, but heroes are people who make history. Time makes heroes but dissolves celebrities."

3 Boorstin's heroes include Thomas Jefferson, Abraham Lincoln and William James, the psychologist and philosopher. "They symbolize the receptive, open mind," he said. "They considered that mankind is capable of things that have not been revealed in the past."

4 **Richard Parsons,** 47, president of Time Warner, believes people discover their heroes early in life, largely through personal experience. "You don't sit down with a child and say, 'Look, let me tell you what heroes are about,' " he said. "Young people make that judgment for themselves because they know who they're attracted to, who they want to be like."

5 Parsons' father, Lorenzo, an electronics technician, has been the one constant hero of his life, even when Parsons realized his dad's limitations. "There is an expression," Parsons explained: " 'Never get to know your hero too well.' My father was not a businessman. There were points when I realized I had to turn to someone else for guidance, because he just didn't come from the world I was entering."

6 **Jackie Joyner-Kersee,** 33, a track and field star and winner of three Olympic gold medals, is seen as a hero by many. It disturbs her that this label often is given for her image alone.

7 Joyner-Kersee frequently returns to her hometown of East St. Louis, Ill., to speak to young people. She tells them, " 'If you think of me as your hero, it's important that you emulate Jackie Joyner-Kersee the person, not the athlete you read about.' I want kids to understand my values—that I was able to accomplish my goals by working hard—and to realize that, for me to do that, I needed people who believed in me."

8 "The true sense of 'hero' is someone who really has made a difference in your life," she went on. "The person could be your parent or grandparent. They might not be great in someone else's eyes, but to you they are great." Rosa Parks, the civil-rights activist, is a hero to Joyner-Kersee. "Parks made people realize they do have a voice," she explained. "She proved that people can be strong if they work together."

9 But the larger-than-life heroes of the past—such as Franklin Delano Roosevelt and John F. Kennedy—may be gone today, said **Jules Feiffer,** 66, a political cartoonist known for satirizing our foibles and the author of several books and plays. With today's public nature of private lives, "we can't closet our inconsistencies or hypocrisies as easily as we once could," he continued. "If you're looking for a leader or hero, and you ask for one who's had no experience or temptations, then you're asking for a return to an innocence we can never go back to."

10 I.F. Stone, the journalist and philosopher, and Fred Astaire are two of Feiffer's heroes. "Stone taught me to find ways to tell the unpleasant truths and make them seem palatable," Feiffer explained. As for Astaire, he added: "During the Depression, he could dance his way through life and make it seem effortless. As I grew older, I realized the amount of work that went into this effortlessness. It became a standard for me."

11 **Joan Chen,** 34, played Empress Wan Jung in the film *The Last Emperor* and was seen on the TV show *Twin Peaks.* She grew up in Shanghai during China's Cultural Revolution, when heroes such as Mao were state-mandated. "In the Communist system," explained the actress, "heroes were so important. By giving us heroes, the Communists wanted us to emulate them."

12 True heroes—unlike the Communist images or U.S. celebrities—are strong in moments of choice, Chen said, and make the morally right choice. "So often we make compromises in life," she explained. "Often, these choices go against our principles. Heroes rise above."

13 The Burmese opposition leader Daw Aung San Suu Kyi is one such person. She won the Nobel Peace Prize in 1991 and recently was freed from house arrest after almost six years. Aung San Suu Kyi is a hero, said Chen, because "she took action and sacrificed a lot—physically, materially and emotionally—for the cause she steadfastly believed in."

14 Heroes guide us to achieving our dreams, said **John Leguizamo,** 30, the Colombian-born actor and playwright: "When you feel like the world is against you or you give up hope, you look at your heroes and say, 'They were able to do it. They had hard times and a lot of opposition, but they got through it.' Then you feel, 'I can do it too.' "

15 Leguizamo—who wrote, produced and starred in Fox TV's Latin comedy show *House of Buggin'*—said he has different heroes for different things: some for comedy, others for sports or playwriting. They're heroes for what they've accomplished, added Leguizamo, but also because they have overcome obstacles. He described Richard Pryor as one of his heroes: "Pryor took the urban experience and made it very funny, yet touching at the same time." Julio César Chávez, the Mexican boxer, is another. "He came from a small town and had a dream to become the best boxer he could be," said Leguizamo. "He also gives back to his community. I respect that."

16 For **Brandy Norwood,** the 16-year-old pop singer whose songs "Best Friend" and "Baby" reached the top of the charts, there's no question who rates as heroes: "My parents are everything a child would want," she said. "They teach me principles, morals and values, and about self-confidence. And they're with me all the time, by my side."

17 Other than her parents, Norwood admires Whitney Houston—but not because of the pop icon's fame. Rather, it is for Houston's moral integrity. "Whitney is so powerful, and she carries herself as a positive woman," noted Norwood. "She doesn't use sex to sell records. I want to be like her in my own way."

18 At 26, **Awadagin Pratt** won the 1992 Naumburg International Piano Competition and became a celebrated classical musician. While he has inspired many performers, Pratt prefers to avoid the term 'hero,' because he believes it has lost its meaning through overuse. He admitted, however, "At different points in my life, there were people whose work I admired and relied upon to provide me with inspiration."

19 The late classical pianist Glenn Gould and the composer Beethoven have affected Pratt deeply. They are heroes, he said, because of their ability to maintain an independent spirit in the face of pressures to conform to the conventions of their day. Pratt also admires Arthur Ashe, the tennis star who became an AIDS activist and died in 1993 from an HIV-related infection. "Ashe was a person with great dignity and character," Pratt said. "He was an activist who dealt with a lot of adverse situations."

20 The poet **Maya Angelou,** 67—whose works include the autobiography *I Know Why the Caged Bird Sings* and "On the Pulse of Morning," the poem she read at President Clinton's inauguration—also doesn't use the word "hero." She prefers the term "hero/shero," because "hero" too often is

thought of as male. "Young women and young men need to know that there are women who give encouragement and succor, nourishment and insight," explained Angelou. "A hero/shero encourages people to see the good inside themselves and to expand it."

21 Angelou lists Eleanor Roosevelt, the author Pearl S. Buck and the abolitionist Frederick Douglass among her heroes. "They confronted societies that did not believe in their ideas and faced hostile adversaries," she said. "At times they were angry. Anger is very good—but I have not seen any case where any of them became bitter."

22 We can develop the heroic in ourselves, Angelou continued, by seeking to do right by others. "Are you concerned about the poor, the lonely and the ill?" she asked. "Do you follow your concern with action? I try to act as I would want my hero/shero to act. I want to display courtesy, courage, patience and strength all the time. Now, I blow it 84 times a day. But I'm trying."

Vocabulary Highlights

contemporaries (1)
receptive (3)
emulate (7)
satirizing (9)
foibles (9)
hypocrisies (9)
palatable (10)
mandated (11)
adverse (19)
succor (20)
adversaries (21)

Discussion and Critical Thinking

1. According to Daniel Boorstin, what is the difference between a celebrity and a hero?
2. What do the celebrity and the hero reveal about human possibilities?
3. From Boorstin's view, how do celebrities relate to history and time?
4. What does Jackie Joyner-Kersee say about values and achievements in relation to heroism?
5. Are state-mandated heroes really heroes? (See paragraphs 11–13.)
6. Why does Maya Angelou use the term *hero/shero*?
7. As a person trying to be heroic, what qualities does Angelou try to display?

Reading-Related Writing

1. Using Boorstin's definition, write about a hero from history.
2. Using one of Joyner-Kersee's definitions in paragraph 8, write an extended example of a hero.
3. Using the heroic traits offered by Angelou (courtesy, courage, patience, and strength) or similar traits, define your hero through an extended example.
4. Using the definitions offered by any author in this article or using your own definition, write a piece discussing an exemplary person and his or her heroic traits. You may choose to use the term *role model* instead of *hero.*

Connections

1. Apply Daniel Boorstin's definition of the hero from "Who Are Our Heroes?" to the essay "Susan B. Anthony: Hero in Bloomers."
2. Apply Maya Angelou's definition of the hero from "Who Are Our Heroes?" to one or both of the other two reading selections in this chapter.
3. Apply Maya Angelou's definition of "hero" to Mrs. Flowers in Angelou's "Liked for Myself" on p. 271.

19

The Joy and Grief of Work (Process Analysis)

Work is inseparable from life. There is a German saying—"You are what you eat." There should be another saying—"You are what you do for a living." After all, one reason we change jobs is that we say the work is adversely affecting other parts of our lives. The effects are not just a matter of stress. Whatever procedures, attitudes, and thought processes we develop at work are likely to find their way into our everyday lives. For instance, a professor's teacherish behavior at times emerges even when he or she is relating to loved ones.

Work can also be full of repetition, a necessary condition of almost any job, but more so in some. If we are involved in repetition, we may perceive it as tedium and imagine that out there somewhere are exciting careers teeming with intellectual stimulation and creativity. But regardless of the job, if a person does it long enough, it will probably become to an important extent a "been-there, done-that" activity. Once I talked to a heart specialist, telling him of my gratitude for his doing just the right thing in saving the life of my relative. With a dismissing wave of his hand, he said, "It's all a matter of procedures. I respond to each symptom and choose a procedure. It's as automatic and procedural as fixing a car. I don't have much choice."

Whether we love our work or not, we are likely to talk about it—our coworkers, our bosses, our tasks, our security, our triumphs, our embarrassments. We swap stories. We provide examples from work to support our views on human behavior and values. Some of our funniest and saddest stories are work-related.

Taking advantage of this interest, for the last twenty years or so, popular literature and much media entertainment have used the workplace as a setting. Recently many popular TV programs have been work-related: *Frasier, Home Improvement, Wings, Cheers*. We like to know about what others do and how they feel about what they do. Some people can perform seemingly monotonous jobs for long times and not be bored. How do they do that? we wonder. Does it not take some imagination, a strong will, and even some courage not to burn out?

Ponder Questions

1. Is work essential to the typical person's psychological well-being?
2. What would be your ideal job?
3. Is it possible for any job never to be boring?
4. Why is work by its very nature likely to be a matter of procedure or process?
5. As you look back on your jobs, what are you most proud of?
6. What was the most embarrassing thing you ever did or saw at work?

Nothing is more central to the idea of *work* than process analysis: how something was done or how to do it. Process analysis is one of the most practical forms of writing to master, but everyone who has read those directions in boxes marked "easy to assemble" knows that, at least for many, process analysis is not "easy to write."

Process Analysis

If you have any doubt about the frequency of the use of process analysis, just think about how many times you have heard people say, "How do you do it?" or "How is [was] it done?" Even when you are not hearing those questions, you are posing them yourself when you need to make something, cook a meal, assemble an item, take some medicine, repair something, or figure out what happened. In your college classes, you may have to discover how osmosis occurs, how a rock changes form, how a mountain was formed, how a battle was won, or how a bill goes through the legislature.

If you need to explain how to do something or how something was (is) done, you will write a paper of *process analysis*. You will break down your topic into stages, explaining each so that your reader can duplicate or understand the process.

Two Types of Process Analysis: Directive and Informative

The questions How do I do it? and How is (was) it done? will lead you into two different types of process analysis—directive and informative.

Directive process analysis explains how to do something. As the name suggests, it gives directions and tells the reader how to do something. It says, for example, "Read me, and you can bake a pie (tune up your car, read a book, write an essay, take some medicine)." Because it is presented directly to the reader, it usually addresses the reader as "you," or it implies the "you" by saying something such as, "First [you] purchase a large, fat wombat, and then [you] . . ." In the same way, this textbook addresses you or implies "you" because it is a long how-to-do-it (directive process analysis) statement.

Informative process analysis explains how something was (is) done by giving data (information). Whereas the directive process analysis tells you what to do in the future, the informative process analysis tells you what has occurred or what is occurring. If it is something in nature, such as the formation of a mountain, you can read and understand the process by which it emerged.

Working with the Stages

Preparation In this first stage of the directive type of process analysis, list the materials or equipment needed for the process and discuss the necessary setup arrangements. For some topics, this stage will also provide technical terms and definitions. The degree to which this stage is detailed will depend on both the subject itself and the expected knowledge and experience of the projected audience.

The informative type of process analysis may begin with background or context rather than with preparation. For example, a statement explaining how mountains form might begin with a description of a flat portion of the earth made up of plates that are arranged like a jigsaw puzzle.

Steps The actual process will be presented here. Each step must be explained clearly and directly, and phrased to accommodate the audience. The language, especially in directive process analysis, is likely to be simple and concise; however, avoid dropping words such as *and, a, an, the,* and *of,* and thereby lapsing into "recipe language." The steps may be accompanied by explanations about why certain procedures are necessary and how not following directions carefully can lead to trouble.

Order The order will usually be chronological (time based) in some sense. Certain words are commonly used to promote coherence: *first, second, third, then, soon, now, next, finally, at last, therefore, consequently,* and—especially for informative process analysis—words used to show the passage of time such as hours, days of the week, and so on.

Writer's Checklist for Process Analysis

- Decide whether your process analysis type is mainly directive or informative, and be appropriately consistent in using pronouns and other designations.

  Use second person for the directive as you address the reader (*you, your*).

  Use first person for the informative; do not address the reader (use *I*); or

  Use third person for the informative; do not address the reader (use *he, she, it, they, them,* individuals, the name of your subject).

- Consider using this form for the directive process (with topics such as how to cook something or how to fix something).

  I. Preparation

  A.

  B.

  C.

  II. Steps

  A.

  B.

  C.

  D.

- Consider using this form for the informative process (with topic such as how a volcano functions or how a battle was won).

  I. Background or context

  A.

  B.

  C.

II. Change or development (narrative)

A.

B.

C.

D.

- In explaining the stages and using technical terms, take into account whether your audience will be mainly well informed, moderately informed, or poorly informed.
- Explain reasons for procedures whenever you believe explanations will help.
- Use transitional words indicating time or other progression (such as *finally, at last, therefore, consequently,* and—especially for the informative process analysis—words used to show passage of time, such as hours, days of the week, and so on).
- Avoid recipe language; in other words, do not drop *the, a, an,* or *of.*

Topics for Process Analysis

- How to eat (and perhaps, select, as well) a food item such as watermelon, pizza, Chinese food, cotton candy, popcorn, dips, snails, fried chicken, sushi, taffy, peppers, or liver.
- How to fix your own hair, nails, or face.
- How to deal with a person who is angry, sexually aggressive (against your wishes), pouting, or controlling.
- How to fix a ___________________.
- How to cook ___________________.

King of Klutziness

STUDENT PARAGRAPH by Joel Bailey

Joel Bailey is now a confident and competent person at work in a computer store, but he remembers the first day of his first job. It began with apprehension, turned to excitement as a celebrity appeared, and then ended in chaos.

Topic sentence <u>It was my first day of what would be a memorable day at work in Carl's Jr., a fast-food place by Universal Studio near Hollywood.</u> I was assigned to the front counter because another worker was late. There I was at noon, the busiest time of the day, with no training, **Situation** scared, and nervous. In the beginning, things went well. Orders were routine, and I filled them and made change. As time passed, the lines got short, and I was still doing great because, after all, the job didn't require the mentality of a rocket scientist. Several counter people left their registers to help out in back. Then a lot of people came in at one time. Only two of us were taking orders. I was nervous. I served three persons, hardly

Simple procedure

looking up as I punched the keys, called out orders, and made change. After barely glancing at the next person, I heard *his* voice ordering, a familiar voice. It was Alex Benson, a reporter for a TV channel I frequently watched.

Repeated procedure

I repeated his order so it would be perfect, and I took his money. After I gave him his change, he stared at the receipt and said with more than a touch of irritation,

Conflict/dialogue

"You made a mistake. You charged me for two chicken burgers." I apologized and gave him a refund. "What about the tax," he growled. "You didn't refund the tax." I was really getting nervous. He always laughed and smiled on TV. I gave him the tax money. I grabbed someone else's chicken order just so I could give him quick service, but when I handed him the tray, my hand slipped and I spilled

Blunder/more conflict

his Coke on his trousers. Quickly I grabbed a napkin and ran around the counter and wiped at the Coke stain. Unfortunately the napkin I grabbed had catsup on it. Now I had added a condiment to the Coke stain. By that time I might as well have salted and peppered him. Beyond anger, and looking at me wildly, he fled with his tray to a distant booth and sat with his back to the wall. I decided not to ask for an autograph.

Discussion and Critical Thinking

1. Is Bailey really klutzy or is this just the first-day jitters?
2. Is the problem with procedures or execution of the procedures?
3. Was this a funny situation at the time?

Reading-Related Writing

1. Write about a time when just about everything went wrong at work for you.
2. Write about a time when just about everything went wrong at work for a friend.
3. Write about a time when just about everything went wrong when you were being served in an establishment such as a restaurant, department store, gas station or an airport.

McDonald's—We Do It All for You

Barbara Garson

In this essay from *The Electronic Sweatshop*, Barbara Garson interviews a former McDonald's griddleman, who explains why he quit and will never return. It's an inside look at the workplace that produces that burger the same way every time, no matter where you are. A well-established and highly regarded playwright and journalist, Garson has recently focused her attention on workers in a computerized society of service-oriented jobs.

Jason Pratt:

1 "They called us the Green Machine," says Jason Pratt, recently retired McDonald's griddleman, " 'cause the crew had green uniforms then. And that's what it is, a machine. You don't have to know how to cook, you don't have to know how to think. There's a procedure for everything and you just follow the procedures."

2 "Like?" I asked. I was interviewing Jason in the Pizza Hut across from his old McDonald's.

3 "Like, uh," the wiry teenager searched for a way to describe the all-encompassing procedures. "O.K., we'll start you off on something simple. You're on the ten-in-one grill, ten patties in a pound. Your basic burger. The guy on the bin calls, 'Six hamburgers,' so you lay your six pieces of meat on the grill and set the timer." Before my eyes Jason conjures up the gleaming, mechanized McDonald's kitchen. "Beep-beep, beep-beep, beep-beep. That's the beeper to sear 'em. It goes off in twenty seconds. Sup, sup, sup, sup, sup, sup." He presses each of the six patties down on the sizzling grill with an imaginary silver disk. "Now you turn off the sear beeper, put the buns in the oven, set the oven timer and then the next beeper is to turn the meat. This one goes beep-beep-beep, beep-beep-beep. So you turn your patties and then you drop your re-cons on the meat, t-con, t-con, t-con." Here Jason takes two imaginary handfuls of reconstituted onions out of water and sets them out, two blops at a time, on top of the six patties he's arranged in two neat rows on our grill. "Now the bun oven buzzes [there are over a half dozen different timers with distinct beeps and buzzes in a McDonald's kitchen]. This one turns itself off when you open the oven door so you just take out your crowns, line 'em up and give 'em each a squirt of mustard and a squirt of ketchup." With mustard in his right hand and ketchup in his left, Jason wields the dispensers like a pair of six-shooters up and down the lines of buns. Each dispenser has two triggers. One fires the premeasured squirt for ten-in-ones—the second is set for quarter-pounders.

4 "Now," says Jason, slowing down, "now you get to put on the pickles. Two if they're regular, three if they're small. That's the creative part. Then the lettuce, then you ask for a cheese count ('cheese on four please'). Finally the last beep goes off and you lay your burger on the crowns."

5 "On the *crown* of the buns?" I ask, unable to visualize. "On top?"

6 "Yeah, you dress 'em upside down. Put 'em in the box upside down too. They flip 'em over when they serve 'em."

7 "Oh, I think I see."

8 "Then scoop up the heels [the bun bottoms] which are on top of the bun warmer, rake the heels with one hand and push the tray out from underneath and they land (plip) one on each burger, right on top of the re-cons, neat and perfect. [The official time allotted by Hamburger Central, the McDonald's headquarters in Oak Brook, Ill., is ninety seconds to prepare and serve a burger.] It's like I told you. The procedures make the burgers. You don't have to know a thing."

9 McDonald's employs 500,000 teenagers at any one time. Most don't stay long. About 8 million Americans—7 per cent of our labor force—have worked at McDonald's and moved on.[1] Jason is not a typical ex-employee.

[1]These statistics come from John F. Love, *McDonald's Behind the Golden Arches* (New York: Bantam, 1986). Additional background information in this chapter comes from Ray Kroc and Robert Anderson, *Grinding It Out* (Chicago: Contemporary Books, 1977), and Max Boas and Steve Chain, *Big Mac* (New York: Dutton, 1976).

In fact, Jason is a legend among the teenagers at the three McDonald's outlets in his suburban area. It seems he was so fast at the griddle (or maybe just fast talking) that he'd been taken back three times by two different managers after quitting.

10 But Jason became a real legend in his last stint at McDonald's. He'd been sent out the back door with the garbage, but instead of coming back in he got into a car with two friends and just drove away. That's the part the local teenagers love to tell. "No fight with the manager or anything . . . just drove away and never came back. . . . I don't think they'd give him a job again."

11 "I would never go back to McDonald's," says Jason. "Not even as a manager." Jason is enrolled at the local junior college. "I'd like to run a real restaurant someday, but I'm taking data processing to fall back on." He's had many part-time jobs, the highest-paid at a hospital ($4.00 an hour), but that didn't last, and now dishwashing (at the $3.35 minimum). "Same as McDonald's. But I would never go back there. You're a complete robot."

12 "It seems like you can improvise a little with the onions," I suggested. "They're not premeasured." Indeed, the reconstituted onion shreds grabbed out of a container by the unscientific-looking wet handful struck me as oddly out of character in the McDonald's kitchen.

13 "There's supposed to be twelve onion bits per patty," Jason informed me. "They spot check."

14 "Oh come on."

15 "You think I'm kiddin'. They lift your heels and they say, 'You got too many onions.' It's portion control."

16 "Is there any freedom anywhere in the process?" I asked.

17 "Lettuce. They'll leave you alone as long as it's neat."

18 "So lettuce is freedom; pickles is judgment?"

19 "Yeah but you don't have time to play around with your pickles. They're never gonna say just six pickles except on the disk. [Each store has video disks to train the crew for each of about twenty work stations, like fries, register, lobby, quarter-pounder grill.] What you'll hear in real life is 'twelve and six on a turn-lay.' The first number is your hamburgers, the second is your Big Macs. On a turn-lay means you lay the first twelve, then you put down the second batch after you turn the first. So you got twenty-four burgers on the grill, in shifts. It's what they call a production mode. And remember you also got your fillets, your McNuggets. . . ."

20 "Wait, slow down." By then I was losing track of the patties on our imaginary grill. "I don't understand this turn-lay thing."

21 "Don't worry, you don't have to understand. You follow the beepers, you follow the buzzers and you turn your meat as fast as you can. It's like I told you, to work at McDonald's you don't need a face, you don't need a brain. You need to have two hands and two legs and move 'em as fast as you can. That's the whole system. I wouldn't go back there again for anything."

Discussion and Critical Thinking

1. Jason Pratt says, "The procedures make the burgers." Is that bad for the burger customers or bad for the burger makers? Or both?
2. Do you think Pratt is a typical McDonald's employee? What positive things might be said about the company?
3. How are McDonald's procedures different from other procedures you have encountered?

4. How do you account for the fact that some people work at McDonald's, even doing grill duty, for a long time? Do they like to work there? Do some people thrive on the repetition? Have some people learned to deal creatively with the repetition?

Reading-Related Writing

1. Write a paragraph about the procedures you have used at a job you have now or have had.
2. If the procedures you have worked with at a job are not written down, write them in concise, numbered parts.
3. Using some of the same terminology used by Jason Pratt, write a procedural statement of how to eat the McDonald's burger. Refer to the parts of the burger as it is to be consumed. Include sound effects. Use buzzers if you like. Time each stage.

One More Time

Gary Soto

University of California professor and celebrated author of poetry, fiction, and nonfiction, Gary Soto writes especially of his experiences growing up as a Mexican-American in the 1950s and 1960s in the San Joaquin Valley around Fresno. As a child he had seen the Mexican workers in the fields and vineyards. He had seen his mother go there for work, and he had worked one summer picking grapes for the Sun-Maid Raisin Company. Determined never again "to stoop like a Mexican" doing field labor, he said, at first, he would rather wear old clothes to school than earn money that way. But then he relented and went to the field, this time chopping cotton.

1 Along with my brother and sister I picked grapes until I was fifteen, before giving up and saying that I'd rather wear old clothes than stoop like a Mexican. Mother thought I was being stuck-up, even stupid, because there would be no clothes for me in the fall. I told her I didn't care, but when Rick and Debra rose at five in the morning, I lay awake in bed feeling that perhaps I had made a mistake but unwilling to change my mind. That fall Mother bought me two pairs of socks, a packet of colored T-shirts, and underwear. The T-shirts would help, I thought, but who would see that I had new underwear and socks? I wore a new T-shirt on the first day of school, then an old shirt on Tuesday, then another T-shirt on Wednesday, and on Thursday an old Nehru shirt that was embarrassingly out of style. On Friday I changed into the corduroy pants my brother had handed down to me and slipped into my last new T-shirt. I worked like a magician, blinding my classmates, who were all clothes-conscious and small-time social climbers, by arranging my wardrobe to make it seem larger than it really was. But by spring I had to do something—my blue jeans were almost silver and my shoes had lost their form, puddling like black ice around my feet. That spring of my sixteenth year, Rick and I decided to take a labor bus to chop cotton. In his old Volkswagen, which was more noise than power, we drove on a Saturday morning to West Fresno—or Chinatown as some call it—parked, walked slowly toward a bus, and stood gawking at the winos, toothy

blacks, Okies, *Tejanos* with gold teeth, whores, Mexican families, and labor contractors shouting "Cotton" or "Beets," the work of spring.

2 We boarded the "Cotton" bus without looking at the contractor who stood almost blocking the entrance because he didn't want winos. We boarded scared and then were more scared because two blacks in the rear were drunk and arguing loudly about what was better, a two-barrel or four-barrel Ford carburetor. We sat far from them, looking straight ahead, and only glanced briefly at the others who boarded, almost all of them broken and poorly dressed in loudly mismatched clothes. Finally when the contractor banged his palm against the side of the bus, the young man at the wheel, smiling and talking in Spanish, started the engine, idled it for a moment while he adjusted the mirrors, and started off in slow chugs. Except for the windshield there was no glass in the windows, so as soon as we were on the rural roads outside Fresno, the dust and sand began to be sucked into the bus, whipping about like irate wasps as the gravel ticked about us. We closed our eyes, clotted up our mouths that wanted to open with embarrassed laughter because we couldn't believe we were on that bus with those people and the dust attacking us for no reason.

3 When we arrived at a field we followed the others to a pickup where we each took a hoe and marched to stand before a row. Rick and I, self-conscious and unsure, looked around at the others who leaned on their hoes or squatted in front of the rows, almost all talking in Spanish, joking, lighting cigarettes—all waiting for the foreman's whistle to begin work. Mother had explained how to chop cotton by showing us with a broom in the backyard.

4 "Like this," she said, her broom swishing down weeds. "Leave one plant and cut four—and cut them! Don't leave them standing or the foreman will get mad."

5 The foreman whistled and we started up the row stealing glances at other workers to see if we were doing it right. But after awhile we worked like we knew what we were doing, neither of us hurrying or falling behind. But slowly the clot of men, women, and kids began to spread and loosen. Even Rick pulled away. I didn't hurry, though. I cut smoothly and cleanly as I walked at a slow pace, in a sort of funeral march. My eyes measured each space of cotton plants before I cut. If I missed the plants, I swished again. I worked intently, seldom looking up, so when I did I was amazed to see the sun, like a broken orange coin, in the east. It looked blurry, unbelievable, like something not of this world. I looked around in amazement, scanning the eastern horizon that was a taut line jutted with an occasional mountain. The horizon was beautiful, like a snapshot of the moon, in the early light of morning, in the quiet of no cars and few people.

6 The foreman trudged in boots in my direction, stepping awkwardly over the plants, to inspect the work. No one around me looked up. We all worked steadily while we waited for him to leave. When he did leave, with a feeble complaint addressed to no one in particular, we looked up smiling under straw hats and bandanas.

7 By 11:00, our lunch time, my ankles were hurting from walking on clods the size of hardballs. My arms ached and my face was dusted by a wind that was perpetual, always busy whipping about. But the work was not bad, I thought. It was better, so much better, than picking grapes, especially with the hourly wage of a dollar twenty-five instead of piece work. Rick and I walked sorely toward the bus where we washed and drank water. Instead of

eating in the bus or in the shade of the bus, we kept to ourselves by walking down to the irrigation canal that ran the length of the field, to open our lunch of sandwiches and crackers. We laughed at the crackers, which seemed like a cruel joke from our Mother, because we were working under the sun and the last thing we wanted was a salty dessert. We ate them anyway and drank more water before we returned to the field, both of us limping in exaggeration. Working side by side, we talked and laughed at our predicament because our Mother had warned us year after year that if we didn't get on track in school we'd have to work in the fields and then we would see. We mimicked Mother's whining voice and smirked at her smoky view of the future in which we'd be trapped by marriage and screaming kids. We'd eat beans and then we'd see.

8 Rick pulled slowly away to the rhythm of his hoe falling faster and smoother. It was better that way, to work alone. I could hum made-up songs or songs from the radio and think to myself about school and friends. At the time I was doing badly in my classes, mainly because of a difficult stepfather, but also because I didn't care anymore. All through junior high and into my first year of high school there were those who said I would never do anything, be anyone. They said I'd work like a donkey and marry the first Mexican girl that came along. I was reminded so often, verbally and in the way I was treated at home, that I began to believe that chopping cotton might be a lifetime job for me. If not chopping cotton, then I might get lucky and find myself in a car wash or restaurant or junkyard. But it was clear; I'd work, and work hard.

9 I cleared my mind by humming and looking about. The sun was directly above with a few soft blades of clouds against a sky that seemed bluer and more beautiful than our sky in the city. Occasionally the breeze flurried and picked up dust so that I had to cover my eyes and screw up my face. The workers were hunched, brown as the clods under our feet, and spread across the field that ran without end—fields that were owned by corporations, not families.

10 I hoed trying to keep my mind busy with scenes from school and pretend girlfriends until finally my brain turned off and my thinking went fuzzy with boredom. I looked about, no longer mesmerized by the beauty of the landscape, no longer wondering if the winos in the fields could hold out for eight hours, no longer dreaming of the clothes I'd buy with my pay. My eyes followed my chopping as the plants, thin as their shadows, fell with each strike. I worked slowly with ankles and arms hurting, neck stiff, and eyes stinging from the dust and the sun that glanced off the field like a mirror.

11 By quitting time, 3:00, there was such an excruciating pain in my ankles that I walked as if I were wearing snowshoes. Rick laughed at me and I laughed too, embarrassed that most of the men were walking normally and I was among the first timers who had to get used to this work. "And what about you, wino," I came back at Rick. His eyes were meshed red and his long hippie hair was flecked with dust and gnats and bits of leaves. We placed our hoes in the back of a pickup and stood in line for our pay, which was twelve fifty. I was amazed at the pay, which was the most I had ever earned in one day, and thought that I'd come back the next day, Sunday. This was too good.

12 Instead of joining the others in the labor bus, we jumped in the back of a pickup when the driver said we'd get to town sooner and were welcome to

join him. We scrambled into the truck bed to be joined by a heavy-set and laughing *Tejano* whose head was shaped like an egg, particularly so because the bandana he wore ended in a point on the top of his head. He laughed almost demonically as the pickup roared up the dirt path, a gray cape of dust rising behind us. On the highway, with the wind in our faces, we squinted at the fields as if we were looking for someone. The *Tejano* had quit laughing but was smiling broadly, occasionally chortling tunes he never finished. I was scared of him, though Rick, two years older and five inches taller, wasn't. If the *Tejano* looked at him, Rick stared back for a second or two before he looked away to the fields.

13 I felt like a soldier coming home from war when we rattled into Chinatown. People leaning against car hoods stared, their necks following us, owl-like; prostitutes chewed gum more ferociously and showed us their teeth; Chinese grocers stopped brooming their storefronts to raise their cadaverous faces at us. We stopped in front of the Chi Chi Club where Mexican music blared from the juke box and cue balls cracked like dull ice. The *Tejano,* who was dirty as we were, stepped awkwardly over the side rail, dusted himself off with his bandana, and sauntered into the club.

14 Rick and I jumped from the back, thanked the driver who said *de nada* and popped his clutch, so that the pickup jerked and coughed blue smoke. We returned smiling to our car, happy with the money we had made and pleased that we had, in a small way, proved ourselves to be tough; that we worked as well as other men and earned the same pay.

15 We returned the next day and the next week until the season was over and there was nothing to do. I told myself that I wouldn't pick grapes that summer, saying all through June and July that it was for Mexicans, not me. When August came around and I still had not found a summer job, I ate my words, sharpened my knife, and joined Mother, Rick, and Debra for one last time.

Vocabulary Highlights

irate (2)

perpetual (7)

clot (5)

taut (5)

predicament (7)

mesmerized (10)

excruciating (11)

demonically (12)

chortling (12)

cadaverous (13)

Discussion and Critical Thinking

1. Why does Soto decide to chop cotton?
2. What kinds of people are on the truck headed for the fields?
3. What is the procedure for chopping cotton? Who are the teachers?
4. Does the work involve a procedure almost as exact as making a hamburger in McDonald's?

5. How does Soto avoid boredom and persevere? How long do those techniques work?
6. Does he finally give up on field work?

Reading-Related Writing

1. Write about an occasion when you did some work you had sworn not to do, such as cooking fast foods, mowing lawns, doing common labor, baby sitting, or car washing.
2. At first, Soto had ways of avoiding the boredom in the fields. Write about how you managed to endure a "boring" job by using your imagination.
3. Write about the satisfaction that Soto derived from his experiences in the field. Refer directly to the story for support.

Connections

1. Compare the attitudes of the two workers in "McDonald's—We Do It All for You" and "One More Time." Why is each one working? How does each one feel about the kind of work he is doing? How does each one feel about the boredom associated with the work? How does each one deal with the problem of boredom? How does each one look upon work?

20

Girls and Guys in Gangs (Cause-and-Effect Analysis)

> "The gang mentality alienates these youths from their families and from the community. Their mind-set has them in a constant battlefield superconsciousness, like soldiers in battle, that numbs them to the sensitivities and the needs of others."

That characterization is by Carlos A. Chavez and Antonio H. Rodriguez. They call it *"La Vida Loca:* Crazy Life." Just why and how do youngsters select this crazy life? In "Girls and Gangs," Portland policewoman Dorothy Elmore says, "If we could get the girls to stop associating with the male gang members, we wouldn't have any gangs." From a distance the problem is not so difficult to describe, and the solutions are fairly clear. From up close, we see that gang culture is part of society in the same way that a cancer can be part of a body. But it is often not easy to find the clear causes and cure of cancer within that body, and, similarly, it is not easy to find the clear causes and cure for gangs, as their destructive elements multiply like malignant cells.

Gangs weaken and destroy neighborhoods and families of all classes and colors. Hadley McGraw says she came from a stable middle-class home, but she became involved with a gang member and now "Everyone Pays the Price." Linda Yang says her uncle and aunt could not believe their "college prep" son was a gang member—until he was arrested for murder. In her words, "Then denial went away to prison with their son."

Ponder Questions

1. For various ethnic groups, what are the major motives for joining gangs?
2. What is meant by the term *gang mentality*?
3. How would you rank some of the basic reasons for gang membership: family, protection, crime, women, respect, unemployment, low self-esteem, immaturity?
4. Why is gang membership more appealing to males than females?

The mention of any topic regarding gangs is likely to generate questions about why people join and what happens to those who do. The appropriate form of writing for those matters is cause-and-effect analysis.

Cause-and-Effect Analysis

If you wish to explain the causes or effects of some event, happening, or result, you should write an analysis by causes or by effects. Cause-and-effect relationships are common in our daily lives. A single situation may raise questions about both causes and effects:

> The car won't start. Why? (cause)
>
> What now? (effect)

In a short piece of writing, you will probably concentrate on one, though you may mention both. Because you cannot write about all causes or all effects, you should try to identify and develop the most important ones. Consider that some causes are immediate, others remote; some visible, others hidden. Any one or a group of causes can be the most important. The effects of an event can also be complicated. Some may be immediate, others long-range. The sequence of events is not necessarily important. *B* (inflation) may follow *A* (the election of a president), but that sequence does not mean that *A* caused *B*.

One useful approach to developing a cause-or-effect analysis is listing. Write down the situation or trend you are concerned about. Then on the left side, list the causes and on the right side list the effects. Looking at the two lists, you can then determine the best side (causes or effects) for your study.

Causes	Situation	Effects
Bad habits		Financial problems
In-law problems		Liberation
Religious differences		Financial success
Career decision		Safety
Personal abuse	*Divorce*	New relationships
Infidelity		Social adjustment
Sexual incompatibility		Vocational choice
Politics		Problems for children
Money		Independence

Then you would choose about three of the most immediate causes or effects and proceed. One cause such as personal abuse, may in turn have its own (remote, hidden, or underlying) cause or partial cause: frustration over job loss, mental problems, tumor on the brain, drug addiction, bad parenting, or weak character. In short papers, one usually deals with immediate causes such as in-law problems, money, and personal abuse. (These same principles can be applied to effects.)

The causes could be incorporated into a *topic sentence,* and then developed in an *outline.*

The main causes of my divorce were in-law problems, money, and personal abuse.

I. In-law problems
   A. Helped too much
   B. Expected too much
II. Money
   A. Poor management
   B. Low-paying job

III. Personal abuse
   A. Verbal
   B. Physical

Writer's Checklist for Cause-and-Effect Analysis

Apply these ideas to your writing.

- Have your purpose clearly in mind.
- Be sure that you have sufficient knowledge of the subject to develop it.
- Distinguish clearly between causes and effects by using three columns:

Causes	Situation	Effects

- Usually concentrate on either causes or effects.
- Do not conclude that something is an effect merely because it follows something else.
- Distinguish between immediate and underlying causes.
- Distinguish between immediate and long-range effects.

Topics for Cause-and-Effect Analysis

- Write about the causes of crime (for one individual involved in crime), unemployment (one person who is out of work), leaving home (one person who has left home), emigrating (one person or family), poverty (one person who is poor), school dropout (one person), going to college (one who did), or success or product or program on television (about one).
- Write about the effects of disease (a particular disease, perhaps on just one person), fighting (one or two people involved in a dispute), fire (a particular one), alcoholism (a certain alcoholic), getting a job (a person with a particular job), early marriage (a person who married very young), teenage parenthood (one person or a couple), or dressing a certain way (one person and his or her style).

Young Model-Minority Gangster

Student Paragraph by Linda Yang

Gangs are equal opportunity organizations. Though there may be little ethnic diversity within individual gangs, there are gangs for all ethnic groups, even the groups that have a reputation for dedicated scholarship and family obedience. Student Linda Yang knows. Here she writes of her Asian-American cousin, who is now doing nine years in prison for a gang-related crime.

Topic sentence Some people in the community were really surprised when my cousin was arrested for a gang-related shooting. They were surprised because he's Asian-American, the so-called model minority and all that. Even his parents said they were surprised. They'd seen some of the signs: the baggy clothing he'd been wearing when he went out with **Effects** his friends, some evidence that he'd been drinking, and a few times that he'd had some dope. He even kept coming up with this extra money for a '92 Prelude—he told his parents he'd raised the money by buying and selling used computers. As for his clothes, he said he could make better sales when he was dressed the way young people do on TV. To his parents, he was a young business person. They wouldn't believe any of the signs of gang activity were serious. My cousin was almost a straight "A" student. The fact is that he was living two lives. Like lots of Asian-American youths, he was torn between cultures. His family was important enough that he was an obedient son, but his **Cause** need for rebellion was strong enough that he was a teen gang-type after school. His grades didn't drop. He didn't go to continuation school. But he had problems. His family was one source. They were very middle class, but both **Cause** his mother and father were busy making money. He got discipline from them and he got expectations from them, but he didn't get time and real attention. Because of their **Cause** long hours, he had time on his hands. And the school **Cause** offered classes, but he didn't make connections otherwise. After his first year he wasn't involved in any clubs or other activities. One of his friends said after the arrest that my cousin at first wasn't accepted by many of the popular students in school, and then later he rejected them. In my part of town most Asian-American gang members are similar to my cousin in that they live two lives. They don't go openly against their parents, but they can be just as heartless as my cousin when they **Effects** go against society and other gangs. My cousin and his friends were stealing computers and selling them. There was a double cross, and there was a shooting. Time, lack of supervision and affection, temptation, money, and peer pressure—for the next nine years his parents will be thinking about some of those things. Denial went away to prison with their son. My cousin must realize that others with far less parental concern did not become gangsters. He will have plenty of time to think about personal responsibility.

Discussion and Critical Thinking

1. Why didn't the parents of Yang's cousin suspect there were problems?
2. Many other youngsters have far worse home situations and do not turn to crime or gangs. Why do you think Yang's cousin did?
3. Does Yang imply that she suspected her cousin's being in some kind of trouble?
4. Toward the end of the paragraph, Yang brings together the causes of her cousin's fall. What are they?
5. In your view, which is the most important?

Reading-Related Writing

1. Write about someone you know who was leading two lives—gang and conventional—until he or she got caught.
2. Discuss to what extent this selection questions the idea of model minority persons.
3. Rewrite this paragraph and emphasize the idea of personal responsibility throughout.

Everyone Pays the Price

STUDENT ESSAY by Hadley McGraw

Sitting in a college classroom, Hadley McGraw doesn't remind one of the stereotypical gang member. Apparently tattoo- and puncture-free, she is fair-skinned, well-groomed, and soft-spoken. She does her homework, contributes to class discussion, and writes well. So much for stereotypes!

It is ten o'clock and time for me to start my day. I put an *X* on my calendar to signify that another twenty-four hours has passed. I now have one hundred and nine days until Martin, my boyfriend, comes home. He has been in jail for the last year. I guess you could say I was not surprised by his sentence. This is not the first time, and I'm afraid it will not be the last. Eighteen months of our three-and-a-half-year relationship, he has spent in correctional institutions. Martin is a gang member. He has been a gang member for nine years now. **Thesis** Gang membership of a loved one affects everyone around that person. Three-and-a-half years later I live each day in fear and grief.

Topic sentence I guess what attracted me to Martin at first was his bad-boy image and his carefree way of life. He was good looking and well known. He was tough and exciting. I, on the other hand, was good and obedient. I had been told often that I was pretty. I made good grades and came from a good home. My parents, still married and drug-free, lived comfortably in a middle-class neighborhood.

Causes Martin, on the contrary, came from a broken home. His parents hated each other. His father was a cold, heartless man, and his mother was a "flakey" drug addict. His uncles and cousins were all members of a very large gang who "controlled" an area where he lived. Soon so was he a gang member.

Effects Martin quit school when he was a freshman and spent his days on a street corner drinking Olde English forty-ouncers. Soon I was joining him. I began ditching school to hang out. In no time I was a gang member myself, and as

Effects I look back, I see what an awful person I became. We used drugs all day and all night. I didn't care about anything and neither did he. I left home and devastated my family and lost my friends. I didn't care because I had a new family and new friends. Martin spent his nights committing crimes and dealing drugs. I was by his side, carrying his gun. The drugs made him irritable and violent, and small disagreements turned into huge battles between us. Jail sentences made him angrier and closer to his gang. Each day Martin became farther from me. Life was a nonstop party with his homeboys, and I was his woman. It was exciting and risky. It was self-destructive.

Topic sentence My breaking point was one year ago. Martin and I were at a party. Everyone was drinking and joking. Oldies were playing and a noisy, wild game of poker was taking place. Suddenly a car was approaching us rapidly. Martin told me to run and hide, so I did. The homeboys began reaching for their guns. I heard five gunshots before the car drove away. I ran to the front of the house where Martin's cousin lay bleeding. I tried to wake him, speak to him. He wasn't responding. I screamed for an ambulance. Finally Martin appeared from behind a car and ran inside

Effects to call 911. When the ambulance arrived, I was hysterical and covered in blood. They took Martin's cousin to the hospital where he was pronounced dead. Because of the gunshot wounds, the funeral was a closed casket affair and very hard on everyone. It made Martin stronger, meaner, and colder, and it made me wiser. Martin was out committing crimes again, and two months later would be jailed again.

It is hard for me to imagine what I did to myself, knowing that any day I could have died senselessly. It is even harder for me to accept the fact that my boyfriend would die for a dirty, trashy street gang, but not for me.

Topic sentence — This last year I have been moving back to the right track.

Effects — I have gotten sober, started college, and returned home. I have nightmares about things I have seen and things I have done. I struggle everyday to stay sober, to do the right thing. I'm doing a lot of thinking. I live each day in fear of Martin's safety as well as my own. I fear for our future in a society that doesn't understand us. I count down the days until Martin can see the sunlight. I pray every day that this time will be the last time he goes to jail. I pray Martin will trade his gun

Effects — for me, even get an education. I cry every night and try to live every day.

Discussion and Critical Thinking

1. Why did McGraw become associated with Martin and finally become a gang member?
2. Do you suspect there were deeper reasons for her dropping out of mainstream, middle-class society and joining a gang?
3. What were the effects on her life and those who were close to her?
4. What happened before the killing to set the stage for her change?
5. To what extent has she changed?
6. Why doesn't she leave Martin?
7. What is your reaction to the statement "I fear for our future in a society that doesn't understand us"?

Reading-Related Writing

1. In a short piece of writing, discuss the causes or effects of gang membership in relation to the writer of "Everyone Pays the Price."
2. Discuss the possible implications in the quotation in question 7 above.
3. Pretend you are a psychologist at McGraw's college and give her some guidance in a written statement.
4. Write about someone you know who has had similar experiences to Hadley's or Martin's.

Girls Form Backbone of Gangs

Holley Gilbert

When reporting or discussing gang activities, newspapers and the other media are usually concerned with males. Yet we also hear comments that gangs have their own community, their own society. If so, then where are the females? Are there gang "families" in a traditional sense? The following article goes beyond the lurid headlines of violent gang activities to the all-too-frequently lurid reality that has become the everyday life of women in male-controlled gangs.

1 Hundreds of young women and girls have hooked up with the Bloods and Crips in Portland, giving their boyfriends safe haven and sometimes joining them in the violence of gang culture.

Police say the future of gangs may hinge on these young women, who dress their children—especially little boys—in gang colors, teach them hand signs and nurture an allegiance to vendettas.

2 "If we could get the girls to stop associating with the male gang members, we wouldn't have any gangs," Portland policewoman Dorothy Elmore says bluntly.

A few, like Denise, a young black woman who lives in Northeast Portland, take an active role in the gangs. She pulled the trigger in drive-by shootings that she now regrets.

"I was scared," she says. "Me, shooting this gun, my hand sticking out and the police could be hiding anywhere."

3 Like Anne, who grew up with the Crips in the Columbia Villa housing project, some girls in the gang world are white. Like Sal, a former Blood, some are Hispanic.

The real names of the former girl gang members are not being used.

Some, like Denise, say they have left the wild and sometimes dangerous lifestyle they embraced two and three years ago when they became enamored of young men in the gangs. But there are others to take their place.

4 "Girls are the backbone of gangs," says Elmore, who works with the Portland Police Bureau's Gang Enforcement Team.

"Girls give the males a place to lay their heads. Girls shelter them. Girls feed them. They protect them. They nurture them. Girls carry their guns and their dope. They are the key.

"In return, what they get is someone who they can claim as their own. A boyfriend. Someone they can say, 'He's mine.' That's all it is."

5 The price the girls pay for this sense of belonging is high.

Gang rape is sometimes part of a girl's initiation into membership. Other assaults and rapes occur. Pregnancy is a symbol of status for the girls. But in the end, the men are likely to go to jail—or be killed—leaving the girls and their babies alone.

6 There are no programs specifically aimed at keeping girls out of gangs.

"If we'd begun with the girls or put as much focus on the girls as the boys, our gang problem wouldn't be eliminated, but it wouldn't be where we are now," Elmore says.

"We didn't pay attention to the girls because we didn't see them as the shooters. But they were the nucleus.

"We missed the boat on that, and we're still missing the boat."

7 No one can even say accurately how many girls have joined gangs or run with the hundreds of men who are gang members in Portland.

One counselor estimates that, of 250 cases carried by the Multnomah County's gang resource team, as many as 50 are young women. She thinks that's only a small indication of the problem.

"I meet girls all the time that are with the boys on my caseload, girls that are wearing the colors, having the babies," said Lonnie Nettles, a counselor with the Juvenile Court's Gang Resource Intervention Team.

"I know that for every boy that's out there banging, they've got a girl involved with them. So you know the girls are out there."

8 Of 10 gang girls on Nettles' caseload recently, half were in the court system for felonies, such as assault, car theft, drug violations and robbery. Half were there for misdemeanors.

Typically, gang girls in the juvenile court system have a string of minor offenses or delinquent behavior. They may not continue to commit crimes, but often they do not comply with the rules of their probation. Maybe they've skipped school, dropped out of sight or stayed out all night with their boyfriends.

9 By hooking up with gang members, Nettles said, "the girls more often are seeking love and emotional fulfillment."

Sex and children will assure that the girls will be protected and provided for, they believe. They don't see the long-range consequences of a pregnancy.

"In this circle, it's not a negative thing. It's a positive thing," Nettles said. "It's like instant status for these girls. I made a baby. I'm having *his* baby."

10 But the young men may have a handful of girlfriends pregnant at the same time. "Then they go to prison and leave them with a welfare check," Elmore said.

Or they die.

Gang workers said that after Crip leader Arthur Lee Davis Jr. was shot and killed in February, numerous young women claimed he was the father of their child. Who wouldn't be proud to have a baby by such a powerful gang member who gave his life for his colors?

11 Some gang members initiate girls into a set by forcing her to have sex with all the boys and men, said Sal, an 18-year-old former Bloods gang member who didn't want her last name used.

Girls are raped. They are slapped around. And they generally are unfazed by their mistreatment.

"They don't see it that way," Nettles said. "It's so much an expectation, it's like what comes with the territory. They're in love and that's positive."

12 As part of the court's supervision program, all youths work with adults to develop their self-esteem. The girls' program also pays particular attention to women's issues.

In addition, Portland needs homes for girls similar to the House of Umoja, a building on Northeast Albert Street that is being renovated as a group home for gang members and gang-affected boys, said Alberta Phillips, director of Christian Women Against Crime.

"Girls are real frustrating," Elmore said. "Being female and being a black female, I find it frustrating to see so many black females in a predicament where they have no sense of hope, no aspirations. I can see them doing much better."

13 Black women, Elmore said, must take the lead.

"We need to start from the beginning and work up," she said. "And we as black women need to do it and stop relying on men. And we as black women need to do it without relying on other races."

14 The first girl gang member to come through the courts in Portland was convicted last year for piloting a car in an August 1988 drive-by shooting, when she was 17. Loretta S. Rogers was tried as an adult and sentenced to seven years in prison.

Her case was unprecedented.

"That's a real out-of-control behavior for the court to see in a girl," Nettles said. "When you see a real different kind of case that doesn't fit the norm, you feel the person's more a risk to society and needs to come out."

Rogers, now 19, denies she was ever a gang member or was guilty in the shooting.

"I don't really (see) myself as being a gang member, like they say I'm the first gang girl," she said in an interview at the Oregon Women's Correctional Center in Salem. "To me, I think they just blew it out of proportion."

Since then, no young woman has received such a stiff punishment, and the hardest girls essentially can be counted on one or two hands.

15 In late 1988 and early 1989, a group of five girls terrorized the area along Northeast Prescott Street between 12th and 15th avenues, police said. Led by two girls, 15 and 17, the group claimed allegiance to the Bloods and called themselves Bloodettes, as many girls do.

They have been involved in at least two stabbings and one walk-by shooting, police said.

"They were the roughest set of girls I've seen in the system, period," Nettles said.

Now dispersed, the girls were what officials consider the city's closest thing to an all-girl gang.

16 But a gang of girls may be in the making again, this time in the Southeast Asian community.

The young women, ages 14 to 19, were involved in crimes in Southern California and cause trouble "everyplace they go" in the Portland area, said Officer Stew Winn, who tracks Southeast Asian gang activity.

But, again, most of the young women are hanging out with the Asian gangs because their boyfriends are members.

17 Among Skinheads, nearly half of the approximately 300 active in the Portland area are young women, said Loren Christensen, a gang enforcement police officer.

One Skinhead girl was accused last month in Clark County, Wash., of the juvenile equivalent of first-degree murder and robbery in the beating death of a 19-year-old man, another Skinhead.

18 A 16-year-old girl in the Bloods gang is considered more dangerous than many boys held in the county's new 30-day juvenile court assessment program for gang members, said Wil Willhite, who also works on the gang resource team.

And because they have little self-esteem and few positive role models, Nettles says, the problem of girl gangsters will not go away.

"When they're acting out, getting pregnant, sleeping around, prostituting, it's usually they who are the victims," she says.

"Almost any way you can look at it, they are the victims."

Vocabulary Highlights

haven (1)

allegiance (1)

vendettas (1)

enamored (3)

nurture (4)

renovated (12)

unprecedented (14)

dispersed (15)

assessment (18)

self-esteem (18)

Discussion and Critical Thinking

1. Which paragraph in the article first presents the main idea clearly?
2. What are the author's main sources of information?
3. How reliable and convincing are those sources?
4. How many different ethnic groups are involved in the gangs discussed in this article?
5. Is the article essentially optimistic or pessimistic?
6. What possible solutions are offered?
7. Give some examples of facts and opinions the author uses.

Reading-Related Writing

1. Propose a solution to the problem.
2. Discuss how this article comments on the way women are regarded in society.
3. Explain how this article illuminates what you have read about elsewhere, heard about, or experienced.
4. Pretend that you are a counselor or a columnist like "Dear Abby." Offer your advice to some of the young women who are featured in the article.
5. You are a politician running for office and a voter has asked what society should do about youth gangs. Write a speech.
6. You are a social worker. Imagine that you are on the street with some of these gang women. Write an account.

La Vida Loca: Crazy Life, Crazy Death

Carlos A. Chavez and Antonio H. Rodriguez

How can we be hopeful for young men whose lives are marginalized by the fatalistic mentality of barrio warfare? Carlos A. Chavez, director of community and public relations at Occidental College, and Antonio H. Rodriguez, civil rights attorney, search for hope and solutions in the midst of chaos.

1 For the last week we've held vigil over Jaramillo Rodriguez, our 19-year-old nephew. His body lies inert, invaded by tubes and tethered to electronic machines that do the basic biological work that this strapping, 6-foot-4 boy is currently incapable of sustaining. Once a promising athlete, he lies near death, another young victim to the brutal gang warfare plaguing the City of Angels.

2 He and his two "homies" were cut down by gunfire from rival gang members over disputes that are totally baffling even to those familiar with the self-destructive lifestyle called *la vida loca*, the crazy life. It's irrelevant whether the dispute was over control of territory (usually involving short stretches of bleak barrio asphalt), or personal insult (perceived as violating the integrity of an exaggerated sense of pride and honor) or simply the chance encounter by rival members of kamikaze-like youth gangs.

3 What is shocking is the degree to which this formerly romanticized rite-of-passage lifestyle has degenerated into a self-destructive, alienated, fatalistic ideology that holds sway over so many of our children. Spawned by the fraying fabric of barrio life and fueled by popular culture's steady diet of conflict resolution through violence, this view of life as mayhem is causing too many of our intelligent, eager school-age kids to mutate into teen warriors without a cause.

4 During the early part of the Chicano power movement in the late '60s, the *vato loco* (crazy guy) was cast as the embodiment of resistance to sinister cultural aggression. His unconventional clothing, colorful *caló* dialect—a unique blend of Spanish and English—and insolent demeanor made him the definition of "cool" in the barrio. Chicano college student activists adopted the cool look: white T-shirts under plaid Pendleton wool shirts with a military press and sharply creased khakis or jeans.

5 But in those days, most *vatos* became *veteranos* by their 20s and outgrew the crazy life. Some led a dual life, going to school or work during the week and hanging out in the neighborhood on weekends. Guns were a rare commodity and drive-bys were just beginning to be used as a gang tactic. Most *veteranos* made the transition to the work force as semiskilled and skilled laborers and as professionals. While Los Angeles was just as segregated and racist a city as it is now, there were job opportunities and the evidence for believing in the future was found on every Eastside street: Guys working for a living as did their fathers and grandfathers before them.

6 The loss of blue-collar jobs, combined with the curtailment of social spending, has eroded employment and educational opportunities for our children to the point that they are extremely marginalized. In the process, the adolescent lifestyle for many of them appears to have become a life sentence.

7 Barrio life for most gang youths is marked by self-destructive activity often terminated by incarceration or death. Confronted by armed gangsters on one side and police on the other, a homie's life is dictated by a live-for-today attitude in which the goal is to stay alive by warding off attacks and inflicting attacks on rivals without getting arrested. Behind bars, the mayhem and, often, killing continue.

8 These children have no hope. For them, fatalism has replaced faith. At the hospital this week, one of our nephew's friends commented on the tragedy: "It's messed up, hey, but everybody has to go some day. I know it may happen to me. But that's all right. I'll die for my barrio." The young man was no older than 15, but he already presented a chilling and disheartening combination of attitudes: childlike idealism and a reckless disregard for human life.

9 The gang mentality alienates these youths from their families and from the community. Their mind-set has them in a constant battlefield superconsciousness, like soldiers in battle, that numbs them to the sensitivities and the needs of others. When they grieve for their fallen friends, a frequent occurrence, they do so profoundly, intensely, but only for a very brief period—they must remain hypervigilant and combat ready in the low-intensity warfare their lives have become. To relax or drop your guard could mean death.

10 As we wrestle with the pain, the remorse and self-reproach about how we could have done more to prevent the tragedy, the deadly hold that gang life has is haunting us. Our nephew and his friend were hit after they had made a commitment to bail out of the gang-banger life. Our nephew had begun to make arrangements to move out of Southern California. His

friend, also on life support, had gone back to night school to earn a diploma and qualify for the armed forces. He had about one month to go. (The other friend has recovered from his wounds.)

11 Where can we find hope in the future when young men like this see none for themselves? Our family's tragedy is but one of many in this city. And like so many other families, we continue our vigil for a young man on life support, with a hope born in an earlier era.

Vocabulary Highlights

irrelevant (2)
mayhem (3)
mutate (3)
sinister (4)
insolent (4)
demeanor (4)
transition (5)
marginalized (6)
terminated (7)
fatalism (8)
remorse (10)

Discussion and Critical Thinking

1. How do the writers characterize the attitudes of the gang members (par. 3)?
2. What do the authors say are the causes of this self-destructive behavior?
3. What is the difference between the gang members now and the *vatos loco* of the '60s?
4. What social changes affected the outlets for rebellious youth?
5. What is the homie's "live-for-today" attitude?
6. Why do the gang members say they will die for their barrios?
7. Are gang members supported by their communities and families?
8. Do the authors have a solution? Do you?

Reading-Related Writing

1. Using an example or examples, write a piece in which you agree or disagree with Chavez and Rodriguez.
2. Discuss practical solutions to the main problems mentioned by the authors.
3. Write in some detail about the barrio gangsters being in a state of perpetual warfare. How does that mentality affect the way they judge education, family, community, laws, and even church?

Connections

1. Write about the views in *"La Vida Loca"* in relation to the situation of the author in "Everyone Pays the Price."
2. Wite about the views in *"La Vida Loca"* in relation to the situation in "Young Model-Minority Gangster." Which views fit?
3. Write about the validity of the following statement as it applies to *"La Vida Loca":* "If we could get the girls to stop associating with the male gang members, we wouldn't have any gangs."

21

Cross-Cultural Encounters (Comparison and Contrast)

Culture here is used in the broad sense to indicate groups of people with recognizable identities. That means generation, ethnic, gender, sexual preference, physical and mental condition, age, and region. As we meet those who are different from us, we may discover up close the enormous range of differences and at the same time recognize the far greater degree of commonality in human beings. Of course, we can't put an individual into one slot. Each of us, especially in a culturally diverse society, must reflect the experiences we have had and the persons we have met, and, consequently, we come away being parts of many cultural groups. A person could be an older, female, Asian-American, slightly deaf, Southern, heterosexual individual and thereby comprise six different cultures just with those considerations.

The cultural encounters that we are most aware of are those that concern our closest associates—our friends and family. Jennifer Leynes writes of the difficulties and satisfactions of her cultural transformation in "Like a Butterfly." Marie G. Lee discovers the multiple levels of culture when she returns to Korea with her Korean-American father and sees him become Korean again. This experience is the subject of her essay "My Two Dads." Rose Del Castillo Guilbault deals with cultural misunderstandings. She says that the meaning of *macho* "depends on which side of the border you come from."

Ponder Questions

1. How many cultures are you part of?
2. To what extent are you a product of a culturally diverse society?
3. What cultures do people most frequently misunderstand? Why?
4. It has been said that we are almost all hyphenated (ethnically mixed) and, therefore, no one should be classified as a single ethnic culture. Do you agree?
5. If by *culture* we mean "a group of people who have a certain characteristic or characteristics in common that make them significantly different from others," how many cultures can you name?

The title of this chapter, "Cross-Cultural Encounters," suggests the most relevant form of discourse: comparison and contrast.

Comparison and Contrast

Comparison and contrast is a method of showing similarities and dissimilarities between subjects. *Comparison* is concerned with organizing and developing points of similarity; *contrast* has the same function for dissimilarity. In some instances a writing assignment may require that you cover only similarities or only dissimilarities. Occasionally, an instructor may ask you to separate one from the other. Usually, you will combine them within the larger design of your paragraph or essay. For convenience, the term *comparison* is often applied to both comparison and contrast, because both utilize the same techniques and are usually combined into one operation.

This chapter will help you deal with topics and choose strategies in writing comparison and contrast.

Generating Topics and Working with the 4 *Ps*

Comparison and contrast is basic to your thinking. In your daily activities, you consider similarities and dissimilarities between persons, things, concepts, political leaders, doctors, friends, instructors, schools, nations, classes, movies, and so on. You naturally turn to comparison and contrast to solve problems and make decisions in your affairs and in your writing. Because you have had so many comparative experiences, finding a topic to write about is likely to be only a matter of choosing from a great number of appealing ideas. Freewriting, brainstorming, and clustering will help you generate topics that are especially workable and appropriate for particular assignments.

Many college writing assignments will specify a topic or ask you to choose one from a list. Regardless of the source of your topic, the procedure for developing your ideas by comparison and contrast is the same. That procedure can be appropriately called the "4 *Ps*": *purpose, points, pattern,* and *presentation.*

Purpose

Are you trying to show relationships (how things are similar and dissimilar) or to show that one side is better?

Let's say you have been watching the two fathers on television: Bill Cosby as Dr. Cliff Huxtable on "The Cosby Show" and Al Bundy on "Married with Children." Your purpose might be to show relationships, not to show that one is better.

Points

Next you would come up with ideas that you could apply somewhat equally to the two sides. For a short paper you might select two or three. After a bit of listing, you might come up with these points:

family members

attitude toward family

judgment in solving family problems

Pattern

Then you would want to organize the material. There are two basic patterns: subject-by-subject and point-by-point. The **subject-by-subject** presents all of one side and then all of the other, with cross-references.

I. Dr. Cliff Huxtable
   A. Family members
   B. His attitude toward family
   C. His judgment in solving family problems

II. Al Bundy
   A. Family members
   B. His attitude toward family
   C. His judgment in solving family problems

The **point-by-point** shows the points in relation to the sides (subjects) one at a time. This is the more common pattern.

I. Family members
   A. Dr. Cliff Huxtable
      1. Details (For a short paper, you may omit the support in the outline as we have done here.)
      2. Details
   B. Al Bundy
      1.
      2.

II. Attitude toward family
   A. Dr. Cliff Huxtable
      1.
      2.
   B. Al Bundy
      1.
      2.

III. Judgment in solving family problems
   A. Dr. Cliff Huxtable
      1.
      2.
   B. Al Bundy
      1.
      2.

Presentation

Here you use your outline (or other alternative such as a cluster or list) and begin writing your paper. You would use appropriate explanations, details, and examples for support. As with the reading selections in this section of the anthology, this study would be based on cross-cultural matters, in this case, class. The following paragraph shows point-by-point development.

Different Dads

Cliff Huxtable from "The Bill Cosby Show" and Al Bundy from "Married with Children" are both dads, but the similarity ends with that biological fact. Whether the television viewer sees these dads in relation to their family **Topic sentence** members, attitudes toward the family, or judgment in solving family problems, the two dads face each other as **I. Family members** opposites, standing more than channels apart. Each one **A. Cliff** does have a complete family—wife and children. Cliff has a wife who is charming, stylish, loving, and loyal, and **B. Al** his children are lovable, agreeable, and kind. Al Bundy is not so fortunate. His brood are contentious, self-**II. Attitude toward family** centered, and mean-minded. Both dads have an appropriate attitude toward their family. **A. Cliff** Cliff is affectionate to his wife and protective of his family. He believes that he is there to share with his wife and to nurture his children; so he gives quality and quantity time. Al has a **B. Al** different situation (perhaps one he deserves); he must deal with a lazy, self-serving wife, whose idea of loveliness is a gold lamé miniskirt, see-through blouse, and four-inch spike heels—in the kitchen. His sluttish daughter and delinquent son give him a hard time and he **III. Judgment in solving family problems** returns it, if possible. Of course, both dads have family problems to solve. **A. Cliff** Cliff helps his family cleverly with problems big and small. Whether a goldfish has died or the children are torn between values, Dad is there with **B. Al** guidance and jokes. Al is also there when problems arise, but the guidance is nonexistent, and the jokes are mostly on him. The family comes to him mainly for money, and he never has enough. Oddly, both families seem to work, one on the basis of love, the other on the basis of self-interest. In each instance, we viewers (who will be seeing them in reruns forever) can safely say that the family members deserve each other.

Eric Martin

Writer's Checklist

Work with the 4 *P*s:

- **Purpose:** Are you trying to inform (show relationships) or persuade (show that one side is better)?
- **Points:** What ideas will you apply to each side?
- **Pattern:** Will you use subject-by-subject or point-by-point organization?
- **Presentation:** To what extent should you develop your ideas? Be sure to use cross-references to make connections and to use examples and details to support your views.

Topics for Comparison and Contrast

Be as specific as you can when you compare and/or contrast such topics as two automobiles, cultures, social classes, friends, bosses, actors, singers, musicians, comedians, policemen, teachers, doctors, apartments, marriages, movies, commercials, songs, families, parties, dates, habits.

Like a Butterfly

STUDENT PARAGRAPH by Jennifer Leynnes

For several years now, student Jennifer Leynnes has been in the process of becoming, "like a butterfly." An immigrant from the Philippines, she started as someone with potential, then became someone unattractive, and finally became someone who is "pleasing" to herself, a person with "an open mind and an open heart."

Topic sentence Like a butterfly, I have gone through some ugly stages and become something pleasing. Immediately after we arrived to live in America, I was enrolled in elementary **Adjustment** school. It was a time of adjustment. Every day, I appreciated the freedom I felt in America. I could play with whomever I wanted, whenever I wanted. I developed many friendships with Americans, Mexican-Americans, and African-Americans. Soon I was the one helping my parents with their English. As I progressed, so did my attitude. I took advantage of my freedom. I became rebellious. I talked back to my parents, slapped my brother around, and ridiculed whatever my grandmother said. I only wanted things my way. I wanted to go out with my friends and not stay home. Pretty soon, I looked like my friends, talked like them, and even began to think like them. It was then that I became aware of my need to feel and be accepted. I **Rejection** just wanted to blend in. I didn't want to be seen as a foreigner with a really bad accent. In other words, I didn't want to be Filipino anymore. I wanted to be white, sometimes Mexican-American, and other times African-American. I gradually turned away from my own identity. I was very confused. By this time, my parents were having problems with my sister and me. They said we were becoming uncontrollable, and they wished we had never come to the United States. They said we were forgetting what they had taught us. I realized that wanting to be accepted **Self-Recognition** wasn't the problem. The problem was that I was trying to be someone I wasn't. If I could only be myself and be accepted by others at the same time, I would definitely be the happiest person on this earth. Now I can say that growing up in an environment filled with people of different ethnic backgrounds has been a good experience for me. Not only have I learned from different cultures, but I have also learned to be proud of who I am—a Filipino and a Filipino-American. I can learn from others, and, in turn, they can also learn from me. I have developed an open mind and an open heart. I can relate to others and not pretend anymore. I can let me be me. I can unfold my wings and fly.

Discussion and Critical Thinking

1. Leynnes's experiences are those of an immigrant, and her struggle for identity involves ethnic considerations. Do other young people who are not immigrants face a similar struggle? Discuss.
2. Could she have become the strong person she is now without having gone through these stages of adjustment and rejection?
3. What is her final position of which she is proud?

Reading-Related Writing

1. Write about your own quest for self-identity as you struggled with the pressures brought by peers, parents, or tradition.
2. Compare your own identity (including the search for it, if you like) with that of someone who has a similar background.
3. Compare your own identity (including the search for it, if you like) with that of someone who has a different background or is of a different generation.

My Two Dads

Marie G. Lee

A first-generation Korean American, Marie G. Lee is the author of two novels and the winner of the 1993 Friends of American Writers Award. Here she writes about a trip she took to Korea with her father, a person she thought she knew well, but within his native culture she witnessed another father emerge.

1 I am a first-generation Korean-American. On my first trip to Korea at age twenty-six, I found that I had two fathers. One was the Dad I'd always known, but the second was a Korean father I'd never seen before—one surprising and familiar at the same time, like my homeland.

2 I was born and raised in the Midwest, and to me, my Dad was like anyone else's. He taught my brothers to play baseball, fixed the garage door, and pushed the snowblower on chilly February mornings. If there was anything different about him, to my child's eyes, it was that he was a doctor.

3 Growing up, my siblings and I rarely came into contact with our Korean heritage. Mom and Dad spoke Korean only when they didn't want us to know what they were saying. We didn't observe Korean customs, except for not wearing shoes in the house, which I always assumed was plain common sense. I'd once seen a photograph of Dad in a traditional Korean costume, and I remember thinking how odd those clothes made him look.

4 With my parents' tacit encouragement, I "forgot" that I was Korean. I loved pizza and macaroni and cheese, but I had never so much as touched a slice of kimchi.[1] All my friends, including my boyfriend, were Caucasian. And while I could explain in detail everything I thought was wrong with Ronald Reagan's policies, I had to strain to remember the name of Korea's president.

5 Attempting to learn the Korean language, *bangukmal,* a few years ago was a first step in atoning for my past indifference. I went into it feeling smug because of my fluency in French and German, but learning Korean knocked me for a loop. This was a language shaped by Confucian rules of reverence, where the speaker states her position (humble, equal, superior) in relation to the person she is addressing. Simultaneously humbling myself and revering the person with whom I was speaking seemed like a painful game of verbal Twister. To further complicate the process, I found there are myriad titles of reverence, starting with the highest, *sansengnim,* which loosely means "teacher/doctor," down to the ultra-specific, such as *waysukmo,* "wife of mother's brother."

6 Armed, then, with a year's worth of extension-school classes, a list of polite phrases and titles, and a Berlitz tape in my Walkman, I was as ready as I'd ever be to travel with my family to Korea last year.

7 When we arrived at Kimpo Airport in Seoul, smiling relatives funneled us into the customs line for *wayguksalam,* "foreigners." I was almost jealous watching our Korean flight attendants breeze through the line for *banguksalam,* "Korean nationals." With whom did I identify more—the flight attendants or the retired white couple behind us, with their Bermuda shorts and Midwestern accents? My American passport stamped me as an alien in a land where everyone looked like me.

8 I got my first glimpse of my second father when we began trying to hail cabs in downtown Seoul. Because the government enforces low taxi fares, the drivers have developed their own system of picking up only individual passengers, then packing more in, to increase the per-trip profit. The streets are clogged not only with traffic but also with desperately gesticulating pedestrians and empty taxis.

9 Even my mother was stymied by the cab-hailing competition. When Mom and I traveled alone, cabs zoomed blithely past us. When we finally got one, the driver would shut off his meter, brazenly charge us triple the usual fare and ignominiously dump us somewhere not very close to our destination.

10 But traveling with Dad was different. He would somehow stop a taxi with ease, chitchat with the driver (using very polite language), then shovel us all in. Not only would the cabbie take us where we wanted to go, but some of the usually-taciturn drivers would turn into garrulous philosophers.

[1]*Kimchi:* a food made from fermented cabbage.

11 I began to perceive the transformation of my father from American dad to functioning urban Korean. When we met with relatives, I noticed how Dad's conversational Korean moved easily between the respect he gave his older sister to the joviality with which he addressed Mom's younger cousin. My brother Len and I and our Korean cousins, however, stared shyly and mutely at each other.

12 Keeping company with relatives eased my disorientation, but not my alienation. Korea is the world's most racially and culturally homogeneous country, and although I was of the right race, I felt culturally shut out. It seemed to me that Koreans were pushy, even in church. When they ate, they slurped and inhaled their food so violently that at least once during every meal, someone would have a sputtering fit of coughing.

13 Watching my father "turn Korean" helped me as I tried to embrace the culture. Drinking *soju*[2] in a restaurant in the somewhat seedy Namdaemun area, he suddenly lit into a story of the time when Communists from North Korea confiscated his parents' assets. Subsequently, he became a medical student in Seoul, where each day he ate a sparse breakfast at his sister's house, trekked across towering Namsan Mountain (visible from our room in the Hilton), and studied at Seoul National University until night, when he would grab a few hours of sleep in the borrowed bed of a friend who worked the night shift.

14 I have always lived in nice houses, gone on trips, and never lacked for pizza money. But as my father talked, I could almost taste the millet-and-water gruel he subsisted on while hiding for months in cellars during the North Korean invasion of Seoul. Suddenly, I was able to feel the pain of the Korean people, enduring one hardship after another: Japanese colonial rule, North Korean aggression, and dependence on American military force. For a brief moment, I discerned the origins of the noble, sometimes harsh, Korean character. Those wizened women who pushed past me at church were there only because they had fought their way to old age. The noises people made while eating began to sound more celebratory than rude.

15 And there were other things I saw and was proud of. When we visited a cemetery, I noticed that the headstones were small and unadorned, except for a few with small, pagoda-shaped "hats" on them. The hats *(cbinsa),* Dad told me, were from a time when the country's leaders awarded "national Ph.D.'s," the highest civilian honor.

16 "Your great-grandfather has one of those on his grave," Dad mentioned casually. I began to admire a people who place such a high value on hard work and scholarship. Even television commercials generally don't promote leisure pursuits, such as vacations or Nintendo, but instead proclaim the merits of "super duper vitamin pills" to help you study longer and work harder.

17 After two weeks, as we prepared to return to the U.S., I still in many ways felt like a stranger in Korea. While I looked the part of a native, my textbook Korean was robotic, and the phrases I was taught—such as, "Don't take me for a five-won plane ride"—were apparently very dated. I tried to tell my Korean cousins an amusing anecdote: in the Lotte department store in Seoul, I asked for directions to the restroom and was directed instead to the

[2]*Soju:* a traditional potato vodka popular in Korea.

stereo section. But the story, related once in English and once in halting Korean, became hopelessly lost in the translation.

18 Dad decided he would spend an extra week in Korea, savoring a culture I would never fully know, even if I took every Berlitz course I could afford. When I said good-bye to him, I saw my Korean father; but I knew that come February, my American dad would be back out in our driveway, stirring up a froth of snow with his big yellow snowblower.

Vocabulary Highlights

reverence (5)
simultaneously (5)
myriad (5)
gesticulating (8)
stymied (9)
brazenly (9)
ignominiously (9)
taciturn (10)
homogeneous (12)
wizened (14)

Discussion and Critical Thinking

1. Does Lee seem to regret that she was never taught the Korean language and taught to be Korean?
2. What is her first glimpse of her father as a Korean?
3. How was he transformed when he was around his Korean relatives?
4. Why do his stories about growing up take on a special meaning to Marie?
5. What does she get to know about her father and Korean culture?
6. What did she learn?

Reading-Related Writing

1. Write a comparison and contrast involving an experience when you or a person you know has returned to an area and reclaimed a culture left behind, but not far behind. This culture need not be a foreign one. It can be regional, rural, urban, or class. For points of comparison you might select from these: language, behavior, manners, appearance.

Americanization Is Tough on "Macho"

Rose del Castillo Guilbault

What does *macho* mean to you? If someone calls you or a person you respect "macho," are you pleased or offended? Or are you perhaps unsure and listen on, reserving judgment and trying to determine what the speaker means. The fact is that *macho* has two distinctly different meanings. This essay gives one Hispanic perspective on the different definitions.

1 What is *macho*? That depends which side of the border you come from.

2 Although it's not unusual for words and expressions to lose their subtlety in translation, the negative connotations of *macho* in this country are troublesome to Hispanics.

3 Take the newspaper descriptions of alleged mass murderer Ramon Salcido. That an insensitive, insanely jealous, hard-drinking, violent Latin male is referred to as *macho* makes Hispanics cringe.

4 *"Es muy macho,"* the women in my family nod approvingly, describing a man they respect. But in the United States, when women say, "He's so macho," it's with disdain.

5 The Hispanic *macho* is manly, responsible, hardworking, a man in charge, a patriarch. A man who expresses strength through silence. What the Yiddish language would call a *mensch.*

6 The American *macho* is a chauvinist, a brute, uncouth, selfish, loud, abrasive, capable of inflicting pain, and sexually promiscuous.

7 Quintessential *macho* models in this country are Sylvester Stallone, Arnold Schwarzenegger and Charles Bronson. In their movies, they exude toughness, independence, masculinity. But a closer look reveals their machismo is really violence masquerading as courage, sullenness disguised as silence and irresponsibility camouflaged as independence.

8 If the Hispanic ideal of *macho* were translated to American screen roles, they might be Jimmy Stewart, Sean Connery and Laurence Olivier.

9 In Spanish, *macho* ennobles Latin males. In English it devalues them. This pattern seems consistent with the conflicts ethnic minority males experience in this country. Typically the cultural traits other societies value don't translate as desirable characteristics in America.

10 I watched my own father struggle with these cultural ambiguities. He worked on a farm for twenty years. He laid down miles of irrigation pipe, carefully plowed long, neat rows in fields, hacked away at recalcitrant weeds and drove tractors through whirlpools of dust. He stoically worked twenty-four-hour days during harvest season, accepting the long hours as part of agricultural work. When the boss complained or upbraided him for minor mistakes, he kept quiet, even when it was obvious the boss had erred.

11 He handled the most menial tasks with pride. At home he was a good provider, helped out my mother's family in Mexico without complaint, and was indulgent with me. Arguments between my mother and him generally had to do with money, or with his stubborn reluctance to share his troubles. He tried to work them out in his own silence. He didn't want to trouble my mother—a course that backfired, because the imagined is always worse than the reality.

12 Americans regarded my father as decidedly un-*macho.* His character was interpreted as nonassertive, his loyalty, non-ambition, and his quietness, ignorance. I once overheard the boss's son blame him for plowing crooked rows in a field. My father merely smiled at the lie, knowing the boy had done it, but didn't refute it, confident his good work was well known. But the boss instead ridiculed him for being "stupid" and letting a kid get away with a lie. Seeing my embarrassment, my father dismissed the incident, saying "They're the dumb ones. Imagine, me fighting with a kid."

13 I tried not to look at him with American eyes because sometimes the reflection hurt.

14 Listening to my aunts' clucks of approval, my vision focused on the qualities America overlooked. "He's such a hard worker. So serious, so responsible." My aunts would secretly compliment my mother. The unspoken comparison was that he was not like some of their husbands, who drank and womanized. My uncles represented the darker side of *macho*.

15 In a patriarchal society, few challenge their roles. If men drink, it's because it's the manly thing to do. If they gamble, it's because it's how men relax. And if they fool around, well, it's because a man simply can't hold back so much man! My aunts didn't exactly meekly sit back. But they put up with these transgressions because Mexican society dictated this was their lot in life.

16 In the United States, I believe it was the feminist movement of the early '70s that changed *macho*'s meaning. Perhaps my generation of Latin women was in part responsible. I recall Chicanas complaining about the chauvinistic nature of Latin men and the notion they wanted their women barefoot, pregnant and in the kitchen. The generalization that Latin men embodied chauvinistic traits led to this interesting twist of semantics. Suddenly a word that represented something positive in one culture became a negative prototype in another.

17 The problem with the use of *macho* today is that it's become an accepted stereotype of the Latin male. And like all stereotypes, it distorts truth.

18 The impact of language in our society is undeniable. And the misuse of *macho* hints at a deeper cultural misunderstanding that extends beyond mere word definitions.

Vocabulary Highlights

subtlety (2)

connotations (2)

allayed (3)

quintessential (7)

ambiguities (10)

recalcitrant (10)

stoically (10)

upbraided (10)

transgressions (15)

embodied (16)

Discussion and Critical Thinking

1. What is Hispanic *macho*?
2. What is American *macho*?
3. What other examples of the different definitions of *macho* can you provide?
4. The author's father worked "stoically." What does the word *stoical* imply about how a person looks at life with its many problems?
5. How does the author relate the word *macho* to the feminist movement?
6. Would the word *patriarch* be regarded differently by people with different cultural and/or political views?

7. What makes the author's view valuable?
8. To what kind of audience is this piece directed?

Reading-Related Writing

1. Write a paragraph defining *macho,* by explaining what is and what is not macho. Consider beginning with the author's definition. Use examples.
2. Discuss two people who have different definitions of *macho,* explaining not only the different definitions but also the different backgrounds and experiences of the people who offer the definitions.
3. The author says that the difference of attitudes toward *macho* depends on "which side of the border you come from." Others argue that the "darker side" the author mentions causes severe problems on both sides of the border, the darker side being behavior held by certain males, not necessarily just the Hispanic. Write on the "darker side" versus the other side (1) by comparing two individuals you are familiar with or (2) by comparing the reality (darker side, the way the person's spouse and family would know the person) and the reputation (the other side, the way most people would know the person).

Connections

1. Compare and contrast what Jennifer Leynnes and Marie G. Lee learned about themselves and their cultures. You might want to concentrate on these points: what they learned, how they learned, and how they were changed.
2. Referring extensively to the essays "My Two Dads" and "Americanization Is Tough on 'Macho,'" discuss how one can best understand cultures tied significantly to other countries by examining the values, history, and basic experiences of those cultures.

22

Walking in Different Shoes (Persuasion)

Are there those who do not understand you? And is the problem that those who do not understand simply have not looked at the world from your perspective? Have they not, to use a common expression, "walked in [your] shoes"? That term applies especially to a culturally diverse society. We cannot, of course, view the world from anyone else's perspective, but we can consider what others say about their perspectives. In doing so, we naturally can become more informed, more tolerant, and more considerate. We can also become stronger as we read, listen, and respond, because our visions are expanded as we borrow and adopt ideas, modify our ideas, and offer our own ideas to others.

In this chapter, Michael Holguin gives a personal view of poverty, Lewis Sawaquat explains what it is like being a Native American as he writes a letter to his infant daughter, and Harold Krents tells of being blind.

It will be an instructive and interesting exercise for you to pretend you are the writer of what you read. Try to walk in others' shoes. The shoes will not fit perfectly. They may bind, pinch, irritate, or even blister. But most of us will agree that the journey is more pleasant if we recognize that all must walk the same road, and that all shoes (and all feet) are more similar than they are different.

Ponder Questions

1. What persons do not understand you? Why?
2. What persons do you not understand?
3. What does the expression *walk in my shoes* mean to you?

The author of each of the three selections in this chapter implies, "You would understand me if you could walk in my shoes." **The selections, therefore, are expressions of persuasion, a type of discourse that ranges from the informal persuasive appeal to the tightly structured argument.**

Persuasion and Argument

When you persuade and/or argue, you take a position advocating an action or belief and explain why your position is valid. You may offer advice that no reasonable person would oppose. For example, you might say that everyone who doesn't have a severe disability or special condition should eat a wholesome diet. Reasonable people would certainly agree. In that instance the approach would be one of *persuasion.* But when you take a position on a topic such as abortion, on which reasonable people disagree, then the approach is one of *argument.* All argument is persuasion because you are trying to convince someone, but not all persuasion is argument.

The most common pattern for writing a paper of persuasion or argument is quite direct. The reasons follow the thesis, called the *proposition.* Think of the organization of a simple presentation this way: your proposition is valid because of this reason, because of this reason, and because of this reason. Imagine that each Roman-numeral part of your outline or cluster begins with the word *because.* In a longer piece of argumentative writing, you might want to include a statement of *refutation.* The refutation examines the other side's arguments and points out their incorrectness. This statement should be tactful and brief; do not attempt to give equal treatment.

Proposition: The blood/alcohol count for drunken driving should be lowered to .04.

I. (Because) Driving is a privilege, not a right

II. (Because of) The number of fatalities involving drunk drivers

III. (Because of) The cost to taxpayers and society generally

The supporting evidence can be authoritative statements, statistical information, reasoning, and examples. See "Critical Thinking," in the Appendix, p. A-24, for a discussion of facts and opinions and basic logic.

The persuasive paragraph or essay is often structured much less carefully than the formal argument. It might be an essay of any form intended to influence opinion. The reading selections in this chapter are all informal.

Writer's Checklist

In a formal argument or other persuasive statement, use this pattern:

Background (discussion of the issue, reason for concern, necessary definitions)

Proposition (a thesis or topic sentence that indicates your position on an issue)

Refutation (brief comments on the other side, indicating its fundamental weakness—optional in short papers)

Support (evidence consisting of facts, examples, statistics, opinions of authorities, and reasoning)

In an informal argument, these parts (with refutation optional) will be included, but the structure may be less precise. You will still need to state your view and support it with evidence.

Topics for Persuasion and Argument

The following are broad subject areas; you will have to limit the focus for your writing assignment: birth control, teenage marriages, teenage parenthood, child rearing, education, advertising of tobacco and alcohol products, legalization of drugs, pornography, prayer in public schools, racism, affirmative action, surrogate mothers, welfare/workfare, AIDS, gun control, abortion, child support, speed limits, minimum wage, sports and drugs, censorship, capital punishment, foreign trade, dieting, exercise, personal responsibility, dress code, pride, discrimination.

Being Poor

STUDENT PARAGRAPH by Michael Holguin

Student Michael Holguin says there is more to being poor than being without money. Being poor affects every aspect of one's life—home, neighborhood, school. This paragraph was written in response to a reading of Jo Goodwin Parker's provocative essay "What Is Poverty?"

Topic sentence <u>What is being poor? I'll tell you what being poor is</u>. Being poor is going to school in the same clothes your four older brothers wore before you. Being poor is wearing socks that were sewn back together in six different places. **Clothes** It's carrying pitchers to the homes of neighbors to fill with water because the water's been shut off . . . again. **Water** It's gathering towels so you and your brothers can go shower at a friend's house. It's being happy when you have both rice and beans for dinner. **Food** It's enjoying the Sunday dinner of tomato soup. It's shamefully asking for something to eat at your friend's house because you know there will be little to eat at home. Being poor is your oldest brother stealing vegetables from a neighbor's garden. It's climbing in garbage bins behind grocery stores, looking for discarded food. Being poor is hearing your mother call local churches to ask for help to feed her children. It's hearing your mother cry late at night because she doesn't know what she'll do for breakfast the next morning. **School** It's the embarrassment of your teacher asking, "What did you get for Christmas?" It's being the only one in your class who didn't know who Speed Racer is, or have anything to show and tell about, for that matter. It's your mother washing and erasing the filth from discarded school text books so they look new on Christmas morning. **Transportation** It's your mother walking five miles to visit you in the hospital and five miles home because she doesn't have a car or even the price of a bus ticket. Those are only a few details about being poor.

Discussion and Critical Thinking

1. What kind of support does Holguin use?
2. What is unusual about Holguin's sentences?
3. What is his main point?

Reading-Related Writing

1. Using a subject other than being poor, write your own definition. Consider using Holguin's pattern of development by examples and repetition of sentence structure. Suggestions for topics: being depressed, addicted, dyslexic, anorexic, sightless, deaf, mute, physically handicapped.

For My Indian Daughter

Lewis Sawaquat

This author writes of two discoveries: the meaning of being an Indian and the extent of society's prejudice against Indians. These discoveries, with comments on how he made them, are written with his daughter in mind, because she will one day face much of what he has faced.

1 My little girl is singing herself to sleep upstairs, her voice mingling with the sounds of the birds outside in the old maple trees. She is two and I am nearly 50, and I am very taken with her. She came along late in my life, unexpected and unbidden, a startling gift.

2 Today at the beach my chubby-legged, brown-skinned daughter ran laughing into the water as fast as she could. My wife and I laughed watching her, until we heard behind us a low guttural curse and then an unpleasant voice raised in an imitation war whoop.

3 I turned to see a fat man in a bathing suit, white and soft as a grub, as he covered his mouth and prepared to make the Indian war cry again. He was middle-aged, younger than I, and had three little children lined up next to him, grinning foolishly. My wife suggested we leave the beach, and I agreed.

4 I knew the man was not unusual in his feelings against Indians. His beach behavior might have been socially unacceptable to more civilized whites, but his basic view of Indians is expressed daily in our small town, frequently on the editorial pages of the county newspaper, as white people speak out against Indian fishing rights and land rights, saying in essence, "Those Indians are taking our fish, our land." It doesn't matter to them that we were here first, that the U.S. Supreme Court has ruled in our favor. It matters to them that we have something they want, and they hate us for it. Backlash is the common explanation of the attacks on Indians, the bumper stickers that say, "Spear an Indian, Save a Fish," but I know better. The hatred of Indians goes back to the beginning when white people came to this country. For me it goes back to my childhood in Harbor Springs, Mich.

5 **Theft:** Harbor Springs is now a summer resort for the very affluent, but a hundred years ago it was the Indian village of my Ottawa ancestors. My grandmother, Anna Showanessy, and other Indians like her, had their land there taken by treaty, by fraud, by violence, by theft. They remembered how whites had burned down the village at Burt Lake in 1900 and pushed the Indians out. These were the stories in my family.

6 When I was a boy my mother told me to walk down the alleys in Harbor Springs and not to wear my orange football sweater out of the house. This way I would not stand out, not be noticed, and not be a target.

7 I wore my orange sweater anyway and deliberately avoided the alleys. I was the biggest person I knew and wasn't really afraid. But I met my comeuppance when I enlisted in the U.S. Army. One night all the men in my bar-

racks gathered together and, gang-fashion, pulled me into the shower and scrubbed me down with rough brushes used for floors, saying "We won't have any dirty Indians in our outfit." It is a point of irony that I was cleaner than any of them. Later in Korea I learned how to kill, how to bully, how to hate Koreans. I came out of the war tougher than ever and, strangely, white.

8 I went to college, got married, lived in La Porte, Ind., worked as a surveyor and raised three boys. I headed Boy Scout groups, never thinking it odd when the Scouts did imitation Indian dances, imitation Indian lore.

9 One day when I was 35 or thereabouts I heard about an Indian powwow. My father used to attend them and so with great curiosity and a strange joy at discovering a part of my heritage, I decided the thing to do to get ready for this big event was to have my friend make me a spear in his forge. The steel was fine and blue and iridescent. The feathers on the shaft were bright and proud.

10 In a dusty state fairground in southern Indiana, I found white people dressed as Indians. I learned they were "hobbyists," that is, it was their hobby and leisure pastime to masquerade as Indians on weekends. I felt ridiculous with my spear, and I left.

11 It was years before I could tell anyone of the embarrassment of this weekend and see any humor in it. But in a way it was that weekend, for all its silliness, that was my awakening. I realized I didn't know who I was. I didn't have an Indian name. I didn't speak the Indian language. I didn't know the Indian customs. Dimly I remembered the Ottawa word for dog, but it was a baby word, *kahgee,* not the full word, *muhkahgee,* which I was later to learn. Even more hazily I remembered a naming ceremony (my own). I remembered legs dancing around me, dust. Where had that been? Who had I been? "Suwaukquat," my mother told me when I asked, "where the tree begins to grow."

12 That was 1968, and I was not the only Indian in the country who was feeling the need to remember who he or she was. There were others. They had powwows, real ones, and eventually I found them. Together we researched our past, a search that for me culminated in the Longest Walk, a march on Washington in 1978. Maybe because I now know what it means to be Indian, it surprises me that others don't. Of course there aren't very many of us left. The chances of an average person knowing an average Indian in an average lifetime are pretty slim.

13 **Circle:** Still, I was amused one day when my small, four-year-old neighbor looked at me as I was hoeing in my garden and said, "You aren't a real Indian, are you?" Scotty is little, talkative, likable. Finally I said, "I'm a real Indian." He looked at me for a moment and then said, squinting into the sun, "Then where's your horse and feathers?" The child was simply a smaller, whiter version of my own ignorant self years before. We'd both seen too much TV, that's all. He was not to be blamed. And so, in a way, the moronic man on the beach today is blameless. We come full circle to realize other people are like ourselves, as discomfiting as that may be sometimes.

14 As I sit in my old chair on my porch, in a light that is fading so the leaves are barely distinguishable against the sky, I can picture my girl asleep upstairs. I would like to prepare her for what's to come, take her each step of the way saying, there's a place to avoid, here's what I know about this, but much of what's before her she must go through alone. She must pass through pain and joy and solitude and community to discover her own inner self that is unlike any other and come through that passage to the place where she sees all people are one, and in so seeing may live her life in a brighter future.

Vocabulary Highlights

essence (4)

lore (8)

iridescent (9)

culminated (12)

moronic (13)

discomfiting (13)

Discussion and Critical Thinking

1. Sawaquat gives several examples of prejudice from personal experience. Which one made the deepest impression on him?
2. He says that he now knows what it is to be an Indian, but he does not explain. In your opinion, what *does* it mean?
3. Sawaquat says he came out of the Korean War "strangely, white" (par. 7). What does he mean?
4. How can he forgive the "moronic man on the beach"?
5. According to the author, how much can he help his daughter grow up and what must she do and learn herself?

Reading-Related Writing

1. This piece was written in 1983 when the author's daughter was two years old. Pretend that you are his daughter now, and respond to some of his concerns. What have you already learned and what parts of this piece do you especially appreciate?
2. Reflect on what the author has said and use your imagination to assume the point of view of Lewis Sawaquat. In one paragraph, attempt to explain what it means to be an Indian.
3. He writes, "We came full circle to realize other people are like ourselves, as discomfiting as that may be sometimes" (par. 13). Have you too had that experience? For example, after having matured in some important way (perhaps in developing a sensitivity to discrimination against a particular race, women, an age group, or the handicapped), have you observed that at one time you were as insensitive as some still are? Write a paragraph about that experience.
4. Assume the person of the author and expand paragraph 10 from three sentences to about ten to fifteen. Give descriptive details. Refer to page 282 if you need some instructions on writing a descriptive paragraph.
5. Write a short journal-entry letter to a child (your own, one you know, or an imaginary one) in which you relate some of your own learning experiences.

Darkness at Noon

Harold Krents

Blind from birth, Harold Krents graduated from Harvard College and became a lawyer. He was the subject of Leonard Gershe's play and film *Butterflies Are Free.* Until his death in 1986, he worked to promote the employment of handicapped people.

1 Blind from birth, I have never had the opportunity to see myself and have been completely dependent on the image I create in the eye of the observer. To date it has not been narcissistic.

2 There are those who assume that since I can't see, I obviously also cannot hear. Very often people will converse with me at the top of their lungs, enunciating each word very carefully. Conversely, people will also often whisper, assuming that since my eyes don't work, my ears don't either.

3 For example, when I go to the airport and ask the ticket agent for assistance to the plane, he or she will invariably pick up the phone, call a ground hostess and whisper: "Hi, Jane, we've got a 76 here." I have concluded that the word "blind" is not used for one of two reasons: Either they fear that if the dread word is spoken, the ticket agent's retina will immediately detach, or they are reluctant to inform me of my condition of which I may not have been previously aware.

4 On the other hand, others know that of course I can hear, but believe that I can't talk. Often, therefore, when my wife and I go out to dinner, a waiter or waitress will ask Kit if "*he* would like a drink" to which I respond that "indeed *he* would."

5 This point was graphically driven home to me while we were in England. I had been given a year's leave of absence from my Washington law firm to study for a diploma in law degree at Oxford University. During the year I became ill and was hospitalized. Immediately after admission, I was wheeled down to the X-ray room. Just at the door sat an elderly woman—elderly I would judge from the sound of her voice. "What is his name?" the woman asked the orderly who had been wheeling me.

6 "What's your name?" the orderly repeated to me.

7 "Harold Krents," I replied.

8 "Harold Krents," he repeated.

9 "When was he born?"

10 "When were you born?"

11 "November 5, 1944," I responded.

12 "November 5, 1944," the orderly intoned.

13 This procedure continued for approximately five minutes at which point even my saint-like disposition deserted me. "Look," I finally blurted out, "this is absolutely ridiculous. Okay, granted I can't see, but it's got to have become pretty clear to both of you that I don't need an interpreter."

14 "He says he doesn't need an interpreter," the orderly reported to the woman.

15 The toughest misconception of all is the view that because I can't see, I can't work. I was turned down by over forty law firms because of my blindness, even though my qualifications included a cum laude degree from Harvard College and a good ranking in my Harvard Law School class.

16 The attempt to find employment, the continuous frustration of being told that it was impossible for a blind person to practice law, the rejection letters, not based on my lack of ability but rather on my disability, will always remain one of the most disillusioning experiences of my life.

17 Fortunately, this view of limitation and exclusion is beginning to change. On April 16, the Department of Labor issued regulations that mandate equal-employment opportunities for the handicapped. By and large, the business community's response to offering employment to the disabled has been enthusiastic.

18 I therefore look forward to the day, with the expectation that it is certain to come, when employers will view their handicapped workers as a little child did me years ago when my family still lived in Scarsdale.

19 I was playing basketball with my father in our backyard according to procedures we had developed. My father would stand beneath the hoop, shout, and I would shoot over his head at the basket attached to our garage. Our next-door neighbor, aged five, wandered over into our yard with a playmate. "He's blind," our neighbor whispered to her friend in a voice that could be heard distinctly by Dad and me. Dad shot and missed; I did the same. Dad hit the rim: I missed entirely: Dad shot and missed the garage entirely. "Which one is blind?" whispered back the little friend.

20 I would hope that in the near future when a plant manager is touring the factory with the foreman and comes upon a handicapped and nonhandicapped person working together, his comment after watching them work will be, "Which one is disabled?"

Vocabulary Highlights

narcissistic (1)

conversely (2)

retina (3)

cum laude (15)

disillusioning (16)

mandate (17)

Discussion and Critical Thinking

1. Since Krents was blind, people knew that he could not see. What else did some assume?
2. How did misconceptions affect his job opportunities?
3. To what extent did he feel handicapped?
4. What is the purpose of this persuasive article? What does he use for support?
5. Do you think federal laws have corrected most of the employment problems for the handicapped?

Reading-Related Writing

1. Write about a handicapped person other than someone who is blind. How is that person misunderstood and discriminated against? Include some short narrative examples.
2. Write about a time when, because of appearance, ethnicity, or age, you were not understood or treated fairly.

Connections

1. Discuss the similarities among all the persuasive writers in this chapter. The topics are sight handicap, poverty, and racial discrimination. Just what do all these writers have in common in the way they are treated? If you had to state the solution or the beginning of the solution in one word, what word would it be? Then how would you proceed from that word?
2. Compare any two pieces for similarities and dissimilarities of problem and solution.

23

Mixed Bag

These readings represent a variety of perceptions, experiences, and tastes. With each reading incorporating several forms, they are intended to stimulate thought, serve as models, and be subjects for analysis and comparative studies.

American Space, Chinese Place

Yi-Fu Tuan

What can you learn about people by studying the design of their homes? According to Yi-Fu Tuan, you can learn a great deal.

1 Americans have a sense of space, not of place. Go to an American home in exurbia, and almost the first thing you do is drift toward the picture window. How curious that the first compliment you pay your host inside his house is to say how lovely it is outside his house! He is pleased that you should admire his vistas. The distant horizon is not merely a line separating earth from sky, it is a symbol of the future. The American is not rooted in his place, however lovely: his eyes are drawn by the expanding space to a point on the horizon, which is his future.

2 By contrast, consider the traditional Chinese home. Blank walls enclose it. Step behind the spirit wall and you are in a courtyard with perhaps a miniature garden around the corner. Once inside the private compound you are wrapped in an ambiance of calm beauty, an ordered world of buildings, pavement, rock, and decorative vegetation. But you have no distant

view: nowhere does space open out before you. Raw nature in such a home is experienced only as weather, and the only open space is the sky above. The Chinese is rooted in his place. When he has to leave, it is not for the promised land on the terrestrial horizon, but for another world altogether along the vertical, religious axis of his imagination.

3 The Chinese tie to place is deeply felt. Wanderlust is an alien sentiment. The Taoist classic *Tao Te Ching* captures the ideal of rootedness in place with these words: "Though there may be another country in the neighborhood so close that they are within sight of each other and the crowing of cocks and barking of dogs in one place can be heard in the other, yet there is no traffic between them; and throughout their lives the two peoples have nothing to do with each other." In theory if not in practice, farmers have ranked high in Chinese society. The reason is not only that they are engaged in the "root" industry of producing food but that, unlike pecuniary merchants, they are tied to the land and do not abandon their country when it is in danger.

4 Nostalgia is a recurrent theme in Chinese poetry. An American reader of translated Chinese poems may well be taken aback—even put off—by the frequency, as well as the sentimentality of the lament for home. To understand the strength of this sentiment, we need to know that the Chinese desire for stability and rootedness in place is prompted by the constant threat of war, exile, and the natural disasters of flood and drought. Forcible removal makes the Chinese keenly aware of their loss. By contrast, Americans move, for the most part, voluntarily. Their nostalgia for home town is really longing for childhood to which they cannot return: in the meantime the future beckons and the future is "out there," in open space. When we criticize American rootlessness we tend to forget that it is a result of ideals we admire, namely, social mobility and optimism about the future. When we admire Chinese rootedness, we forget the word "place" means both location in space and position in society: to be tied to place is also to be bound to one's station in life, with little hope of betterment. Space symbolizes hope; place, achievement and stability.

Vocabulary Highlights

exurbia (1)

vistas (1)

ambiance (2)

terrestrial (2)

axis (2)

Taoist (3)

wanderlust (3)

pecuniary (3)

nostalgia (4)

lament (4)

social mobility (4)

symbolizes (4)

Discussion and Critical Thinking

1. According to the author, if you visit a traditional American home, what will your host invite you to enjoy? Why?
2. On the contrary, if you visit a Chinese home, what will your host invite you to enjoy? Why?
3. Why do the Chinese admire their farmers?
4. In the same vein, what station in life do Americans admire?
5. What are the different views, good and bad, held by Chinese and Americans on moving?
6. What do you see that is positive and negative in both the American and Chinese views?

Reading-Related Writing

1. Write a paragraph about your own (or your idealized) home, room, or apartment. In what ways does it reflect your philosophy of life?
2. The author writes about exurbia (suburbia, outside the city) and traditional homes. In one paragraph discuss how well his ideas can be applied to urban living, perhaps to apartment buildings, condos, and projects.
3. Write a paragraph about the diversity of views regarding housing as held by several people of a single ethnic group. Consider your family members, friends, and relatives.

Rambos of the Road

Martin Gottfried

Martin Gottfried is concerned about what happens to us—all of us—when we get behind the steering wheel of a car. We are transformed. What emerges is often something ugly and something mean. We become "Rambos of the Road."

1 The car pulled up and its driver glared at us with such sullen intensity, such hatred, that I was truly afraid for our lives. Except for the Mohawk haircut he didn't have, he looked like Robert DeNiro in "Taxi Driver," the sort of young man who, delirious for notoriety, might kill a president.

2 He was glaring because we had passed him and for that affront he pursued us to the next stoplight so as to express his indignation and affirm his

masculinity. I was with two women and, believe it, was afraid for all three of us. It was nearly midnight and we were in a small, sleeping town with no other cars on the road.

3 When the light turned green, I raced ahead, knowing it was foolish and that I was not in a movie. He didn't merely follow, he chased, and with his headlights turned off. No matter what sudden turn I took, he followed. My passengers were silent. I knew they were alarmed, and I prayed that I wouldn't be called upon to protect them. In that cheerful frame of mind, I turned off my own lights so I couldn't be followed. It was lunacy. I was responding to a crazy *as* a crazy.

4 "I'll just drive to the police station," I finally said, and as if those were the magic words, he disappeared.

5 **Elbowing fenders:** It seems to me that there has recently been an epidemic of auto macho—a competition perceived and expressed in driving. People fight it out over parking spaces. They bully into line at the gas pump. A toll booth becomes a signal for elbowing fenders. And beetle-eyed drivers hunch over their steering wheels, squeezing the rims, glowering, preparing the excuse of not having seen you as they muscle you off the road. Approaching a highway on an entrance ramp recently, I was strong-armed by a trailer truck so immense that its driver all but blew me away by blasting his horn. The behemoth was just inches from my hopelessly mismatched coupe when I fled for the safety of the shoulder.

6 And this is happening on city streets, too. A New York taxi driver told me that "intimidation is the name of the game. Drive as if you're deaf and blind. You don't hear the other guy's horn and you sure as hell don't see him."

7 The odd thing is that long before I was even able to drive, it seemed to me that people were at their finest and most civilized when in their cars. They seemed so orderly and considerate, so reasonable, staying in the right-hand lane unless passing, signaling all intentions. In those days you really eased into highway traffic, and the long, neat rows of cars seemed mobile testimony to the sanity of most people. Perhaps memory fails, perhaps there were always testy drivers, perhaps—but everyone didn't give you the finger.

8 A most amazing example of driver rage occurred recently at the Manhattan end of the Lincoln Tunnel. We were four cars abreast, stopped at a traffic light. And there was no moving even when the light had changed. A bus had stopped in the cross traffic, blocking our paths: it was a normal-for-New-York-City *gridlock.* Perhaps impatient, perhaps late for important appointments, three of us nonetheless accepted what, after all, we could not alter. One, however, would not. He would not be helpless. He would go where he was going even if he couldn't get there. A Wall Street type in suit and tie, he got out of his car and strode toward the bus, rapping smartly on its doors. When they opened, he exchanged words with the driver. The doors folded shut. He then stepped in front of the bus, took hold of one of its large windshield wipers and broke it.

9 The bus doors reopened and the driver appeared, apparently giving the fellow a good piece of his mind. If so, the lecture was wasted, for the man started his car and proceeded to drive directly *into the bus.* He rammed it. Even though the point at which he struck the bus, the folding doors, was its most *vulnerable* point, ramming the side of a bus with your car has to rank very high on a futility index. My first thought was that it had to be a rented car.

10 **Lane merger:** To tell the truth, I could not believe my eyes. The bus driver opened his doors as much as they could be opened and he stepped directly onto the hood of the attacking car, jumping up and down with both his feet. He then retreated into the bus, closing the doors behind him. Obviously a man of action, the car driver backed up and rammed the bus again. How this exercise in absurdity would have been resolved none of us will ever know for at that point the traffic unclogged and the bus moved on. And the rest of us, we passives of the world, proceeded, our cars crossing a field of battle as if nothing untoward had happened.

11 It is tempting to blame such belligerent, uncivil and even neurotic behavior on the nuts of the world, but in our cars we all become a little crazy. How many of us speed up when a driver signals his intention of pulling in front of us? Are we resentful and anxious to pass him? How many of us try to squeeze in, or race along the shoulder at a lane merger? We may not jump on hoods, but driving the gantlet, we seethe, cursing not so silently in the safety of our steel bodies on wheels—fortresses for cowards.

12 What is within us that gives birth to such antisocial behavior and why, all of a sudden, have so many drivers gone around the bend? My friend Joel Katz, a Manhattan psychiatrist, calls it, "a Rambo pattern. People are running around thinking the American way is to take the law into your own hands when anyone does anything wrong. And what constitutes 'wrong'? Anything that cramps your style."

13 It seems to me that it is a new America we see on the road now. It has the mentality of a hoodlum and the backbone of a coward. The car is its weapon and hiding place, and it is still a symbol even in this. Road Rambos no longer bespeak a self-reliant, civil people tooling around in family cruisers. In fact, there aren't families in these machines that charge headlong with their brights on in broad daylight, demanding we get out of their way. Bullies are loners, and they have perverted our liberty of the open road into drivers' license. They represent an America that derides the values of decency and good manners, then roam the highways riding shotgun and shrieking freedom. By allowing this to happen, the rest of us approve.

Vocabulary Highlights

delirious (1)

notoriety (1)

affront (2)

behemoth (5)

gridlock (8)

vulnerable (9)

belligerent (11)

neurotic (11)

gantlet (11)

seethe (11)

bespeak (13)

derides (13)

Discussion and Critical Thinking

1. What is Gottfried's main idea?
2. What major support does the author use?
3. To what authority (expert) does he appeal? Why is the authority appropriate or inappropriate?
4. How convincing is his support?
5. For what kind of audience is this article intended?
6. To what extent is the author different from the drivers he writes about?

Reading-Related Writing

1. Write a reaction statement in which you agree or disagree with Gottfried's views. Refer directly to his statements by using quotations, and if you use your own driving experiences as support, be specific.
2. Take one example, such as the one in paragraph 6 or in paragraphs 8 and 9, and relate it to your own experiences.
3. Do some personal research. During your next drive of more than thirty minutes, takes notes (*mental* notes, if you are the driver!) of Rambo drivers and of your own reactions to "competitive" driving situations. Then write a response of several paragraphs in which you evaluate your feelings and behavior, and that of others, on the road.
4. Discuss your worst day of driving or riding as a passenger.
5. Discuss some reasonable techniques for combating feelings of aggression relating to "auto-macho" stress.

Listening to the Air

John (Fire) Lame Deer and Richard Erdoes

John Lame Deer's message for us is to withdraw from the "conveniences" that have made us "civilized" and "advanced" and contemplate nature and our place in it. He says human beings have set up barriers that have diminished us as people and have altered and destroyed much of our natural world. He wants us to rethink our roles and our responsibilities and to spend more time "listening to the air." His message comes through journalist Richard Erdoes.

1 Let's sit down here, all of us, on the open prairie, where we can't see a highway or a fence. Let's have no blankets to sit on, but feel the ground with our bodies, the earth, the yielding shrubs. Let's have the grass for a mattress, experiencing its sharpness and its softness. Let us become like stones, plants, and trees. Let us be animals, think and feel like animals.

2 Listen to the air. You can hear it, feel it, smell it, taste it. *Woniya waken*—the holy air—which renews all by its breath. *Woniya, woniya waken*—spirit, life, breath, renewal—it means all that. *Woniya*—we sit together, don't touch, but something is there; we feel it between us, as a presence. A good way to start thinking about nature, talk about it. Rather talk to it, talk to the rivers, to the lakes, to the winds as to our relatives.

3 You have made it hard for us to experience nature in the good way by being part of it. Even here we are conscious that somewhere out in those hills there are missile silos and radar stations. White men always pick the few unspoiled, beautiful, awesome spots for the sites of these abominations. You have raped and violated these lands, always saying, "Gimme, gimme, gimme," and never giving anything back. You have taken 200,000 acres of our Pine Ridge reservation and make them into a bombing range. This land is so beautiful and strange that now some of you want to make it into a national park. The only use you have made of this land since you took it from us was to blow it up. You have not only despoiled the earth, the rocks, the minerals, all of which you call "dead" but which are very much alive; you have even changed the animals, which are part of us, part of the Great Spirit, changed them in a horrible way, so no one can recognize them. There is power in a buffalo—spiritual, magic power—but there is no power in an Angus, in a Hereford.

4 There is power in an antelope, but not in a goat or in a sheep, which holds still while you butcher it, which will eat your newspaper if you let it. There was a great power in a wolf, even in a coyote. You have made him into a freak—a toy poodle, a Pekingese, a lap dog. You can't do much with a cat, which is like an Indian, unchangeable. So you fix it, alter it, declaw it, even cut its vocal cords so you can experiment on it in a laboratory without being disturbed by its cries.

5 A partridge, a grouse, a quail, a pheasant, you have made them into chickens, creatures that can't fly, that wear a kind of sunglasses so that they won't peck each other's eyes out, "birds" with a "pecking order." There are some farms where they breed chickens for breast meat. Those birds are kept in low cages, forced to be hunched over all the time, which makes the breast muscles very big. Soothing sounds, Muzak, are piped into these chicken hutches. One loud noise and the chickens go haywire, killing themselves by flying against the mesh of their cages. Having to spend all their lives stopped over makes an unnatural, crazy, no-good bird. It also makes unnatural, no-good human beings.

6 That's where you fooled yourselves. You have not only altered, declawed, and malformed your winged and four-legged cousins; you have done it to yourselves. You have changed men into chairmen of boards, into office workers, into time-clock punchers. You have changed women into housewives, truly fearful creatures. I was once invited into the home of such a one.

7 "Watch the ashes, don't smoke, you stain the curtains. Watch the goldfish bowl, don't breathe on the parakeet, don't lean your head against the wallpaper; your hair may be greasy. Don't spill liquor on that table: it has a delicate finish. You should have wiped your boots; the floor was just var-

nished. Don't, don't, don't . . ." That is crazy. We weren't made to endure this. You live in prisons which you have built for yourselves, calling them "homes," offices, factories. We have a new joke on the reservation: "What is cultural deprivation?" Answer: "Being an upper-middle-class white kid living in a split-level suburban home with a color TV."

8 Sometimes I think that even our pitiful tar-paper shacks are better than your luxury homes. Walking a hundred feet to the outhouse on a clear wintry night, through mud or snow, that's one small link with nature. Or in the summer, in the back country, leaving the door of the privy open, taking your time, listening to the humming of the insects, the sun warming your bones through the thin planks of wood; you don't even have that pleasure anymore.

9 Americans want to have everything sanitized. No smells! Not even the good, natural man and woman smell. Take away the smell from under the armpits, from your skin. Rub it out, and then spray or dab some nonhuman odor on yourself, stuff you can spend a lot of money on, ten dollars an ounce, so you know this has to smell good. "B.O.," bad breath, "Intimate Female Odor Spray"—I see it all on TV. Soon you'll breed people without body openings.

10 I think white people are so afraid of the world they created that they don't want to see, feel, smell, or hear it. The feeling of rain and snow on your face, being numbed by an icy wind and thawing out before a smoking fire, coming out of a hot sweat bath and plunging into a cold stream, these things make you feel alive, but you don't want them anymore. Living in boxes which shut out the heat of the summer and the chill of winter, living inside a body that no longer has a scent, hearing the noise from the hi-fi instead of listening to the sounds of nature, watching some actor on TV having a make-believe experience when you no longer experience anything for yourself, eating food without taste—that's your way. It's no good.

11 The food you eat, you treat it like your bodies, take out all the nature part, the taste, the smell, the roughness, then put the artificial color, the artificial flavor in. Raw liver, raw kidney—that's what we old-fashioned full-bloods like to get our teeth into. In the old days we used to eat the guts of the buffalo, making a contest of it, two fellows getting hold of a long piece of intestines from opposite ends, starting chewing toward the middle, seeing who can get there first; that's eating. Those buffalo guts, full of half-fermented, half-digested grass and herbs, you didn't need any pills and vitamins when you swallowed those. Use the bitterness of gall for flavoring, not refined salt or sugar. *Wasna*—meat, kidney fat, and berries all pounded together—a lump of that sweet *wasna* kept a man going for a whole day. That was food, that had the power. Not the stuff you give us today: powdered milk, dehydrated eggs, pasteurized butter, chickens that are all drumsticks or all breast; there's no bird left there.

12 You don't want the bird. You don't have the courage to kill honestly—cut off the chicken's head, pluck it and gut it—no, you don't want this anymore. So it all comes in a neat plastic bag, all cut up, ready to eat, with no taste and no guilt. Your mink and seal coats, you don't want to know about the blood and pain which went into making them. Your idea of war—sit in an airplane, way above the clouds, press a button, drop the bombs, and never look below the clouds—that's the odorless, guiltless, sanitized way.

13 When we killed a buffalo, we knew what we were doing. We apologized to his spirit, tried to make him understand why we did it, honoring with a prayer the bones of those who gave their flesh to keep us alive, praying for their return, praying for the life of our brothers, the buffalo nation, as well

as for our own people. You wouldn't understand this and that's why we had the Washita Massacre, the Sand Creek Massacre, the dead women and babies at Wounded Knee. That's why we have Song My and My Lai now.

14 To us life, all life, is sacred. The state of South Dakota has pest-control officers. They go up in a plane and shoot coyotes from the air. They keep track of their kills, put them all down in their little books. The stockmen and sheepowners pay them. Coyotes eat mostly rodents, field mice and such. Only once in a while will they go after a stray lamb. They are our natural garbage men cleaning up the rotten and stinking things. They make good pets if you give them a chance. But their living could lose some man a few cents, and so the coyotes are killed from the air. They were here before the sheep, but they are in the way; you can't make a profit out of them. More and more animals are dying out. The animals which the Great Spirit put here, they must go. The man-made animals are allowed to stay—at least until they are shipped out to be butchered. That terrible arrogance of the white man, making himself something more than God, more than nature, saying, "I will let this animal live, because it makes money"; saying, "This animal must go, it brings no income, the space it occupies can be used in a better way. The only good coyote is a dead coyote." They are treating coyotes almost as badly as they used to treat Indians.

Discussion and Critical Thinking

1. How should we begin to start thinking about nature, according to Lame Deer?
2. How have we made it hard to experience nature in the good way by being part of it?
3. Lame Deer says, "You have not only altered, declawed, and malformed your winged and four-legged cousins; you have also done it to yourselves." Explain that.
4. In what ways are Native American primitive home conditions better than those of urban people in Lame Deer's view?
5. How do Native Americans, according to Lame Deer, regard killing and life?

Reading-Related Writing

1. Summarize what Lame Deer said and evaluate it. Emphasize the main points of his concern.
2. Lame Deer makes some strong statements about domesticated animals (par. 4). Agree or disagree in a brief written statement.
3. Discuss what part(s) of Lame Deer's message can and should be applied in a practical sense.

Soul Food at a Black American Family Reunion

Sheila Ferguson

Sheila Ferguson is the author of *Soul Food: Classic Cuisine from the Deep South.* Let her tell you about soul food in the proper setting, the Black American family reunion.

1 Soul food . . . is a legacy clearly steeped in tradition; a way of life that has been handed down from generation to generation, from one black family to another, by word of mouth and sleight of hand. It is rich in both history and variety of flavor.

2 "To cook soul food you must use all of your senses. You cook by instinct but you also use smell, taste, touch, sight, and, particularly, sound. You learn to hear by the crackling sound when it's time to turn over the fried chicken, to smell when a pan of biscuits is just about to finish baking, and to feel when a pastry's just right to the touch. You taste, rather than measure, the seasonings you treasure; and you use your eyes, not a clock, to judge when that cherry pie has bubbled sweet and nice. These skills are hard to teach quickly. They must be felt, loving, and come straight from the heart.

3 "Ah, but when you taste good soul food then it'll take ahold of your soul and hang your unsuspecting innards out to dry. It's that shur-'nuf everlovin' down-home stick-to-your-ribs kinda food that keeps you glued to your seat long after the meal is over and done with, enabling you to sit back, relax, and savor the gentle purrings of a well satisfied stomach, feeling that all's right with the world. . . .

4 It was down South . . . that I went to my first family reunion. Now, I know I should be telling you that the highlight of this affair was the prayers that one member was chosen to deliver. But if I were to tell the gospel truth, and I think I'm a-gonna, it was definitely the dishes that everybody turned out. Oh, dear, I'm making myself sound like some kinda pagan, but all that food, spread out majestically, on a long banquet-sized picnic table, sure was one sight for a small girl to behold. The table at the farm on Blanton Street in Charlotte kinda sloped with the terrain, but that didn't stop us from keeping the food well balanced and from swatting the flies away from the pecan pies, stacked a mile high, I might add. With one long and narrow slice you had a hunk of pie big enough to last you for quite a spell.

5 I should explain, though, that a black American family reunion stands for a great deal more than just the sharing of a really fine meal. It is a testimonial both to the past and to what the future holds in store for the entire family. We gather to share all that is most precious to us, especially with those family members we don't get to see that often. We eat, we drink, and we pray, but also we encourage each other and lift our heads in praise of what our offspring have accomplished. We share in each other's joys and good fortunes and offer solace when the chips are down. We comfort each other and this enables us to retain a special kind of closeness, even when we're hundreds of miles apart.

6 Everytime our family gets together we try to pay some humble tribute to the accomplishments of our race in one way or another. My family, for example, after discovering the existence of my great-great-grandfather Dennison Harrell, now meets annually for a grand family reunion expressly in his honor. We come together from all over the States—and in my case from across the Atlantic each time—tracing new family members we have never met before, as we continue to pay homage to the man who founded our family in America. Everyone who attends gives in the best of spirit and puts all of their personality into the dishes they concoct. At the same time, we are remembering all of our forebears and all that they gave, often against apparently insurmountable odds.

7 This is precisely why we feel we must get down to some real serious cookin' at the time of a family reunion. It represents sharing the very best

with those we love the very most and that love is best conveyed in the pride we take in preparing our food. By now, it has become a family tradition. And believe you me, can we burn when we cook. Everyone is asked to bring a dish, usually their specialty, and each cook has to maintain an exceedingly high standard of cooking, baking, and innovation. One dish just walks all over and surpasses another, and we always delight in sharing and comparing recipes. Once Aunt Peacie brought along her 'Jesse Jackson Sweet Potato Pie.' Well, it was gone before you had a chance to take a good look. Man, that pie was 'the T'—the talk of the day. But another thing is for dang sure: if your cooking isn't quite up to scratch, you sure as shootin' won't be asked to bring a dish next time round! You'll be nicely passed over with, 'Oh, honey, that's OK, why don't you just sit this one out.'

8 Even if it's not a big family reunion, it is still considered an extreme insult if you don't put yourself out and cook a fine and exquisite meal. I wouldn't dream of presenting my family and friends with a meal consisting of frozen fried chicken, frozen collard greens, store-bought cartons of buttermilk sausage biscuits and gravy made out of some sorry old box of granules. Oh, they'd eat it all right. But they would just feel so put down and outright insulted that they would commence telling me off, royally, right on the spot. Then, they would continue to talk about me for fifteen more years! My folks pull no punches when it comes to telling you off and they don't necessarily wait until they're politely out of earshot either. I can just hear them signifying now: 'Well, she sure didn't sweat long over that sad plate of stuff.' 'Do you call that food? Sure was pathetic.' 'I don't care how busy the girl is, she could certainly take a little time to think about her family once in a while, humph!' That is the spirit through which soul food traditions continually evolve—*pressure!*

Discussion and Critical Thinking

1. How does one use all five senses to prepare soul food?
2. According to Ferguson, why is soul food, soul food?
3. What does a black American family reunion stand for?
4. What has Ferguson done on a personal level?
5. What are the standards in cooking?

Reading-Related Writing

1. Write about the tradition of reunions in your family.
2. Write about a particular reunion you have gone to.
3. Write about the equivalent of soul food in another culture. Use Ferguson's description as a framework for your discussion.

The Incense Bowl

STUDENT ESSAY by Nguyet Anh Nguyen

In this beautifully evocative essay, student Nguyet Anh Nguyen writes of a family heirloom. She says it is not valuable in a monetary sense, but to her family it is beyond cost. It is an incense bowl, an object of beauty that ties her to her family and her revered ancestors. In this book dedicated to help students write well, it is appropriate to end the anthology section with an example of a highly effective essay by a student, one that is just as moving and revealing of culture as any these authors have read.

I don't know exactly when the incense bowl came to my house. It was there when I was born. This incense bowl, together with a set of two candlesticks, is a family heirloom, so it has been kept and maintained carefully by all the descendants in my family, even though most people would see it as a simple, common object. As a child, I was told that my father was the unexpected heir to the bowl and had a right to keep it because his oldest brother had died early without having children. Of course, my only brother will be the next heir following my father. According to Vietnamese custom, daughters are

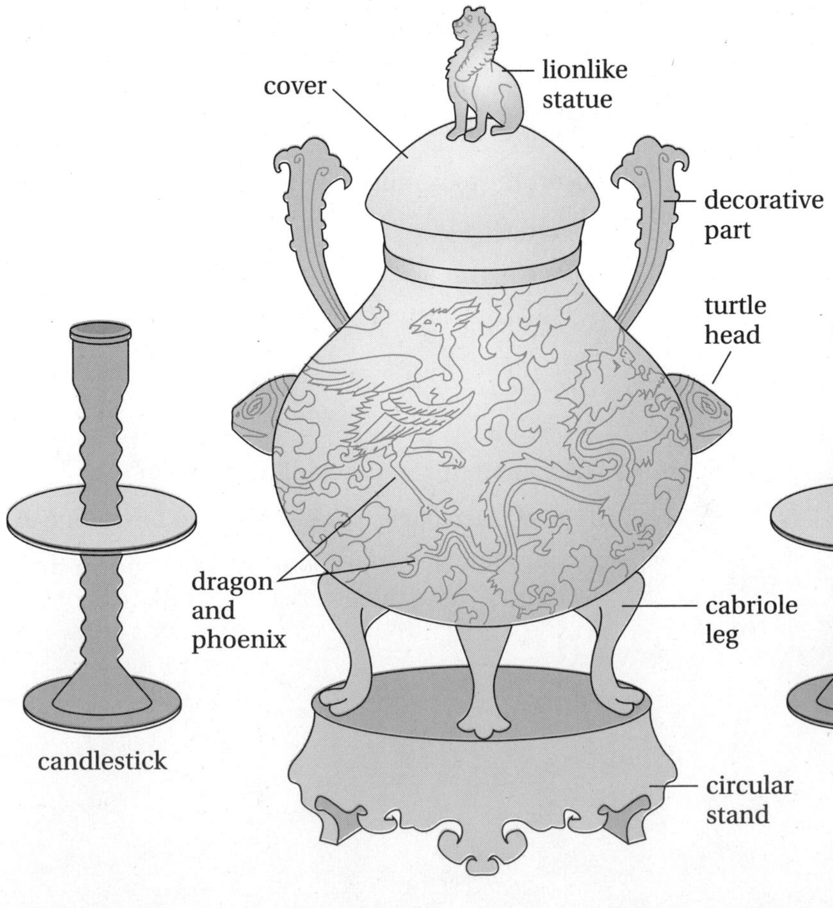

seldom allowed to become heiresses, so my sister and I will never have a chance to own the bowl.

Made of copper and used to burn incense, the incense bowl is round, golden in color, heavy, and compact, with a diameter of about fifteen inches. It sits on a prayer table, which is wide and strong enough to hold it. Before every ceremony, my father cleans and polishes the incense bowl and candlesticks by hand at home rather than bringing them to a cleaning service store. This task takes him several hours to finish. First, he uses lemon liquid to clean the outside of the bowl before rubbing the polish on it. This method is very effective. The copper surface of the bowl becomes dull after being exposed to the air for a long time. The acid in lemon liquid can wash away the outer layer of copper oxide. Then, after rinsing the bowl with water, he rubs it again with a soft towel and polish. The harder he rubs, the brighter it becomes. By watching my father's work, I can understand how much he esteems his ancestors and deceased parents. And his manner is unintentionally transferred directly to my soul without using language.

The cleaning process takes much time because the outer surface of the incense bowl is not smooth. Each side of the bowl is decorated with the relief figures of a flying dragon and a dancing phoenix-like creature blending well with carved cloud and flower images. The incense bowl is supported by three S-shaped cabriole legs, which fit into a circular stand made of copper as well. On top of the incense bowl's cover, there is a separate part, a copper statue of a sitting lion-like creature, which is attached to serve as the handle. We occasionally use this cover when the bowl contains only burning sandalwood, and put it aside when using stick incense. Also, two turtle head figures are carved on opposite sides of the bowl to use as its handles. These creatures—the dragon, the phoenix-like bird, the turtle heads, and the lion-like animal—are the four Chinese mythical animals that have the magical power to bring peace and good fortune to people according to ancient belief. Besides those creatures, the incense bowl is decorated with features of Chinese classical architecture.

In our family, the incense bowl is also a witness of all notable events such as birthdays, weddings, new years, funerals, anniversaries of the deaths of deceased ancestors, and even simple prayers of my family. On the important ceremonial days, we usually place on the prayer table some fresh flowers and tropical fruits, varied according to the season, such as durian, longans, mangoes, pineapple, watermelon, green oranges, bananas, custard apples, coconuts, persimmons, mangosteens, mulberries, grapes, grapefruits, plums, papayas, Jacknut tangerines, and so on, together with a tray of plentiful food, and some hot tea or wine as an offering to our ancestors. One candlestick is placed on the left and one on the right side of the incense bowl, which is located at the center of the prayer table. Then the candles are lighted. In the solemn atmosphere, the whole family stands in line and bows formally in front of the table while the aromatic white smoke of burning incense and smoldering sandalwood fly up to the air (from the incense bowl). In this worship, we believe that the smoke transmits our prayers to our ancestors.

This incense bowl has shared intimately with my family in difficult times. Once, my father was very poor. He had to toil hard to maintain his family's well being. However, he never thought about selling this copper bowl for money. Such behavior, which is common among most Vietnamese people, can be compared with the Asian Indians' love for cows. Even those who are starving in India refuse to eat their sacred cows. In much the same spirit, the incense bowl has been handed down from generation to generation, no matter what the family's situation.

As one can see, the copper incense bowl has a special position in my family, even though it is not very valuable. Definitely, it carries much cultural meaning and is a symbol of the sentiment or bond shared through the generations. And more importantly, the incense bowl's history embraces both the prosperity and poverty of our lives.

Discussion and Critical Thinking

1. Does Nguyen seem disappointed that she will never own the bowl? Why?
2. How are the description and narration blended in this essay?
3. Why is the bowl beyond price?

Reading-Related Writing

1. Describe a family heirloom (ring, watch, wedding dress, religious item, silverware, dishes, tools) or another relic that is being passed down from generation to generation in your family and explain why it is prized by you (or explain your apprehension about being responsible for it).
2. Describe another object such as a picture album that depicts relatives from different generations and represents the "roots" of your family. Include descriptions of some of your favorite pictures.

Connections

1. Discuss how John Lame Deer might feel about the behavior of people in "Rambos of the Road."
2. Compare the ideas in "Soul Food" with "Listening to the Air." Are they more similar or different? Consider being natural, valuing tradition, and depending mightily on the emotions.
3. Compare the ideas of "American Space, Chinese Place" with those of "Listening to the Air." Answer the question, "To what extent is the way we look at our environment dependent on our conditioning?" If we have American space and Chinese place, what do we have for the Native American? Sort it out.
4. Compare "The Incense Bowl" with "Soul Food." What does each one say about family, traditions, and roots? In what different ways do they make family connections?

Appendixes

Appendix A: Spelling

Some people are born good spellers. They see a word and can spell it correctly forever; others struggle. If you are not a great speller, you probably never will be, but the good news is that you can be a competent speller—with work. This appendix offers you a systematic approach and several separate strategies to spelling well in a language that is inconsistent to a significant degree. Some words just don't look the way they sound; in other words, they are not phonetic, and they do not pattern in ways parallel with other words of the same spelling. This anonymous poem shows some of the problems:

> When in the English language we speak
> Why is *break* not rhymed with *freak?*
> Will you tell me why it's true
> That we *sew,* but we also saw *few?*
> And why cannot makers of verse
> Rime the word *horse* with *worse?*
> *Beard* sounds much different from *heard*
> *Cord* is so different from *word*
> *Cow* is *cow,* but *low* is *low.*
> *Shoe* never rhymes with *foe;*
> And think of *hose,* and *dose,* and *lose.*
> And think of *goose* and yet of *choose.*
> *Doll* and *roll,* and *home* and *some.*
> And since *pay* is rimed with *say,*
> Why *paid* and *said,* I pray?
> *Mould* is not pronounced like *could*
> And *done* is not like *gone* and *lone.*
> If there is one *tooth* and a whole set of *teeth*
> Why shouldn't the plural of *booth* be *beeth?*
> If the singular is *this* and the plural is *these*
> Should the plural of *kiss* be *kese?*
> We speak of masculine pronouns *he, his, him,*
> Why not *she, shis,* and *shim?*

If the plural of *box* is *boxes*
Why is it *oxen* instead of *oxes?*
If the plural of *mouse* is *mice*
Why doesn't *house* become *hice?*
If the plural of *man* is *men*
Why is it *pans* instead of *pen?*
If the plural of *foot* is *feet,*
Why is it *boots* instead of *beet?*
To sum it all up, it seems to me
That sounds and letters just do not agree.

Despite these problems inherent in our language, you can be an effective speller. Unfortunately, for those who are not, there are unhappy consequences. In a society as literate as ours, if you are a poor speller, you will find yourself with a serious handicap. The professions and trades, as well as the schools, are demanding that individuals spell well and write effectively. If you write *thier* for *their* or *definately* for *definitely* in compositions, term reports, examinations, letters of application, or business reports, you will draw unfavorable attention from your audience.

Use these steps as a guide to efficient spelling:

1. Make up your mind that you are going to spell well.
2. Keep a list of words you misspell; work on spelling them correctly.
3. Get into the habit of looking up new words in the dictionary for correct spelling as well as for meaning.
4. Look at each letter in the word carefully and pronounce each syllable; that is, *change-a-ble, con-tin-u-ous, dis-ap-pear-ance.*
5. Visualize how the word is made up.
6. Write the word correctly several times. After each writing, close your eyes and again visualize the word.
7. Set up frequent recall sessions with problem words. Become aware of the reasons for your errors.

Do not omit letters.

Many errors occur because of mispronunciations of words in which certain letters are omitted. Observe the omissions in the words below. Then concentrate on learning the correct spellings.

Incorrect	Correct	Incorrect	Correct
agravate	ag*g*ravate	ajourned	a*d*journed
aproved	a*p*proved	aquaintance	a*c*quaintance
artic	ar*c*tic	comodity	co*m*modity
efficent	effic*i*ent	envirnment	envir*o*nment

Incorrect	Correct	Incorrect	Correct
familar	famil*i*ar	irigation	ir*r*igation
libary	lib*r*ary	paralell	paral*l*el
parlament	parl*i*ament	paticulaly	pa*r*ticula*r*ly

readly	read*i*ly	sophmore	soph*o*more
stricly	stric*t*ly	unconsious	uncons*c*ious

Do not add letters.

Incorrect	Correct	Incorrect	Correct
ath*e*lete	athlete	co*m*ming	coming
drown*d*ed	drowned	folk*e*s	folks
occa*s*sionally	occasionally	om*m*ission	omission
pas*t*time	pastime	privile*d*ge	privilege
simil*i*ar	similar	tra*d*gedy	tragedy

Do not substitute incorrect letters for correct letters.

Incorrect	Correct	Incorrect	Correct
benefi*s*ial	beneficial	bull*i*tins	bulletins
*s*ensus	census	d*i*scription	description
d*e*sease	disease	dissen*t*ion	dissension
it*i*ms	items	offen*c*e	offense
peculi*e*r	peculiar	re*s*itation	recitation
scre*a*ch	screech	sustan*s*ial	substantial
surpri*z*e	surprise	techn*a*cal	technical

Do not transpose letters.

Incorrect	Correct	Incorrect	Correct
alu*nm*i	alumni	child*er*n	children
dup*il*cate	duplicate	irre*vel*ant	irrelevant
kindel	kindle	p*re*haps	perhaps
p*er*fer	prefer	p*er*scription	prescription
princip*el*s	principles	y*ei*ld	yield

Note: Whenever you notice other words that fall into any one of these categories, add them to the list.

Apply the spelling rules for spelling *ei* and *ie* words correctly.

Remember the poem?

Use *i* before *e*
Except after *c*
Or when sounded as *a*
As in *neighbor* and *weigh*

i* Before *e			
achieve	belief	believe	brief
chief	field	grief	hygiene

niece	piece	pierce	relief
relieve	shield	siege	variety

Except After *c*

ceiling	conceit	conceive	deceit
deceive	perceive	receipt	receive

Exceptions: *either, financier, height, leisure, neither, seize, species, weird.*

When Sounded as *a*

deign	eight	feign	feint
freight	heinous	heir	neigh
neighbor	rein	reign	skein
sleigh	veil	vein	weigh

Apply the rules for dropping the final *e* or retaining the final *e* when a suffix is added.

Words ending in a silent *e* usually drop the *e* before a suffix beginning with a vowel; for example, *accuse* + *-ing* = *accusing.* Some common suffixes beginning with a vowel are the following: *-able, -al, -age, -ary, -ation, -ence, -ing, -ion, -ous, -ure.*

admire + *-able* = admirable	arrive + *-al* = arrival
plume + *-age* = plumage	imagine + *-ary* = imaginary
explore + *-ation* = exploration	precede + *-ence* = precedence
come + *-ing* = coming	locate + *-ion* = location
fame + *-ous* = famous	please + *-ure* = pleasure

Exceptions: *dye* + *-ing* = *dyeing* (to distinguish it from *dying*), *acreage, mileage.*

Words ending in a silent *-e* usually retain the *e* before a suffix beginning with a consonant; for example: *arrange* + *-ment* = *arrangement.* Some common suffixes beginning with a consonant are the following: *-craft, -ful, -less, -ly, -mate, -ment, -ness, -ty.*

state + *-craft* = statecraft	hate + *-ful* = hateful
hope + *-less* = *hopeless*	safe + *-ly* = safely
stale + *-mate* = stalemate	manage + *-ment* = management
like + *-ness* = likeness	entire + *-ty* = entirety

Exceptions: Some words taking the *-ful* or *-ly* suffixes drop the final *e;* for example:

awe + *-ful* = awful	due + *-ly* = duly
true + *-ly* = truly	whole + *-ly* = wholly

Some words taking the suffix *-ment* drop the final *e;* for example:

acknowledgment	argument	judgment

Words ending in silent *-e* after *c* or *g* retain the *e* when the suffix begins with the vowel *a* or *o*. The final *-e* is retained to keep the *c* or *g* soft before the suffixes.

advantag*e*ous	courag*e*ous
notic*e*able	peac*e*able

Apply the rules for doubling a final consonant before a suffix beginning with a vowel.

Words of one syllable:

blot	blotted	brag	bragging	cut	cutting
drag	dragged	drop	dropped	get	getting
hop	hopper	hot	hottest	man	mannish
plan	planned	rob	robbed	run	running
sit	sitting	stop	stopped	swim	swimming

Words accented on the last syllable:

acquit	acquitted	admit	admittance	allot	allotted
begin	beginning	commit	committee	concur	concurring
confer	conferring	defer	deferring	equip	equipped
occur	occurrence	omit	omitting	prefer	preferred
refer	referred	submit	submitted	transfer	transferred

Words that are not accented on the last syllable, or words that do not end in a single consonant preceded by a vowel, do not double the final consonant (whether or not the suffix begins with a vowel).

Frequently Misspelled Words

1. absence	15. beginning	29. dependent	43. environment
2. across	16. belief	30. develop	44. especially
3. actually	17. benefit	31. development	45. etc.
4. a lot	18. buried	32. difference	46. exaggerate
5. all right	19. business	33. disastrous	47. excellent
6. among	20. certain	34. discipline	48. exercise
7. analyze	21. college	35. discussed	49. existence
8. appearance	22. coming	36. disease	50. experience
9. appreciate	23. committee	37. divide	51. explanation
10. argument	24. competition	38. dying	52. extremely
11. athlete	25. complete	39. eighth	53. familiar
12. athletics	26. consider	40. eligible	54. February
13. awkward	27. criticism	41. eliminate	55. finally
14. becoming	28. definitely	42. embarrassed	56. foreign

57. government
58. grammar
59. grateful
60. guarantee
61. guard
62. guidance
63. height
64. hoping
65. humorous
66. immediately
67. independent
68. intelligence
69. interest
70. interfere
71. involved
72. knowledge
73. laboratory
74. leisure
75. length
76. library
77. likely
78. lying
79. marriage
80. mathematics
81. meant
82. medicine
83. neither
84. ninety
85. ninth
86. nuclear
87. occasionally
88. opinion
89. opportunity
90. parallel
91. particular
92. persuade
93. physically
94. planned
95. pleasant
96. possible
97. practical
98. preferred
99. prejudice
100. privilege
101. probably
102. professor
103. prove
104. psychology
105. pursue
106. receipt
107. receive
108. recommend
109. reference
110. relieve
111. religious
112. repetition
113. rhythm
114. ridiculous
115. sacrifice
116. safety
117. scene
118. schedule
119. secretary
120. senior
121. sense
122. separate
123. severely
124. shining
125. significant
126. similar
127. sincerely
128. sophomore
129. speech
130. straight
131. studying
132. succeed
133. success
134. suggest
135. surprise
136. thoroughly
137. though
138. tragedy
139. tried
140. tries
141. truly
142. unfortunately
143. unnecessary
144. until
145. unusual
146. using
147. usually
148. Wednesday
149. writing
150. written

Confused Spelling/Confusing Words

The following are more words that are commonly misspelled or confused with one another. Some have similar sounds, some are often mispronounced, and some are only misunderstood.

a: An article adjective that is used before a word beginning with a consonant or a consonant sound, as in "I ate *a* donut."

an: An article adjective that is used before a word beginning with a vowel sound (*a, e, i, o, u*) or with a silent *h*.

and: A coordinating conjunction, as in "Sara *and* I like Johnny Cash."

accept: A verb meaning "to receive," as in "I *accept* your explanation."

except: A preposition meaning "to exclude," as in "I paid everyone *except* you."

advice: A noun meaning "guidance," as in "Thanks for the *advice*."

advise: A verb meaning "to give guidance," as in "Will you please *advise* me of my rights?"

all right: An adjective meaning "correct" or "acceptable," as in "It's *all right* to cry."

alright: Misspelling.

all ready: An adjective that can be used interchangeably with *ready,* as in "I am *all ready* to go to town."

already: An adverb meaning "before," which cannot be used in place of *ready,* as in "I have *already* finished."

a lot: An adverb meaning "much," as in "She liked him *a lot,*" or a noun meaning "several," as in "I had *a lot* of suggestions."

alot: Misspelling.

altogether: An adverb meaning "completely," as in "He is *altogether* happy."

all together: An adverb meaning "as one," which can be used interchangeably with *together,* as in "The group left *all together.*"

choose: A present-tense verb meaning "to select," as in "Do whatever you *choose.*"

chose: The past-tense form of the verb *choose,* as in "They *chose* to take action yesterday"

grammar: A noun meaning "how words are arranged," as in "I must work on my *grammar.*"

grammer: Misspelling.

hear: A verb indicating the receiving of sound, as in "I *hear* thunder."

here: An adverb meaning "present location."

it's: A contraction of *it is,* as in "*It's* time to dance."

its: A possessive pronoun, as in "Each dog has *its* day."

know: A verb usually meaning "to comprehend" or "to recognize," as in "I *know* the answer."

no: An adjective meaning "negative," as in "I have *no* potatoes."

led: The past-tense form of the verb *lead,* as in "I *led* a wild life in my youth."

lead: A present-tense verb, as in "I *lead* a stable life now" or a noun referring to a substance, such as "I sharpened the *lead* in my pencil."

loose: An adjective meaning "without restraint," as in "He is a *loose* cannon."

lose: A present-tense verb from the pattern *lose, lost, lost,* as in "I thought I would *lose* my senses."

paid: The past-tense form of *pay,* as in "He *paid* his dues."

payed: Misspelling.

passed: The past-tense form of the verb *pass,* meaning "went by," as in "He *passed* me on the curve."

past: An adjective meaning "formerly," as in "that's *past* history now."

patience: A noun meaning "willingness to wait," as in "Job was a man of much *patience.*"

patients: A noun meaning "people under care," as in "The doctor had fifty *patients.*"

peace: A noun meaning "calm" or "without strife," as in "The guru was at *peace* with the world."

piece: A noun meaning "particle," as in "I gave him a *piece* of my mind."

quiet: An adjective meaning "silent," as in "She was a *quiet* child."

quit: A verb meaning "to cease" or "to withdraw," as in "I *quit* my job."

quite: An adverb meaning "very," as in "The clam is *quite* happy."

receive: A verb meaning "to accept," as in "I will *receive* visitors now."

recieve: Misspelling.

stationary: An adjective meaning "not moving," as in "Try to avoid running into *stationary* objects."

stationery: A noun meaning "paper material to write on," as in "I bought a box of *stationery* for Sue's birthday present."

than: A conjunction, as in "He is taller *than* I am."

then: An adverb, as in "She *then* left town."

their: An adjective, as in "They read *their* books."

there: An adverb, as in "He left it *there,*" or a filler word as in "*There* is no time left."

they're: A contraction of *they are,* as in "*They're* happy."

to: A preposition, as in "I went *to* town."

too: An adverb meaning "having exceeded or gone beyond what is acceptable," as in "You are *too* late to qualify for the discount," or "also," as in "I have feelings, *too.*"

two: An adjective of number, as in "I have *two* jobs."

thorough: An adjective, as in "He did a *thorough* job."

through: A preposition, as in "She went *through* the yard."

truly: An adverb meaning "sincerely" or "completely," as in "He was *truly* happy."

truely: Misspelling.

weather: A noun meaning "condition of the atmosphere," as in "The *weather* is pleasant today."

whether: A conjunction, as in "*Whether* he would go or not was of no consequence."

write: A present-tense verb, as in "Watch me as I *write* this letter."

writen: Misspelling.

written: A past-participle verb, as in "I have *written* the letter."

you're: A contraction of *you are,* as in "*You're* my friend."

your: A possessive pronoun, as in "I like *your* looks."

EXERCISE 1

Underline the correct word or words. (See Answer Key for answers.)

1. I cannot (hear, here) the answers.
2. She is taller (then, than) I.
3. They left town to find (their, they're, there) roots.
4. Sam went (through, thorough) the initiation.
5. I am only asking for a little (peace, piece) of the action.
6. Whatever you say is (alright, all right) with me.
7. I (passed, past) the test and now I'm ready for action.
8. That smash was (to, too, two) hot to handle.
9. I did not ask for her (advise, advice).
10. I found (a lot, alot) of new ideas in that book.
11. She has (all ready, already) left.
12. I (chose, choose) my answer and hoped for the best.
13. I knew that I would (recieve, receive) fair treatment.
14. Juan was (quit, quite, quiet) happy with my decision.
15. Maria went to the store for some (stationary, stationery).
16. Marlin knew they would (lose, loose) the game.
17. I've heard that (it's, its) a good movie.
18. June would not (accept, except) my answer.
19. I did not (know, no) what to do.
20. Sean (paid, payed) his bill and left town.

EXERCISE 2

Underline the correct word or words.

1. She said that my application was (alright, all right).
2. Sheriff Dillon worked hard for (peace, piece) in the valley.
3. She was the first woman to (recieve, receive) a medal.
4. He spoke his mind; (then, than) he left.
5. The cleaners did a (through, thorough) job.
6. After the loud explosion, there was (quit, quiet, quite).
7. The nurse worked diligently with his (patience, patients).
8. They were not (altogether, all together) happy.
9. The cowboys (led, lead) the cows to water.
10. For my hobby, I study (grammar, grammer).
11. Elvis (truly, truely) respected his mother.
12. Zeke asked for the (whether, weather) report.
13. I never (advise, advice) my friends about gambling.
14. You should (accept, except) responsibility for your actions.
15. Joan inherited (alot, a lot) of money.
16. We waited for the gorilla to (chose, choose) a mate.
17. Virginia thinks (its, it's) a good day for a party.
18. It was a tale of (to, too, two) cities.
19. I went (they're, their, there) to my childhood home.
20. It was the best letter Kevin had ever (writen, written, wrote).

Appendix B: Vocabulary Building

When you encounter a word you have not seen before, what do you usually do? Be honest. That's right. You skip it. You just pretend it doesn't exist. You even conveniently forget that you have skipped a word. We all do this at times. That's why often, soon after we take the time to learn a new word, we see it in print. Coincidence? Probably not. It's more likely that we have seen it in print many times, but now we are "noticing" it.

Obviously, it would be better to acquire a large vocabulary, because if we skip words that are important, we will miss significant meaning. But we may not have the time or opportunity to use the dictionary for all our vocabulary improvement. The good news is that we acquire most of our vocabulary *without* using the dictionary.

Word Analysis

Some of our vocabulary growth comes from comparisons. The precise term is *word analysis.* We see words and we make comparisons with other words. We see the word *synchronize* for example, and we observe that it has parts: *syn, chron,* and *ize.* We know that *syn* can be found in *synonym,* meaning "same word," or *synthetic,* meaning "same construction." Therefore, *syn* must have something to do with *same* or *sameness.* The second part of the word, *chron* means "that which lasts over time," as in "chronic cough." We also recognize *chron* in *chronological, chronicle,* and *chronology,* all pertaining to time. The *-ize* part as in *energize,* means "to do or make" and is a verb form. *Synchronize,* then, means "to cause to occur at the same time," as in "We should synchronize our watches."

We don't have to be linguists to make those discoveries. When we see or hear new and difficult words but cannot or choose not to use a dictionary, we should try to analyze them, to recognize their parts. The three parts we are concerned with are *prefixes, roots,* and *suffixes.* Consider the simple word *unloading:*

un-	load	-ing
prefix	*root*	*suffix*
This modifies the root and changes its meaning. In this case it gives *load* an opposite meaning.	This carries the basic meaning; there may be more than one.	This shows that the word can be a verb if there is a helping verb, as in "He is unloading the truck." Or it can be a noun, as in "Unloading the truck is hard work."

The following table lists some common prefixes, suffixes, and roots.

Common Word Parts

Prefix	Meaning	With Word
de-	away, from	*de*tract
inter-	between	*inter*vene

Prefix	Meaning	With Word
post-	after	*post*erior
pre-	before	*pre*marital
re-	back, again	*re*gain
trans-	across	*trans*fer
dis-	away, not	*dis*like
mis-	bad, wrong	*mis*taken
un-	not	*un*do
multi-	many	*multi*faceted

Root	Meaning	With Word
cap	take, seize	*cap*ture
dic	tell, say	*dic*tate
mit	send	trans*mit*
port	carry	trans*port*
scrib, script	write	in*script*ion
terr, terre	earth, land	*terre*strial
ven, vent	come	con*vene*
vis	see	*vis*ible
voc	call	*voc*ational

Suffix	Likely Part of Speech	With Word
-able	adjective	favor*able*
-ic	adjective	com*ic*
-ion	noun	act*ion*
-ment	noun	enjoy*ment*
-ous	adjective	joy*ous*
-ure	verb	nurt*ure*
-er	noun	employ*er*
-ate	verb	activ*ate*
-ive	adjective	suggest*ive*
-al	adjective	occasion*al*
-ly	adverb	slow*ly*

EXERCISE 1

Try word analysis on these words. Can you come up with some basic meanings? The roots, prefixes, and suffixes come from the table. Begin by dividing the words into parts.

deportation: ______________________________

____

____

transmission: ______________________________

____

____

prescription: ______________________________

____

____

multivision: ______________________________

____

____

recapture: ______________________________

____

____

remit: ______________________________

____

____

captivate: ______________________

____

____

interdict: ______________________

____

____

intervention: ______________________

____

____

postscript: ______________________

____

____

Contextual Clues

Another way of determining basic word meaning is by using contextual clues, hints from the passage where the word appears. These are some of the most common kinds of clues you will be able to take advantage of:

1. **Contrast** If a person says, "I don't like *enigmatic* leaders; I want to be able to understand how they think," you can determine what *enigmatic* means from the rest of the sentence. It means "that which is not easily understood." The clue is one of contrast.

2. **Definition** If a person says, "I can't stand him because of his *arrogance.* He thinks he's better than everyone else and lets it show," you can tell what *arrogance* means even if it's new to you. The word is actually explained by definition.

3. **Example** You might find an example in the context: "He's a *traitor,* a real Benedict Arnold." If you know anything about Benedict Arnold, you know what a *traitor* is.

4. **Synonym** The contextual clue may be a synonym: "She is *devoid* of, absolutely without, any charm." There the definition, "without," follows the unfamiliar word.

5. **Logic** Then you may read a passage in which sheer logic provides the definition. "Bart's *pugnacious* behavior would not go unpunished. School was a place where fighting was not permitted." The passage makes sense only if *pugnacious* means "combative" or "physically aggressive."

We acquire most of our vocabulary by using contextual clues. As children, before we learned to read, we acquired our vocabulary by listening and imitating. After we learned to read, we then had opportunities to learn words pertaining to many areas outside the family concerns.

Dictionary Usage

You can systematically strengthen your vocabulary through dictionary use by making vocabulary cards. This method also provides flexibility. You should develop a card format that fits your needs both specifically for classes and generally for lifetime learning.

Consider this form:

On one side of the card write the word.

Side 1

hypocrite

On the other side of the card, include other information: (1) pronunciation, (2) definition, (3) word origin, and (4) word used in a sentence.

Side 2

(1) hip a krit

(2) a person who pretends to hold beliefs, feelings, or virtues he or she does not have

(3) Ancient Greek; meant an actor, one who was pretending on the stage

(4) He appears on many television benefit programs to help the poor, but he always gets paid, and he never donates money. Even his fans have started to call him a hypocrite.

Anyone who is serious about vocabulary improvement should be using all three of these methods—word analysis, contextual clues, and dictionary usage—extensively. Often a combination of methods can be used profitably.

Of these methods, the use of contextual clues is the main source of vocabulary growth. It naturally follows then that the key to the greatest improvement is extensive reading of different kinds of material. That experience will expose the reader to new concepts and, therefore, new words.

The English language contains approximately two million words. No one person knows more than about ninety thousand. The average college freshman can use more than twenty thousand. Many students enter college with a rich and varied vocabulary, having experienced a doubling of words during high school. Others, those who were not in the strongest high school academic program and did not read widely, enter college with a much smaller vocabulary. The encouraging note is that because of college reading requirements in general education and other courses, significant vocabulary growth is bound to occur. The person who takes the time to read beyond required assignments will experience even more growth.

Your systematic approach to expanding your vocabulary through word analysis, contextual clues, and dictionary use will enhance your ability to acquire words. Having a stronger vocabulary will enable you to read better, write better, and think more clearly.

Appendix C: Taking Tests

Good test-taking begins with good study techniques. These techniques involve, among other things, how to read, think, and write effectively. Those skills have been covered in this book. Here we will deal only with a few principles that apply directly and immediately to the test situation.

At the beginning of the semester, you should discover how you will be tested in each course. Match your note-taking and underlining of texts to the kind or kinds of tests you will take. Objective tests will usually require somewhat more attention to details than will subjective or essay tests.

For both types of tests—and you will probably have a combination—you should carefully apportion your time, deciding how much to spend on each section or essay, and allowing a few minutes for a quick review of answers. For both, you should also read the directions carefully, marking key words (if you are permitted to do so) as a reminder to you for concentration.

Objective Tests

Here are some tips on taking objective tests:

- Find out whether you will be graded on the basis of the number of correct answers or on the basis of right-minus-wrong. This is the difference: If you are graded on the basis of the number of correct answers, there is no penalty for guessing; therefore, if you want the highest possible score, you should leave no blanks. But if you are graded on the basis of right-minus-wrong (meaning one or a fraction of one is subtracted from your correct answers for every miss), then answer only if the odds of being right are in your favor. For example, if you know an answer is one of two possibilities, you have a 50 percent chance of getting it right; consequently, guess if the penalty is less than one because you could gain one by getting it right and lose less than one by getting it wrong. Ask your teacher to explain if there is a right-minus-wrong factor.
- If you are going to guess and you want to get some answers correct, you should pick one column and fill in the bubbles. By doing that, you will almost certainly get some correct.

- Studies show that in a typical four-part multiple choice test section, more answers are B and C than A and D.
- Statements with absolutes such as *always* and *never* are likely to be false, whereas statements with qualifications such as *usually* and *probably* are more likely to be true.
- If you don't know an answer, instead of fixating on it and getting frustrated, mark it with what seems right, put a dot alongside your answer, and go back later for a second look if time permits.
- When (and if) you go back to check your work, do not make changes unless you discover that you obviously marked one incorrectly. Studies have shown that first hunches are usually more accurate.

Subjective or Essay Tests

Here are some tips on taking subjective tests:

- Consider the text, the approach taken by the instructor in lectures, and the overall approach in the course outline and try to anticipate essay questions. Then, in your preparation, jot down and memorize simple outlines that will jog your memory during the test if you have anticipated correctly.
- Remember to keep track of time. A time-consuming A+ essay that does not allow you to finish the second half of the exam will result in a failing grade.
- Study the essay questions carefully. Underline key words. Each essay question will have two parts: the subject part and the treatment part. It may also have a limiting part. If you are required, for example, to compare and contrast President Carter and President Bush on their environmental programs, you should be able to analyze the topic immediately in this fashion:

  The *subject* is President Carter and President Bush.

  The *limitation* is their environmental programs.

  The *treatment* is comparison and contrast.

  Hence, you might mark it in this fashion:

  treatment — limitation

  Compare and contrast the environmental programs of

  subject

  President Carter and President Bush.

  The treatment part (here "compare and contrast") may very well be one of the forms of discourse such as definition, classification, or analysis, or it may be something like "evaluate" or "discuss," in which a certain form or forms would be used. Regardless of what the treatment word is, the first step is to determine the natural points of division and to prepare a simple outline or outline alternative for organization.
- In writing the paper, be sure that you include specific information as support for your generalizations.

Appendix D: Making Application

Two forms of practical writing that you may need even before you finish your college work are the letter of application and the résumé. They will often go together as requirements by an employer. In some instances the employer will suggest the form and content of the letter and résumé; in others, you will receive no directions and should adjust your letter and résumé to match the requirements and expectations as you perceive them. The models on pp. A-22–A-23 are typical of what job applicants commonly submit.

Letter of Application

A few basic guidelines will serve you well:

- Use standard letter-size paper and type.
- Do not apologize, and do not brag.
- Do not go into tedious detail, but do relate your education, work experience, and career goals to the available job.
- Begin your letter with a statement indicating why you are writing the letter and how you heard about the job opening.
- End the letter by stating how you can be contacted for an interview.

Résumé

Employers are especially concerned about your most recent work experiences and education, so include them first, as indicated in the example on page A-22. The heading "College Activities" can be replaced with "Interests and Activities." Your main concern is presenting relevant information in a highly readable form. Always end with a list of references.

Benjamin Johanson
203 Village Center Avenue
Glendora, California 91740
(818) 987-5555

WORK EXPERIENCE:

1994-96 Lab Assistant in the Mt. San Antonio College Computer Lab
1994-96 Sales and Stock Technician in the Mt. San Antonio College Book Store

EDUCATION:

1994-96 Full-time student at Mt. San Antonio College
1990-94 High school diploma from Glendora High School

COLLEGE ACTIVITIES:

Hackers' Club (1993-95)
Chess Club (1993-95)
Forensics Club (1994-96)— twice a regional debate champion

REFERENCES:

Stewart Hamlen
Chairperson, Business Department
Mt. San Antonio College
Walnut, California 91789
(714) 594-5611 Extension 4707

Bart Grassmont
Personnel Director, Book Store
Mt. San Antonio College
Walnut, California 91789
(714) 594-5611 Extension 4706

Howard McGraw
Coach, Forensics Team
Mt. San Antonio College
Walnut, California 91789
(714) 594-5611 Extension 4575

203 Village Center Avenue
Glendora, California 91740
July 11, 1996

Mr. Roy Ritter
Computers Unlimited
1849 N. Granada Avenue
Walnut, California 91789

Dear Mr. Ritter:

I am responding to your advertisement in the Los Angeles *Times* for the position of salesperson for used computers. Please consider me as a candidate.

In one more semester I will have completed my A.A. degree at Mt. San Antonio College with a major in Business Management and a minor in Computer Technology.

My experience relates directly to the job you offer. As a result of my part-time work for two years as lab technician at Mt. San Antonio College, I have come to know the operations of several different computers. I have also learned to explain the operations to people who have very little knowledge of computers. In my business classes, I have studied the practical approaches to advertising and sales while also learning theory. Each semester for the past two years, I have worked in the college book store where I helped customers who were buying various products, including computers.

This job would coincide perfectly with my work at school, my work experience, and even my goal of being a salesperson with a large company.

Enclosed is my resumé with several references to people who know me well. Please contact them if you want information or if you would like a written evaluation.

I am available for an interview at your request.

Sincerely yours,

Benjamin Johanson

Benjamin Johanson

Appendix E: Critical Thinking

Critical thinking is the systematic examination and evaluation of ideas. It pertains to all you will do in this book. Critical thinking reflects back on reading and looks forward to writing and its related skills. In assignments as diverse as reading a chapter in your history text and preparing a written lab report for geology, you need to use critical thinking. In short, it is an essential part of effective reading and writing.

To develop your critical thinking skills, you need to understand the framework of this systematic examination and evaluation of ideas, which is the purpose of this appendix. *Systematic* means "organized," which in this case indicates that you will ask certain questions, often in a particular order. You will ask yourself whether the ideas you are dealing with are main or supporting ideas. Moreover, you will ask which statements are based on facts and which ones on opinion. You will consider the most basic patterns of thought and some specific common errors in thinking, called logical fallacies. Finally, you will examine causes and effects in relation to situations and instances.

Main and Supporting Ideas

Your ability to distinguish between main and supporting ideas is paramount. Whether you are working with the paragraph or the essay, reading or writing, these ideas and their relationships will establish the boundaries for your critical thinking. The principles of identifying, developing, and organizing main and supporting ideas are set down and illustrated throughout this book.

Literal and Implied Meanings

The main ideas of an essay or paragraph may be supported directly or indirectly. At one level you will want to know whether you are dealing with facts or opinions. At another you need to know the difference between a simple literal meaning (what the words say) and an implied meaning (what all the characteristics of a passage represent). For example, on your worst day of the decade, if someone says to you,

"You really look great today," the word *great* may have an implied meaning opposite to its literal meaning. You very naturally pick up clues if you are part of an audience and drop clues if you are addressing an audience.

Facts and Opinions

***Facts** are based on verifiable information.* Facts may concern events that have been reliably observed and recorded. They may be perceived by one or more of the senses—sight, smell, hearing, tasting, feeling (though at times we may be misled by our own perceptions). They may be scientific findings that we can duplicate. Usually facts will be presented in concrete terms and/or numbers, and they often take the form of dates, place names, and statistics. Their sources are frequently encyclopedias, dictionaries, and other reference books.

*Whereas facts are objective, **opinions** are subjective, representing personal views.* They may indicate likes and dislikes. They may compare and evaluate. Instead of using concrete and specific words, opinions are likely to be stated in terms of descriptive words such as *best, worst, greatest, unfair, fair, wrong, incompetent, pretty, unpleasant,* and *ugly.*

No one deals entirely with facts or opinions. We all mix them. We base many opinions on facts. We often treat facts and opinions with the same respect. Problems occur, however, when we *confuse* facts and opinions. We seldom argue about certain facts. If we have the appropriate sources, we can check on information and settle the question. The first *Guinness Book of Records* was compiled by the owner of the Guinness liquor products, who also owned bars. His patrons frequently engaged in arguments, sometimes in fights, over factual matters. His book was intended to be used by his bartenders to settle arguments and bets. Opinions cannot be dealt with that easily. Now we are certainly not advancing the idea that facts are good and opinions are bad. The objective of critical thinking here is to understand the nature of facts as information that can be reliably verified and sound opinions as views that are based on adequate evidence and logic.

EXERCISE 1

Identify the italicized statements as fact (F) or (O).

_______ 1. *Elvis deserves to be called the King of Rock and Roll. Born in 1935 in*
1

_______ 2. *Tupelo, Mississippi,* he went on to become *the greatest entertainer of the*
2 3

_______ 3. *mid-twentieth century. Eighteen of his songs were No. 1.* His movie
4

musicals

_______ 4. are still seen and loved by television viewers. Who can watch *Viva Las*

Vegas and not admire his versatility? His fans are still enthusiastic.

More

_______ 5. *than 500,000 people go to Graceland each year* to visit his grave and
5

see his

_______ 6. former home, and *every month after fifty letters arrive there,* all
6
addressed

_______ 7. to Elvis Presley. *That kind of attention is appropriate for the King.*
7

EXERCISE 2

Identify each sentence as one based on fact (F) or opinion (O).

_______ 1. As recently as 1950, 90 percent of mothers with children under the age of six did not work for pay.

_______ 2. By the mid-1980s, 44 percent of all wage earners were women.

_______ 3. Women have long been exploited in the work place.

_______ 4. In 1980 women accounted for only 14 percent of lawyers.

_______ 5. Betty Friedan was a spokesperson for women's rights in 1963.

_______ 6. In fact, Ms. Friedan was the most influential spokesperson of that decade.

_______ 7. The Civil Rights Act of 1964 prohibited sexual discrimination by employers.

_______ 8. Women benefited greatly from that piece of legislation.

_______ 9. The armed services now includes more than 200,000 enlisted women and more than 30,000 female officers.

_______ 10. The emerging new role of women adds up to a revolution comparable to the coming of industrialization or the freeing of the slaves.

EXERCISE 3

Identify each sentence as one based on fact (F) or opinion (O).

_______ 1. Blue jeans were first worn by miners in the 1849 Gold Rush.

_______ 2. They were made of canvas that originally had been ordered to use in constructing tents.

_______ 3. They became the best pants the miners ever wore.

_______ 4. Later, jeans were sold to American farmers.

_______ 5. By the 1960s, blue jeans caught on with several prominent fashion designers.

_______ 6. Europeans adopted blue jeans as the natural clothes style for rock-and-roll music.

_______ 7. Blue jeans are still scarce in Eastern Europe.

_______ 8. They were once smuggled in and sold there on the black market.

_______ 9. Some people apparently regarded blue jeans as a symbol of rebellion.

_______ 10. The love of blue jeans will never end.

Logical Fallacies

Certain flawed patterns in inductive and deductive thought, commonly called **logical fallacies,** are of primary concern in critical thinking.

These are among the most common logical fallacies:

1. *Post hoc, ergo, propter hoc* (After this, therefore, because of this): In other words, when one happening precedes another in time, the first is assumed to cause the other.

   Examples: "I knew I'd have a day like this when I saw that black cat run across the driveway this morning."

   "See what I told you. We elected him president, and now we have high inflation."

2. *False analogy:* False analogies ignore differences and stress similarities, often in an attempt to prove something.

   Examples: "People have to get a driver's license because unqualified people could have bad effects on society. Therefore, couples should also have to get a license to bear children because unqualified parents can produce delinquent children."

   "The leader of that country is a mad dog dictator, and you know what you do with a mad dog. You get a club and kill it."

3. *Hasty generalization:* This is a conclusion based on too few reliable instances.

   Examples: "Everyone I've met this morning is going to vote for the incumbent. The incumbent is going to win."

   "How many people did you meet?"

   "Three."

4. *False dilemma:* This fallacy presents the reader with only two alternatives from which to choose. The solution may lie elsewhere.

   Examples: "Now, only two things can be done with the savings and loan places. You either shut them down now or let them go bankrupt."

   "The way I see it, you either bomb them back into the Stone Age or let them keep on pushing us around."

5. *Argumentum ad hominem* (Arguing against the person): This is the practice of abusing and discrediting your opponent instead of keeping to the main issues of the argument.

   Examples: "Who cares what he has to say? After all, he's a wild-eyed liberal who has been divorced twice."

   "Let's put aside the legislative issue for a moment and talk about the person who proposed it. For one thing he's a southerner. For another he's Catholic. Enough said."

EXERCISE 4

Each of the following sentences is based on a logical fallacy. Identify the logical fallacies with these labels: PH (post hoc), FA (False analogy), HG (Hasty generalization), FD (False dilemma), or AH (Ad hominem).

_______ 1. It's no wonder she had a terrible honeymoon. She didn't wear something blue during the wedding ceremony.

_______ 2. My kids' loud music is driving me crazy. There are only two possible solutions: either the boom boxes go or the kids go.

_______ 3. After reading two Harlequin romances, I can say that the French are the most romantic people in the world.

_______ 4. I'm not surprised. You elect a liberal mayor, and now taxes have gone up.

_______ 5. Even Tommy Lasorda says that practice makes perfect. So I plan to get married lots of times before I settle down.

_______ 6. I can't recommend the fiction of F. Scott Fitzgerald. What could an admitted alcoholic have to say that would be of value?

_______ 7. I'm not surprised. I knew I'd win the Pillsbury bake-off when I found that lucky penny this morning.

_______ 8. Today I met a group of ten Russian tourists. Now I can see why people say the Russians are friendly.

_______ 9. Joe DiMaggio has always liked his coffee, and now he's in the Hall of Fame. Obviously the secret to becoming a great baseball player is in your coffee maker.

_______ 10. How can you take Heavy Metal music seriously? The musicians that play that stuff are druggies with long hair and tattoos.

EXERCISE 5

Each of the following sentences is based on a logical fallacy. Identify the logical fallacies with these labels: PH (Post hoc), FA (False analogy), HG (Hasty generalization), FD (False dilemma), or AH (Ad hominem).

_______ 1. I trained my dog not to wet on the carpet by rubbing his nose in the "mess" he created; therefore, I will potty train my children by rubbing their noses in the "messes" they make.

_______ 2. The continued use of nuclear energy will lead to either nuclear war or catastrophic nuclear accidents.

_______ 3. Everyone in the front office is dipping Lippy Snuff. I figure it's the hottest item on the market.

_______ 4. Our dog eats only once a day, and look how healthy he is. I don't know why you kids keep yellin' for three meals a day.

_______ 5. No wonder she's been going around crying all day. Yesterday the government slapped a tax on Lippy Snuff.

_______ 6. I refuse to listen to his musical interpretation of the Yalta Conference because he's a card-carrying member of the ACLU.

_______ 7. Either we cave in to the terrorist demands, or we strike back with nuclear weapons.

_______ 8. After watching the high school kids on the bus today, I would say that the whole education system could use a required course in manners.

_______ 9. It's no wonder my Winnebago exploded today. Yesterday I bought a tank of cheap gasoline.

_______ 10. I wouldn't trust him as far as I can throw a heifer. He rides a Harley and drinks Rebel Yell.

Cause and Effect

Causes and effects are often prime concerns in critical thinking. Many of our most common questions begin with *why*, indicating that we want to understand the cause(s), and just as many questions begin with *what if*, indicating that we want to know the effect(s). Of course, one situation or condition or instance may provoke questions in both directions—causes and effects.

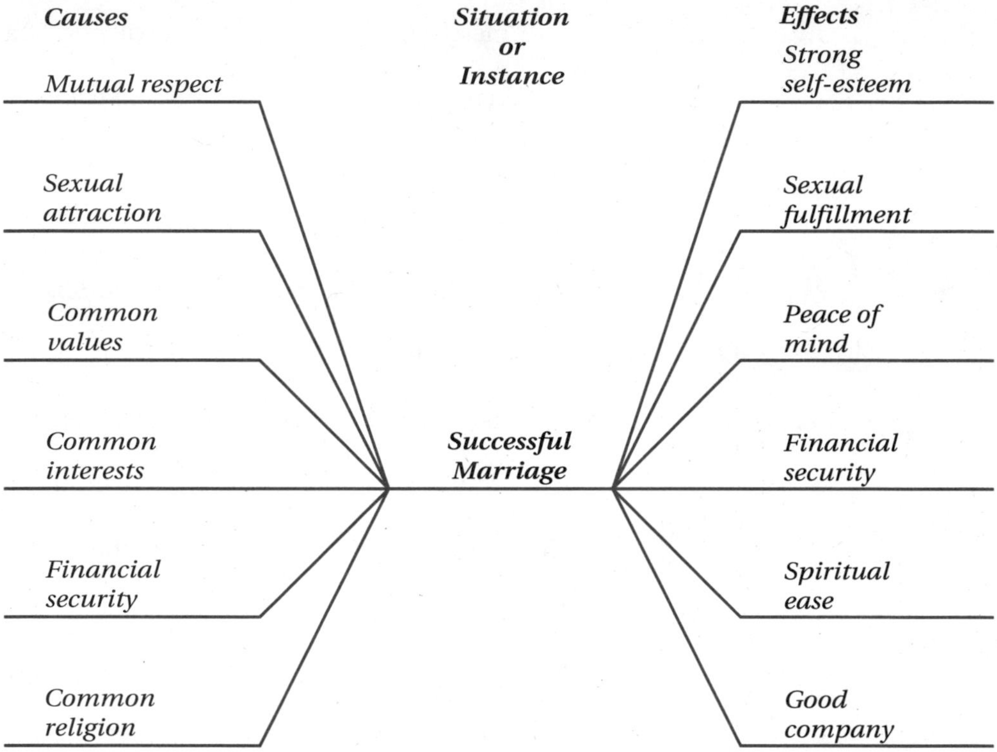

The *why's* and *what if's* in the figure are only some of the possible causes and effects of successful marriage. Naturally, not all would fit every situation, and of the ones that would fit, some would be more important than others. Some causes, such as money or religion, might not be principal factors but they could certainly be contributing ones. Common values, mutual respect, and common interests are more likely to be principal causes.

As a critical thinker, you should be able to distinguish between principal and contributing causes, between immediate and remote causes, and even between major and minor effects.

EXERCISE 6

State two situations or instances and write them on the center lines below. (Suggestions: unemployment, boredom, wealth, popularity, true love, drugs, fighting.) Then, through brainstorming, list at least six causes and six effects of each situation.

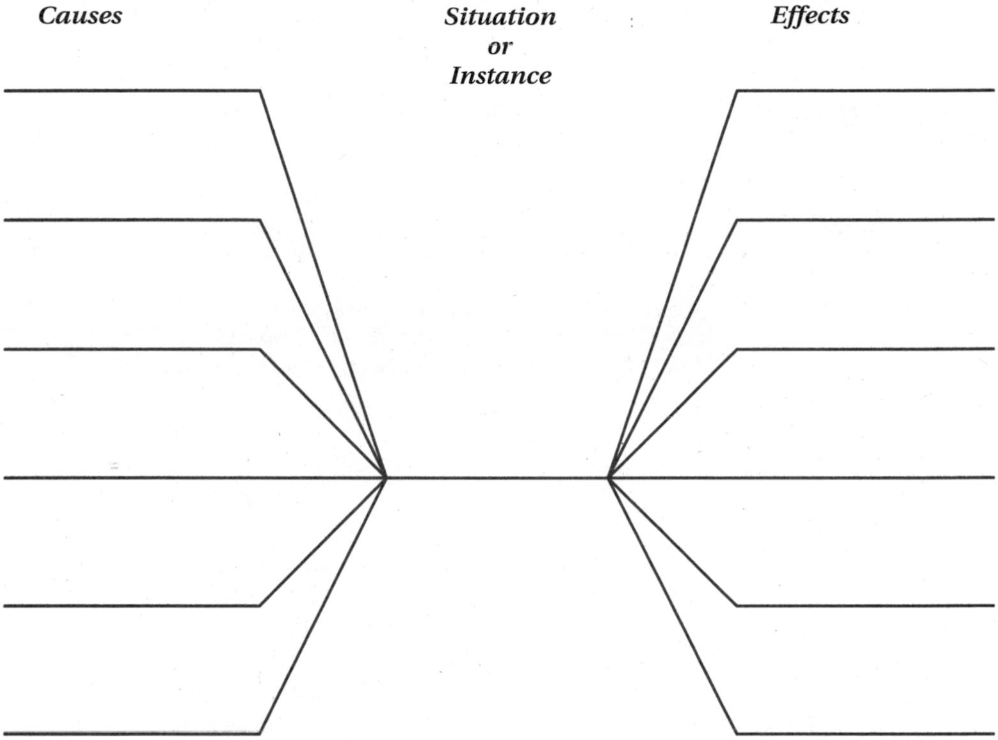

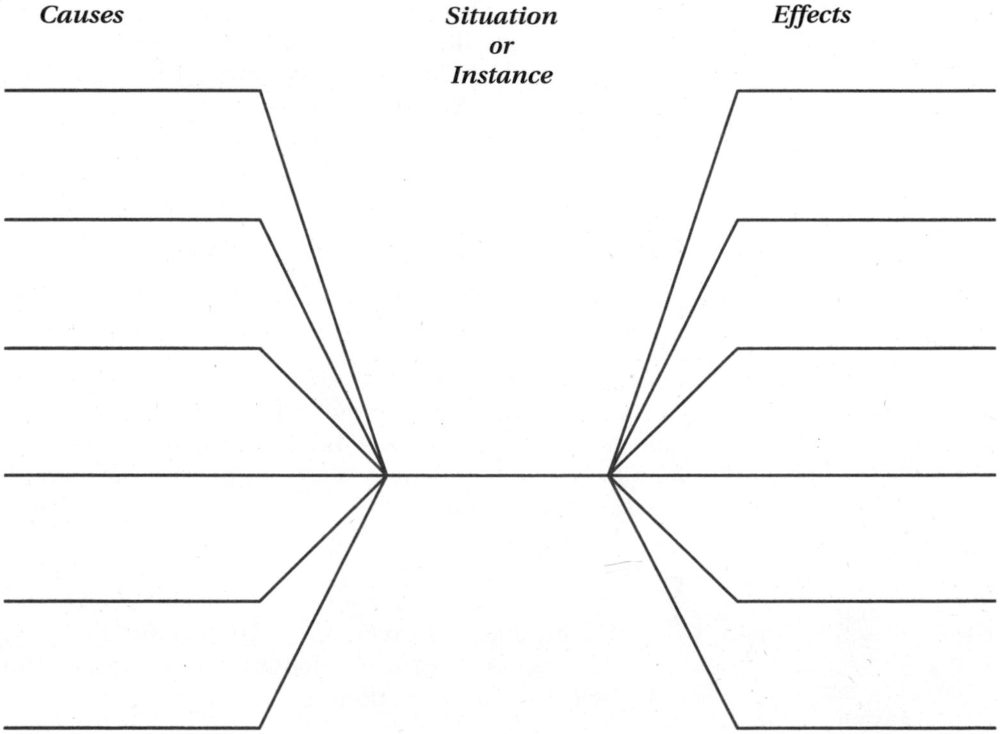

Appendix F: Brief Guide for ESL Students

If you came to this country knowing little English, you probably acquired vocabulary first; then you began using that vocabulary within the basic patterns of your own language. If your native language had no articles, you probably used no articles; if your language had no verb tenses, you probably used no verb tenses, and so on. Using the grammar of your own language with your new vocabulary may have initially enabled you to make longer and more complex statements in English, but eventually you learned that your native grammar and your adopted grammar were different. You may have even learned that no two grammars are the same, and that English has a bewildering set of rules and an even longer set of exceptions to those rules. Chapters 1–10 present grammar (the way we put words together) and rhetoric (the way we use language effectively) that can be applied to your writing. The following are some definitions, rules, and references that are of particular concern to writers who are learning English as a second language.

Using Articles in Relation to Nouns

Articles: Articles are either indefinite (*an, a*) or definite (*the*). Because they point out nouns, they are often called noun determiners.

Nouns: Nouns can be either singular (*book*) or plural (*books*) and are either count nouns (things that can be counted, such as "book") or noncount nouns (things that cannot be counted, such as "homework"). If you are not certain whether a noun is a count noun or a noncount noun, try placing the word *much* before the word. You can say, "much homework," so *homework* is a noncount noun.

Rules:

- ***Use an indefinite article** (a or an) **before singular count nouns and not before noncount nouns.*** The indefinite article means "one," so you would not use it before plural count nouns.

  CORRECT: I saw a book. (count noun)

  CORRECT: I ate an apple. (count noun)

INCORRECT: I fell in a love. (noncount noun)

CORRECT: I fell in love. (noncount noun)

INCORRECT: I was in a good health. (noncount noun)

CORRECT: I was in good health. (noncount noun)

- ***Use the definite article*** (*the*) ***before both singular and plural count nouns that have specific reference.***

CORRECT: I read the book. (a specific one)

CORRECT: I read the books. (specific ones)

CORRECT: I like to read a good book. (nonspecific, therefore the indefinite article)

CORRECT: A student who works hard will pass. (any student, therefore nonspecific)

CORRECT: The student on my left is falling asleep. (a specific student)

- ***Use the definite article with noncount nouns only when they are specifically identified.***

CORRECT: Honesty (as an idea) is a rare commodity.

CORRECT: The honesty of my friend has inspired me. (specifically identified)

INCORRECT: I was in trouble and needed the assistance. (not specifically identified)

CORRECT: The assistance offered by the paramedics was appreciated. (specifically identified)

- ***Place the definite article before proper nouns (names) of:***

oceans, rivers, and deserts. (for example, *the Pacific Ocean* and the *Red River*)

countries, if the first part of the name indicates a division. (*the United States of America*)

regions. (*the South*)

plural islands. (*the Hawaiian Islands*)

museums and libraries. (*the Los Angeles County Museum*)

colleges and universities when the word *college* or *university* comes before the name. (*the University of Oklahoma*)

These are the main rules. For a more detailed account of rules for articles, see a comprehensive ESL book in your library.

Sentence Patterns

Chapter 4, Types of Sentences, defines and illustrates the patterns of English sentences. Some languages include patterns not used in standard English. The following principles are well worth remembering:

- Unlike patterns in certain other languages, the conventional English sentence is based on one or more clauses, each of which must have a subject (sometimes with the implied "you") and a verb.

INCORRECT: Saw the book. (subject needed even if it is obvious)

CORRECT: I saw the book.

- English does not repeat a subject, even for emphasis.

  INCORRECT: The book that I read it was interesting.

  CORRECT: The book that I read was interesting.

Verb Endings

- *English indicates time through verbs.* Learn the different forms of verb tenses and the combinations of main verbs and helping verbs.

  INCORRECT: He watching the game. (A verblike word ending in *-ing* cannot be a verb all by itself.)

  CORRECT: He is watching the game. (Note that a helping verb such as *is, has, has been, will,* or *will be* always occurs before the main verb.)

- *Take special care in maintaining consistency in tense.* (These points are covered with explanations, examples, time lines, and exercises in Chapter 7, Verbs.)

  INCORRECT: I went to the mall. I watch a movie there. (verb tenses inconsistent)

  CORRECT: I went to the mall. I watched a movie there.

Idioms

Some of your initial problems with writing English are likely to arise from trying to adjust to a different and difficult grammar. If the English language employed an entirely systematic grammar, your learning would be easier, but English has patterns that are both complex and irregular. Among them are idioms, word groups that often defy grammatical rules and mean something other than what they appear to mean on the surface.

The expression "He kicked the bucket," does not mean that someone struck a cylindrical container with his foot; instead, it means that someone has died. That example is one kind of idiom. Because the expression suggests a certain irreverence, it would not be the choice of most people who want to make a statement about death; but if it is used, it must be used with its own precise wording, not "He struck the long cylindrical container with his foot," or "He did some bucket-kicking." Like other languages, the English language has thousands of these idioms. "Gee, Francine, you eat like a bird" contains one. Expressions such as "the more the merrier" and "on the outs" are ungrammatical. They are also very informal expressions and, therefore, would seldom be used in college writing, though they are an indispensable part of a flexible, effective, all-purpose vocabulary. Because of their twisted meanings and illogic, idioms are likely to be among the last parts of language that a new speaker learns well. A speaker must know the culture thoroughly in order to understand when, where, and how slang and other idiomatic expressions work.

If you listen carefully and read extensively you will learn idioms. Your library has dictionaries that explain them.

Suggestions for ESL Writers

1. Read your material aloud and try to detect the inconsistencies and awkward phrasing.
2. Have others read your material aloud for the same purposes.

3. If you have severe problems with grammatical awkwardness, try composing shorter, more direct sentences until you become more proficient in phrasing.
4. Keep a list of problems you have (such as articles, verb endings, clause patterns), review relevant parts of this chapter, and concentrate on your problem areas during your drafting, revising, and editing.

EXERCISE 1

Make corrections in the use of articles, verbs, and phrasing.

George Washington at Trenton

One of most famous battles during War of Independence occur at Trenton, New Jersey, on Christmas Eve of the 1776. The colonists outmatched in supplies and finances and were outnumbered in troop strength. Most observers in other countries think rebellion would be put down soon. British overconfident and believe there would be no more battles until spring. But George Washington decide to fight one more time. That Christmas, while large army of Britishers having party and thinking about the holiday season, Americans set out for surprise raid. They loaded onto boats used for carrying ore and rowed across Delaware River. George Washington stood tall in lead boat. According to legend, drummer boy floated across river on his drum, pulled by rope tied to boat. Because British did not feel threatened by the ragtag colonist forces, they unprepared to do battle. The colonists stormed living quarters and the general assembly hall and achieved victory. It was good for the colonists' morale, something they needed, for they would endure long, hard winter before they fighting again.

Appendix G: The DCODE Writing Process

DCODE (pronounced "decode," as in "decoding your ideas") is a systematic process for writing. In this appendix, it will be applied to developmental paragraphs, but it can be applied to writing essays. Flexible enough to accommodate different kinds of assignments, **DCODE** provides a set of strategies that will help you in generating topics and in developing them for effective paragraphs and essays.

The **DCODE** writing process has five stages:

D *Delve:* Freewrite, brainstorm, and cluster in order to generate and investigate topics.

C *Concentrate:* Narrow your topic and state your topic sentence or thesis.

O *Organize:* Develop an outline or a section of the **Delve** cluster.

D *Draft:* Write and revise as many times as necessary for **c**oherence, **l**anguage, **u**nity, **e**mphasis, **s**upport, and **s**entence structure (**cluess**).

E *Edit:* Correct problems in **c**apitalization, **o**missions, **p**unctuation, and **s**pelling (**cops**).

DCODE helps you move naturally from exploring relevant ideas and generating a topic; to stating a topic sentence or thesis precisely; to organizing the material; to writing and revising; and finally to editing. It also allows for recursive movement: you can go back and forth as you rework your material. In short, **DCODE** systematizes what you as a good writer should do. Paying attention to its components will remind you of the importance of writing as a process. Initially, you may approach **DCODE** somewhat mechanically, but as you become accustomed to its logical progression, through the useful repetition provided by the worksheets you will begin following it with natural ease.

Keep in mind that one of the most useful features of **DCODE** is its *flexibility.* You can emphasize, deemphasize, or even delete strategies according to the needs of your assignments.

WORKSHEET

NAME: Cyrus Norton

Writing in DCODE

D
Delve

Generate your topic, or ideas for your topic, by delving into your subject area through:

- ***Freewriting***—writing sentence after sentence, nonstop and spontaneously
- ***Brainstorming***—jotting down answers to Who? What? Where? When? Why? and How? and then listing words and phrases in relation to those answers.
- ***Clustering***—connecting bubbled ideas with lines to show strings of relationships, producing each new bubble item in response to the question, What comes to mind?
- ***Combining*** any of these approaches, as directed by your instructor.

Freewriting

Magic Johnson was the greatest I've ever seen in the NBA. He was always moving, always thinking, always smiling. I've seen him lots of times at the Forum. He was the greatest player in lots of ways. He was great at shooting the ball and when the team needed a basket, he was usually the one that got the ball. If he hadn't been so unselfish he would have scored even more points, but he seemed to love passing the ball as much as shooting it. He was famous for his no-look passes that almost always hit their mark. Then he used a lot of energy on rebounds and many times he was in double digits, which isn't so surprising when you think that he was six feet and nine inches tall with a strong body.

Brainstorming

Who: Magic Johnson
What: great basketball player
Where: the NBA
When: for more than ten years
Why: love of game and great talent
How: shooting, passing, rebounding, leading

Clustering

C
Concentrate

Concentrate your work by stating your topic in one sentence that is not too broad, narrow, or vague to be developed. Base this sentence (which may become the topic sentence for your paragraph or the thesis for your essay) on an idea emerging from the **Delve** stage. You may have to try several statements here before you formulate one that is best for your writing task. Be sure that your final statement covers your assignment or intent and specifies both your subject (what you are writing about) and treatment (what aspect you will focus on). Label the *subject* and *treatment* parts.

subject **treatment**

Magic Johnson was a great NBA star because he was excellent in shooting, passing, rebounding, and leading.

O
Organize

Complete an outline or a cluster, as directed by your instructor. The cluster should be a section from, or a refined version of, the **Delve** clustering. Regardless of the strategy you use, the organizational pattern should indicate a division of your topic into parts that will, in turn, be further subdivided for support as necessary to address a particular audience on your concentrated topic.

```
  I. Shooting
     A. Short shots
     B. Long shots
     C. Free throws
 II. Passing
     A. No-look
     B. Precise
III. Rebounding
     A. Tall
     B. Rugged
 IV. Leading
     A. Energy
     B. Spirit
```

D
Draft

On separate paper, write and then revise your assignment as many times as necessary for **c**oherence, **l**anguage (usage, tone, and diction), **u**nity, **e**mphasis, **s**upport, and **s**entence structure (**cluess**).

E
Edit

Correct problems in fundamentals such as **c**apitalization, **o**missions, **p**unctuation, and **s**pelling (**cops**). Before writing the final draft, read your paper aloud to discover oversights and awkwardness of expression.

First Draft

Magic Johnson

Some ~~NBA~~ National Basketball Association players are good because they ~~are good~~ have a special talent in one area such as shooting, passing, or rebounding. Magic Johnson was great because he ~~was good~~ had talent in all of those things and more. As a shooter few have ~~ever been able to do what he could~~ equaled him. He could slam, shovel, hook, and fire from three-point range; all with deadly accuracy. ~~When it came to~~ As for free throws, he led all NBA players in shooting percentage in 1988-89. ~~Then he averaged~~ While averaging more than twenty points per game, he helped others become stars. As the point (the quarterback of basketball) guard he was always near the top in the league in assists and was famous for his "no-look" passes, which often surprised even his teammates with their precision. A top rebounding guard is unusual, but Magic, ~~standing~~ at six feet nine inches ~~tall~~, could bump shoulders and ~~jump~~ leap with anyone. These three qualities made him probably the most spectacular triple-double threat of all time. "Triple-double" means reaching two digits in scoring, assists, and rebounding. Magic didn't need more for greatness in the NBA, but he had more. He was also an inspirational team leader with his everlasting smile and boundless energy. ~~Always believing~~ He always believed in himself and his team. When his team was down by a point and three seconds ~~were left, you always~~ remained on the clock, the fans looked for Magic to get the ball. Then ~~you~~ they watched as "he dribbled once, he faded, he leaped, he twisted, and he hooked one in from twenty feet!" That was magic. ~~That was Magic.~~

Final Draft

Magic Johnson

Cyrus Norton

Some National Basketball Association (NBA) players are good because they have a special talent in one area such as shoot-
topic sentence ing, passing, or rebounding. Magic Johnson was great because he had talent in all of those areas and more. As a shooter few
Part 1: shooter have ever equaled him. He could slam, shovel, hook, and fire from three-point range-all with deadly accuracy. As for free throws, he led all NBA players in shooting percentage in 1988-89. While averaging more than twenty points per game, he helped
Part 2: passes others become stars. As the point guard (the quarterback of basketball), he was always near the top in the league in assists and was famous for his "no-look" passes, which often surprised even his teammates with their precision. A top
Part 3: rebounding rebounding guard is unusual in professional basketball, but Magic, at six feet nine inches, could bump shoulders and leap with anyone. These three qualities made him probably the most

spectacular triple-double threat of all time. "Triple-double" means reaching two digits in scoring, assists, and rebounding. Magic didn't need more for greatness in the NBA, but he had

Part 4: leader

more. With his everlasting smile and boundless energy, he was also an inspirational team leader. He always believed in himself and his team. When his team was down by a point and three seconds remained on the game clock, the fans looked for Magic to get the ball. Then they watched as "he dribbled once, he faded, he leaped, he twisted, and he hooked one in from twenty feet!" That was magic. That was Magic.

WORKSHEET

NAME: ____

Writing in DCODE

D

Delve

Generate your topic, or ideas for your topic, by delving into your subject area through:

- ***Freewriting***—writing sentence after sentence, nonstop and spontaneously
- ***Brainstorming***—jotting down answers to Who? What? Where? When? Why? and How? and then listing words and phrases in relation to those answers.
- ***Clustering***—connecting bubbled ideas with lines to show strings of relationships, producing each new bubble item in response to the question, What comes to mind?
- ***Combining*** any of these approaches, as directed by your instructor.

C
Concentrate

Concentrate your work by stating your topic in one sentence that is not too broad, narrow, or vague to be developed. Base this sentence (which may become the topic sentence for your paragraph or the thesis for your essay) on an idea emerging from the **Delve** stage. You may have to try several statements here before you formulate one that is best for your writing task. Be sure that your final statement covers your assignment or intent and specifies both your subject (what you are writing about) and treatment (what aspect you will focus on). Label the *subject* and *treatment* parts.

O
Organize

Complete an outline or a cluster, as directed by your instructor. The cluster should be a section from, or a refined version of, the **Delve** clustering. Regardless of the strategy you use, the organizational pattern should indicate a division of your topic into parts that will, in turn, be further subdivided for support as necessary to address a particular audience on your concentrated topic.

D
Draft

On separate paper, write and then revise your assignment as many times as necessary for **c**oherence, **l**anguage (usage, tone, and diction), **u**nity, **e**mphasis, **s**upport, and **s**entence structure (**cluess**).

E
Edit

Correct problems in fundamentals such as **c**apitalization, **o**missions, **p**unctuation, and **s**pelling (**cops**). Before writing the final draft, read your paper aloud to discover oversights and awkwardness of expression.

Self-Evaluation Chart

Organization/ Development/ Content	Spelling	Grammar/ Sentence Structure	Punctuation

Basic Problems I Need to Work on in My Writing

Spelling	Grammar	Punctuation

Answer Key

Chapter 1

Exercise 1

1. n n	4. task flesh
2. x n	5. crows food (road kill)
3. n n	6. smell buzzards

Exercise 2

1. pro x	4. who him
2. x pro	5. them it
3. x pro	6. he her

Exercise 3

1. v v	4. shook sang
2. v x	5. drove took
3. v x	6. starred made

Exercise 4

1. n v	11. v pro
2. x pro	12. v x
3. v n	13. v n
4. x v	14. x v
5. x n	15. x v
6. n v	16. n v
7. pro v	17. x v
8. v n	18. n v
9. v pro	19. n n
10. x x	20. v x

Exercise 6

1. adj adj	4. clear novelty
2. adj x	5. Many silly
3. adj adj	6. better ridiculous

Exercise 7

1. adv x	4. Finally highly
2. x adv	5. immediately foul
3. adv adv	6. not bitterly

Exercise 8

1. adj adj	6. adv adj
2. adv adv	7. adj adj
3. adj adj	8. adv adj
4. adv adj	9. adv adj
5. adj x	10. adv adj

11.	adv	adj	16.	adj	x
12.	adv	adv	17.	adj	x
13.	adj	x	18.	adv	adv
14.	x	adj	19.	adj	x
15.	adj	adv	20.	adv	adj

Exercise 10

1.	prep	prep	4.	Up	of
2.	prep	x	5.	by	for
3.	prep	prep	6.	in	of

Exercise 11

1.	conj	conj	4.	Although	because
2.	x	conj	5.	and	and
3.	conj	x	6.	and	because

Exercise 12

1.	conj	prep	11.	conj	conj
2.	prep	prep	12.	conj	x
3.	prep	conj	13.	prep	prep
4.	prep	conj	14.	conj	prep
5.	conj	prep	15.	conj	prep
6.	conj	prep	16.	prep	conj
7.	x	conj	17.	prep	prep
8.	conj	conj	18.	prep	prep
9.	conj	prep	19.	prep	prep
10.	prep	conj	20.	prep	conj

Review 1

1.	n	prep	11.	adj	adj
2.	adj	v	12.	adj	n
3.	adv	prep	13.	pro	adj
4.	conj	adj	14.	adj	prep
5.	prep	adj	15.	conj	conj
6.	pro	v	16.	v	conj
7.	adj	n	17.	adj	n
8.	v	adj	18.	adj	adj
9.	pro	conj	19.	conj	n
10.	adj	adj	20.	v	n

Chapter 2

Exercise 1

1. live, travel
2. varies
3. is
4. spend
5. make
6. will beat
7. are, live

8. finds, hoots, shakes
9. hear, go
10. can use
11. are

Exercise 3

1. Mahatma Gandhi
2. he
3. You (understood)
4. good
5. fasting
6. He
7. Gandhi
8. British
9. leaders
10. Gandhi

Exercise 5

1. You (understood) Read, learn Aztec ruled
2. cities were
3. Government, religion were blended
4. was difference
5. They built, sacrificed
6. ceremonies related
7. society had
8. family included
9. boys went girls went, learned
10. Aztec wore they lived they ate
11. Scholars developed
12. calendars arc prcscrved
13. language was
14. language was, represented
15. religion, government required
16. soldiers could capture enlarge
17. Hernando Cortez landed
18. He was joined
19. Aztec rebelled
20. Spaniards killed they defeated

Review 1

1. You (understood) read
2. What causes
3. can they do
4. name suggests earthquakes shake
5. is answer

6. earth is covered
7. they are
8. plates bump, pass
9. rocks get squeezed, stretched
10. They pull, pile cause
11. breaks are called
12. formation is
13. wave travels
14. vibrations are
15. force is
16. scientists have tried
17. has been success
18. Earthquakes are identified they occur
19. regions experience
20. quake is you read

Chapter 3

Exercise 1

Because her handwriting was bad, she decided to type. Although she typed on an electric typewriter, her typing was slow. Moreover, she still made many errors. It took her hours to complete her work. That she was frustrated is an understatement. When she bought a computer, she did so as a last resort. Because she had little money, she worked hard. During the two months since she purchased the computer, she has experienced both success and failure. How she might go wrong was a concern from the beginning. She was doing well until she bought some computer games. Then she became preoccupied with the games, and her school work suffered. She knew she would fail in school unless she learned to discipline herself before it was too late.

Exercise 3

Answers will vary.

1. Because he was the best driver, he won the race.
2. Although he did not own the car, he loved it.
3. That he was cool under pressure was obvious.
4. When he was challenged, he responded.
5. She left long after the game had ended.
6. Since he moved to town, she prospered.
7. She knew how to make friends in a hurry.
8. She waited till he went for refreshments.
9. She would forgive him unless he made the same mistake again.
10. Before he would do it, she would warn him.

Exercise 5

The armadillo looks like a prehistoric animal. Wearing a suit of armor. The armadillo's shell is constructed. Of hard, bony plates. It is not suitable for a pet. Livi in the wild. It is contented. Though having a fierce appearance. The armadillo is not a good fighter. Designed only for chewing. The armadillo's teeth are far back in its mouth. It uses its claws to burrow into soil for tunnels and nests. When it is attacked, it scurries for its tunnel or rolls up into a ball. A ball about the size of a basketball. The armadillo is common in Texas and Oklahoma. Two states with warm weather.

Exercise 7

1. In a large automobile with furry dice hanging from the rear view mirror.

   Harry sat in a large automobile with furry dice hanging from the rear view mirror.

2. Leaving in a dense puff of dust.

   Leaving in a dense puff of dust, Harry went to Jane's house.

3. To go to the opening game.

   To go to the opening game was her fondest desire.

4. A never-to-be-forgotten experience.

   It would be a never-to-be-forgotten experience.

5. Being seen on diamond vision.

   Being seen on diamond vision would give her a moment of fame.

6. Buying peanuts and popcorn.

   Soon Harry was buying peanuts and popcorn.

7. To catch a well-hit ball.

   She brought a glove to catch a well-hit ball.

8. To hear and see heroes.

   She had brought a portable TV to hear and see heroes.

9. With the sound of the bat on ball.

   With the sound of the bat on ball, she took a seat.

10. Seeing the rain clouds.

    Seeing the rain clouds, she was fearful that the game would be canceled.

Exercise 9

Fleas are remarkable animals. Though they do not have wings, they jump more than twelve inches. Fleas ~~living~~ live on many kinds of animals. They ~~Suck~~ suck blood from their victims. They often move from pets to human beings. They do not discriminate. They land on poets, politicians, physicians, and anyone else in close proximity. They ~~Carry~~ carry germ-ridden blood and spread diseases. Fleas were and still are the main spreader of the bubonic plague. Rodents, including those infected with diseases, ~~providing~~ provide fleas with transportation and food. Nowadays one attacker is called the *human flea.* This creature lives in houses where it lays eggs on the carpet. It ~~Often~~ often bites human beings. Another kind of flea is the *chigoe.* It ~~Burrows~~ burrows under the skin and lays its eggs. For flea control, cleanliness and insecticide are important. Our pets, mainly our cats and dogs, are among the main carriers of fleas in the typical household.

Exercise 11

Answers will vary.

1. One of the two main industries in Florida is tourism.
2. People are going to Florida to visit Disney World.
3. Others go to watch sporting events such as the Orange Bowl.
4. Tourists regard the Everglades National Park as a national wonder.
5. St. Augustine has the oldest house in the United States.
6. Many major league baseball teams go to Florida for spring training.
7. Tourists can see a living coral reef formation at a state park.
8. Tours, demonstrations, and displays are available at the John F. Kennedy Space Center.
9. Some people visit Florida for the pleasant weather and good beaches.
10. Circus World offers opportunities for amateurs.

Exercise 14

1. RT	6. OK
2. CS	7. CS
3. OK	8. OK
4. CS	9. RT
5. CS	10. RT

Exercise 16

CS 1. In 1846 a group of eighty-two settlers headed for California with much optimism, but a hard road lay ahead.

RT 2. They had expected to cross the mountains before winter, and they were in good spirits.

OK 3. They would not arrive in California before winter, nor would some of them get there at all.

RT 4. When they encountered a heavy snowstorm, they stopped to spend the winter, yet they still thought they would be safe.
RT 5. They made crude shelters of logs and branches, and some also used moss and earth.
RT 6. They had trouble managing, for they had not encountered such problems before.
RT 7. They ran out of regular food, so they ate roots, mice, shoe leather, and their horses.
RT 8. Thirty-five members of the Donner Party died that winter, and the survivors were so hungry that they ate the dead bodies.
RT 9. They were weak, sick, and depressed, but they did not give up.
RT 10. Fifteen people set out to get help, and seven survived and returned to rescue friends and relatives.

Exercise 18

RT 1. Although Chris Evert was one of the most successful tennis players of the 1970s and 1980s, she was not physically powerful.
CS 2. Because she was intelligent and well coordinated, she became a top player.
RT 3. While she was still in her teens, she won major championships.
RT 4. She attracted much attention in 1974 when she won fifty-five consecutive matches.
RT 5. When she reached the top, she had much competition there.
RT 6. Although Evonne Goolagong was Evert's main competition at first, Martina Navratilova soon assumed that role.
RT 7. Financially Chris Evert's career was notable because she made more than six million dollars.
OK 8. Chris Evert helped to make women's tennis what it is today, and she will not be forgotten.
RT 9. She was called the "ice princess" because she did not show her emotions.
OK 10. She is regarded as one of the greatest athletes of the last thirty years.

Exercise 20

CS 1. Madonna Louise Veronica Ciccone became one of the biggest pop stars in the 1980s; however, she is known to most people as Madonna.
RT 2. Madonna was talented in dance; moreover, she even won a dance scholarship to the University of Michigan in the mid-1970s.
CS 3. She was not interested in staying in school; therefore, with a mere thirty-five dollars in her possession she moved to New York City.
OK 4. After working in several small bands, she finally made her first album in 1983.
OK 5. When her first album became number one on the *Billboard* list in 1984, she immediately had new opportunities.
CS 6. Madonna continues to be a very popular singer; moreover, she can also act.
RT 7. She has performed well in the comedy movie *Desperately Seeking Susan;* she was also a hit in the comic strip drama *Dick Tracy.*
CS 8. Madonna is an expert at manipulating the media; consequently, she increases her popularity each time she changes her image.
CS 9. Her show business career has prospered; however, she has had problems in her private life.
RT 10. She continues to promote herself; similarly, other people do too.

Exercise 22

CS 1. About a hundred and fifty years ago, the British soldiers wore a bright red coat. They also wore a black hat and white trousers.
RT 2. The soldiers looked good in parades. The queen was very proud.
OK 3. On the battlefield, the situation was different, and the uniform was regarded differently.
RT 4. The coat could be seen at a great distance. Enemies aimed at the red coats.
OK 5. This had long been a problem, even in the days of the American Revolution.
CS 6. No one in high position was willing to change the colors of the uniform. The soldiers decided to take action.
CS 7. A solution was at hand. The soldiers would wear the red coats but change the colors.
CS 8. At the time of their experiment, they were serving in India. They would use natural elements to solve their problem.
OK 9. In the dry season they would rub yellow-brown dust on their uniforms, and in the wet season they would use mud.
RT 10. They liked the camouflage color so much they finally changed the color of their uniforms to the drab color. They called it *khaki*, the Indian word for dust.

Chapter 4

Exercise 1

1. S
2. Cp
3. Cx
4. S
5. CC
6. S
7. S
8. Cp
9. Cx
10. Cp

Exercise 3

1. S
2. Cp
3. S
4. Cx
5. CC
6. S
7. S
8. Cx
9. Cx
10. S

Review 1

1. Cp
2. Cp
3. S
4. CC
5. CC
6. Cx
7. Cx
8. S
9. Cp
10. S

Chapter 5

Exercise 1

1. The shepherd has a cooperative flock of sheep. [, and] They will cheerfully donate their wool.
2. The clown has the hardest job in the rodeo. [, but] At least he gets much gratitude from the bull riders.
3. Hamburgers will be served in the cafeteria today. [, so] You should get in line early.
4. Young Billy will surely get first prize in the science fair. [, for] He has developed a milkshake that tastes good and is not filling.
5. The aardvark does not make a good pet. [, but] It gets rid of ants.
6. Secure all the hatches. [, or] Your ship might sink.
7. The couple liked their new house. [, but] They didn't like the spiders.
8. Children should not play with fire. [, and] They should not play with power tools.
9. The entire junior class will be punished. [, but] They already feel miserable.
10. After taking a memory course, Sam memorized one hundred phone numbers. [, but] He can't remember the names to go with them.

Exercise 3

1. The revolution was a nasty affair. [; however,] The revolutionaries were polite when asking locals for directions.
2. You look peculiar wearing clown shoes. [; however,] I'll still go to the concert with you.
3. The singing was so bad that almost everyone booed. [; in fact,] One person applauded the booing.
4. Instructors love Chia Pets. [; therefore,] The campus store specializes in selling such items.
5. Clowns first add whipped cream to ready-made pie crusts. [; then] They throw the creations at other clowns.
6. Some music critics believe that Roy Rogers is the best singing cowboy. [; however,] Others think that Gene Autry reigns supreme.

; then

7. The soldiers packed up their equipment. They left town.

; however,

8. No one knows why the heavy metal band Screaming Death has lost popularity. Some point to the illness of their pet python, Ziggy.

; therefore,

9. He believes in his own greatness. On his last birthday, he sent his parents a message of congratulations.

; therefore,

10. Pancake makeup poses no health threat to the user. Clowns and mimes use it liberally without worry.

Exercise 5

because

1. The air traffic controller took a break. There were apparently no planes in the area.

, though

2. The vacationers did have a good time. The bears destroyed a few tents and ate people's food.

because

3. The teenagers loved their senior prom. The band played well.

because

4. Farmers gathered for miles around. Jeff had grown a fifty-pound cucumber.

if

5. In the new car, back seat drivers can be ejected from the vehicle. They make unwanted suggestions.

Because ,

6. The marriage counselor often gave bad advice. He charged only half price.

because

7. The clients refused to pay. They were not satisfied at all.

Because ,

8. The hurricane would hit during the night. The residents checked their flashlights.

When ,

9. The ice sculptor displayed his work in the dining hall. The customers applauded.

After ,

10. Someone stole the artwork of ice. No evidence was found.

Exercise 7

Although ,

1. A grumpy bear had stalked the grounds. Summer camp had been a great experience for the campers. (, and) They vowed to return.

After , , and

2. The stuffed cabbage ran out. The party ended. The guests went home.

3. It was a costume party. All guests at the party dressed as movie legends. Ten were Elvis impersonators.

4. A new Elvis theme park opened in our town. I attended. I think I saw the King.

5. My father encouraged me to take up a hobby. I began collecting stamps. Now my hobby has become a business.

6. They were in a wilderness camp. They were not allowed to bring pets. They were allowed to bring toys.

7. He had no leather shoes to wear. Young Stu could not go to the prom. He hoped there would be a next year.

8. People were hungry. They ate mass quantities of hot dogs at the game. They knew the dogs were made of mystery meat.

9. The ambulance drivers were taking a break. A man had a choking fit. The drivers came to his rescue.

10. The film was filled with scenes of violence. It included a charming love story. It became a tremendous hit.

Review 1

1. The Mercury Comet was judged the winner. ~~It had~~ imitation zebra-skin seat covers. ~~It had~~ an eight-ball shift knob.
2. Becky had a great plan to make some money. There was one problem. She had no money to develop her plan.
3. The mixture could not be discussed openly. Competitors were curious. Corporate spies were everywhere.
4. Nancy's bowling ball is special. It is red and green. It is decorated with her phone number in metal-flake.
5. The young bagpiper liked Scottish food. He enjoyed doing Scottish dances. Wearing a kilt in winter left him cold.

6. Ruby missed the alligator farm. She fondly remembered the hissing and snapping of the beasts as they scrambled for raw meat, but her neighbors were indifferent about the loss.
7. Although many people are pleased to purchase items with food preservatives, others are fearful because they think these chemicals may also preserve consumers.
8. Joanne loves her new in-line roller skates because they look and perform much like ice skates, but they are not as safe as her conventional roller skates.
9. Fish sold at Discount Fish Market were not of the highest quality because some of them had been dead for days without refrigeration and ~~They~~ were suitable only for bait.
10. Jerry wanted to impress his date, so he splashed on six ounces of He-Man cologne and ~~He~~ put on his motorcycle leathers and a flying scarf.

Chapter 6

Exercise 1

1. vicious, relentless, and inexplicable
2. family moves and they find
3. to make and to ignore
4. invited but neglected
5. has and has caused
6. separates and is hated
7. twin is and other is
8. embittered and vindictive
9. unreasoning, angry, and brutal
10. crashes and devours

Exercise 3

1. x eating
2. x escaping
3. x he finds
4. x having
5. P
6. x they sat down
7. x upsetting
8. x who had
9. P
10. x becoming

Exercise 5

1. color amazement
2. action-packed
3. how to save them
4. to live
5. joys sorrows
6. truth, justice, freedom
7. survives triumphs
8. love care
9. fly float
10. loves sends

Exercise 6

1. hulking unrelenting
2. to destroy
3. life woman
4. survive
5. humans are the slaves
6. begins
7. attack
8. to destroy
9. ugly harmless
10. arrogant obnoxious

Exercise 7

1. not only robbed rich but also gave poor
2. both Humphrey Bogart and Katharine Hepburn
3. either himself or Mr. Hyde
4. neither jobs nor compassion
5. either die or go
6. either develop or go
7. not only gets but also goes
8. both who framed and who is
9. not only heartaches but also joy
10. either dignity or life

Chapter 7

Exercise 1

1. talk, talks
2. talked, talked
3. talked, talked
4. walked, walked
5. walk, walks
6. is, am
7. are, were
8. do, does
9. have, have
10. does, do

Exercise 4

1. had received
2. had worked
3. walked
4. had
5. could have gone
6. will have completed
7. are considering
8. has had
9. had built
10. will go

Exercise 10

1. are
2. was
3. celebrates
4. becomes
5. have
6. are
7. knows
8. fill
9. is
10. refuses

Exercise 13

The hottest game show in TV-Land ~~was~~ is called "Guess My Shoe Size." At the beginning of each show, the renowned quiz show host, Vic Binkly, introduces a guest whose feet ~~were~~ are concealed in enormous clown shoes. Guest-celebrity panelists, whose identities are also disguised with masks, then ~~asked~~ ask the mystery guest questions for five minutes. At this point, the guest ~~revealed~~ reveals his or her shoe size, and then the audience ~~responded~~ responds to the proceedings with questions. In one program, the audience ~~is~~ was stunned because they thought the guest ~~wears~~ wore a $6\frac{1}{2}$D when in reality she ~~wears~~ wore a $5\frac{1}{2}$EE. If the guest stumps the celebrity panel, he or she ~~received~~ receives a year's supply of fine footwear. The critics have proclaimed this show a winner. And, of course, the Vic Binkly fans ~~were~~ are pleased that their hero has another show after his "Guess My Hat Size" show failed when the audience ~~cannot~~ could not hear the contestants talking through the paper bags on their heads.

Exercise 16

1. P The young lad named the pit bull Homicide.
2. P
3. P Reporters questioned the warden as he left the scene of the execution.
4. P The solemn judge sentenced the noisy rappers to listen to a hundred waltz records.
5. P Hungry bears interrupted the picnic.
6. P As the picknickers scattered, the bears grabbed the food.
7. P I have given you your last warning; the next time you leave a mess in your room, I will yodel for the rest of the day.
8. P
9. A
10. P You should eat the souffle before it hardens to the processed cheese spread that it once was.

Exercise 18

1. My watch runs slowly.
2. My computer costs little.
3. The horse ran swiftly.
4. They wrote well.
5. The dog sleeps on the bed.
6. Mr. Hawkins sells real estate.
7. Jose attends Rancho Santiago College.
8. I like this assignment.
9. We students succeeded here.
10. She combs her hair.

Chapter 8

Exercise 1

1. her	6. We
2. She, I	7. We, him
3. he	8. I
4. them, us	9. who
5. me, us	10. me

Exercise 3

1. We	6. me
2. who	7. she, us
3. me, us	8. I
4. who, me	9. he
5. I	10. They, who

Exercise 5

1. Whom	6. who
2. whom	7. who
3. whom, I	8. Whom
4. whom	9. who
5. who	10. Who

Exercise 7

	From	*To*
1.	you	they
	you	they
2.	you	she
3.	you	I
4.	you	they
5.	you are	he or she is
6.	you	we
	you	we
7.	you	they
8.	you	they
9.	you	she
10.	you	he

Exercise 9

1. its	6. their
2. he or she	7. his or her
3. his or her	8. their
4. it	9. her
5. his	10. its

Exercise 11

1. they, us	6. they
2. they	7. his or her
3. their	8. they
4. their	9. his
5. their	10. his or her

Exercise 13

1. (a) V
   (b) OK
2. (a) OK
   (b) V
3. (a) V
   (b) OK
4. (a) V
   (b) OK
5. (a) V
   (b) OK
6. (a) V
   (b) OK
7. (a) OK
   (b) V
8. (a) V
   (b) OK
9. (a) V
   (b) OK
10. (a) OK
    (b) V

Chapter 9

Exercise 5

1. really well
2. most
3. biggest
4. any
5. worse
6. friendlier
7. well
8. more
9. more
10. well

Exercise 7

	From	To
1.	real	really
2.	no	any
3.	worst	worse
4.	no	any
5.	well	good
6.	real	really
7.	more	more nearly
8.	never	ever
9.	real	really
	horribler	more horrible
10.	most nastiest	nastiest

Exercise 9

D 1. As we drove through the field, the wild jackrabbits were excited.
M 2. Carrying fresh meat, the delivery truck drove past the library.
D 3. Walking through the meadow, we observed that the satisfied wolverines slept deeply after gorging on the road kill.
M 4. Hoping to meet an available female, he went for a walk with his cute puppy.
M 5. Watching a television program, I saw a slimy monster.
M 6. Nursing a head wound inflicted by crazed weasels, the lass ran home to her parents.
M 7. I fearfully began to unwrap the ticking package from my loved one.
M 8. I watched the plane trailing smoke and flames.
M 9. I saw the men, soaked to the bone, remove their boots at the front door.
D 10. Understanding the need for medical attention, the captain allowed the galley slaves ten minutes to dip their wounds in salt water.

Chapter 10

Exercise 1

1. .
2. !
3. .
4. !
5. !
6. .
7. .
8. .
9. ?
10. .

Exercise 3

1. beasts,
2. records,
3. you, big,
4. coach, hand, enthusiastically,
5. cheerful, squirming,
6. rink,
7. dog, dreary,
8. bright,
9. belief, attractive
10. jerky, tarot cards,

Exercise 5

1. years,
2. all, interesting,
3. inexpensive, nutritious,
4. young,
5. day, beautiful,
6. Maxine, handsome, Pierre,
7. Rimkin, attorney, week,
8. bright,
9. television,
10. court,

Exercise 6

1. consideration,
2. cowpokes, hungry,
3. belief,
4. Barstow, California, Las Vegas,
5. decided, therefore,
6. Winthrop, match, Cleveland,
7. marshmallows, Pies,
8. small,
9. gang, bored,
10. knew, course,

Exercise 8

1. hobby;
2. went,
3. sidewalks;
4. restaurants,
5. presents; moreover,
6. Shawnee,
7. skill,
8. clouds;
9. Santa Ana, California; Grants Pass, Oregon; and Kelso,
10. legend;

Exercise 11

1. Professor Jones said,"Now we will read from The Complete Works of Edgar Allan Poe."
2. The enthusiastic students shouted,"We like Poe! We like Poe!"
3. The professor lectured for fifty-seven minutes before he finally said,"In conclusion, Poe was an unappreciated writer during his lifetime."

4. The next speaker said, "I believe that Poe said, 'A short story should be short enough so that a person can read it in one sitting.' "
5. Then, while students squirmed, he read "The Fall of the House of Usher" in sixty-eight minutes.
6. "Now we will do some reading in unison," said Professor Jones.
7. Each student opened a copy of The Complete Works of Edgar Allan Poe.
8. "Turn to page 72," said Professor Jones.
9. "What parts do we read?" asked a student.
10. "You read the words, or maybe I should say 'word,' of the raven," said the professor.

Exercise 13

1. Ben Jonson (1573–1637) wrote these poems: "On My First Son" and "Though I Am Young and Cannot Tell."
2. William Blake (1757–1827)—he is my favorite poet—wrote "The Tyger."
3. In that famous poem, he included the following words: "Tyger, Tyger, [the spelling of his time] burning bright / In the forests of the night."
4. Rudyard Kipling (1865–1936) wrote in several forms: short stories, poems, and novels.
5. Robert Frost (1874–1963)—he is probably America's best-loved poet—lived in New England for most of his life.
6. He wrote about many subjects in his environment: trees, walls, spiders, and ants.
7. Poet, philosopher, speaker—Frost had many talents.
8. Dylan Thomas (1914–1953) was a great poet and a flamboyant individual.
9. Thomas acquired a reputation—some say he didn't deserve it—for being a drunk.
10. One of Thomas's most moving poems, "Fern Hill," begins with this line: "Now I was young and easy under the apple boughs."

Exercise 15

1. "I've heard that you intend to move to el paso, texas," my brother-in-law said.
2. "My date of departure on united airlines is july 11," I said.
3. "Then you've only thirty-three days remaining in california," he said.
4. My mother gave me some samsonite luggage, and dad gave me a ronson razor.
5. Jennifer does not know i am leaving for the university of texas at el paso.
6. Jennifer, my mother's dog, is one-quarter poodle and three-quarters cocker spaniel.
7. That dog's immediate concern is almost always food rather than sentimentality.
8. I wouldn't have received my scholarship without the straight A's from my elective classes.

9. I am quite indebted to professor jackson, a first-rate teacher of english and several courses in speech.
10. I wasn't surprised when grandma gave me a box of stationery and a note asking me to write mother each friday.

Chapter 15

Exercise 1

The Leadership of Martin Luther King, Jr.

1 On December 1, 1955, in Montgomery, Alabama, a black woman named Rosa Parks was arrested for refusing to give up her bus seat to a white man. In protest, Montgomery blacks organized a year-long bus boycott. The boycott forced white city leaders to recognize the black's determination and economic power.

2 One of the organizers of the bus boycott was a Baptist minister, the Reverend Martin Luther King, Jr. King soon became a national leader in the growing civil rights movement. With stirring speeches and personal courage, he urged blacks to demand their rights. At the same time, he was completely committed to nonviolence. Like Gandhi, . . . he believed that justice could triumph through moral force.

3 In April 1963, King began a drive to end segregation in Birmingham, Alabama. He and his followers boycotted segregated businesses and held peaceful marches and demonstrations. Against them, the Birmingham police used electric cattle prods, attack dogs, clubs, and fire hoses to break up marches.

4 Television cameras brought those scenes into the living rooms of millions of Americans, who were shocked by what they saw. On May 10, Birmingham's city leaders gave in. A committee of blacks and white oversaw the gradual desegregation of the city and tried to open more jobs for blacks. The victory was later marred by grief, however, when a bomb exploded at a Birmingham church, killing four black children.

—Jantzen *et al.*, *World History: Perspectives on the Past*

Appendix: Spelling

1. hear
2. than
3. their
4. through
5. piece
6. all right
7. passed
8. too
9. advice
10. a lot
11. already
12. chose
13. receive
14. quite
15. stationery
16. lose
17. it's
18. accept
19. know
20. paid

Text Credits

Sheila Ferguson. From *Soul Food* by Sheila Ferguson. Copyright © 1989 by Sheila Ferguson. Used by permission of Grove/Atlantic, Inc.

John Fire/Lame Deer. Reprinted with the permission of Simon & Schuster from *Lame Deer Seeker of Visions* by John Fire/Lame Deer and Richard Erdoes. Copyright © 1972 by John Fire/Lame Deer and Richard Erdoes.

Barbara Garson. Reprinted with the permission of Simon & Schuster from *The Electronic Sweatshop* by Barbara Garson. Copyright © 1988 by Barbara Garson.

Holley Gilbert. "Girls Form the Backbone of Gangs" by Holley Gilbert, *The Oregonian,* September 30, 1990. Copyright 1990 Oregonian Publishing Company, reprinted by permission.

Martin Gotfried. "Rambos of the Road" by Martin Gotfried, *Newsweek,* 9/8/86. Reprinted by permission of the author.

Rose Del Castillo Guilbault. "Americanization Is Tough on 'Macho' " by Rose Del Castillo Guilbault from *This World,* a weekly magazine of the *San Francisco Chronicle,* 1989. Reprinted by permission of the author.

Maxine Hong Kingston. From *The Woman Warrior: Memoirs of a Girlhood Among Ghosts* by Maxine Hong Kingston. Copyright © 1975, 1976 by Maxine Hong Kingston. Reprinted by permission of Random House, Inc.

Lewis Johnson (Sawaquat). "For My Indian Daughter" by Lewis Sawaquat, *Newsweek,* September 1983.

Harold Krents. "Darkness At Noon" by Harold Krents. Copyright © 1978 by The New York Times Company. Reprinted by permission.

Marie G. Lee. "My Two Dads" by Marie G. Lee. First appeared in *Brown Alumni Monthly,* April 1991. Reprinted by permission of the author.

Ponchitta Pierce. "Who Are Our Heroes?" by Ponchitta Pierce. Reprinted by permission of the author and the author's agents, Scovil Chichak Galen Literary Agency, Inc., 381 Park Avenue South, New York, New York 10016. Also reprinted with permission from *Parade,* copyright © 1995.

Gary Soto. "The Jacket" from *A Summer Life.* Copyright © 1990 by University Press of New England. Reprinted by permission. "One More Time." Copyright © 1985 by Gary Soto. From *Living Up the Street* (Dell, 1992). Used by permission of the author.

Sally Squires. "How Families Stay Afloat" by Sally Squires, *The Washington Post,* May 16, 1989, pp. 12–15. Copyright © 1989, Washington Post Writers Group. Reprinted with permission.

Yi-Fu Tuan. "American Space, Chinese Place" by Yi-Fu Tuan. Copyright © 1974 by *Harper's Magazine.* All rights reserved. Reproduced from the July issue by special permission.

Index

Page numbers preceded by a letter: letters indicate the section of the Appendix where the topic can be found. D-25 refers you to Appendix D, page 25.